BETTANE & DESSEAUVE
THE WORLD'S GREATEST WINES

STEWART, TABORI & CHANG
NEW YORK

Introduction

This book is dedicated to all those winemakers who get up in the morning filled with the intense desire to make a great wine and go to bed in the evening wondering what they can do the next day to make it even better. In particular, it is dedicated to the memory of Denis Mortet, one of the very best.

Our claim to have selected the world's greatest wines will no doubt be seen by many wine lovers as a challenge to draw up their own selections. And at least where their own favorite country or region is concerned, these selections will probably be just as relevant as ours. We therefore owe our readers some explanation of the principles on which our choice of producers is based. The main criterion, of course, is the intrinsic quality of a wine or wines. The remarkable stroke of fate that enabled us to make a career out of our passion for fine wine all those years ago has also provided us with the opportunity to explore vineyards throughout the world, to meet countless winemakers and taste their wines and those of their friends and neighbors. This exceptional opportunity has been incredibly enriching, thanks to the deep and harmonious fraternity that has developed within the world of wine – one that transcends national borders and continents. It has also enabled us to compare the different levels of pleasure we experience as tasters and occasionally to organize this pleasure into hierarchies, to exploit our natural universal curiosity in order to avoid (as far as possible) the pitfalls of chauvinism, and ultimately to establish for each country or region a collection of personal choices that we wish to share with other wine lovers. It is astonishing and extremely gratifying to see just how far the desire to produce wine of the best possible quality has spread to vineyards all over the planet, benefiting from the experimentation and advances made by international agronomy and enology but always driven by the enthralling passion of the men and women who make the wine.

How do we assess this quality? The purpose of this introduction is not to theorize about different styles of wine but let us just say that aromatic purity, freshness, finesse, silkiness of tannins (in the case of red) and length on the palate are key elements and more universal than, for example, richness, and power. We never lose sight of the fact that the main purpose of a wine is to be enjoyed!

While essential, passion, technique, and resources are not enough in themselves to guarantee quality. Numerous other factors come into play. The ancient or modern history of a wine certainly has a key role. Even more important in determining the excellence of a wine, however, is terroir, embracing soil, subsoil, exposure, and climate. Like it or not, nothing is more inegalitarian than the varying potential of different vineyard sites to produce great wine and this undeniable fact explains why certain regions are better represented than others.

Nevertheless, the purpose of our second main selection criterion has been to demonstrate the extent to which the desire to produce great wine has become universal over the last few decades. We therefore felt we had to reflect this delicious diversity in our choices, and the contents section of this book shows just how far the world of wine has opened up – at the risk, it is often said, of bringing about a standardization of taste and styles. Actually, if the first stage in the process of viticultural emancipation is to take inspiration from existing models, once they achieve a certain renown, many vineyards and winemakers take great pains to reinvent their own local traditions. Similarly, while a handful of grape varieties have become a universal key to success, regardless of which continent they are grown on, it would be ridiculous to describe the balance of a Cabernet Sauvignon from California's Napa Valley as being identical to that of a Cabernet Sauvignon from the Maipo Valley in Chile, Bolgheri in Tuscany, or Pauillac in Bordeaux. We believe that each of the wines we present in this guide possesses its own distinct personality.

Finally, given that this book is aimed at a wide audience of lovers of good and great wines, we thought it necessary to write about realities rather than myths. Even if we have the greatest admiration for a particular micro-cru, we will have ruled it out if its distribution is too small for anyone to have a real chance of tasting it. Conversely, we have taken account of the representativeness of a brand or very widely distributed name where we believe that the quality of all or a part of that firm's production is assured.

This book therefore presents the reader with famous wines from regions long hallowed as the source of the most exotic crus, with enormous producers and tiny vineyards, with wines capable of immediately seducing a wide international public and others whose subtlety can only be properly appreciated with a degree of knowledge. All, though, in their different ways, tell the same story: that of the rich and wonderful culture of wine.

Page 1 : *A cluster of Pinot Noir grapes, the magical variety at the heart of great Burgundy, in an Aloxe-Corton vineyard.*
Page 2 : *Rino Sottimano tasting a Barbaresco at his property in Neive at the heart of the Piedmont region.*
Opposite : *Klein Constantia, one of South Africa's legendary sweet white wines was resurrected at the end of the 20th century with the aim of restoring it to its former glory.*

France

While those areas of France where the wine made continues to be of the characterful but somewhat rustic type are struggling to cope with the realities of aggressive and dynamic international competition, others have, in the last two decades, attained a level of perfectionism that gives them a well-deserved place among the very best wine producers of the world. The majority of the prestige domaines have experienced a generational change during this period, with vignerons who were hitherto more concerned with quantity than quality handing over the reins to a son or a daughter. This new generation comes with a sound university education in enology, and is seeking to combine ideals of quality with a greater focus on techniques and styles. In a parallel development, new producers – ranging from individual enthusiasts to major industrial groups – have breathed new life into many other once-famous wines, and, in so doing, have encouraged others to do the same.

Both new and well-established producers have benefited from the extraordinary potential of the French vineyards. No other country is able to offer such a variety of terroirs, noble grape varieties, and climatic conditions, and it is these that make it possible to produce so many uniquely nuanced and great wines. This is not the place to summarize the characteristics of each region and each type, since many paragraphs could be devoted to each. That said, the best French wines have a character that unites them over and above their individual personalities, whether it be the aristocratic brilliance of a Médoc, the velvety smoothness of a Saint-Émilion or a Pomerol, the perfumed refinement of a Burgundy, the generous fullness of a wine from the Rhône Valley, the sparkle of a Champagne, the intensity of a Riesling from Alsace, or the delicious fruitiness of a Loire wine. There is no doubt that the link between all these wines is their freshness and harmonious finish. A great French wine may be powerful or light, aromatic or austere, but it is never heavy, and it never leaves a sensation of sugariness or alcohol in its finish. This liveliness and elegance of flavor makes French wine the perfect accompaniment to food, an integral part of an attractively decorated dining table or the particular atmosphere of a special occasion, reminding us of its vital role in the centuries-old and constantly renewed art of civilized living.

BURGUNDY

CHAMPAGNE

JURA

SAVOY

LANGUEDOC

Domaine
Marcel Deiss

Jean-Michel Deiss is one of a breed of winegrowers who are not happy merely to make great wines but who alter the course of history by introducing new practices. While it is almost a religion in Alsace to emphasize the fruit of the grape varieties peculiar to the region (Riesling, Gewürztraminer, Muscat) or shared with Burgundy, Deiss has sought by every means possible to exalt the individual character of Bergheim's fine terroirs and has resurrected the old tradition of planting different varieties side by side. After a long struggle to gain legal acceptance for this new type of wine and subsequently to convince some of his colleagues to follow suit, he can be proud of his achievements, which are founded on an extremely high standard of viticulture and harvesting at the peak of maturity. His own wines have never been as rich and full of flavor while his fellow Bergheim growers have adopted the practice of blending noble varieties for their Altenberg Grands Crus.

VINE VARIETY

67 acres (27 hectares): Gewürztraminer, Riesling, Pinot Gris, Pinot Blanc, and Pinot Noir in similar proportions.

OUR FAVORITE WINES

All the wines made by Jean-Michel Deiss are worthy of attention and are closely connected to the personality of the individual terroir. But certain terroirs have more character than others. One such is Altenberg de Bergheim, which is splendidly sunny and produces wines that are smooth, unctuous, and deep. The 2001 vintage was an out-and-out success. The 2001 and 2002 Riesling-dominated Schoenenburgs are firmer, more mineral, and destined to age extremely well.

The best vineyards in Alsace are often found on steeply sloping hillsides, their east or southeast aspect ensuring that the local grape varieties reach full maturity.

Domaines
Schlumberger

Domaines Schlumberger is an important local benefactor, maintaining – at great expense – the countless terrace walls that endow the landscape around Guebwiller with a monumentality unique in Alsace. It also has by far and away the largest grand cru holdings of any winery in Alsace, and offers the widest choice of wines. The local soils have a high proportion of Vosges sandstone, which gives the varieties plenty of immediate aromatic power, while their depth favors laying down. The most spectacularly situated of the grand cru vineyards, and no doubt Séverine Beydon-Schlumberger's favorite, is Kitterlé. In terms of sandstone soils, its exquisite wines are unrivaled anywhere in the world. Saering perhaps suits Riesling even better, however, producing a wine of greater delicacy with a fine mineral character. All those familiar with the domaine adore its renowned Anne et Christine cuvées, which display a richness similar to that of the Vendanges Tardives and Sélections de Grains Nobles. The 2002, the latest year tasted, recaptures the sumptuousness and aromatic precision on which their reputation rests.

VINE VARIETY

346 acres (140 hectares): 31% Riesling, 25% Gewürztraminer, 19% Pinot Gris, 15% Pinot Blanc, 8% Sylvaner, 2% Muscat.

OUR FAVORITE WINES

Most of the domaine is made up of grands crus, making the wine lover's choice very difficult indeed. If you like sheer elegance and complexity, you will prefer the Riesling or Gewürztraminer (the 2002 is wonderful) from the Kitterlé vineyard. If density and energy are your thing, the Kessler will soon become indispensable. And what can we say about the magnificent Saering? As for the dry wines, remarkable progress has been made with the Princes Abbés cuvées, and the 2004 and 2005 promise to be thrilling.

Hugel

The Hugel family is known above all for having established the rules of production for Vendanges Tardive and Sélection de Grains Nobles wines, and for securing their official acceptance as categories of Alsace wine. Its know-how remains as great as ever. Despite their richness and complexity, its Schoenenberg Grand Cru Rieslings (which abstain from advertising themselves as such) preserve the characteristic exuberance of the variety, while the Gewürztraminers and Pinot Gris take their magnificent fruitiness to near-immortal levels. Over the last few years, the family has focused on trying to improve the general quality of its dry wines, which have retained their immediate likableness and elegant aromas while acquiring greater richness, maturity, and evenness. The Pinot Blancs in particular combine roundness and a very pleasing finish with a dryness that makes them the ideal complement to any Alsatian starter. The perfect ambassador for Alsatian wine in good restaurants, Hugel maintains a keen eye on the range of possible combinations between its wines and different foods. This encourages it to respect a sense of balance that others seem to have lost.

VINE VARIETY

321 acres (130 hectares) white: 30% Riesling, 27% Gewürztraminer, 12% Pinot Gris, 16% Pinot Blanc, 15% various. 22 acres (9 hectares) red: Pinot Noir.

OUR FAVORITE WINES

This firm's vins de négoce (wines bought in from other growers) are perfectly respectable, but wine lovers will want to try the estate-grown wines. These include the Jubilée cuvées and, of course, the first-rate Vendanges Tardives (late harvest) and Sélections de Grains Nobles (wine made from specially selected, often botrytized, grapes). The 2001 vintage is absolutely magnificent; the 2002 is more immediately fruity; the 2003 has a higher alcohol content and is distinctly more opulent.

The peaceful village of Riquewihr in the heart of the winegrowing area of Alsace, home of the Hugel vineyards, is typical of the charm of this region.

Trimbach

The Trimbach firm is inextricably linked with its home town of Ribeauvillé. The magnificent vineyards of Geisberg and Osterberg are without doubt two of the greatest Riesling locations in the world and produce wines that are vigorous and taut, admittedly less immediately fruity than some others but distinctive for their mineral character. The most eloquent example is Cuvée Frédéric Émile. The soil of Clos Sainte-Hune, slightly different in composition, produces a somewhat rounder wine of more immediately apparent elegance, which has earned it worldwide fame. Well versed in this style and taste, Pierre and Jean Trimbach are skilled at buying in grapes – of all varieties – capable of producing wines of the same character but accessible earlier. These grapes make up the firm's famous Réserve and Réserve Personnelle wines, whose aromatic clarity is rarely found wanting. There is a preference for dry wines here (even those made from Pinot Gris), as they are better suited to typical French and Alsatian starters. Naturally a certain roundness is inevitable in the very rich vintages and Vendanges Tardives. In these cases it is necessary to wait ten years or more for the ideal balance in the mouth to develop.

VINE VARIETY

Own vineyard and bought-in fruit.
222 acres (90 hectares) white: 41% Riesling,
33% Gewürztraminer, 15% Pinot Gris, 10% Pinot Blanc,
1% Muscat.
11 acres (4.5 hectares) red: Pinot Noir

OUR FAVORITE WINES

In common with many other wine lovers, our choice from this comprehensive and consistent range would be the firm's great Rieslings. The Cuvée Frédéric Émile and the extremely rare but incomparable Clos Sainte-Hune are among the greatest dry Rieslings in the world and have incredible aging potential. The 2000 will excel for its austere mineral character; the 2001 for its sophistication; the 2002 for the purity of its fruit. Among older vintages, the 1990 displays unrivaled power.

Domaine
Weinbach

Nestling at the heart of the Alsatian hills, visitors to the beautiful Weinbach estate are always impressed by its calm majesty. This sense of seigneurial grace continues as the visitor's gaze wanders across to the vineyards, which begin with the clos at the foot of the hill and climb steeply up the slopes of the Kaysersberg. Few landscapes evoke the culture of wine and the vine as powerfully as this one. Harmony also emanates from the remarkable trio that presides over the destiny of the domaine: Colette Faller and her two daughters. Catherine greets and looks after visitors while winemaker Laurence is responsible for the domaine's very wide selection of wines. Under Laurence's talented direction, the Rieslings grown on the granite terraces of the Schlossberg vineyard have acquired an unrivaled elegance and sophistication of flavor while the Gewürztraminers from the more marly Furstentum terroirs delight the palate with their wonderful depth without a tendency toward heavier aromas displayed by many wines made from this demonstrative grape.

VINE VARIETY

64 acres (26 hectares) white: 41% Riesling, 26% Gewürztraminer, 15% Pinot Gris, 6% Muscat and Chasselas, 6% Pinot Blanc and Auxerrois, 6% Sylvaner.
2.5 acres (1 hectare) red: Pinot Noir.

OUR FAVORITE WINES

A characteristic of all Domaine Weinbach's wines, even the most modest, is their great finesse. Among the very best are the Sainte-Catherine Riesling from Grand Cru Schlossberg, the Gewürztraminers from grand cru vineyards Furstentum and Mambourg, and among the blends with relatively high residual sugar, Cuvée Laurence and the Vendanges Tardives, and Sélections de Grains Nobles. Thanks to their aromatic perfection, freshness, and purity of expression, these wines, particularly the 2001 and 2003 vintages, verge on the sublime.

Domaine
Zind Humbrecht

This domaine has gone from anonymity to world renown in just 30 years, thanks solely to the quality of its wine. Its original 12 acres (5 hectares) have expanded to 111 acres (45 hectares) situated, with the notable exception of Clos Windsbuhl, the pearl of Hunawihr, on the best slopes to the south of Colmar. Olivier Humbrecht has switched his entire estate over to biodynamic production. Working the soil with absolute respect for the environment yields grapes of an aromatic richness and integrity of expression of terroir character that have elevated Alsace wine to its highest level. Its Brand, Clos Hauserer, and Clos Windsbuhl Rieslings are made from grapes harvested at the peak of their maturity and stand out for their lushness. Most importantly, however, the domaine specializes in Pinot Gris and Gewürztraminers. The best examples of the first are Rangen, which has an unforgettable smoky, spicy bouquet, and Clos Jebsal, lusher with a greater finesse. The second, meanwhile, produces at least three masterpieces: Hengst, dense and extraordinarily vigorous; Goldert, divinely floral and delicate; and Clos Windsbuhl, whose mineral lacework conceals magnificent body. The domaine's simpler, generally dry wines are named after the villages in which they originate. They are notable for their fullness and consistency.

A passionate devotee of fine Alsace wines, Léonard Humbrecht applies meticulous attention to every detail of the process of winemaking.

VINE VARIETY

111 acres (45 hectares): 30% Riesling, 30% Gewürztraminer, 30% Pinot Gris, 10% various.

OUR FAVORITE WINES

It is difficult to select one of this domaine's wines in preference to another, such is their excellence and individuality. There is every chance that this winery will go down in history for demonstrating anew the virtues of the extraordinary Rangen de Thann and its Pinot Gris of unsurpassable body, for Clos Windsbuhl at Hunawihr, or for the harmonious character of its wines in general. We have to own up, however, to a weakness for Clos Jebsal, a small, terraced marvel located behind the family home. Here, limestone has asserted itself over granite, favoring the production of a Pinot Gris of a sophistication unrivaled anywhere in the world. The 2002, 2003, and 2004 all come equally highly recommended.

Château
Angélus

For a long time, Château Angélus was a prime example of what was regarded as a good Saint-Émilion: generous and supple in a good year, fluid and sometimes astringent in a lesser year, with earthy aromas and a discreet rusticity. For more than 15 years, this estate located at the heart of Saint-Émilion has been moving emphatically away from this pleasant but limited profile and has become one of the leading Right Bank clarets, expressing all the different facets of a great modern grand cru through its rich nose and fullness of body. This spectacular transformation is the fruit of the passion and commitment of one man, Hubert de Boüard, who succeeded his father as owner of the property in 1985. Rethinking and often reinventing each stage in the winemaking process from harvesting and vinification to aging, and bringing highly exacting standards to bear, he is one of a small band of winemakers who have transformed not only their own wine but their entire region too.

VINE VARIETY
58 acres (23.5 hectares) red: 50% Merlot, 47% Cabernet Franc, 3% Cabernet Sauvignon.

OUR FAVORITE WINES
Since 1985, this wine has been subject to a process of transformation that has resulted in numerous outstanding vintages including 1989, 1990, 1998, 2000, and 2003. Fullness of body and refinement of texture are two of the wine's major characteristics.

Château
Auspice Ausone

In the 4th century C.E. the Bordelais poet Ausonius accumulated honors and riches during the course of his long life, thereby guaranteeing himself eternal fame. The wines of Château Ausone, named after the Gallo-Roman versifier, share the same philosophy. Their delicate, velvety texture is delightful in their first flush of youth, while their elegant nose and long finish guarantee extended, harmonious aging. Ausone and its vines are located on a small promontory that discreetly overlooks the medieval village of Saint-Émilion (only the initiated know how to find the vineyard). This unique site, clinging to the side of a line of limestone hills that bisects the Saint-Émilion appellation east to west, gives the wine an unrivaled structural finesse magnified – thanks to the painstaking work and artistry of Alain Vauthier, the present owner and winemaker – by sumptuous, silky tannins and ideal maturity of fruit.

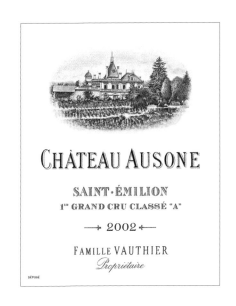

VINE VARIETY
58 acres (23.5 hectares) red: 50% Cabernet Franc, 50% Merlot.

OUR FAVORITE WINES
Legendary vintages abound at Ausone, but since 1995 almost every year has been exceptional, the best being 1998, 2000, 2001, and 2005.

One of the best-situated terroirs producing grand cru Bordeaux wine, the steep Château Ausone vineyards face due south on the limestone hillsides of Saint-Émilion.

Château
Cheval Blanc

Cheval Blanc is the most recent of the leading Bordeaux crus. For a long time it was part of the Figeac lands and only appeared on the books of the Libourne wine brokers at the beginning of the 19th century. Once it had gained its independence, however, it made dazzling progress. Like its neighbor, it owes its success to the fact that its soil differs radically from that of the other Saint-Émilion or even Pomerol properties as it is on the border between the two appellations. Situated on a clay and limestone marl plateau, the vineyard benefits from a deep layer of gravel bearing a closer resemblance to the geology of Médoc than that of the Right Bank and its classic wines. Furthermore, Cheval gets its unrivaled freshness, magnificent fruit, and aristocratic honesty from a preponderance of Cabernet Franc over Merlot. Neither ultra-powerful nor the king of opulence, this wine can be considered a prince of balance.

VINE VARIETY
91 acres (37 hectares) red: 60% Cabernet Franc, 40% Merlot.

OUR FAVORITE WINES
While Cheval Blanc 1947 is without doubt one of the ten most famous wines in the history of Bordeaux, the 1998 also promises to achieve legendary status thanks to its formal perfection and extraordinary depth. The 2003, wonderfully intense and refined, is not far behind and 2005 is sublime.

Château
Pavie

The Côte Pavie is one of the steepest slopes in Saint-Émilion. Indeed, as soon as the first ray of sunshine appears, walkers immediately feel its heat on their heads and necks. This simple fact illustrates the excellence of the property's situation. Its thin layer of gravelly soil rests on a limestone base created by an extraordinary geological fold on which the village of Saint-Émilion is built. Unusually large and with an age-old reputation, Pavie was long regarded as a classic Saint-Émilion – in other words, a supple wine in the traditional style. It was only when it was acquired by Gérard Perse in 1997 that the vineyard entered the modern age and grew in status. Tirelessly hardworking, Perse's ambition from the outset was to produce the very best wine he could. The transformation of Pavie was truly spectacular, resembling the labors of Hercules. Pavie's wines are undeniably unique, but, in addition to their tremendous richness, one cannot help noticing how refined and aristocratic their tannins now seem. A velvet hand inside an iron glove!

1er GRAND CRU CLASSÉ

Château Pavie
SAINT-ÉMILION GRAND CRU
Appellation Saint-Émilion Grand Cru Contrôlée
1998

S.C.A. CHATEAU PAVIE PROPRIÉTAIRE
C. ET G. PERSE, VITICULTEURS A SAINT-ÉMILION, GIRONDE, FRANCE
MIS EN BOUTEILLE AU CHATEAU
PRODUCE OF FRANCE

750 ml   L. 98 4 4 4 4   13,5% by vol.

VINE VARIETY
86 acres (35 hectares) red: 70% Merlot, 20% Cabernet Franc, 10% Cabernet Sauvignon.

OUR FAVORITE WINES
Pavie has been at the peak of its form since 1998 and recent years have all impressed with their velvety texture. Indeed 1998, 2000, 2001, and 2003 can be regarded as being among the very best Bordeaux wines of their respective years.

La Mondotte

This cult wine owes its existence to the Saint-Émilion grand cru classification rule stipulating that the surface area of a cru can only be increased through the planting of adjoining land of the same geological type as the original vineyard. Stefan von Neipperg, the proprietor of Château Canon-La-Gaffelière, also owned a fine parcel of land neighboring Troplong Mondot and Pavie that would have done his famous classified cru no harm whatsoever. However, as he was not allowed to include it he resigned himself to vinifying it separately but with the intention of demonstrating the excellence of the terroir. The small size of the vineyard enabled him to bring to the viticulture and vinification of the wine the perfectionism for which he was already known, and the results – a wine of impressive body and immediate aromatic power very much in keeping with the times – were spectacular from the very first millésime in 1995. The terroir has gradually asserted its character and well-heeled wine lovers soon realized that La Mondotte possessed all the strength and individuality of flavor of its famous neighbors while its limited production volume increased its market value. No one doubts that this vineyard will eventually be classified – maybe even as a premier grand cru!

VINE VARIETY
11 acres (4.5 hectares) red: 80% Merlot, 20% Cabernet Franc.

OUR FAVORITE WINES
The sumptuous body of this cru is well expressed in most of the recent vintages. Our personal preference is for the 1998, 2000, and 2001, which are well-balanced and brilliantly made wines.

Château
Figeac

Figeac is one of the most ancient Saint-Émilion properties. Its name, which other properties have attached to their own, refers to a district in the northwest of the appellation, a vast gravel plateau bordering the Pomerol region. With its planting of two-thirds Cabernet (Franc and Sauvignon), it is often – with justification – said that Château Figeac is the most Médoc-like of the Saint-Émilion wines. The wine is upright, direct, slender, and fresh – a style that contrasts strongly with the roundness and power of many other Right Bank wines (and is not particularly fashionable). Although it bordered on the meager in the 1980s, since 1995 this style has gone hand in hand with a renewed vigor, and – above all – a freshness and balance that are without doubt the prime qualities of a great Bordeaux.

VINE VARIETY

99 acres (40 hectares) red: 35% Cabernet Franc, 35% Cabernet Sauvignon, 30% Merlot.

OUR FAVORITE WINES

Since 1998, this wine has reconnected brilliantly with its glorious vintages of the 1950s (1955 and, most importantly, 1959) and early 1960s (1961 and 1964). The 1998, 2001, and, especially, 2000 are wines that combine honesty, freshness, and elegance.

The unassuming charm of Château Figeac, a property whose elegant and peaceful appearance has been preserved intact since the beginning of the 19th century.

Château
Tertre Roteboeuf

François Mitjaville is one of the great artist-winemakers of Bordeaux. A gentleman farmer who is completely in love with the earth and the vine, Mitjaville wears his overalls with all the elegance of an *ancien régime* dandy. He is an esthete with a highly developed sense of taste and smell that places him in a class of his own, even among a generation of Saint-Émilion and Pomerol owners that is far from lacking in characters. Thanks to a happy quirk of fate, the small Tertre promontory has a very unusual terroir and microclimate. Since 1985, once he had fully appreciated the potential of his vineyard, Mitjaville has been steadily improving his vineyard trellising system in order to make the best of a slow final ripening stage. Harvesting at the very peak of ripeness, once the berries have started to wither, produces a wine of voluptuous texture with a unique nose that paradoxically combines the vibrancy of fresh fruit with the patina of a grape on the verge of decay. Fortunately for a wine of such quality and individuality, Tertre Roteboeuf has escaped the speculation to which cult wines often fall prey. Its devotees prefer to drink it, and who could blame them?

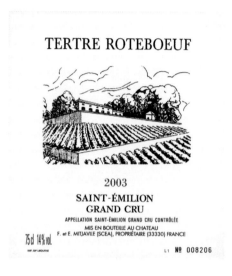

VINE VARIETY

15 acres (6 hectares) red: 85% Merlot, 15% Cabernet Franc.

OUR FAVORITE WINES

The ultimate artist's wine for which every risk is taken each year to harvest the fruit at the very peak of ripeness. The wines are always successful, but in unusual years such as 1997 or 2003 they are even more exciting than in classic years!

Château
Troplong Mondot

Since the French Revolution (if not before), making great wine has not been the exclusive preserve of men – especially in Saint-Émilion and Pomerol, where a good number of famous properties have been run by women. Few female directors, however, have been as omniscient – from vineyard to the winery, from style of wine to general atmosphere – as the present owner of Château Troplong Mondot. Christine Valette took charge of this property (purchased by her great-grandfather from a Monsieur Troplong, who attached his patronymic to the château's original name) at a very early age. With the judicious help of enologist Michel Rolland, she patiently revitalized the vineyard and modernized the cellars. This important work has been rewarded with dazzling success in the form of sleek and succulent wines of depth and generosity that succeeded each other, vintage after vintage, from 1988 onwards. This spirit of excellence is complemented by a general atmosphere of harmony and refinement at the winery.

VINE VARIETY
74 acres (30 hectares) red: 80% Merlot, 10% Cabernet Franc, 10% Cabernet Sauvignon.

OUR FAVORITE WINES
The 1989 and 1990 were unforgettable vintages at Troplong Mondot, as indeed was 1998, which combines refinement, succulence, and an element of sweetness. Moving into the new millennium, 2000 and 2003 have also been impressive

Château
Valandraud

Very few properties have aroused as much passion and debate as Château de Valandraud, created from nothing by Jean-Luc Thunevin, a wine lover who is as entrepreneurial as he is extremely talented. At the end of the 1980s, Thunevin and his wife bought 1.5 acres (0.6 hectares) of vines in Saint-Émilion, and decided to devote the greatest possible care and attention to both the vineyard and the winemaking process. No property had ever been worked with such intensity and no winegrower ever been crazy enough to attempt to overturn the sacrosanct hierarchies of Bordeaux within a mere five years. Nevertheless, Valandraud began to taste international success in 1992, and it was not long before it was crowned with glory. Ultra-ripe, strongly scented, powerful, rich, velvety, and underpinned by a suave wood flavor, Valandraud is a fully evolved wine that is broad-shouldered and generous of spirit while simultaneously displaying all the refinement of a grand cru. While the property has been enlarged, Valandraud remains an original and modern expression of a certain kind of winegrowing perfection.

VINE VARIETY

22 acres (9 hectares) red: 70% Merlot, 25% Cabernet Franc, 3% Cabernet Sauvignon, 2% Malbec.

OUR FAVORITE WINES

The early vintages of the 1990s remain extraordinary for their fullness and refinement. Since then, however (despite the property growing in size), this wine has acquired greater depth and 2000, 2001, and 2003 can be counted among Valandraud's most accomplished offerings.

Château
La Conseillante

Château la Conseillante can have no complaints about its near neighbors, which include Cheval Blanc, Figeac, L'Évangile, and Vieux Château Certan! This is proof positive that its vineyard enjoys one of the best locations in Bordeaux on the border between the Pomerol and Saint-Émilion appellations, an incredible opportunity to benefit from the best of both worlds – the smoothness and softness of Pomerol, and the exquisite textures promoted by Saint-Émilion's gravelly soils. The vineyard's destiny has been lovingly overseen by several generations of the Nicolas family, the most recent of which is without doubt the most highly motivated. Within just a few years the viticulture has become increasingly precise with meticulous control of the density of fruit on the vine and a stricter selection of grapes for the blend. In terms of delicacy and complexity, the wine produced by La Conseillante bears a closer resemblance to its neighbor Cheval Blanc than to any other – although it is perhaps a touch softer, thanks to a higher percentage of Merlot. It also shows a hint of violet and truffle that reveals its Pomerol affiliation.

VINE VARIETY

30 acres (12 hectares) red: 80% Merlot, 20% Cabernet Franc.

OUR FAVORITE WINES

La Conseillante is a wine that is difficult to enjoy when young, as it hides its body and mellowness far more effectively than those of its more powerful neighbors. However, during the course of aging in the bottle, it achieves a level of refinement unusual in a Pomerol. A somewhat greater rigor in the day-to-day work on the estate has allowed the more recent vintages, 2001, 2002, 2003 (generally more balanced), and above all 2004, to recapture the very highest standards.

Château
L'Évangile

Château L'Évangile enjoys an ideal situation on Pomerol's high plateau on the border with Saint-Émilion. Its immediate neighbors are Pétrus and La Conseillante, producing two very different styles of wine. The first is very deep and full-bodied with a truffle flavor, while the second is more refined and subtle in texture and nose. A successful Évangile represents a synthesis of the two. The 1950s and 1960s were kind to the wine despite a certain rusticity of working method – in particular, the absence of maturation in wooden barrels. The following two decades were less consistent, but Rothschild has finally succeeded in bringing the vats and vineyard of this prestigious cru up to date. Its originality is derived from the complexity of its soils: deep clay for body, gravel for firmness and freshness of tannins, and sand for an immediate delicate character. The blending of the three creates a Pomerol that is unique for its superb leather and violet nose and silky texture. This wine appeals in particular to an American clientele due to its astonishingly supple tannins and velvety texture, wherein it represents the very opposite end of the spectrum to a certain tradition of Bordeaux wine.

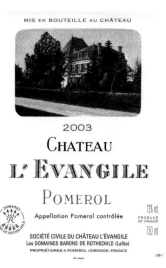

VINE VARIETY
35 acres (14 hectares) red: 78% Merlot, 22% Cabernet Franc.

OUR FAVORITE WINES
The last few years have seen a gradual improvement in terms of clarity of aroma and expression of terroir character. The vineyard was somewhat over-enthusiastically rejuvenated in the 1980s but has started to regain an adequate average age and the 2001, a highly successful year generally in Pomerol, possesses all the velvety texture one would expect. The 2002 and 2004 go even further in terms of purity and complexity, while the very rich and sunny 2003 is without known precedent.

Château
Lafleur

The Lafleur vineyard, adjacent to that of Pétrus, is immediately impressive for its magnificent surface layer of gravel (recalling the soils of the Médoc peninsula), which a freak of nature heaped up on these mere 11 or so acres (4.5 hectares) on top of the famous blue clay of the Certan plateau. This gravel retains the daytime heat, allowing Cabernet Franc to ripen more evenly than elsewhere and therefore to balance the power of the Merlot with its fresh aromas and tannins. It is this balance between the two varieties, unique in Pomerol, that is responsible for the legendary status of this cru, which many wine lovers regard as Pomerol at its richest and most elegant. Jacques Guinaudeau and his wife have been the custodians of Lafleur for a number of years and take their responsibilities extremely seriously. The vineyard's small size means it can be worked like a garden and each vinestock given individual, "personalized" treatment. The same precision is applied to the vinification process, the sole aim of which is to convey the nobility of this exceptional terroir as simply and faithfully as possible. The last few years have produced wines whose texture, purity of style, and beauty of fruit are truly moving.

VINE VARIETY

11 acres (4.5 hectares) red: 50% Merlot, 50% Cabernet Franc.

OUR FAVORITE WINES

The current Lafleurs are dense, elegant gems with a tannic refinement that raises them to premier cru level. The sublime 2001 is one of the three or four best wines of its year, and the 2005 may even surpass it in depth and tannic power.

Pétrus

Pétrus is one of the only properties in Bordeaux that refrains from attaching the epithet château to its name (not only is there no *château*, there is not even a house!). Rather than its architecture (or lack of it), the reputation of this producer rests on its terroir. Formed essentially of a plateau that extends from the northwest of Libourne as far as the western limits of Saint-Émilion, Pomerol is a near-flat and apparently homogeneous region. This surface uniformity nevertheless hides considerable differences beneath the ground. Pétrus's subsoil is almost entirely made up of a seam of blue clay that keeps the roots of its Merlot vines permanently and blessedly cool. Early fruiting and never suffering from a lack of moisture, Pétrus grapes arrive at the winery at the right time and perfectly ripe. In the past, Pétrus was renowned for its heady, juicy intensity. Today, it is the formal perfection of this unctuous liquid that delights wine lovers. And whatever the vintage, it always impresses with its generous and harmonious nose.

VINE VARIETY
28 acres (11 hectares) red: 95% Merlot, 5% Cabernet Franc.

OUR FAVORITE WINES
Since 1998, Pétrus has been in outrageously good form, enabling it to reconnect with the great vintages of the 1920s (1921 and 1929), 1940s (1945, 1947, 1949), and 1960s (1961, 1964), and in particular through its sumptuous and refined 1998, 2000, 2003, and 2004 offerings.

Petrus, the most famous Pomerol cru, is not a château but a quiet vineyard with a recently acquired new winery.

Le Pin

At a time when Bordeaux was so hampered by its own hierarchies it was almost paralyzed by them, Le Pin came along and overthrew a number of accepted ideas. When Jacques Thienpont established the property in 1979, people were amazed at his ambition to take this wine (admittedly produced in minute quantities) to the summit of Pomerol perfection. In the case of a number of local observers, astonishment turned to disbelief when the 1982 vintage went down in legend almost straight away. Château Le Pin is almost impossible to get hold of today, and its price has gone through the ceiling. So what is so extraordinary about this wine? In many respects, Le Pin is the very opposite of what we would normally expect (and sometimes fear) from a Bordeaux. Where most Bordeaux wines display a restrained aromatic palette, Le Pin flaunts an exotic bouquet in which coconut takes over from ultra-ripe black fruit and a roasted, woody flavor unfolds uninhibitedly. Neither is there any austerity or tannic rigor to harden a body that is soft to the point of suavity. Languid and sensual, Le Pin is a Bordeaux from another world.

VINE VARIETY
5 acres (2 hectares) red: 98% Merlot, 2% various.

OUR FAVORITE WINES
While two of the vintages (1982 and 1983) from the early days of this micro-estate remain unsurpassed wonders, recent years possess a velvety texture and highly seductive charm in addition to the wine's customary aromatic exuberance. The 1998, 2000, 2001, and 2005 all stand out for their well-developed roundness.

Château
Trotanoy

Alongside Pétrus, Trotanoy is the other gem in the crown of owner Établissements Jean-Pierre Moueix. Its terroir, more gravelly than Pétrus, places it at the very center of its appellation. At its best – in other words, over the last dozen years or so – this wine possesses a "midway" style that has all the necessary ingredients to appeal to Bordeaux purists who often criticize Pomerol wines for being far too rounded. For while Trotanoy, like the other greats of its appellation, possesses the capacity to instantly seduce with its unctuous body and palette of developed aromas, it also reveals real intensity: it is elegant and silky but undeniably well structured. This fresh, joyful vigor gives the wine surefire aging potential. In the 1980s this aspect was somewhat neglected, but Trotanoy previously enjoyed a reputation as one of the most harmoniously aging of Bordeaux wines.

VINE VARIETY
17 acres (7 hectares) red: 90% Merlot, 10% Cabernet Franc.

OUR FAVORITE WINES
The harmony and freshness of this wine are as legendary as its aging potential. The truly outstanding 1998, 2000, and 2003 vintages will join this estate's list of benchmark wines.

Vieux Château Certan

The Certan district has always been considered a special Pomerol terroir. All that distinguishes it from its next-door neighbor Pétrus is the fact that it is a few feet higher than the rest of the appellation and combines fairly deep, clay-like soils with a shallow layer of gravel. While only Merlot will ripen properly at Pétrus, at Vieux Château Certan the two Cabernet varieties also often reach maturity. Indeed, the Thienpont family was absolutely right to retain the ancient practice of giving Bouchet – the local name for Cabernet Franc – an important role in the blend. This feature gives the wine a rather different character to the other Pomerols, particularly when young: it is more linear, more discreet, even displaying somewhat green tannins at times. However, extended aging in the cellar inevitably does it justice. When mature, the nose is among the most complex and elegant of all the Libournais wines, with cedar and spice notes that provide the perfect complement to the classic aromas of truffle and violet.

VINE VARIETY
35 acres (14 hectares) red: 60% Merlot, 30% Cabernet Franc, 10% Cabernet Sauvignon.

OUR FAVORITE WINES
This wine's most original successes occur during the great Cabernet vintages such as 1986, 1996, and 2000 but more generally the good balance between grape varieties ensures enviable consistency. Of recent vintages, 2001 and 2004 would seem to be the most promising.

Château
Calon-Ségur

The Marquis de Ségur was fond of declaring that his heart belonged to Calon, the third of his grands crus (along with Latour and Lafite). It is easy to see why as this impeccably maintained property, still enclosed by its ancient walls, is truly magnificent. Its terroir is very special, combining the classic deep gravel of the northern Médoc with clay to produce a balanced, powerful but smooth wine that, due to its quality, longevity, and consistency, compares favorably with any premier cru between 1900 and 1960. Following something of a decline in quality between 1961 and the beginning of the 1980s, Calon-Ségur gradually regained its form under the guidance of Madame Gasqueton, an owner with plenty of good country sense. She may not have made any spectacular changes to the daily routines, but her scrupulous respect for all the best Médoc traditions paid dividends. Recent vintages can only increase the universal respect in which this wine is held.

VINE VARIETY
222 acres (90 hectares) red: 60% Cabernet Sauvignon, 30% Merlot, 10% Cabernet Franc.

OUR FAVORITE WINES
Global warming and a steady improvement in grape selection and vinification methods during the 1990s have resulted in a string of five fine vintages since 1998. The 1998, 2002, 2003, 2004, and 2005 should go down in history alongside the legendary 1940 and 1950 vintages.

Château
Cos d'Estournel

Cos d'Estournel was the life's work of Louis-Gaspard d'Estournel, who died bankrupt shortly before the 1855 classification, which placed his château in the second growth but at the head of the Saint-Estèphe properties. Somewhat earlier, after acquiring and reorganizing the vineyard, he constructed an impressive winery building in the style of a pagoda in order to demonstrate to the Bordelais wine merchants that Cos d'Estournel's fame would transcend national borders and win admirers as far away as the exquisite palaces of China. Perched on a hillock (known as a cos in the Gascon language), this proud vineyard, which faces Château Lafite in the Pauillac appellation, benefits from an ideal aspect favored by moderating climatic influences from the ocean and the Gironde estuary. The property's later owners have been more astute than its creator. Bruno Prats, who ran the estate during the final quarter of the 20th century, turned it into one of the most consistent of the higher-ranked Bordeaux crus. Jean-Guillaume, who took over the running of Cos d'Estournel (on behalf of a new owner) from his father, has endowed the wine with even greater density and depth.

VINE VARIETY
166 acres (67 hectares): 60% Cabernet Sauvignon, 40% Merlot.

OUR FAVORITE WINES
Since 1971, Cos has shown impressive consistency with very few bad or even disappointing years. Of the most recent period, 1996, 2000, and 2002 are unquestionably among the most successful Bordeaux wines of their years.

The three turrets of Cos d'Estournel, the instantly recognizable symbol of a vineyard that its founder sought to make universal and unique.

Château
Ducru-Beaucaillou

Like many of the great Médoc estates, Ducru-Beaucaillou acquired its name and independence in the 18th century at a time when the development of viticulture in the region was so intense that the Gironde notables were said to have been seized by a "planting craze." Enjoying (like Beychevelle and Las Cases, its neighbors to the south and north) a splendid site bordering the Gironde, Ducru soon rose to become one of the great Bordeaux wines. While wine merchant Nathaniel Johnston undertook a brilliant modernization of the property in the second half of the 19th century, it was only when the Borie family purchased it in 1941, and with the assistance of the father of modern winemaking, Émile Peynaud, that Ducru was able to show what it was truly capable of. In the 1950s, Ducru shone for its slender elegance and unusual depth. More unusual still is the tannic refinement displayed by many outstanding Ducru vintages. This quintessential Médoc character had faded slightly by the later years of the 20th century, but has now been rediscovered in all its brilliance.

VINE VARIETY

136 acres (55 hectares) red: 70% Cabernet Sauvignon, 25% Merlot, 5% Cabernet Franc.

OUR FAVORITE WINES

This property produced a string of glorious vintages between 1953 and 1985. It rediscovered the splendor of those years with its superb and very deep 1996, and more recently with the brilliantly promising 2003, 2004, and 2005 vintages.

Château
Gruaud Larose

The two Gruaud brothers, one an abbot and the other a judge, merged their lands in the 18th century to form a single vast and ambitious vineyard. Legend has it that the judge built a tower among the vines so that he could keep a closer eye on his workforce and spot any missing vinestocks. The estate rapidly acquired an outstanding reputation, and its wine commanded almost as high a price as that of Lafite, Latour, and Margaux. This glorious past (hence the pompous-sounding motto "the king of wine and the wine of kings") was based on what was and remains a wonderful terroir. Unlike properties such as Beychevelle, Ducru, and Léoville, Gruaud is not located on the edge of the estuary but is set back slightly on a hill of deep gravel that terminates in a plateau – an ideal site for vines. The estate was reunited (having been split in two in the 19th century), thanks to the tenacity of the Cordier family, who proceeded to take it to the highest levels in the 1950s. While the wine did not exactly share in the general progress made by the great Bordeaux estates at the end of the 20th century, it still holds a wonderful trump card in the form of its wonderful and unusual terroir.

VINE VARIETY
203 acres (82 hectares) red: 57% Cabernet Sauvignon, 31% Merlot, 8% Cabernet Franc, 2% Petit Verdot, 2% Malbec.

OUR FAVORITE WINES
Gruaud Larose produced some of the greatest wines of the mid-20th century, culminating in an extraordinary 1959. During recent times, the 2000 and 2003, wines of both power and refinement, have again shown the property at its best.

The countryside around Gruaud Larose, with its broad vistas, is typical of the best Médoc vineyards: the roots of the plants become deeply embedded in the gravelly soil that lies over a layer of marl.

Château
Giscours

A large property in the Margaux appellation, Château Giscours' journey through the 20th century was marked by a certain flamboyance, brilliant highs, and a series of dramatic lows – reminding us that the history of great Bordeaux is a saga dominated by individuals and families. Known to have been in existence as early as the 16th century, the estate passed from owner to owner, from the unusual (it was bought during the Revolution by two American citizens!) to the traditional (for 60 years it was in the hands of the Cruse family of famous Bordeaux wine merchants). But when Nicolas Tari bought the property in 1954, he had to pull up a large area of the vineyard that had been planted with hybrid varieties! His stewardship ushered in a period of considerable success that unfortunately collapsed in major crisis at the end of the century. Subsequently acquired by Dutch businessman Eric Albada, Giscours is once more rising from its ashes. Vintages from the early years of the 21st century have again shown the wine at its best – as a long-distance runner whose pure-bred bouquet and good structure unfold slowly but with rare conviction.

VINE VARIETY
198 acres (80 hectares) red: 55% Cabernet Sauvignon, 40% Merlot, 5% Cabernet Franc.

OUR FAVORITE WINES
It was only at the beginning of the new millennium that Giscours reconnected fully with its glory days. The successful 2000, 2002, and 2003 vintages are wines with depth and great aging potential as is the 2005.

Château
Latour

Throughout the last century, Latour was the most consistent of the premiers crus. But consistency alone does not make a first growth. The property therefore had the good taste to pepper its history and the memories of devoted wine lovers with a number of unusual vintages that in terms of their fullness of body and breadth of nose demolish both the national and international competition with the assurance of giants. Prime examples are the 1961 and 1982, which attracted admiration from their early youth and continue to do so today. Without a shadow of doubt the 2003 is set to follow in their footsteps. Each time they occur, these magical years validate the work and talent of a gifted director and his team. But more than this, they draw something quintessential from what is an exceptional terroir, without doubt the most spectacular in the Médoc region. The natural gifts enjoyed by this classic wine are inherent in the gently curving hilltop dominating the wide estuary (which ensures an even temperature – this stretch of lands never freezes), its deep layer of large, round gravel, and its efficient drainage system.

VINE VARIETY

161 acres (65 hectares) red: 78% Cabernet Sauvignon, 20% Merlot, 1% Petit Verdot, 1% Cabernet Franc.

OUR FAVORITE WINES

The Latour 1961 and 1982 have an assured place in the pantheon of star wines of the 20th century. The 2000 and, with even greater justification, the 2003 and 2005 can be expected to go down alongside them as legendary.

Château
Lafite Rothschild

Properties that present the visitor with such an immediately attractive and harmonious prospect are rare indeed in Médoc, which sometimes seems like a monotonous ocean of vines. Naturally one notices the vines, organized into impeccably neat, tight rows separated by ploughed furrows whose purpose seems to be to allow the earth and its burnished gravel to breathe. But the little park reproduced so faithfully in the etching on the wine label – its lake, its poplars, the château, and above all the huge and complex network of winery buildings conveys an image of serene independence as if Lafite were an independent, self-contained universe of exquisite beauty. It comes as no surprise, therefore, to learn that the wine stands head and shoulders above all its neighbors – including the other Pauillac grand crus. Château Lafite possesses tension, structural dynamism, and a bouquet of unrivaled brilliance. At its best (that is to say mainly since 1995), Lafite is like a drawn bow with a satin arrow.

VINE VARIETY
247 acres (100 hectares) red: 75% Cabernet Sauvignon, 20% Merlot, 4% Cabernet Franc, 1% Petit Verdot.

OUR FAVORITE WINES
Since 1990, Lafite has developed into what is probably the most consistent and immaculate of the leading Bordeaux growths, producing a series of exceptional vintages with an elegance of style that by no means excludes intensity or depth. Of recent years, 1996, 2000, and 2003 in particular, will go down in history alongside legendary vintages such as 1959 and 1982.

Designed by the Catalan architect Ricardo Bofill, the winery at Château Lafite-Rothschild is laid out as an imposing arena.

Château Léoville Barton

Before Anthony there was Ronald. And before Ronald there was Hugh, who succeeded his father Thomas Barton, the founder of a firm of wine traders of the same name who bought Langoa and part of the Léoville domaine, two properties in the village of Saint-Julien. This was in the early years of the 19th century and the Bartons, Irish by birth, had already founded one of the most engaging dynasties in Bordeaux. Anthony Barton, a true gentleman of the wine trade, succeeded his uncle and maintained the domaine with exemplary consistency at almost the highest level of the Médoc growths, the "almost" indicating that only four châteaux could justify a higher ranking at the time of classification. Barton is never the most concentrated, powerful or dazzlingly impressive of wines. However, it is certainly one of the most civilized and best balanced – just like this family straddling two great and ancient cultures.

VINE VARIETY
119 acres (48 hectares) red: 70% Cabernet Sauvignon, 22% Merlot, 8% Cabernet Franc.

OUR FAVORITE WINES
For more than two decades, Château Léoville Barton has produced a succession of immaculate Saint-Juliens, of which 2000 and 2003 are without doubt the most resoundingly joyous.

Château Léoville Las Cases

For decades the indomitable Las Cases, so close to a Latour in terms of its structure as well as the nature of the vineyard, the "grand clos" that makes up the bulk of this great wine, has given the lie to a classification a century and a half old that sought to confine this wine for all eternity to the second division of Médoc wines. The cold rage that motivated Michel Delon throughout his exacting stewardship has given way to the no less determined character of his son and, for nearly 40 years, Léoville Las Cases has helped define great Médoc wine, combining the brilliant, trenchant honesty of elite Cabernet Sauvignon with the luster of Cabernet Franc and the deep mellowness of Merlot – the whole adorned from time to time by a pinch of Petit Verdot. From one year to the next, Las Cases remains living proof of the importance of rigorous standards in winemaking, demonstrating that the creation of a great wine depends on a combination of different factors – including the right terroir, talented winemakers, and attention to detail.

VINE VARIETY

240 acres (97 hectares) red: 65% Cabernet Sauvignon, 19% Merlot, 13% Cabernet Franc, 3% Petit Verdot.

OUR FAVORITE WINES

Lesser vintages are unknown here, as a rigorous selection procedure means it is always possible to vinify great wines for laying down. Since the beginning of the third millennium, the wines made at Château Léoville Las Cases have gained in voluptuousness without forfeiting their legendary rigorous architecture.

Château
Léoville Poyferré

Families from the north of France have played an important role in the Médoc, with the Cuvelier family acquiring Château Léoville Poyferré in 1921. The family member currently in charge is Didier Cuvelier, who took the reins more than 20 years ago. Between the beginning of the 1920s and his arrival, however, the wine had suffered a marked decline as a result of over-cautious, parsimonious management – as was so often the case in the 20th century. Having fallen some way behind its neighbors Las Cases and Barton, Poyferré has slowly but surely climbed back under its new regime. Rehabilitation of the vineyard, respect for exacting agricultural practices, the radical transformation of winery equipment and maturing facilities, new cellars – over the past two decades Poyferré has taken all the necessary steps to achieve excellence again. All this hard work will pay off in the 21st century.

VINE VARIETY

198 (80 hectares) red: 60% Cabernet Sauvignon, 30% Merlot, 8% Petit Verdot, 2% Cabernet Franc.

OUR FAVORITE WINES

Léoville Poyferré has been making steady progress for more than 20 years and is among Médoc's "dead cert" fine wines each year. The 2003 is without doubt one of the property's most successful wines and the 2005 will most likely surpass it.

Château
Lynch-Bages

Few Bordeaux wines are as closely connected with a single family as Lynch-Bages with the Cazes. Not that the Cazes family has always been the owner – in fact, it did not acquire the property until 1934. Since that date, however, the family has taken it to such a high level that Lynch-Bages has outgrown its ranking in the 1855 classification as a fifth growth and has joined the elite group of Bordeaux stars. Consistency is its main virtue. A "vertical" tasting from the 1930s to the 1970s, the years when it enjoyed a merely modest reputation, has shown how consistently impressive the wine was for its roundness and supple fullness. In the 1980s, when Jean-Michel Cazes took over from his father, Lynch-Bages acquired an extra dimension. It became a pioneer of modernity with a deep, generous, fleshy character and seductive bouquet even when young. Today, the Cazes family has taken on another challenge: to revive the village of Bages around the château.

VINE VARIETY

222 acres (90 hectares) red: 73% Cabernet Sauvignon, 15% Merlot, 10% Cabernet Franc, 2% Petit Verdot.
11 acres (4.5 hectares) white: 40% Sauvignon, 40% Sémillon, 20% Muscadelle.

OUR FAVORITE WINES

This wine was already beyond reproach in the decades just before and after the middle of the 20th century. However, there can be no doubt that it reached a turning point in the 1980s with deep, dense, and succulent vintages such as 1985, 1990, 2000, and 2003.

Château
Margaux

Margaux cultivates elegance like no other winery in the world. Nothing exists here that is not the product of an overwhelming desire for refinement and sophistication. The sense of enchantment begins at the bend in the straight, simple lane that leads past Margaux cemetery – the resting place of benevolent onlooker Bernard Ginestet, the former owner – when visitors encounter the tranquil and majestic avenue of plane trees ending in the impressive but slender-columned façade of the château. This impression of serenity continues with the inner courtyards, winery buildings and cellars, which (unlike most in Médoc) have never been subjected to the indignity of drastic remodeling but have been scrubbed from top to bottom in an ongoing desire for perfection. Since its purchase in 1977 by André Menzelopoulos and a spectacular recovery led by his daughter Corinne in conjunction with brilliant director Paul Pontalier, Margaux has redefined elegant Bordeaux as a wine that is slender and yielding but never meager (unlike too many Margaux wines of the past), with a satiny, steely structure, brilliant with good length and displaying an unrivaled freshness of nose.

VINE VARIETY

203 acres (82 hectares) red: 75% Cabernet Sauvignon, 20% Merlot, 3% Petit Verdot, 2% Cabernet Franc. 30 acres (12 hectares) white: Sauvignon.

OUR FAVORITE WINES

Since 2000, one wine that should definitely not be overlooked is the marvelous Pavillon Blanc de Margaux. As for the reds, there have been many great vintages in recent years. Among the leaders are 1985, 1990, 1995, 2000 (perhaps the best), 2001, 2003, and 2005.

In recent years, grands crus such as Château Margaux have paid increasing attention to the selection of one prestige wine, although this may constitute only half of the château's total output.

Château
Montrose

Like Sociando-Mallet to the north and Latour to the south, Château Montrose is one of a handful of Médoc grand crus whose vineyards overlook the immense placid Gironde estuary, descending gently to the fields that separate them from the water's edge. Sites of this kind deal a rare viticultural trump hand. First, there is the soil: a deep bed of alluvial gravel deposited by the river over the course of the preceding millennia, resting on a marly base. Then there is the geographical orientation and natural drainage of water from the vineyards. Finally, there's the mild and stable climate provided by the estuary. These natural advantages, offset prettily by the Charmolüe family with gleaming monastery-like buildings, have helped the wine acquire an enviable reputation. Well-bred to the point of typical Médoc stiffness was a common verdict. In reality, a touch more control over the vineyard and a degree more precision in the vinification process have helped the wine progress spectacularly over recent years. Any harshness has disappeared, leaving the good breeding intact.

VINE VARIETY

168 acres (68 hectares) red: 65% Cabernet Sauvignon, 25% Merlot, 10% Cabernet Franc.

OUR FAVORITE WINES

The 1928 went down in Bordeaux legend, but has since been matched by the brilliant 1990. It now looks likely that the 2000 and 2003 vintages will surpass both with their impressive depth and elegant texture.

Château
Palmer

After the Battle of Waterloo, British general Charles Palmer arrived in Bordeaux and decided to stay. He bought the Gasq estate at Issan, rechristened it Palmer after building a delightful and spectacular château, replanted the vineyard, restored the cellars and, just as the wine was starting to make a reputation for itself, went bankrupt! These tumultuous beginnings clearly did no long-term damage to the property, and testify to the fact that the château was one of the most brilliant in the 1960s and 1970s not just by the 1961 but by a dozen or so others – including the 1966, 1970, and 1975. The wine continues to owe a good measure of its success to its truly individual style, which derives from an unusually high proportion – by Margaux standards – of Merlot. Its suave and engaging nose, with a profusion of exquisite fruit aromas, seduces immediately while the wine has a melting, velvety sweetness in the mouth. This personality, which would be compromised by the least element of casualness, has forged a link in recent years with the Château Palmer of the 1960s.

VINE VARIETY
126 acres (51 hectares) red: 47% Cabernet Sauvignon, 47% Merlot, 6% Petit Verdot.

OUR FAVORITE WINES
The 1961 is the Château Palmer vintage par excellence. In 1998, however, the wine started to achieve an impressive consistency that has enabled it to make nearly every year since then a success. The 2000 and 2001 in particular display an extraordinarily melting, velvety texture surpassing even that of the 2005.

Château
Mouton Rothschild

Mouton's predominant characteristic is its exuberance. The château of Brane-Mouton (the *Mouton* indicating not that these were once sheep-grazing lands but, more appropriately for wine, that the site was dominated by a mound referred to as a *motton* in old French) changed its name to Mouton Rothschild when Baron Nathaniel de Rothschild acquired it in 1855. He was the first great figure in Mouton's history. The second was Philippe de Rothschild, who, from his arrival at the property in 1922 to his death in 1987, literally reinvented the wine, its legend, its marketing, and its personality. The decision to commission a different artist to design each label – the only exceptions being 1945, the "victory vintage," and 2005, the 150th anniversary year – made an important contribution to the estate's unique status. But the main factor was the wine itself, which resembles no other. The immediate charm of its bouquet, its powerful spiciness, its generous body in the mouth, and its rich tannins (which sometimes – as around the turn of the 1990s – bordered on the hard) add up to something unique. Strangely inconsistent in the past, the wine seems to have discovered a new and more harmonious rhythm in the 21st century.

VINE VARIETY
193 acres (78 hectares) red: 77% Cabernet Sauvignon, 11% Merlot, 10% Cabernet Franc, 2% Petit Verdot.
10 acres (4 hectares) white: 51% Sauvignon Blanc, 47% Sémillon, 2% Muscadelle.

OUR FAVORITE WINES
The 1945, "the victory vintage" as the famous label proudly proclaims, has gone down in wine legend. More recently the 1959, 1982, 1990, and above all 2000, 2002, 2003, and 2005 have reconnected with this glorious history.

Fine Bordeaux wines are matured in oak casks – sometimes, as at Mouton, entirely newly made each year – and allowed to age for 20 or more months.

Château
Pichon-Longueville

The noble Pichon dynasty was famous in Bordeaux as long ago as the Middle Ages. When Baron Pichon de Longueville created the domaine at the beginning of the 18th century, the property (not yet divided) was immediately regarded as one of the most important Médoc estates. When the property was divided, this male half (the baron bequeathed Pichon-Longueville to his sons and Pichon-Comtesse to his daughters!) was nevertheless long considered to be a "feminine" Pauillac – with everything this implies in terms of unacceptable male chauvinism. In other words, that "Pichon-Baron," as it was generally known at the time, lacked body and depth. It was not until the property was bought by insurance company AXA that it began to reveal its true character as a typical Pauillac – succulent, intense, long, with a Havana cigar and mocha nose that gradually turns to cedarwood over time – under the strict guidance of Jean-Michel Cazes. Three centuries after its creation, Pichon-Baron is in better health than ever.

VINE VARIETY
180 acres (73 hectares) red: 60% Cabernet Sauvignon, 35% Merlot, 4% Cabernet Franc, 1% Petit Verdot.

OUR FAVORITE WINES
Pichon-Longueville has made brilliant progress since the end of the 1980s, producing a great 1989 and an even greater 1990. Since then the most accomplished and distinguished wine from this great property has been the 2000; 2005, however, looks promising.

Château Pichon-Longueville Comtesse de Lalande

Having originally been created by Virginie de Pichon-Longueville, a woman of considerable willpower and talent, "Pichon-Comtesse" (as it is known in Bordeaux) was later given a new lease of life by another woman of great character: May-Eliane de Lencquesaing. Virginie was the youngest of Baron de Pichon-Longueville's three daughters, who were left three-fifths of the original estate by their father. She built the château, a rare example of Romantic architecture in the Médoc, and managed the estate with extraordinary dedication. In 1978, more than a century after her death, history repeated itself when May-Eliane de Lencquesaing (née Mialhe) inherited the estate after drawing lots for the family property with her brothers and sisters. With impressive dynamism and an iron will, she reclaimed a place among the dozen or so star Haut-Médocs while retaining a planting mix that contrasts strongly with the other great Pauillacs traditionally dominated by Cabernet Sauvignon.

VINE VARIETY

173 (70 hectares) red: 45% Cabernet Sauvignon, 35% Merlot, 12% Cabernet Franc, 8% Petit Verdot.

OUR FAVORITE WINES

This wine started to make spectacular progress in the mid-1980s. However, it was not until the 1990s that it achieved a certain formal perfection with the very deep and refined 1995, 1996, 2000 and, most importantly, the marvelous 2003.

Château
Pontet-Canet

One of the most significant events to have occurred in the Médoc over the last 15 years is the drastic improvement in quality achieved by this classic Pauillac, the next-door neighbor of Mouton Rothschild. Alfred Tesseron manages the property with passion and tenacity, and has turned it into a pioneering venture on a number of accounts. Work in the vineyard has reached a degree of rigor and precision previously considered impossible on such a large scale. At harvest time the utmost respect is shown for the grapes, which are collected in small crates, and a new, fully gravity-fed winery respects the estate's complex division into parcels with an array of vats adapted to the size of each parcel. Michel Rolland was brought in as a consultant, as a result of which the aging process has been substantially improved, and judicious slow and regular oxygenation in the barrel has refined the texture of the flagship wine, endowing it with silky and highly seductive tannins. This terroir produces highly aromatic Cabernet Sauvignon with an emphasis on the variety's core cedar and Havana tobacco character, which only fully develops after long aging.

VINE VARIETY
198 acres (80 hectares) red: 61% Cabernet Sauvignon, 32% Merlot, 5% Cabernet Franc, 2% Petit Verdot.

OUR FAVORITE WINES
Starting in 1990, this wine gradually rediscovered the full opulence of body and nobility of flavor of its exceptional terroir. Of recent vintages, our personal favorite is for 2000, 2004, and 2005, followed by 2001 and 2002 (which are barely inferior to 1998).

Some of the vats used in winemaking at Pontet-Canet are made of wood, while others are of concrete. In both cases they have a truncated shape that is particularly suitable for fermenting Bordeaux wines.

Château
Rauzan-Ségla

Like Rauzan-Gassies, the other half of what was once a single property, Château Rauzan-Ségla owes its name to Pierre des Mesures de Rauzan, who acquired the estate in 1661. It stayed in the family for two centuries before passing to the Cruse family of Bordeaux wine merchants, in whose hands it remained for almost a century. After a temporary interruption, this family continuity seems to have resumed with the purchase of the property in 1994 by the Wertheimer family (the owners of Chanel). In the meantime, the progress of this historic wine toward fulfilling its potential (along with Château Margaux it can be described as one of the purest of the Margaux wines) was inevitably set back. Thanks to some painstaking work in the vineyard and cellars, and despite often remaining enigmatic and closed during its early years, the wine has now been able to fulfill this potential. Never solid or heavy, Rauzan-Ségla evolves slowly, developing tannins of great silkiness, brilliant acidity, and rigorous grip. This classic profile of a great Margaux is occasionally complemented by licorice and red berry aromas evolving toward cedarwood and tobacco.

VINE VARIETY
128 acres (52 hectares) red: 54% Cabernet Sauvignon, 41% Merlot, 4% Petit Verdot, 1% Cabernet Franc.

OUR FAVORITE WINES
The delicate, distinguished character of this wine never fails to materialize after a few years of aging. Indeed, the progress made from the beginning of the 1990s onward has produced dazzling results that can be seen in vintages such as 1990, 1996, 1998, 2000, 2001, and 2003.

Honest, rounded, reserved, and elegant, Rauzan-Ségla is one of the finest representatives of Margaux wines.

Château
Sociando-Mallet

Little did Jean Gautreau know when he bought a few acres of land on the banks of the Gironde on which he planned to build a summer house that he would go down in history as the creator of the best new Médoc cru since the 1855 classification. His first wines, made from a small collection of old vines, struck this "pure-bred" Médocain as so characteristic of their variety that he threw himself into a project to plant 75 acres (30 hectares). He gradually added to the vineyard until it grew to its current size of 161 acres (65 hectares) of vines. The terroir consists of more or less clayey gravel and the vines benefit from an exceptional estuary microclimate. This energetically vinified wine, which is luxuriously aged in new oak, possesses the body and density of the best Pauillacs or Saint-Estèphes along with the aging potential and classic cedar and graphite aromas of the finest Cabernet Sauvignons. Its originality stems from the power of expression of the Merlot, which envelops the terroir's strong minerality in an extremely voluptuous texture. Another factor in the cru's worldwide success is its consistency – lesser years are unheard of!

VINE VARIETY

161 acres (65 hectares) red: 55% Cabernet Sauvignon, 42% Merlot, 2% Cabernet Franc, 1% Petit Verdot.

OUR FAVORITE WINES

The consistency of Sociando-Mallet over the last 25 years has made it one of the most admired and sought-after of Médoc producers. Merlot gives even the lesser years an exceptional roundness and volume, but the true character of the terroir is only fully revealed in the great Cabernet years such as 1990, 1996, 2004, and 2005, when this cru bourgeois can be just as good as certain famous Pauillac or Saint-Estèphe second growths.

Château Haut-Bailly

Haut-Bailly is a jewel from every point of view. Located on a plateau of deep gravel mixed with a ferruginous soil particular to (and typical of) a number of Pessac-Léognan wines, the superb vineyard unfolds around the château in a single sweep. If Pessac is Graves' first historic pole, Haut-Bailly is at the center of its second, this vast plateau that begins above the village of Léognan with Malartic-Lagravière and ends at Martillac with Latour-Martillac. The château – or more precisely fine charterhouse – has been restored charmingly and without excessive display. So too have the cellars, which are now a model of viticultural efficiency. Dedicated to reds, and moreover to the uncompromising brilliance of Cabernet, for a long time the estate was owned first by one and then by another gentleman of wine. Jean Sanders was followed by Robert Wilmers, an American who fell in love with the vineyard and its surroundings. Haut-Bailly is still run by his daughter, the discerning Véronique Sanders. This serene continuity is fully expressed through the consistency and harmonious personality of the wines, which are among the finest on the Left Bank.

GRAND VIN DE BORDEAUX

CHATEAU HAUT-BAILLY

GRAND CRU CLASSÉ
PESSAC-LÉOGNAN

2003

MIS EN BOUTEILLE AU CHATEAU

VINE VARIETY
79 (32 hectares) red: 65% Cabernet Sauvignon, 25% Merlot, 10% Cabernet Franc.

OUR FAVORITE WINES
This highly consistent property produced superb Graves in 1989, 1990, 1996, 1998, 2000, and 2003 although the years in between have been almost on a par. The deep wines made here show refined tannins, length rather than breadth, and an aromatic freshness that is the hallmark of great claret. The 2005 promises to be sublime.

Domaine de
Chevalier

Chevalier, which is somewhat removed from the winemaking centers, is set in a landscape dominated by pine trees and moorland that opens up toward Gascony. It is a world apart, a tiny wine principality with its own well-defined borders. But its terroir alone, a gravel hilltop impressive for its homogeneity, justifies the unusual location. Despite the fact that production has easily been dominated by red, Chevalier has always been one of the best specimens of great dry white Bordeaux. Even when production of dry white was almost universally mediocre in Bordeaux (during the 1960s and 1970s), Chevalier stood out for its clear, frank style that shone without showing off. This remains true today. The reds, which have never been swayed by any kind of trend, share a similar profile. Chevalier is an aristocrat that pursues its own independent path with supreme nonchalance.

VINE VARIETY
82 acres (33 hectares) red: 65% Cabernet Sauvignon, 30% Merlot, 2.5% Petit Verdot, 2.5% Cabernet Franc. 11 acres (4.5 hectares) white: 70% Sauvignon, 30% Sémillon.

OUR FAVORITE WINES
Chevalier's white, along with that of Laville, has been one of the most brilliant and consistent whites over the last 30 years and more. Among recent vintages, 2000 and 2004 have been particularly successful. Its red always needs to age for a few years for its aristocratic reserve to open out. That said, its 2002, 2003, 2004, and 2005 are already showing great promise.

In his unusual circular winery, Chevalier has opted for stainless steel vats for his red wines. The white wines are matured in casks.

Château
Haut-Brion

Samuel Pepys, the apparently prudish high-ranking British naval administrator, was actually a hellraiser, a seducer of servant girls, and a frequenter of taverns. Recording his turpitudes in his secret diary (discovered two centuries after his death), he describes his encounter with a wine "that hath a good and most particular taste that I never met with" named "Ho Bryan." His spelling may have been somewhat shaky, but it is clear that by April 10, 1663 Haut-Brion was already making a name for itself on English tables. Located close to Bordeaux – so close, in fact, that it now falls firmly within the city's suburbs – Haut-Brion has been an undisputed star among wines ever since. And its status is richly merited. The careful balance between Cabernet and Merlot allows a unique personality to shine through, featuring truffle notes and a smoky quality, which is the preserve of this wine and its special terroir. Maturing at a slow, wise pace, its full character unfolds slowly and quietly in the cellar. And the very rare Haut-Brion white offers further opportunities to shine, as if Haut-Brion were trying to establish itself as the ultimate yardstick for great wine.

VINE VARIETY
107 acres (43.2 hectares) red: 45% Cabernet Sauvignon, 37% Merlot, 18% Cabernet Franc.
7 acres (2.7 hectares) white: 63% Sémillon, 37% Sauvignon.

OUR FAVORITE WINES
Famous for its very high degree of consistency, Haut-Brion has attained peaks of excellence in its recent history with its 1989, 2000, and 2002 vintages. However, its reds and nearly all its whites are of exceptional quality nearly every year. The red and white wines in 2005 are superb.

Famous for its red wine – such as this wonderful 1996 – with its hints of truffle and remarkable reliability, Haut-Brion also produces limited quantities of a delicious white wine.

Château
La Mission Haut-Brion

Located directly opposite its sister property, Haut-Brion, La Mission is a "next-door" wine that is keen to assert its own personality. Yes, its terroir and mix of varieties are very similar to those of its illustrious neighbor, whose characteristic smokiness and supple, harmonious depth it shares. Yes, the owners of Haut-Brion – the Duc and Duchesse de Mouchy – acquired the property more than a quarter of a century ago and entrusted the impressive perfectionist Jean Delmas, the manager of Haut-Brion, with the technical stewardship. Having succeeded his father in this role, Delmas has in turn passed the baton to his son, who now looks after the two châteaux. Despite these strong similarities, La Mission possesses in its youth a velvet softness and mellowness on the palate that makes it more immediately charming than its more celebrated counterpart. This wine possesses a discreet, altogether aristocratic gaiety that is even more in evidence in the great vintages.

CHATEAU
LA MISSION HAUT-BRION

2000

MIS EN BOUTEILLE AU CHATEAU

DOMAINE CLARENCE DILLON S.A.
PROPRIETAIRE

VINE VARIETY
52 acres (21 hectares) red: 48% Cabernet Sauvignon, 45% Merlot, 7% Cabernet Franc.

OUR FAVORITE WINES
Less intense and less well-structured than Haut-Brion, La Mission is nevertheless an extremely voluptuous and elegant wine. The 2000 surpasses all other recent vintages for its intensity and superb breeding.

Château
Pape Clément

In the Middle Ages, Bertrand de Got was a Bordelais clergyman who became Clement V, the first Avignon pope. Although he did not live on this estate, he owned it and bequeathed it to the Bordeaux archbishopric, which in turn named it after its donor. Hardly any further from the center of Greater Bordeaux than Haut-Brion, Château Pape Clément is one of three vineyards (Carmes Haut-Brion is the third) in the built-up town of Pessac. It benefits from the pure gravelly soil that gives the wines of this area their very strong identity in terms of aroma. This potential nevertheless needs to be properly and fully exploited. Until 1985, when Bernard Magrez took over the running of the estate from his father, this was far from the case. This iron-willed manager is currently head of a very impressive winemaking business. At the time, this cru classé was very much the exception in a portfolio of business interests oriented toward branded wines and spirits. In 1986, however, the wine rediscovered superb form and has continued to progress ever since. The viticulture and vinification are carried out in highly impressive style and Château Pape Clément is now one of the biggest names in Bordeaux.

VINE VARIETY
74 acres (30 hectares) red: 60% Cabernet Sauvignon, 40% Merlot.
6 acres (2.5 hectares) white: 49% Sauvignon, 48% Sémillon, 3% Muscadelle.

OUR FAVORITE WINES
Château Pape Clément only really started producing great wines in 1986. These were outstanding, but its quality rose even higher with the 2000 vintage. The 2002, 2003, 2004, and 2005 are very great wines that combine a superb velvety texture with sheer expressive power.

Château
Malartic-Lagravière

The heart of this splendid Léognan property is one of the best locations for a vineyard in the whole of Bordeaux: a gravelly rise enjoying a perfect aspect and ideal drainage. It takes more than simply a great terroir to make great wine, however, and since acquiring the property, the Bonnie family has spent large sums of money on improving every stage of the production process. The remarkable technical facilities are based on a gravity-feed system and are designed to respect the integrity of the harvest while the sound advice of enologist Michel Rolland has transformed what was previously a distinguished though somewhat austere wine into something more appealing.

The reds have made enormous progress in terms of structure, ripeness of fruit, and terroir character over the last few years while retaining the aging potential on which the cru's fame rests. The white, dominated by Sauvignon Blanc, has also changed in style. Delicate, pure, subtly spiced but occasionally rather lean, it has gained in solidity without losing its delicate though highly expressive and distinctive muskiness. This type of wine is always drunk too young. It needs five or six years in the bottle for its qualities to develop fully.

GRAND CRU CLASSÉ DE GRAVES
CHATEAU
MALARTIC LAGRAVIERE
2003
PESSAC-LÉOGNAN
APPELLATION PESSAC-LÉOGNAN CONTRÔLÉE
PRODUCE OF FRANCE
SOCIÉTÉ CIVILE DU CHÂTEAU MALARTIC-LAGRAVIÈRE PROPRIÉTAIRE À LÉOGNAN (GIRONDE) · A & B BONNIE · GÉRANT
MIS EN BOUTEILLE AU CHATEAU

VINE VARIETY
91 acres (37 hectares) red: 50% Merlot, 40% Cabernet Sauvignon, 10% Cabernet Franc.
17 acres (7 hectares) white: 85% Sauvignon Blanc, 15% Sémillon.

OUR FAVORITE WINES
Since 1998 the reds have enjoyed uninterrupted success, the 2002 and 2004 vintages in particular displaying a refined elegance and astonishing body for this appellation. The whites underwent a change of style in 2002 as the result of a quest for greater ripeness of fruit.

The grapes at the spectacular and innovative winery at Château Malartic-Lagravière are delivered to the vats by gravity alone, a method that prevents the fruit being damaged.

Château
Smith Haut-Lafitte

Smith Haut-Lafitte, in the commune of Martillac, is located on one of the superb and extensive gravel plateaus that gave this entire winegrowing region the name "Caillou" (meaning stone or pebble). Dominating a number of major properties that fan out below (Bouscaut, Carbonnieux, La Louvière, and slightly farther south Haut-Bailly), Smith Haut-Lafitte is a salutary reminder that while there can be no great wine without a great terroir, a great terroir is nothing without the will to work it properly. For a period of many years when it was owned by wine merchants Eschenauer, Château Smith Haut-Lafitte was a wine without soul or style. Purchased in 1989 by a couple of dynamic entrepreneurs, Daniel and Florence Cathiard, not only has it caught up with the pack, but also it has become something of a model producer. Previously lacking in substance, it was reborn in the 1990s as a powerful, dense, and intense wine, and has now added subtlety and balance to those qualities.

VINE VARIETY

111 acres (45 hectares) red: 45% Cabernet Sauvignon, 35% Merlot, 20% Cabernet Franc.
27 acres (11 hectares) white: 90% Sauvignon Blanc, 5% Sauvignon Gris, 5% Sémillon.

OUR FAVORITE WINES

Since 1990 this wine – both red and white – has made enormous progress. The 2000, 2002, and above all 2003 vintages of both colors have shown an impressive level of perfection.

Château
Climens

Some wine lovers, with all the enthusiasm (but also the received ideas) of recent converts, judge the quality of a vin liquoreux by its color. The more intense and golden the nectar, the more worthy of praise they believe it to be. They will inevitably be disappointed, therefore, with this premier cru wine from Barsac, a small appellation adjacent to Sauternes and sometimes confused with it. A delicate, translucent yellow in its youth, Climens seems to defy the years and if, after a number of decades, it deigns to take on an amber hue, it still retains a certain diaphanous quality. Added to this eternally youthful air are a fresh nose, an elegance of texture, and a lack of heaviness that give the wine a cheerful, graceful character. Made by Bérénice Lurton, Climens possesses that very feminine quality, elegance, to the highest degree.

VINE VARIETY

74 acres (30 hectares) white: Sémillon.

OUR FAVORITE WINES

Delicacy and freshness are the perennial qualities of this vin liquoreux (a rich, syrupy category of sweet wine) of individual character. The 1997, 2001, 2002, and extraordinary 2003 and 2005 (perhaps the most accomplished of them all) have taken this wine to a stunning level.

Château
Coutet

Château Coutet, a model wine within the Barsac appellation, owns two old pneumatic winepresses over which the proprietors keep an extremely close watch. Now almost antiques, they were once among the most exciting developments in modern winemaking. They are vertical, like the winepresses of times gone by (as depicted in medieval engravings) as opposed to the modern ones, which are large machines with a horizontal drum, although the pressing action is effected by pneumatic pistons. This method is both gentle and extremely precise as grape pressing can be stopped at the exact moment the juice loses its initial purity. It therefore plays a fundamental role in the creation of a fine sweet wine in which only the juice of botrytized grapes is wanted. This excellent equipment was installed more than half a century ago by the previous owners, who manufactured the machines in their factory in Lyon, and helps Château Coutet to continue to shine today.

VINE VARIETY

95 acres (38.5 hectares) white: 75% Sémillon, 22% Sauvignon, 3% Muscadelle.

OUR FAVORITE WINES

In great years, Château Coutet's wines display an exemplary balance between opulence and freshness. The best examples are 1989, 1997, and 2001. The 2005 promises to be outstanding.

Botrytis, a minute fungus visible on some of the grapes in this bunch, gradually dissolves the skin of the fruit, and it is this that accounts for the inimitable taste of the finest Barsacs and Sauternes.

Château
Rieussec

Rieussec is the first estate visitors see on entering *le Sauternais*. Its château, which resembles a Gascon manor house, sits on a hilltop and keeps proud watch over the road that connects Sauternes with Langon and Bordeaux. It is also a wine that is easy to identify in comparative tastings, so emphatic are its qualities of opulence, syrupy richness, and roasted meat aroma. The geographical situation and orientation of the vineyards have made an important contribution to the construction of this strong personality, for although the wine has improved significantly in terms of consistency since the château was acquired by Eric de Rothschild in 1984, power was already a major characteristic of the great vintages prior to this date. From 1985, this power was subdued and civilized by Charles Chevallier, a great servant of Bordeaux wine who was handed the reins at Château Rieussec ten years before also taking charge at Lafite. Unlike many winemakers who apply the same recipe to any wine they make, Chevallier adapts to the fundamental personality of each wine and is thus able to respect Rieussec's richness while exalting the taut and slender character of a Lafite.

VINE VARIETY
185 acres (75 hectares) white: 90% Sémillon, 8% Sauvignon, 2% Muscadelle.

OUR FAVORITE WINES
Of legendary opulence and richness of body, Rieussec has been particularly impressive in good botrytis years such as 1997 and 2001.

Château
d'Yquem

While the unofficial but seldom disputed title of "best wine in the world" confers obvious advantages, this dominant status necessitates a standard of absolute excellence that is constantly being tested, scrutinized, and imitated. Although Yquem may not be superior to other wines in every respect, its supremacy is based on factors that help define the wine's lineage. Consistency is clearly its dominant characteristic, and this alone places it on another planet. Run-of-the-mill years are extremely rare. Furthermore, Yquem vintages always seem to be at their best regardless of their age. In terms of style, even the least syrupy examples display impressive volume in the mouth, unctuousness, and a profuse aroma. This triple opulence – of body, flesh, and nose – is the wine's hallmark. Despite this, the wine exhibits a near-perfect harmony whatever the vintage: Yquem is always Yquem. While the personnel, methods, and follow-up procedures may change (though relatively little compared to other wines), Yquem's character remains the same, transcending the human contribution with ease.

VINE VARIETY
255 acres (103 hectares) white: 80% Sémillon, 20% Sauvignon.

OUR FAVORITE WINES
Perfection in a bottle, Yquem can boast a longer succession of extraordinary vintages than any other wine. The legendary years are legion – the fabled 1811, 1921, 1928, 1937, 1967, and 1990. But its triumphs are by no means all in the past, as 1997 and 2001 have already shown themselves to be among the most glorious the property has produced. And 2005 has shown its exceptional potential from the very beginning!

Château Yquem still retains the aristocratic appearance that it must have had in the late 18th century when the future president of the United States, Thomas Jefferson, came here.

Château Suduiraut

Geographically speaking, Suduiraut has taken up a forward position and is keeping a close watch on Yquem. On the very edge of the vast vineyard that is Bordeaux, Sauternes – an area that is entirely given over to the special art of making fine sweet wine – is preserved a uniquely serene and secretive atmosphere. A neighbor of the undisputed king of Sauternes, Suduiraut is a simultaneously faithful and ambitious vassal of Yquem. Faithful, because in great years its opulence is in no way inferior to Yquems; ambitious, because the wine's nobility of aroma, its harmony and unctuousness reach the very peak of perfection in such years. Admittedly, for a long time Suduiraut was a wine for great vintages only. This reputation was magnified moreover by the rare special selection blend known as Cuvée Madame – another way of saying that many others were not that good. In truth it was not until the château was bought by insurance company AXA that the means to improve matched the desire to improve. Significant investment and an influx of talent started to bear fruit in the middle of the 1990s. Suduiraut had finally thrown off its vassalage!

VINE VARIETY

222 acres (90 hectares) white: 90% Sémillon, 10% Sauvignon.

OUR FAVORITE WINES

The 1997, 2001, 2003, and 2005 have earned themselves a place on the property's roll of honor (alongside the marvelous Cuvée Madame 1989) with their fullness of body and stupendously rich nose.

The deep golden color of a fine Sauternes makes this wine unique even before you have tasted it.

Domaine
Raveneau

In Chablis, where most of the domaines have significantly increased their area under vine and hence their production, the two Raveneau brothers have remained faithful to the 18.5 acres (7.5 hectares) they inherited from their parents, believing it would be impossible to maintain the same quality if they were to increase production. Every action performed here respects the Burgundy winemaking tradition: every decision is in keeping with the nature of each individual cuvée. The brothers' stock of vines is confined to the best terroirs within the commune of Chablis – the grands crus Les Clos, Blanchot, and Valmur, and the premiers crus Vaillons, Butteaux, Montée de Tonnerre, and Chapelot, unanimously regarded as those in which the minerality of the chalk soils is most forcefully expressed. One could spend forever wondering what sleights of hand were responsible for producing such matchless wines that after 10 to 15 years of aging form a perfect blend between the honey of ripe Chardonnay and slightly salty minerality contributed by the soil, and tertiary notes of oyster and meadow mushroom.

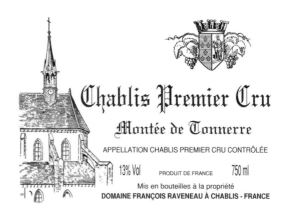

VINE VARIETY

18.5 acres (7.5 hectares) white: Chardonnay.

OUR FAVORITE WINES

This unfailingly consistent domaine brings out the best in every vintage. The 2000 excels with its fatness and fullness. The 2001, a more classic Chablis with notes of moist chalk, and the very well-balanced but tender 2002, should be drunk first. There is no wine we would hesitate to recommend, but the Clos et Montée de Tonnerre often displays rather more finesse and a more pronounced minerality than the others.

Domaine William Fèvre

The history of this great Chablis domaine falls into two distinct periods: that of its creation and that of its qualitative renewal. Responsible for the first was William Fèvre, who fought untiringly for proper recognition of the great Chablis terroirs, which had been badly affected by the geographical expansion of the appellation. With 37 acres (15 hectares) of grand cru vines (out of a total of 247 acres, or 100 hectares) and around 32 acres (13 hectares) of premier cru vines, this domaine has established itself as one of the leading properties. But it was only with its purchase in 1998 by Joseph Henriot (who already owned Bouchard Père et Fils as well as the Champagne house that bears his name) that it experienced a dramatic leap in quality and became a model for good Chablis. This northern terroir benefits from limestone soils and bedrock, and climbs up steeply from either side of the Serein river. Free from artifice and heaviness, the domaine's Chablis now possesses a straight and brilliant body that expresses the purity of this unusual terroir with astonishing freshness. Since the change of proprietor, every year has been dazzling.

VINE VARIETY

116 acres (47 hectares) white: Chardonnay.

OUR FAVORITE WINES

The year 1998 marked a turning point in the quality of this domaine's wines – from its simple Chablis all the way to its grands crus. Since then, every year has been successful, with 2002 particularly worthy of mention. Among the domaine's wide assortment of crus, its Les Clos impress with their grandeur and its Preuses with their honesty.

The young spring buds are sprayed with water so that they become encased in ice, a technique that, paradoxically, protects them from overnight frosts.

Domaine
Bernard Dugat-Py

Apainstaking artisan, Bernard Dugat-Py has turned his small Gevrey-Chambertin domaine into an enchanted garden devoted to viticulture and runs it with unrivaled discipline. The grapes are harvested and sorted at the peak of their maturity and produce wines that – for those fortunate enough to have tasted them – recall the great Burgundies of the first half of the 20th (and even 19th) centuries. His Gevreys, from the "Village" blend to the Mazis Grand Cru, possess a very distinct style. They are almost black with sumptuous body, sometimes a little unsmiling in their youth but often sublime after lengthy aging. Assisted by his wife and son, Bernard Dugat-Py is a master who works with the humility and passion of a bygone age, taking his art to a level of exactingness seldom equaled.

VINE VARIETY

20 acres (8 hectares) red: Pinot Noir.

OUR FAVORITE WINES

Since 1995 the general standard here has been magnificent and entirely worthy of the domaine's reputation – sublime Mazis-Chambertins and Gevrey Premiers Crus, a monumental Charmes-Chambertin, and a strangely austere but deeply spicy Gevrey Coeur de Roy sculpted in marble by its Brochon terroir.

Domaine
Charlopin

The proprietor of this Gevrey-Chambertin domaine, the friendly and garrulous Philippe Charlopin, is a very fine winemaker indeed. Both modernist in his practices, knowing how to extract color and body from the highly capricious and delicate Pinot Noir, but also highly respectful of the great terroirs, he has endowed his wine with a personality that is as original as it is seductive. His wines, made in a consistent style since 1990, combine a marvelous silky texture with the deep flavor of very ripe grape. The wood, which could sometimes be a little too baroque in the early years, ultimately melts into the wine. Having just a small area of vines at his disposal when he began his career as a winemaker, he has patiently assembled a stock that includes numerous crus in his own village as well as in neighboring Côte de Nuits sites. He is thus a micro-producer of Chambertin, Mazis, Charmes, Clos Saint-Denis, Bonnes-Mares, Échezeaux, and Clos de Vougeot grands crus, as well as a number of magnificent "Village" offerings including a superb *cuvée vieilles vignes* produced in far from trifling volumes!

VINE VARIETY

37 acres (15 hectares) red: Pinot Noir.
3 acres (1.3 hectares) white: Chardonnay.

OUR FAVORITE WINES

Made in very small quantities, Philippe Charlopin's grands crus possess a generous, velvety and richly aromatic character that is the hallmark of this winemaker. Among them the Chambertin and the Charmes-Chambertin are particularly captivating – most of all the 1999, 2002, and 2003 examples. The Charlopin style can also be discovered in his delicious Gevrey-Chambertin cuvée vieilles vignes.

Domaine
Dujac

When, at a very young age, he had to think of a name for the Morey-Saint-Denis domaine he had just acquired, Jacques Seysses christened it simply and phonetically "Dujac" in wry homage to the Burgundian locals who referred to it as the "domaine du Jacques." It took a good measure of both originality and courage to throw himself into the winemaking profession, particularly in 1967 and especially as there was no winemaking tradition in the family. And he chose to do his own bottling, too! Seysses did not lack virtue and ten years later did not shy away from embarking on further study in order to improve his knowledge of enology. Working today with his son Jérémy and his daughter-in-law, he has established a very personal style that exalts the Pinot Noir's aromatic finesse and allows its elegance to seduce from the word go.

VIN NON FILTRÉ
DECANTATION
RECOMMANDÉE

MIS EN BOUTEILLE
AU
DOMAINE

CLOS DE LA ROCHE
GRAND CRU
APPELLATION CLOS DE LA ROCHE CONTRÔLÉE

1999
ALC.13%
BY VOL.

DOMAINE DUJAC
750 ML.

DOMAINE DUJAC S.A. - MOREY - ST. DENIS - FRANCE
RED BURGUNDY WINE · PRODUCE OF FRANCE

VINE VARIETY

27 acres (11.25 hectares) red: Pinot Noir.
4 acres (1.5 hectares) white: Chardonnay.

OUR FAVORITE WINES

The two Clos de Morey – Clos de la Roche and Clos Saint-Denis – are, with the Charmes-Chambertin, this domaine's greatest wines, although the cuvées de village share the same seductive style. Of recent years, 1996, 1999, and 2002 have been particularly successful.

Domaine des
Lambrays

Morey-Saint-Denis is not the best-known of the Côte de Nuits villages, yet the commune can boast at least four grands crus and possibly a fifth as Bonnes-Mares starts here before essentially ending up in Chambolle-Musigny. Located immediately above the village, the grands crus Saint-Denis, La Roche, and Tart et Les Lambrays all bear the prefix "Clos," although it has been many years since the first two were enclosed by walls. The Clos des Lambrays is wholly owned by the domaine that bears its name. It enjoyed considerable fame before the war thanks to the then owner Camille Rodier, founder of the *Confrérie des Chevaliers du Tastevin* (Brotherhood of the Knights of the Tasting-Cup) and author of the following line, which deserves to be heeded during these difficult times: "Our wines aren't selling, so we may as well invite our friends round for a glass or two!" Today the wines produced by the Clos des Lambrays sell well because they have rediscovered what made them so good before: superlative finesse, the very opposite of the mammoth wines trampling all over the world today.

VINE VARIETY

25 acres (10 hectares) red: Pinot Noir.
1.6 acres (0.65 hectares) white: Chardonnay.

OUR FAVORITE WINES

The years 2002 and 2003 helped this domaine produce its best-balanced "clos" wines for decades, displaying magnificent delicacy of texture and subtlety of fragrance. Another wine that should not be missed is the rare but delicious white produced by the domaine at Puligny – the Clos des Caillerets Premier Cru.

Domaine
Leroy

Domaine Leroy is a Burgundy beacon. It serves as a benchmark for anyone wishing to judge the style of a particular vintage or discover the character of the region's most celebrated terroirs. Its collection of grand cru and premier cru wines is impressive and covers both Côtes. Failing disaster, biodynamic viticulture produces grapes that are incredibly rich in perfume and terroir character. Vinification using uncrushed grapes that are destemmed – where necessary – by hand on a sorting table preserves the Pinot Noir's freshness and nobility. Lalou Bize-Leroy is without doubt the most demanding, knowledgable and experienced of Burgundy tasters, and has done everything in her power to create the wine of her dreams. Her first vintages, produced between 1988 and 1993, astonished with their deep color and (occasionally slightly rigid) monumentality. Subsequent vintages produced wines of a rather different style, displaying greater refinement and suppleness with more delicate tannins and better integrated wood.

VINE VARIETY

44 acres (18 hectares) red: Pinot Noir.
10 acres (4 hectares) white: 70% Aligoté, 30% Chardonnay.

OUR FAVORITE WINES

Other than 2004, when the domaine declassified a large number of cuvées, the last five years have been glorious. The 2000 and 2001 in particular have been exceptional, displaying a wonderful delicacy and clarity in their expression of terroir. Wealthy collectors will pounce on the Chambertin, Musigny, Richebourg, and Romanée Saint-Vivant grands crus, while others should not overlook the more reasonably priced Savigny-Narbantons or Nuits-Saint-Georges Villages.

Domaine
Denis Mortet

In the 1960s, Burgundy sank into a mediocre routine from which only a very small number of properties or firms remained aloof. Even in the most celebrated villages of the Côte de Nuits, the viticultural heart of the region, banality was the order of the day and was sometimes even deliberately targeted as a more modern style better adapted to changing tastes. This altered as a new generation of winemakers succeeded their fathers and dared to call into question their work in the vineyard and cellars. Denis Mortet, fired by idealism but also bringing unusually exacting standards to the task, was at the spearhead of this renewal. His wines of spectacular color and aroma became progressively more sophisticated throughout the 1980s and have now achieved a serene, consensual maturity. The bulk of his production is from "Village" wines of incomparable quality that enjoy ideal hillside sites. After the tragic death of Denis in January 2006, his son Arnand is determined to continue his father's outstanding work.

VINE VARIETY
25 acres (10 hectares) red: Pinot Noir.
2.5 acres (1 hectare) white: 70% Chardonnay, 30% Aligoté.

OUR FAVORITE WINES
The Lavaux-Saint-Jacques, a Gevrey premier cru, offers a perfect illustration of the flavor and velvety texture that are the hallmarks of Denis Mortet's wines. His brilliant mastery of this style is revealed by all the property's wines since 1993 – in particular the glorious 1995, 1996, 1999, 2000, 2002, and 2003 vintages – from the simple Burgundy to the Chambertin.

Domaine de la
Romanée-Conti

The reputation of this domaine, the most famous in Burgundy, rests above all on its unrivaled range of grand cru wines from the village of Vosne-Romanée, including La Tâche and Romanée-Conti, of which it is the exclusive proprietor. Nowhere else in the world does Pinot Noir achieve such a nobility of aroma. Mindful of both their responsibility and extraordinary opportunities, the members of the non-trading company that owns the domaine and its current head, Aubert de Villaine, have steadily improved the quality of the grapes over the last 20 years. This has allowed them to vinify in the simplest manner in the world. The Échezeaux and Grands Échezeaux conjure with delicate aromas and nobility of texture. The Romanée-Saint-Vivant goes further down the same path, while the Richebourg and La Tâche display more body without sacrificing any of their exquisite perfumes. As for the Romanée-Conti, its *prima ballerina* grace conceals a richness of structure and even greater aging potential. The domaine's only white is a Montrachet no less. Its almost extravagant richness, obtained by harvesting as late as possible, gives it a style of its own. At no point in the last 50 years or so has the domaine better justified the respect it has worldwide than today.

SOCIÉTÉ CIVILE DU DOMAINE DE LA ROMANÉE-CONTI
PROPRIÉTAIRE A VOSNE-ROMANÉE (COTE-D'OR) FRANCE

ROMANÉE-CONTI
APPELLATION ROMANÉE-CONTI CONTROLÉE

5.548 Bouteilles Récoltées

LES ASSOCIÉS-GÉRANTS

BOUTEILLE Nº
ANNÉE 2002

Mise en bouteille au domaine

VINE VARIETY

62 acres (25 hectares): 95% Pinot Noir, 5% Chardonnay.

OUR FAVORITE WINES

An evolution in style toward greater naturalness and aromatic freshness over the last few years has made these wines even more appealing than their predecessors to discriminating wine lovers. With its 2001, 2002, and 2003 vintages, even the Échezeaux belies its status as the domaine's first-level wine to reach a pinnacle of finesse one would have thought unsurpassable. And yet each of the other grands crus goes further. If we had to choose one, it would be the Romanée-Saint-Vivant for its sublime elegance.

The use of egg whites as a fining agent, drawing the particles in suspension in the wine to the bottom of the barrel, is still practiced at the Romanée-Conti domaine.

Domaine
Armand Rousseau

This fine family domaine came into being at the beginning of the last century. Under the direction of Armand and then Charles Rousseau, it was one of the first to win respect for top-quality Burgundy from small producers during a time when the region was dominated by the blends of the wine merchants. Possessing wonderful parcels of vines in all the best Gevrey-Chambertin terroirs, the domaine developed a style based on finesse of aroma, purity of terroir character, and elegance of texture. However, with the exception of its two Chambertins, its wines sometimes lacked body or developed disappointingly in the bottle. Under the influence of Eric Rousseau and his sister, serious improvements have been made to the standards of viticulture and the wines are gradually regaining their fullness.

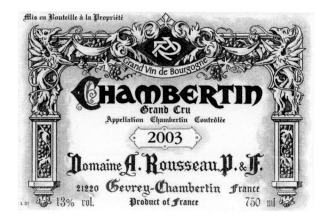

VINE VARIETY
35 acres (14 hectares) red: Pinot Noir.

OUR FAVORITE WINES
In 2002 and 2003 this domaine succeeded magnificently across its entire range of crus and cuvées. At the top are the two grands crus Chambertin and Chambertin-Clos de Bèze. While offering no surprises, these wines display an incredible refinement of bouquet.

Clos de Tart

Along with its neighbor Clos des Lambrays, Clos de Tart is one of the two great monopoly vineyards of Morey-Saint-Denis. It is owned by a single proprietor, the Mommessin family, which can therefore work it along Bordeaux lines, selecting only the best vats for its *grand vin*. Under the intelligent direction of Sylvain Pitiot, the vineyard has notched up success after success over the last ten years: the vines are old, impeccably maintained and above all consist of extremely fine Pinot Noir clones that are indispensable for a refined aroma and texture. Vinification takes place in an extremely modern vat-house and is as precise as possible in order to extract the best of the fruit's color and perfume and to create wines that are balanced, fleshy, velvety, and extremely long in the mouth. Corresponding to the vineyard's geographical situation, the style of wine made here is a successful combination of aromatic refinement, the silky texture of the Chambolle-Musignys, and the energy and depth of the best Chambertins.

VINE VARIETY
19 acres (7.5 hectares) red: Pinot Noir.

OUR FAVORITE WINES
While Clos de Tart's wonderful situation enables it to harvest ripe grapes every year, global warming has also made a significant contribution to the astonishing succession of fine vintages produced here since 1995. In our view the most distinctive are 1997, which is tender and voluptuous; 1999, which is deep and dense; 2001, which is extremely elegant; and the sumptuous 2003, which is the stuff of legend.

Winter landscape, Vosne Romanée. With Gevrey-Chambertin, this village in Côte de Nuits has the greatest number of grands crus.

Domaine
Jean et Jean-Louis Trapet

Here is a domaine belonging to an old and noble tradition that has taken a long, hard look at the way it does things and changed almost all its practices from the tending of vines to bottling. Its soils are once again ploughed (sometimes by horses) and reinvigorated with biodynamic preparations. The grapes are harvested when fully mature, and sorted and vinified with the minimum element of mechanization in order to avoid the extraction of rough tannins. Moreover, this level of care was demanded by the domaine's stock of vines – including fine parcels of Chambertin at the heart of the cru and holdings in two great neighbors (Latricières-Chambertin and Chapelle-Chambertin) that produce wines similar in character but a little more supple and that open up more readily. The premiers crus, such as Petite-Chapelle and Clos Prieur, are more sophisticated than previously, while a rigorous selection by terroir allows for the production of two or three different blends of Gevrey "Village" that are not yet "up there" with the best of their type. Jean-Louis Trapet and his wife display a combination of courage and modesty to a degree that is rare at this level of celebrity; they will most certainly continue to make progress.

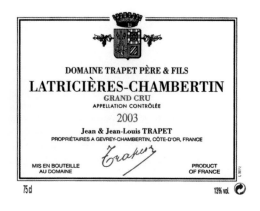

VINE VARIETY
32 acres (13 hectares): 95% Pinot Noir, 5% Chardonnay.

OUR FAVORITE WINES
Switching this domaine's prestigious vineyards to biodynamic methods has resulted in significant changes in style over recent years. Perfumes are released earlier on, and the tannins have acquired considerably more finesse and suppleness. The domaine's specialty is without doubt its well-balanced Chambertin, but its Latricières and Chapelle are increasingly closing the gap and its premier cru wines, far more polished than they once were, are also worthy of attention. To date, the vintage that best expresses the property's potential is the 2002.

Château de
la Tour

More than anywhere else, the Clos-Vougeot symbolizes the complex and turbulent history of viticulture in Burgundy. These 124 acres (50 hectares) of vineyard, rising very gently at first and then gaining in steepness behind the Cistercian manor, were laid out back in the 12th century by monks from Cîteaux Abbey. The walled vineyard was parceled out at the time of the French Revolution, but a banker named Ouvrard succeeded in reuniting it. This lasted until 1889 when it was split up again. Today it is worked by more than 70 producers. Of these, Château de la Tour, with its 15 acres (6 hectares) distributed around the small but very real château in the middle of the clos, is the most important. François Labet, who has run the company for nearly 20 years, has overseen considerable improvements in the quality of the wines, whose density, structure, and succulence have helped to establish them as the leading Clos-Vougeot. This is especially true of the *vieilles vignes* cuvée, which offers an incredibly complex nose and velvety texture.

VINE VARIETY

15 acres (6 hectares) red: Pinot Noir.

OUR FAVORITE WINES

While the classic version of Château de la Tour has shown itself since the beginning of the 1990s to be a great Clos-Vougeot, the vieilles vignes (old vines) cuvée attains a new level of breeding, intensity, and depth – particularly in the extraordinary 1990, 1993, 1996, 1999, 2002, and 2003 vintages.

Domaine de la
Vougeraie

The merging of the Boisset family's properties into a single domaine was a major event in Burgundy's recent history. It resulted in the creation of a large, leading domaine that brings together a range of grand and premier cru wines, the assertion of an individual style based on the structural vigor of each cuvée, and a desire to bring out the unique characteristics of the respective terroir. Canadian Pascal Marchand was the ideal person to accomplish this. A remarkable taster and an unconventional personality with a loathing of routine, Marchand poured his heart and expertise into the creation of the ideal vathouse and incessantly fine-tuned the wine he made therein. The type of viticulture he practiced was increasingly inspired by the principles of biodynamics. The domaine's ambition is, one day, to match the quality of the wines produced by Domaine Leroy. Marchand's first few vintages were highly expressive but over-powerful. Subsequent vintages have been truly stunning – slightly less extracted and more respectful of the individual textures of each cru. We hope Marchand's successor will continue in the same spirit.

VINE VARIETY
91 acres (37 hectares): 83% Pinot Noir, 17% Chardonnay.

OUR FAVORITE WINES
Pascal Marchand's wines grow more and more refined from year to year. His 2003, 2004, and 2005 offerings show an even better tannic balance and loyalty to terroir character than previously. Wine lovers may be perplexed by his long list of wines. In addition to the grands crus, dominated by a brilliant Musigny (produced in tragically small quantities!), we would happily recommend the Gevrey-Evocelles, Beaune, and Savigny premier cru reds, and the Clos Blanc de Vougeot Chardonnay. The Terre de Famille Pinot Noir offers exceptional value for money.

Domaine d'Auvenay

Auvenay is the second domaine run by Lalou Bize and is fully owned by her, while Domaine Leroy belongs to a company owned jointly by Ms Bize, her sister, and their Japanese partners. Its size and production are minuscule, but for those who have the opportunity to taste these wines, there is nothing to compare. The domaine specializes in white wine. At the bottom of the range is an Aligoté that could easily be mistaken for a prestigious premier cru. Progressing upwards, the Auxey-Duresses captivate with their concentrated intensity and nobility of flavor. As for the Meursault, Puligny, and grands crus, it is better never to have tasted them in order to prevent any dissatisfaction creeping in with the quality of the others! The secret of this domaine's remarkable success is its tiny yields (often lower than 30hl/ha) and minimal intervention in the cellar. The two grand cru reds (barely 1,500 bottles between them!) – Mazis-Chambertin and Bonnes Mares – are every bit as wonderful as those of Vosne-Romanée.

VINE VARIETY

1 acre (0.5 hectare) red: Pinot Noir.
7 acres (3.5 hectares) white: 90% Chardonnay, 10% Aligoté.

OUR FAVORITE WINES

Grand cru wines are produced here in minute quantities and are practically unaffordable. Those fortunate enough to have tasted the merest drop of Chevalier-Montrachet or Criots-Bâtard 2000, 2001, and 2002 will know that there are no better dry whites in the world. The Auxey-Duresses are particularly tempting, as those made here are the equal of other producers' grands crus!

Winter pruning plays an essential role in determining and controlling the productivity of the plant the following summer.

Domaine
Bonneau du Martray

With its hill, like that of Hermitage a couple of hundred miles farther south, Corton is one of the most spectacular elements of the (apparently widely misunderstood) appellation d'origine system. Approaching from either Dijon or Beaune, visitors cannot help noticing the broad, brutally truncated cone dominating the quiet village of Aloxe-Corton below. While the plateau-like summit (which reaches a height of 1,312 feet, or 400 meters) is covered with wood, its entire south and southwestern slopes have, since time immemorial, been devoted to the vine. The magnificent whiteness of the southern flank, known as Charlemagne, reveals the slope's pure limestone bedrock. Domaine Bonneau du Martray's 20-odd acres of Chardonnay are majestically located at the heart of this terroir. The owner, Jean-Charles Beau de la Morinière, draws out the quintessence of this ideal site – from its soil and subsoil that are constantly fed with water – with all the tact and respect that such a major landmark deserves.

VINE VARIETY

23 acres (9.5 hectares) white: Chardonnay.
4 acres (1.5 hectares) red: Pinot Noir.

OUR FAVORITE WINES

Extremely pure and upright but previously a little austere, from 1995 onwards the Corton-Charlemagne acquired an additional, superior dimension that earned it a place among the world's greatest Chardonnays. The 1995, 1997, 1999, 2000, and 2002 were all dazzling. In terms of reds, the Corton has made considerable progress, attaining its highest level in 1999, 2002, and 2003.

Domaine
Jean-François Coche-Dury

An obsessive winemaker, but an admirably modest and sensitive human being, Jean-François Coche-Dury produces wines in his own image that sadly fall prey to speculators as soon as they leave the estate, such is their worldwide fame. Coche-Dury laid down the guiding principles of his work at a very early stage. These principles help to explain his highly individual style: harvesting grapes at the perfect moment of sugar–acidity balance; pressing and vinification designed to protect the wine from any oxidation (through meticulously controlled fermentation alone); and long, slow, careful aging in casks made of wood he has chosen himself. As the domaine does not possess extensive grand cru or premier cru holdings, Coche-Dury has been forced to take the same degree of care over his "Village" wines, and this hard work has been rewarded with exceptional, long-lived wines with a refined bouquet – especially those from the Rougeot and Narvaux sites. But neither should we neglect his delicious Monthélie, Auxey-Duresses, and Volnay reds in which the exquisite Pinot Noir fruit is shown all the respect it deserves.

VINE VARIETY

27 acres (11 hectares): 80% Chardonnay, 15% Pinot Noir, 5% Gamay et Aligoté.

OUR FAVORITE WINES

Many people will be surprised by the sophistication of the reds being made by this domaine, as Jean-François Coche-Dury is considered primarily to be a great Chardonnay master. He is responsible for a style of wine that is inimitable and stands out from all the rest, featuring pure, clean aromas of hazelnut and grilled almond carried by a very pure, sinewy body showing a clarity of definition in terms of origins and vintage that astonishes time after time. The Meursault "Village" wines find their most perfect expression here; this was true even of the very sunny 2003 vintage. The supremely refined 2002 examples have already become legendary.

Bouchard Père et fils

In the 19th century, Bouchard Père was the great Beaune firm that established the canons of Burgundy wine. It was taken over at the end of the 20th century and confirmed its status in the early years of the 21st. Unforgettable wines testify to both these facts. The firm's wine collection is housed in a cellar at the Château de Beaune, a fiefdom of the company, and is stuffed with treasures that are regularly opened for the fortunate few, recalling the occasions when famous vintages from the past – 1846, 1865, 1893, 1929, 1945, and 1947 – displayed an intensity, depth, and aging potential very far removed from today's continual talk of the fragility of Pinot Noir and Chardonnay. Many of the company's latter-day wines, which are magnificently vinified by a team that brings an impressive precision to all its work from the vine to the cellar, originate in terroir of stunning quality: of the firm's holdings of 322 acres (130 hectares), 30 acres (12 hectares) are in grand cru vineyards (Montrachet, Chevalier-Montrachet, Corton, Clos de Vougeot and others), and 183 acres (74 hectares) in premier cru vineyards, with a significant proportion in Beaune including the famous Vigne de l'Enfant Jésus.

The merchant house of Bouchard Père et fils also owns its own extensive vineyards that are particularly well-stocked with grands crus and premiers crus.

VINE VARIETY

213 acres (86 hectares) red: Pinot Noir
109 acres (44 hectares) white: 80% Chardonnay, 20% Aligoté.

OUR FAVORITE WINES

The year 2003 represented the high point of the efforts undertaken by this firm over the course of 15 years. Wines like the Corton, Bonnes-Mares, Nuits-Saint-Georges Les Cailles, Vosne-les-Suchots, and Beaune l'Enfant Jésus reds, and the Chevalier-Montrachet la Cabotte, Le Montrachet, and Corton-Charlemagne whites (which were also wonderful in 2002) attained the lofty heights of the firm's mythical vintages such as the unforgettable 1865 – a few bottles of which are still to be found in its cellars.

Domaine des
Comtes Lafon

As its name implies, this important southern Côte de Beaune domaine is a family business. It was started by Jules Lafon (mayor of Meursault and founder of the village's famous Fête de la Paulée) at the beginning of the 20th century. Jules was made a *Comte Pontifical* by the Pope and the title came to honor the domaine's wine label. However, it is the nobility of the profession of winemaker that his grandson René (who took over the domaine at a time when his father was thinking of selling it) and his great-grandson Dominique (who has achieved the highest levels of international recognition with it) reveal with greatest panache. Possessing a superb stock of vines, Dominique has made his range of Meursaults (rich, deep, and displaying a rare elegance of aroma) absolute models of Chardonnay perfection for wine lovers all over the world. And the domaine's rare Montrachet (only four-fifths of an acre – one-third of an hectare) is without doubt one of just two or three examples that reveal the cru's true greatness. Of the reds, similar can be said of the Volnay blends, which since the end of the 1980s have been displaying a fullness and refinement of flavor that represent the very quintessence of the Burgundy renewal.

MONTRACHET
GRAND CRU
APPELLATION MONTRACHET GRAND CRU CONTRÔLÉE

2000

DOMAINE DES COMTES LAFON

*Mis en bouteilles
à la Propriété*

CLOS DE LA BARRE
21190 MEURSAULT
FRANCE

13,5% vol.

PRODUIT DE FRANCE
L 00 01

75 cl

VINE VARIETY

20 acres (8 hectares) white: Chardonnay.
15 acres (6 hectares) red: Pinot Noir.

OUR FAVORITE WINES

This domaine's Meursault, from premier cru vineyards Perrières, Charmes and Genevrières, has notched up a string of brilliant achievements since the 1960s (1963, 1967, 1973, 1979, 1981, 1982, 1985, 1989, 1990, 1992, 1995, 1996, 1999, 2000, 2002), even if some of the vintages from the 20th century have developed somewhat faster than anticipated. So too has its Montrachet. As for the reds, the first of the great Volnay-Santenots vintages emerged in 1989.

Not all oak is suitable for making good-quality barrels: particularly good oak trees are grown in the Tronçais forest in the département of Allier, and in the Vosges.

Joseph Drouhin

Joseph Drouhin, who was born in the Chablis district, founded the firm that bears his name in Beaune in 1880; 126 years later, it is still, indeed more than ever, a family business. Today it is run by Philippe, Véronique, Laurent, and Frédéric Drouhin (all of whom were born between 1961 and 1968) with their father Robert. They have not neglected the Chablis of their forefather, for the company has long owned a vast domaine in this cru to the north of Burgundy, but has also expanded further afield, establishing Drouhin Estate in Oregon – planted to Pinot Noir, of course. Nevertheless, the heart of its winegrowing operations, which today follows biodynamic principles, remains the Côte d'Or. The style of wine (both white and red) produced here, focusing on finesse, delicacy even, has thus expressed itself more strongly in the last few vintages, gaining in tension and magnitude.

VINE VARIETY
59 acres (24 hectares) red: Pinot Noir.
109 acres (44 hectares) white: Chardonnay.

OUR FAVORITE WINES
The Beaune Clos des Mouches red and white are two of the most famous cuvées from a firm whose star wines nevertheless remain its Musigny and Montrachet Marquis de Laguiche. The 2002 and 2003 are the crowning glory of Drouhin's steady development.

Louis Jadot

An engaging Beaune firm, Louis Jadot has been one of the great ambassadors of Burgundy for many years and, unlike other companies, has not suffered periods of passing weakness. Founded in the mid-19th century and run today by Pierre-André Gagey with the passionate, charismatic collusion of Jacques Lardière (one of Burgundy's most gifted winemakers), Jadot can take pride in an extensive collection of bottles illustrating the Burgundian winemaking genius at work across the ages – from the eternal marvels of the 19th century to the "liquid cathedrals" constructed with consummate skill by Jacques Lardière over the course of a career that began in 1970. Forming the main focus of his work are the vines that either belong to the firm or which it has cultivated and vinified for a long period of time, such as the prestigious Domaine du Duc de Magenta in Chassagne-Montrachet. One of the most fascinating aspects of the work being carried out by Lardière and Jadot is the capacity of each wine to express the personality of its terroir with an incredible richness of nuance, even if only a few acres separate it from that of another wine in the range.

VINE VARIETY

301 acres (122 hectares) red: 55% Pinot Noir, 45% Gamay.
54 acres (22 hectares) white: 98% Chardonnay, 2% Aligoté.

OUR FAVORITE WINES

Jadot offers a very rich selection of Côte d'Or wines. Its reputation is carried high by numerous crus – including Musigny, Clos Saint-Denis, Chambertin-Clos de Bèze, Bonnes-Mares, Corton-Pougets (red), Corton-Charlemagne (white), Chevalier-Montrachet Les Demoiselles, and Montrachet. The most striking of recent vintages are 1989, 1990, 1995, 1996, 1999, and 2002. The extraordinary windmills at the Château des Jacques should not be missed either.

According to the winemaker Jacques Lardière, the convergence of magnetic waves in the center of the Jadot cellars encourages the wines to express their interior vibration.

A great Burgundy, red or white, will age superbly as is demonstrated when some of the famous 19th-century vintages are sampled.

Montrachet
1881

Domaine
Leflaive

If the 19th century belonged to the large firms of Burgundy wine merchants, the 20th witnessed the budding and blossoming of the family-owned domaines. Domaine Leflaive, a veritable sampling stick of the great Puligny-Montrachet terroirs, was closely bound up with this strong movement for the emancipation of family properties. The domaine was founded immediately after the First World War by Joseph Leflaive, an engineer and graduate of the École Polytechnique in Paris, and subsequently developed by his sons, all of whom continued to pursue other professional activities. Since 1990, Anne-Claude Leflaive, one of Joseph's granddaughters, has been in charge. The devoted servant of what is an extraordinary collection of wines (four grands crus, six Puligny premiers crus including Pucelles, Clavoillon and Folatières, and an assortment of Puligny "Village" holdings), she has now adopted biodynamic methods throughout. This preoccupation with the environment has also improved definition of the wines, allowing a pure, brilliant, and uncompromising personality to show through. Additionally, Domaine Leflaive's crus have gained in richness of body, aromatic precision, and transparency of terroir character while retaining the superlative finesse that has made them legendary.

VINE VARIETY

57 acres (23 hectares) white: Chardonnay.

OUR FAVORITE WINES

Thanks to their intensity and precision of flavor, the great 1990s and early 21st-century vintages from this domaine generously endowed with grands crus (Bâtard, Bienvenues-Bâtard, Chevalier, and Montrachet!) have even improved on the great successes of earlier years. The 1992, 1995, 1996, 2000, and 2002 are the best.

Domaine
Marquis d'Angerville

Domaine Marquis d'Angerville, one of the leading properties in Volnay (along with Pommard, the most prestigious red wine village in the southern Côte de Beaune region), is a key domaine for more than one reason. First of all, it has considerable historical significance. Prior to the French Revolution, it formed part of the estate of the Dukes of Burgundy, who had made Volnay their summer residence. In the 19th century it became one of Burgundy's most famous private domaines. Its assortment of premiers crus is all the more impressive as Jacques, and now his son, Guillaume, have made them into serious, well-structured wines with good aging potential. Their style has gradually and intelligently become more modern, gaining in finesse and texture. The subtlety of the Clos des Ducs, the prococity of Taillepieds, the earthy power of Les Champans, the delicacy of Les Fremiets, and the longevity of Les Caillerets can all bear witness to the fact that the individual personality of a cru can often be deeper than we might have suspected.

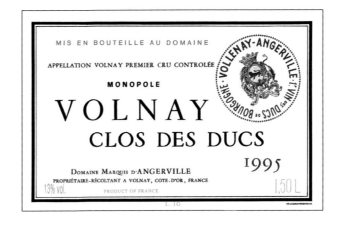

VINE VARIETY
30 acres (12 hectares) red: Pinot Noir.
2.5 acres (1 hectare) white: Chardonnay.

OUR FAVORITE WINES
The 2002 and 2003 were brilliant years across Domaine Marquis d'Angerville's entire range, yielding wines of rare delicacy and elegance of body. They can be expected to age as harmoniously as the domaine's other glorious vintages such as 1989, 1990, 1996, and 1999.

Domaine de
Montille

Before being consecrated as the archetype of the humble but wise winegrower in the film *Mondovino*, Hubert de Montille managed two brilliant careers in parallel. On the one hand, he was a successful lawyer; on the other, he was the devoted servant of his family vineyards in the Côte de Beaune. Mischievous, charming, and eminently Burgundian, Hubert de Montille is one of the most engaging and effective ambassadors and advocates for the specific virtues of great Burgundy in general and that of his own domaine in particular. Domaine de Montille has been one of the most consistent producers over the last 30 years. Its wines are never strong in alcohol and are always tannic. He has now passed the reins to his son, Étienne, who shows impressive rigor and precision in his work and has further refined the domaine's style, increasing the silkiness of texture in the Pommard (Rugiens) and above all Volnay (Champans, Mitans, and Taillepieds) crus.

VINE VARIETY
17 acres (7 hectares) red: Pinot Noir.
2.1 acres (0.85 hectares) white: Chardonnay.

OUR FAVORITE WINES
The Rugiens Pommard and the Taillepieds Volnay represent two different sides of the same honed, nimble character. The first is a robust long-distance runner, while the second is a willowy athlete. Both won laurels in 1985, 1999, and 2003.

The inner surfaces of the casks are gently scorched, the taste and aroma of the wine varying according to the intensity of the heat.

Domaine Jacques Prieur

After being driven forward by Bertand Devillard and Martin Prieur to make significant progress in record time, this fine domaine has now found a good cruising speed. This progress began in the vineyard. Its great Côte de Beaune terroirs possessed an older stock of vines that were easier to bring up to scratch and dominated production in the 1990s, but the prestigious Côte de Nuits grands crus have now fully asserted their superior class. The Chambertin is deep, dense and underpinned by firm but not astringent tannins; the Musigny develops an exciting floral nose; and the ample and earthy Clos de Vougeot has gained a touch more elegance of texture. Work in the cellar has not stood still either, developing a precision and rigor that stem largely from the character of one of the best enologists around, Nadine Gublin. But the domaine is in Meursault, and wine lovers will naturally seek out its whites, which are among the best balanced and most flavorsome Burgundies being made today. They are produced in minute volumes and their staggering prices, linked to the prestige of their terroirs (including a superb Montrachet), sadly make them less accessible.

MUSIGNY
GRAND CRU
APPELLATION MUSIGNY CONTRÔLÉE

MIS EN BOUTEILLE PAR ~ BOTTLED BY
DOMAINE JACQUES PRIEUR
Propriétaire à Meursault (Côte-d'Or) France

13,5% vol   PRODUCE OF FRANCE   750 ml

VINE VARIETY
52 acres (21 hectares): 65% Pinot Noir, 35% Chardonnay.

OUR FAVORITE WINES
Nadine Gublin's masterly wines get the most out of every vintage. The 2002 reds and whites are playfully elegant; the dark, warm 2003 offerings radiate sunshine without any heaviness; and the 2004 vintages have the capacity to astonish with their complexity of aroma and smooth tannins. Highlights among the domaine's more accessible wines are its premier cru Beaune and Meursault Clos du Mazeray.

Domaine Guffens-Heynen

If there is one winemaker who has prodded *le Mâconnais* out of its sleepy routine and drawn attention to the enormous value of its terroirs, it is Belgian Jean-Marie Guffens. A love of great Burgundy and the desire to embark on an exciting adventure with his wife, Maine, led Guffens to the shallow hillside terroirs of the delightful village of Vergisson, sandwiched between two famous rocky outcrops. Here he has practiced a rigorous form of viticulture diametrically opposed to the obsession with productivity that reigned here before. In creating his wine, though, he has not neglected the lessons that can be learned from the science of enology. Natural talent combined with excellent tasting skills have enabled Guffens to take the pressing and fermentation processes to a level of refinement never surpassed (to the best of our knowledge), and no one else has done better justice to the noble minerality of the best Pierreclos and Vergisson sites. Meanwhile, Jean-Marie Guffens' outspokenness and entrepreneurial spirit have led many to emulate him. His founding of the Verget firm of wine merchants, based in Sologny, has enabled him to expand his product range with the same level of commitment but without ever equaling the perfection of the wines produced by his own domaine.

PRODUCT OF FRANCE

Pouilly-Fuissé
"La Roche"
Appellation Pouilly-Fuissé Contrôlée

Récolte 2002

13% VOL.   750 ML ℮

MIS EN BOUTEILLES A LA PROPRIETE
Domaine Guffens - Heynen - 71960 VERGISSON

VINE VARIETY
10 acres (4 hectares): Chardonnay.

OUR FAVORITE WINES
This peerless winemaker has surpassed himself with his recent vintages. His 2002 wines are practically unrivaled in France for their balance of alcohol and acidity. The domaine's Mâcon en Chavigne has established new standards of excellence for the appellation, while its Pouilly-Fuissés sparkle with exquisite, diamond-like brilliance. The 2003 lacks any hint of heaviness, and the delicate lacy 2004 should be tracked down at any price.

Billecart-Salmon

Billecart-Salmon relates how, in the 19th century in Mareuil-sur-Aÿ, a certain Monsieur Billecart and Madame Salmon formed a union for better or for worse based on love and champagne, sealed not only in church but also in the cellar. Fortunately, the "worse" never came to pass although it took some time for the "better" to arrive, since, although the business developed without problems, its wine remained something of a secret, known only to a few fortunate connoisseurs who had been privileged to taste such exquisite vintages as those of 1959 and 1961 – today regarded as the best of the best. The refinement and delicacy of the Billecart-Salmon wines have only begun to become more widely known in the last ten years. These qualities can be found not only in the champagnes produced from three traditional varieties of grape (as in the Cuvée Nicolas-François Billecart), but also in the blanc de blancs and the delicious and well-balanced rosés – particularly the Cuvée Elisabeth Salmon.

VINE VARIETY

74 acres (30 hectares): Pinot Noir, Pinot Meunier, Chardonnay.

OUR FAVORITE WINES

Cuvée Elisabeth Salmon Rosé is one of the most refined and impressive rosé champagnes, with the 1996 vintage of particular note. The blanc de blancs Nicolas-François Billecart, of the same vintage, combines refinement with depth of body.

The round, horizontal presses used in the production of champagne allow the quality of the musts to be carefully controlled.

Bollinger

If there were any doubt that James Bond is no ordinary hero, his favorite champagne alone – Bollinger – would be sufficient to prove the contrary. Very different from some of the more flashy champagnes, this marque represents better than any other the high standards of quality and rigorous production methods required to make a wine of such outstanding purity and honesty. Equally indicative of the producers' belief in their wine is the fact that the house, established in 1829 in Aÿ, is still owned by descendants of the original founder and has never been relocated. Its situation could hardly be bettered, placed as it is at the meeting point of the three greatest champagne-producing terroirs. To the north is Montagne de Reims, while below is the Marne valley and, opposite, Côte des Blancs. The Bollinger style was established early on: based on Pinot Noir grapes, the juice is placed first in small barrels. The wine is then aged *sur pointe* (inverted), remaining in the cellar for several years after fermentation in the bottle has taken place. The famous reputation of this house derives not so much from the excellence of a few outstanding cuvées but from the consistency with which it is able to perpetuate its style throughout its whole range of champagnes, regardless of year. In short, a superstar among champagnes.

The bright golden color and refined but lasting bubbles of a Bollinger make it instantly appealing.

VINE VARIETY
395 acres (160 hectares) red: Pinot Noir 86%, Pinot Meunier 14%.
white: Chardonnay.

OUR FAVORITE WINES
The non-vintage brut Spécial Cuvée. The quality and honesty of this wine make it the archetype of great champagnes. Its style has attained even greater heights of complexity in certain vintage years – including the remarkable Grande Année of 1996, the outstanding 1990 RD cuvées, and the rare and sublime 1998 rosé.

Dom Pérignon

Few wines have attained the mythical status of Dom Pérignon.
Bearing the name of the monk in charge of the wine cellars at
the abbey of Hautvillers who developed the principle of blending
(but who was not, despite popular legend, the inventor of
sparkling wine) at the end of the 17th and beginning of the
18th centuries, this champagne was created in 1936. Since this
time, the methods used have become fixed and unchanging.
Dom Pérignon is a vintage cuvée, produced only in a *grande
année* (great year) – although it must be said that in recent times
there has been a certain inflation in the definition of a *grande
année*, since there have been seven in the decade of the
1990s alone! – of grapes from a grand cru, with slightly larger
amounts of Pinot Noir than Chardonnay. While some of the earlier
vintages (such as the very rich 1959 or the sun-drenched 1976)
have a very individual personality, the cuvée has subsequently
acquired a very reliable style that is light and well-balanced.
It is a pity that it is so frequently drunk while still young, since
Dom Pérignon improves wonderfully with age, as does the
delicious but rare rosé.

VINE VARIETY

*1,899 acres (768 hectares) belonging to Moët & Chandon,
the house producing Dom Pérignon: Pinot Noir, Chardonnay.*

OUR FAVORITE WINES

*When young, Dom Pérignon is a very accessible champagne.
After a few year's maturation in the cellar, its potential develops,
revealing its thoroughbred origins. The 1988, 1990, and 1996
demonstrate this to perfection.*

*The brightest jewel in the crown of the foremost champagne house, Moët et Chandon,
Dom Pérignon is symbolic throughout the world for luxury and refinement.*

Clos des
Goisses

Champagne is generally imagined to be a flat, neat ocean of vines. Nothing could be further from the truth, at least where the best vineyards are concerned – all of which are located on (often steep) slopes. This is true of the two most famous regions (Côte des Blancs and Montagne de Reims), but also of the right bank of the Marne valley, home to a succession of famous crus. Among them, the Clos des Goisses offers what is without doubt the most spectacular view of the river. The vineyard tumbles down a pure chalk slope worthy of the best Mosel sites and enjoys a due southerly exposure. Here, Pinot Noir and Chardonnay ripen more quickly and vigorously than anywhere else in Champagne, giving the resulting wine an unusual power of texture and an aromatic personality. Owned by the firm Philiponnat, which employs respectful and intelligent vinification methods, Clos des Goisses goes extremely well with food. Its pronounced vinosity calms down over time but can never be completely subdued.

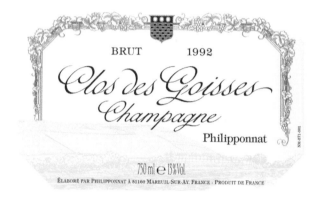

VINE VARIETY
14 acres (5.5 hectares): Pinot Noir 75%, Chardonnay 25%.

OUR FAVORITE WINES
Highly vinous, powerful, deep, and intense, Clos des Goisses is only made in good years and only released for sale after a long period of cellarage. As a result, the wines display a wonderfully mature nose and flavors, and are perfect for drinking with food. The 1989, 1990, and 1992 are out-and-out successes full of vigor and generosity.

Egly-Ouriet

For those who prefer champagnes based mainly on Pinot Noir, Egly-Ouriet is currently one of the most reliable sources. It combines, to an unusual degree, refinement and vinosity. The pedigree of the grapes cannot be bettered, since they come from old vines in the famous vineyards of Ambonnay, Bouzy, and Verzenay and, for the Pinot Meunier, from the remarkable village of Festigny. Few producers can equal Francis Egly in skill and experience, and larger houses cannot hope to emulate the cultivation norms applicable to a single domaine of relatively small size such as this. The vines are cultivated and the loads of grapes regulated in such a way as to favor an unequaled level of maturation. At each new tirage, we cannot but marvel anew at the fullness and precision of fruit of the traditional bruts and the even better blanc de noirs. A proportion of the still wine is matured in wood as it is at Bollinger and for the same reasons: to optimize the vinosity of the wine and ensure its longevity. Finally, the most recent vintages of the red Coteau Champenois have revolutionized the style, proving themselves worthy of comparison with many of the greatest Burgundies.

VINE VARIETY

2 acres (11 hectares): 70% Pinot Noir, 15% Pinot Meunier, 15% Chardonnay.

OUR FAVORITE WINES

Currently, the tirage period, when the non-vintage wine is matured on the lees, is four years. This gives wines of an unusual fullness, particularly apparent in the superb blanc de noirs produced from the very old vines at Les Crayeres. The recent use of Meunier grapes from Festigny has led to the fixing of new norms for the variety. The 1998 vintage promises great things.

Jacquesson

In the past, champagne corks were secured with string. Although effective, the process of tying them was very slow. It was Adolphe Jacquesson who, in 1844, invented the *muselet*, or muzzle. This ingenious wire construction has been used ever since for all types of sparkling wine. At that time, Jacquesson was a famous and important marque, but the 20th century saw a decline in its fortunes, culminating in the takeover of the house in 1974. Wisely, Jean Chiquet, and then his two sons Jean-Hervé and Laurent, did not attempt to increase production, concentrating instead on bringing out the best of a small but high-quality terroir, with excellent vineyards, all classified on the official scale of the Champagne region as premiers or grands crus. In this way they are able to exploit to best effect not only a number of excellent grands crus including Avize, Ay (for Pinot Noir), and Dizy (a pure Chardonnay from grapes grown in a plot of land called Corne Bautray), but also the power and harmony of blends such as the Signature or the wonderful 728 (based on the 2000 vintage), 729 (2001), and so on. The house's self-appointed mission to explore in depth every nuance and subtlety that makes a great champagne can be said to have been entirely successful.

VINE VARIETY

69 acres (28 hectares): Pinot Noir, Pinot Meunier, Chardonnay, and bought-in grapes.

OUR FAVORITE WINES

The excellent Jacquesson vintages from the late 1980s – particularly 1988 and 1989 – are notable for their fullness and freshness. The 1995 is another impressive year.

Krug

While the Krug family still runs the house, it passed first to the cognac- and champagne-producing company Rémy-Martin, then to the luxury goods conglomerate LVMH. It has, nevertheless, preserved its unique and exceptional character. This derives not so much from the use of oak barrels (a process reflecting a much older tradition and one of great interest from the enological point of view), but, more importantly, from the practice of aging the champagnes used in the making of multi-vintage wines. Before a bottle of Grande Cuvée can be tasted by the many worldwide fans of Krug champagne, it will have been slowly matured for at least six years in the deep cellars in Reims. While retaining all the freshness of the great champagnes, Krug has in addition a delightful bouquet of candied fruit, spices, brioche, toast, and honey, with hints of balsam. This profusion of aromas is found combined with that of citrus fruits in the magnificent Clos du Mesnil wines, produced from Chardonnay grapes grown in the heart of Côte des Blancs.

VINE VARIETY

49 acres (20 hectares): Pinot Noir, Pinot Meunier, Chardonnay, and bought-in grapes.

OUR FAVORITE WINES

The Grande Cuvée – not only that produced in the legendary year of 1928, but also in other vintage years such as 1981, 1988, 1989, and 1990 – has a wonderful bouquet and full, smooth body. The outstanding walled vineyard, Clos du Mesnil, produced particularly impressive results in 1988.

Rows of barrels in the courtyard at Reims waiting to be filled with what will become champagne in the inimitable Krug style.

Laurent-Perrier

Most of the famous champagne houses are to be found in Reims or Épernay (the two wine-producing capitals of the Champagne region), while there are others in Aÿ, in the heart of the Marne valley. Only one house, Laurent-Perrier, exists at Tours-sur-Marne, an outlying village situated to the east of the main vineyards. As a result, Laurent-Perrier, born in 1812, had only modest aspirations for the house. This remained true even after his widow, Émilie Perrier, launched it more definitively in the late 19th century. Indeed, until the end of the Second World War, business was precarious. It was finally put on the right track with the arrival of a man of unusually dynamic and enterprising spirit: Bernard de Nonancourt. A modernizer in respect both to wine-making (he was the first, in the early 1950s, to produce wine using stainless steel vats) and to marketing (introducing the fashion first for champagne made without dosage and then rosé champagne), he has succeeded in creating a champagne of the highest possible refinement and elegance: the Grand Siècle cuvée. Generally non-vintage, this blend represents almost an ideal of excellence. It is produced from 12 grands crus planted with almost equal numbers of Chardonnay and Pinot Noir vines.

VINE VARIETY

163 acres (66 hectares) and bought-in grapes: Pinot Noir, Pinot Meunier, Chardonnay.

OUR FAVORITE WINES

All the unalloyed distinction and elegance of structure of the wines produced by this house are found united in the Grand Siècle cuvée, which includes limited vintages such as the wonderful 1990. The very light and delicious Ultra-Brut can also be recommended.

Pol Roger

Pol Roger is one of only two top champagne houses that has remained undisturbed in the hands of the descendants of the original founder. Established in 1849, it immediately found a measure of success. Today it remains one of the small number of prestige marques, never compromising on quality. Described by Winston Churchill as "the world's most drinkable address in the world," the house of Pol Roger benefited from a gentle nudge in the direction of innovation with the appointment of Patrice Noyelle in the mid-1990s. Without apparently altering anything, he has succeeded in reviving the house's innate sense of balance and fullness, now manifest across the whole range of wines. Rather than the strong character or somewhat unsubtle production methods of some champagnes, here we will find a wine that can best be summed up in the words of the poet Baudelaire: *"Luxury, peace, and pleasure …"*.

VINE VARIETY

371 acres (150 hectares): 45% Pinot Noir, 55% Pinot Meunier, 100% Chardonnay, and bought-in grapes.

OUR FAVORITE WINES

While the house owes its reputation to the great vintages of the 1950s and 1960s, those of 1995 and 1996 provide a noble link with a proud history, particularly the full-bodied and well-balanced Sir Winston Churchill Cuvée.

Louis Roederer

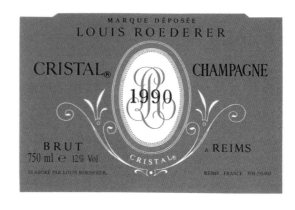

Along with Pol Roger, Louis Roederer is the only great champagne house to have remained a family business. Always well-regarded, it leaped to fame in the latter part of the 20th century as a result of a combination of three singularly positive factors: the magnetic personality of Jean-Claude Rouzaud who took over the reins in 1979; the magic of a prestige cuvée, Cristal, that has enchanted the whole world; and the fabulous heritage of a 500-acre (200-hectare) family vineyard situated in an ideal location (rated 98% on the scale of the Champagne region). The latter has been judiciously used to provide the backbone for a deliberately limited product. First developed for Tsar Alexander II, who wanted a champagne in a clear glass crystal bottle, since 1945 this mythical cuvée has been available to everyone. Using a balanced combination of Chardonnay and Pinot Noir grapes, each vintage of this cuvée seems to have two successive existences: when young it is a bright and festive champagne, light and open in character; if kept for a few years, its honesty and aristocratic brilliance develop, giving a refined pedigree champagne of unusual length.

VINE VARIETY
494 acres (200 hectares): Pinot Noir, Chardonnay, and bought-in grapes.

OUR FAVORITE WINES
Cristal 1996 is a truly memorable wine, in no way inferior to the faultless 1990 for which the house is justly famous. The dazzling 1999 cannot fail to impress.

The second fermentation in the bottle produces a sediment that is gently encouraged to the top of the bottle from where it can be removed or "disgorged."

Salon

Aimé Salon had unerring taste, relying on his own judgment to attain the best. It was for this reason that, in 1911, he decided to make his own champagne, using grapes coming only from carefully selected plots of land and suppliers growing grapes in a cru that he maintained (not unreasonably) was the best of the Champagne region: le Mesnil-sur-Oger. Reserved exclusively for his personal consumption and that of his friends, the Salon S (the only cuvée produced, and only when the vintage was sufficiently good) was to become a marque ten years later, but even then it remained the preserve of the "happy few." Aged for a long time before being put on sale, the robust vigor typical of the Mesnil Chardonnay grape is, in these Salon champagnes, brought to a perfect smoothness. Complex and sensuous, they retain all the mineral freshness of the terroir. When the Laurent-Perrier group took over the marque in 1988, it wisely refrained from changing the essential nature of the wines, seeking only to emphasize their unique personality. The 1995 and 1996 vintages are proof that it has successfully achieved these objectives.

VINE VARIETY

4 acres (1.5 hectares): Chardonnay grapes purchased from the vineyard of Mesnil-sur-Oger.

OUR FAVORITE WINES

While the 1928 has become legendary, the 1982 is another unforgettable vintage – prized for its smoothness, body, and freshness. This, together with the 1990 and, particularly, the dazzling 1995, offer three of the most successful expressions of Chardonnay champagne.

Jacques Selosse

It is thanks to Anselme Selosse, more than any other, that this family of independent winegrowers, producing their own wines, has attained such prestige. With vineyards in the heart of the best terroirs of the Côte des Blancs, Selosse quickly turned to the production of luxury wines in limited series, clearly revealing their origin. He took the courageous decision not only to convert to biodynamic viticulture, regenerating the soil, but also to use wooden barrels to make the wines from the different plots of land. These production methods have yielded wines that are richer and more complex, earning them many fans and giving rise to a number of imitators among the younger generation of wine producers. Now complementary reference points in the production of these characteristic and full-bodied whites, the Avize wines have an intense minerality, while those from Oger and Cramant have a greater delicacy. We can expect great things of Selosse's recent application of his methods to the Pinot Noir grape.

VINE VARIETY

17 acres (7 hectares): 92% Chardonnay, 8% Pinot Noir.

OUR FAVORITE WINES

All the current productions from this domaine border on perfection: the brut made without dosage is redolent of the terroir from which it comes, being pure, refined, and clean; the cuvée Contraste is an exciting newcomer, made from Pinot Noir grapes from Ambonnay and Ay combined with the magnificent Chardonnay grapes of Avize, Oger, and Cramant. We look forward to tasting the 1995 and 1996 vintages, still maturing in the cellars.

Winter pruning in the Champagne region. According to tradition, the discarded vines are burned on the spot in the vineyards.

Taittinger

The most recently established of the great houses, Taittinger was set up in 1932 by Pierre Taittinger when he bought up a business (called Fourneaux) that had already been in existence for some two centuries. The Taittinger family, originally from Lorraine and active in the worlds of both commerce and politics, had long been involved in the distribution and export of champagne. It was a natural development from that to the desire to create its own label. In the post-war period, the house saw its fortunes rise dramatically, soon becoming one of the exclusive circle of the great international marques. This was made possible by the adoption of a clearly identified style, the decision to use Chardonnay grapes from the terroirs of Côte des Blancs, and dynamic marketing at a time when other champagne houses were more restrained. Most importantly, it was able to produce a wonderful prestige cuvée: Comtes de Champagne. This blanc de blancs has a character that is both vigorous and refined, giving a pure and intense champagne worthy of the famous ancestral crus of the Côte des Blancs.

VINE VARIETY
667 acres (270 hectares): Pinot Noir, Pinot Meunier, Chardonnay, and bought-in grapes.

OUR FAVORITE WINES
The white Comtes de Champagne cuvée represents one of the best illustrations of the great Chardonnay champagnes, the particularly full-bodied 1986, 1988, and 1996 vintages being especially fine. The 1996 and 1999 rosé Comtes de Champagne is a wine of true distinction.

Veuve Clicquot Ponsardin

The most celebrated of all champagne widows (and, indeed, perhaps the most famous French widow of any sort), Nicole-Barbe Clicquot, née Ponsardin, was only 27 when, in 1805, she took over as head of the house founded by her recently deceased husband's father. By the time she died, 61 years later, the fame of the house had spread all over Europe and beyond. No less admired today, the acquisition of the house by LVMH in 1987 merely increased the power of the marque (and the size of its estate), as also occurred in the case of the other major player in the group, Moët & Chandon. Despite its size (with a production of more than eight million bottles), Clicquot has managed to preserve its own distinctive taste and style: it is a full-bodied and vinous champagne with a vigorous structure characterized by the black grapes used in its production. While it is found in the non-vintage brut champagnes, it is in the vintage and prestige cuvées – both white and rosé, the latter being a specialty of the house – that this personality is best expressed, with a particular finesse of definition.

VINE VARIETY

902 acres (365 hectares): Pinot Noir, Pinot Meunier, Chardonnay, and bought-in grapes.

OUR FAVORITE WINES

The prestige cuvée Grande Dame is a fine expression of all that is best of the house style – particularly the magnificent vintages of 1988, 1990, and 1996. The rosé champagne of these vintages and of 1995 has a rare elegance.

Domaine
Jean Macle

One of the most picturesque villages in eastern France, Château-Chalon has an ideal situation, perched over its famous vineyards with a view that is worth going out of the way to see. Here, among the old stone houses that evoke an ideal past, life seems timeless. It comes as no surprise to find that the wines from this area are unlike any others and are produced in a unique manner. The flavor of the Savagnin grape, unusual in having a high level of acidity even when harvested very ripe, is here magnified by being given a long maturation period of six years in small barrels, without any topping up. A protective layer of yeasts forms in the barrel, giving a beautiful golden color, and a wine with curious and unusual aromas of walnut, curry, and lightly smoked morel mushrooms. The wines produced from the blue marl soil of Château-Chalon are lighter in color, with a taste recalling the delicious yeasty odors of the bakery and freshly made toast. Jean Macle owns the oldest vines and the best sales and tasting outlet in the village. His wine often has a certain something not found in the others, a model of its kind, with a nobility and long-lived aromas worthy of a Montrachet burgundy.

VINE VARIETY
30 acres (12 hectares) white: 30% Savagnin, 70% Chardonnay.

OUR FAVORITE WINES
Two white wines are produced on this domaine. One is a reasonably priced and full-bodied dry Côtes-du-Jura. When young, it has the typical aromas of dried fruit; with time this becomes more honey-like, well-balanced particularly in the vintages of 2000, 2001, and 2002. The other is the famous Château-Chalon that here has an unequaled delicacy. The 1996 looks set for immortality, while the 1997, opulent and suave with a particularly long finish, is instantly appealing.

Jean Macle, the patient and skilled maker of Château-Chalon, a wine produced in only limited quantities.

Domaine
Louis Magnin

As with many of the more artistic crafts, there are several ways to learn the trade of vigneron. One is to concentrate tirelessly on perfecting the countless details involved in the process of growing grapes and making them into wine, constantly improving and refining the personality of the wines produced. This could be a description of the approach taken by Louis Magnin, who expertly brings out the original character of the wines and grapes of Savoy, so often deprived of the care they deserve. The Roussane grape that he uses in his Chignin-Bergeron takes on the refined, smooth, full-bodied accents found in the very best expressions of this variety. Used in the Arbois and especially in the La Brava cuvées, the Mondeuse grape reminds us of its close relationship to the Syrah of the northern Côtes du Rhône. Tasting the wines, we are immediately struck by the deep bluish color, intense aromas of berries and spices, and the generous but elegant body with a texture that is both firm and velvety. These wines are in an entirely different class from the usual rough table wines that generally accompany a modest meal in the ski resorts of the Alps.

LOUIS MAGNIN

La Brava

VINE VARIETY

10 acres (4 hectares) red: 94% Mondeuse, 6% Gamay.
5 acres (2 hectares) white: 92% Roussanne, 8% Jacquère.

OUR FAVORITE WINES

The Arbin La Brava is a Savoy red of the most harmonious elegance and refinement. All Louis Magnin's expertise and careful work can be found perfectly expressed in the Chignin-Bergeron whites –particularly the Cuvée Grand Orgue.

Nestling at the foot of the Alps, the vineyards of Savoy produce a number of fine wines whose qualities are too little known.

Mas de
Daumas Gassac

The story of Daumas Gassac and its creator Aimé Guibert will forever be inscribed in the history of French wine, so unlikely is it in a country that has always clung so passionately to age-old regulations and fixed hierarchies. This vineyard was created in the 1970s by the charismatic and energetic Guibert in the foothills of the Massif Central, below the Larzac plateau. At that time, this region was ignored by the winegrowers of Languedoc, despite having a perfectly drained but impoverished terroir of glacial formation. With the encouragement of Professors Enjalbert and Peynaud, eminent specialists from Bordeaux, Guibert planted mainly Cabernet vines, producing from them a wine made according to the method used for a Médoc. While its powerful constitution and firm structure are reminiscent of a Pauillac, this cru nevertheless has an authentically Mediterranean personality, noticeable particularly in an aromatic register typical of the *garrigues* (Provençal landscape), displaying berries, spices, and truffles.

VINE VARIETY
79 acres (32 hectares) red: 80% Cabernet Sauvignon, 5% Cabernet Franc, 2% Merlot, 1% Syrah, 1% Malbec, 11% other.
32 acres (13 hectares) white: 20% Chardonnay, 20% Chenin, 20% Petit Manseng, 20% Viognier, 20% other.

OUR FAVORITE WINES
The 1986 is still a wine of astonishing depth and seemingly eternal youthfulness. This fresh and aristocratic crispness can be found in the dazzling 1998 and in the almost-perfect Émile Peynaud Cuvée 2001.

Prieuré de
Saint-Jean-de-Bébian

Although Languedoc is the largest wine-producing area of France, in the early 1980s its wines were thought of as warm but somewhat unsophisticated, suitable only for the large-scale production of table wines. At the same time, the industry was showing disquieting signs of exhaustion. It took a serious reassessment by some of the regional public bodies to enable it to start on the long march toward the production of a quality wine. This process would not have got far had it not been for the efforts of a talented and open-minded group of young winegrowers. By ripping out the ultra-productive grape varieties, used until then to make up the classic palette of the local wines, and replacing them with the most noble southern French varieties – Syrah, Grenache, and Mourvèdre – Alain Roux was able to give new life to this ancient family domaine, paving the way to new levels of quality. Gaining in depth as they became more refined, the Bébian wines rapidly acquired an inimitable personality unlike that of any other wine. This pursuit of excellence was continued by Jean-Claude Le Brun and Chantal Lecouty, who bought the property in 1994. While losing nothing of their vigor and intensity, the wines have gained in precision and refinement of texture, resulting in a model example of the Mediterranean style.

Although better known for the production of table wines for everyday drinking, the regions of Languedoc and Roussillon include some outstanding terroirs that are beginning to be developed by a number of talented winemakers.

VINE VARIETY

67 acres (27 hectares) red: 40% Grenache, 35% Syrah, 15% Mourvèdre, 10% other.
15 acres (6 hectares) white: 60% Roussanne, 10% Bourboulenc, 10% Clairette, 10% Grenache, 10% Picpoul.

OUR FAVORITE WINES

While the domaine's 1989 was without doubt one the finest of the quality wines of Languedoc, since 1995 the cru has achieved a true consistency of production. The best years are the powerful 1995 and 1998, and the more delicate 2001 and 2003. The white, produced in small quantities, is an ambitious wine combining fullness and freshness of expression.

Domaine du
Clos des Fées

Many wine lovers dream of moving across the invisible barrier that separates the enthusiast from the wine producer by establishing or taking over a domaine. Of those who succeed in taking this step, most end up investing as much money as enthusiasm. Hervé Bizeul, who was, at various times, sommelier, restaurateur, publisher, and journalist, had enthusiasm to spare, but very little money. He decided therefore to buy a few acres of vines in the Tautavel valley, a spectacular but desolate limestone basin in the form of an amphitheater. Here, through a mixture of tenacity and skill, he produced rich, ambitious wines, exploding with the aromas of ripe fruit and with a velvety body that was both seductive and monumental. The expression of this style culminated in La Petite Sibérie, a curious and ironic name for a wine produced from a sun-baked terroir. Reflecting the character of their creator – expansive but concentrated, exuberant but secretive, sometimes excessive – Hervé Bizeul's wines have a freedom of tone that is rarely found in French wines.

VINE VARIETY

36 acres (14.5 hectares) red: 30% Carignan, 30% Grenache, 20% Syrah, 10% Lladoner Pelut, 10% Mourvèdre.
6 acres (2.5 hectares) white: 90% Grenache Blanc, 10% Grenache Gris.

OUR FAVORITE WINES

Although a dry wine, the Cuvée La Petite Sibérie has all the richness and aromatic intensity of high-quality port. The Clos des Fées 2001 and 2003 are wines of a more classic type, but possessing a beguiling generosity and lusciousness.

Domaine Gauby

Gérard Gauby's father had so little faith in the future of Roussillon wines, so closely associated with the declining star of the Rivesaltes and other naturally sweet wines, that he went into the construction business in his small village of Calce. The houses he built are still there but, fortunately for wine lovers, his son and daughter-in-law, and subsequently their son, have devoted themselves exclusively to growing grapes and producing wine. Their example, and their creation of a number of rich, generous, fruity, and accessible wines, have given new hope to an entire generation of Roussillon wine producers. The 1995 cuvée of La Muntada shot instantly to international fame. Never one to rest on his laurels, however, Gérard Gauby has returned to the drawing board, seeking to move away from a style based on power in favor of a more perfect expression of harmony, smoothness, and freshness. This act of self-questioning is both courageous and important for the future of wine production in the south of France, where the best wines have too high a level of alcohol to allow them to realize their full potential. Gérard Gauby is to be congratulated for his readiness to further the cause of the wines of his region.

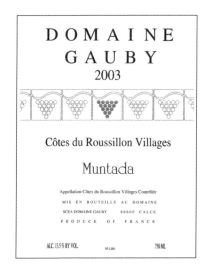

VINE VARIETY

69 acres (28 hectares) red: 47% Carignan, 25% Grenache, 15% Syrah, 7% Mourvèdre, 6% various.
30 acres (12 hectares) white: 50% Muscat, 25% Grenache, 20% Maccabeu, 5% Viognier.

OUR FAVORITE WINES

La Muntada, Gérard Gauby's most celebrated wine, was particularly impressive in 1995 and 1998, with an explosive richness of constitution. The 2001 and 2003 are equally superb wines, having a more distinguished and refined balance.

Mas Amiel

Lying at the foot of the northeastern slopes of the Pyrenees, the Maury estate seems very remote. Unlike those of Rivesaltes and Banyuls (the other two important vineyards producing naturally sweet wine), it is inland from the Mediterranean and no major roads pass through the area. Nevertheless, the schisty terroir and a climate that is both cooler and more protected than other parts of Roussillon are ideally suited for grape growing. Charles Dupuy seized the opportunity to make this vast and beautiful domaine not only the flagship of the appellation, but also the source of one of the best naturally sweet wines in France. These particularly include his oxydative cuvées, wines that are aged for a considerable time in wooden barrels – in the manner used for tawny Ports – or in large demijohns (*bonbonnes*). Acquired by the enterprising Olivier Decelle at the beginning of the 21st century, the basic principles have been maintained while growing methods (now on biodynamic lines) have been further refined, as has the winemaking process. In addition to the full-bodied Maury 15 Ans d'Âge, sensual and expressive vintages are being produced, together with red wines made without *mutage* (where fermentation is halted by the addition of alcohol) of remarkably elegant texture.

VINE VARIETY
353 (143 hectares) red: 81% Grenache, 12% Syrah, 5% Carignan, 2% Mourvèdre.
30 acres (12 hectares) white: 47% Muscat, 33% Grenache Gris, 20% Maccabeu.

OUR FAVORITE WINES
The 2003 vintage, with its deep color, profusion of fruity and spicy aromas, and velvety texture, is an outstanding example of the vintages from this estate – particularly the dazzling Cuvée Charles Dupuy. The 1980 Maury Prestige 1980 and the 15 Ans d'Âge, with their coppery color, are also wines of the highest quality, albeit different in style with aromas of walnut and gingerbread.

Naturally sweet wines can be bottled straight away, as in the case of vintage wines, or left to age in barrels, allowing the deep and aristocratic aroma known as rancio *to develop.*

Domaine
Philippe Alliet

Though Chinon wines were praised for their excellence by the writer Rabelais, Philippe Alliet's domaine does not have such a long history, being one of the most recently created. Established in 1985, it soon began to produce one of the best red wines of the Loire region when, ten years later, it acquired the magnificent Coteau de Noiré terroir, situated on a steep south-facing slope. By replanting and restoring this valuable but difficult vineyard, where pruning was thought to be almost impossible, Alliet accomplished an extraordinary feat that today pays generous dividends. Deep, smooth, perfectly ripe, with an exquisite intensity of taste and delightful bouquet, there is no doubt that the Coteau de Noiré would have met with the approval of Rabelais's hero, Gargantua.

VINE VARIETY
30 acres (12 hectares): Cabernet Franc.

OUR FAVORITE WINES
The 2003 Coteau de Noiré Chinon has a fullness of constitution, velvety texture, and fresh and intense depth that can scarcely be matched by any other wine from the Loire Valley.

Domaine de la
Coulée de Serrant

One of those vineyards that linger in the memory, Coulée de Serrant has a majestic site overlooking the wide, slow-moving waters of the Loire, a few miles outside Angers. It was clear early on that great wines could be produced here, and Curnonsky, "prince of gastronomes," declared it one of the five greatest French white wines. A mere 36 acres (14.5 hectares) of vines, forming part of a single domaine, was given its own unique appellation. Completely renewed in the late 1960s, Coulée de Serrant has been raised to an astounding level of quality by Nicolas Joly, tireless propagandist for biodynamic viticulture. Like other great wine producers who have now followed his example, he works within the context of a vision of nature in which the winemaker seeks as far as possible to understand and respect the terrestrial and cosmic environment of his vines, and to imbue the wine produced with the energy and resonance of its place of origin. To the taste, Coulée de Serrant is a unique wine, long and svelte, ample, and very mature, but offset by a fresh and unrestrained acidity, which develops – particularly after a long decantation – a bouquet of extraordinary complexity.

VINE VARIETY

36 acres (14.5 hectares) white: Chenin.

OUR FAVORITE WINES

Generally a dry wine, Coulée de Serrant has a sweet version that is delightfully unusual. The array of aromas is both subtle and exuberant, combining hints of flowers, honey, curry, and spices, that come out particularly well when drunk with Asian cuisine. The 1989, 1995 (both the dry and the sweet versions), 1997, 1999, 2002, and 2003 are unforgettable wines destined to have a long life.

The Coulée de Serrant vineyards, cultivated along biodynamic lines, have a spectacular site overlooking the Loire.

Domaine
Didier Dagueneau

Didier Dagueneau's greatest strength, in addition to his ability to question the conservatism of wine production, is that of combining the intuition and sense of observation characteristic of the greatest French wine producers – those who have created the types of wines admired and imitated throughout the world – and a perfect understanding of modern enology. The vines are cultivated with the greatest respect for the terroir, while the most up-to-date materials and scrupulous hygiene in the cellars ensures the highest standards of winemaking. The result is wines that verge on perfection. Here the delicate musky flavors characteristic of the appellation Pouilly Fumé are no longer masked by faulty fermentation, lost in a mass of inferior grapes, or made coarse by the use of harvesting machines that damage the fruit. Instead, they are brought out to maximum effect, refinement and faithfulness to the vintage. Tasting the Cuvée Buisson Renard, one is immediately aware of the privileged relationship between this terroir and the Sauvignon grapes, but the wonders of the Silex and Pur-Sang vineyards lead us into another and mysterious universe, that of the true work of art.

VINE VARIETY
28 acres (11.5 hectares) white: Sauvignon.

OUR FAVORITE WINES
Although 2003 was a very hot year, the domaine's wines of this vintage are not marred by excessive heaviness. This is particularly true for the Pur-Sang 2004, made from vines growing on light-colored soil. This wine, more classic and with a greater edge to its character, almost succeeds in repeating the miraculous 2002 vintage with some noteworthy wines from the Saint-Andelain butte. The excellent grape harvest of 2005 looks set to yield some real treats.

Château de
Fesles

With a history dating back to 1070, Fesles, with its splendid 19th-century château, is situated at the top of a hillside long planted with vines. More recently, the property has become the standard bearer of the Bonnezeaux cru. Bonnezeaux owes its name (literally "good waters") to the quality of the local springs and is the most important terroir for sweet wines in the Anjou district. Famous early on for their suitability for the production of wines from late-harvested grapes with an unusual mellowness and richness, the four Fesles hillsides benefit from the micro-climate around the Layon, a small tributary of the Loire river, that favors the growth of the botrytis cinerea fungus. This, in a site well-protected from the wind, is able to establish itself on the grapes as what is called *pourriture noble* (or "noble rot"). Unfortunately, the decline in public interest in sweet wines in the post-war period resulted in some difficult years for the château. Thanks to the energy and enthusiasm of the pâtissier Gaston Lenôtre, who bought the property in the 1980s, Fesles was able to recover from this setback. Now run by Bernard Germain from Bordeaux, this 1,000-year-old cru has never been better.

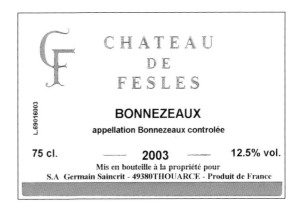

VINE VARIETY

44 acres (18 hectares) white: 95% Chenin, 5% Chardonnay.
42 acres (17 hectares) red: 80% Cabernet Franc, 10% Gamay,
5% Cabernet Sauvignon, 5% Grolleau.

OUR FAVORITE WINES

The 1997 and 2003 Bonnezeaux are very fine sweet wines, with
a fullness of constitution and a richness that will allow them
a life of several decades.

Domaine
Huet

A large wine-producing area – 5,436 acres (2,200 hectares) – Vouvray lies on the plateaus overlooking the right bank of the Loire and the hillsides of the lesser tributaries that have carved a path through this imposing block of limestone. Opposite, on the other side of the Loire, is another vineyard of sweet wines: Montlouis. The vines closest to the cliff edge, where the layer of soil is thinner, are called the *première côte*. A magnificent illustration of the subtle differences between different terroirs, the domaine produces wine from three crus, each with its own unique personality. Bordering the Coteau de Loire, Mont gives a refined and elegant wine that is never overwhelming but which ages wonderfully; Haut-Lieu, with its heavier soil, gives the wine made from its grapes an impressive suppleness; and Bourg, a genuine clos (walled garden), is typical of the *première côte*. This is a deep and structured wine that keeps well. Improved by Gaston Huet, these terroirs were converted by his son-in-law, Noël Pinguet, to biodynamic viticulture in the 1990s. The result was an increase in the precision of this wine's definition.

VINE VARIETY
86 acres (35 hectares) white: Chenin.

OUR FAVORITE WINES
The Huet domaine has, for decades, been the best representative of its appellation. Evidence of this are the countless magical wines produced here, including those of 1933, 1945, 1947, and 1959 that remain today dazzling illustrations of the genius of the mellow Vouvray wines. The more recent 1989, 1990, 1996, 1997, and 2003 will be similarly inscribed in the domaine's roll of honor.

Domaine
Henry Marionnet

Henry Marionnet must certainly be one of the most appealing wine producers of France, producing some of the most sincere wines available. Based in the village of Soing, deep in the hunting forests and moors of La Sologne, this seemed an unpromising area for wine producing. Nevertheless, his faith in the land led Marionnet to replant the entirety of the family vineyards in the 1960s and 1970s, opting for the gaiety and cheerfulness of Gamay and Sauvignon. Designed to be drunk young, time and skill have led to the production of supple and fruity wines with an exceptional velvety depth, and all the honesty and aromatic freedom of wine made with almost no sulfur. Later, when replanting new vines on plots in this sandy terrain, Marionnet took a risky but exciting step, installing old, ungrafted plants (and thus susceptible to attack by phylloxera). In this way he was able to revive flavors forgotten for more than a century after the virtual destruction of Europe's vineyards by the phylloxera aphid. These wines, produced from ancient varieties of Gamay, Cot (also known as Malbec), Chenin, and Romorantin have a lingering taste evocative of a fragile eternity.

VINE VARIETY
99 acres (40 hectares) red: 90% Gamay, 10% Cot.
49 acres (20 hectares) white: 97% Sauvignon, 1.5% Chenin,
1.5% Romorantin.

OUR FAVORITE WINES
Few Gamay wines have such a cheerful, generous, and deep constitution as the Vinifera cuvées (produced from franc de pied, or ungrafted, Gamay vines) and L'épages Oubliés (produced from a rare variety of vine, Gamay de Bouze). Particularly good are the 2003 and 2005 vintages.

Domaine
Alphonse Mellot

Alphonse Mellot Junior runs the family domaine of La Moussière with his father Alphonse Mellot Senior. Nineteen generations of Mellots have ensured that their knowledge of, and dedication to, Sancerre wines, continues to be handed down. The sense of family is so strong among the Mellots that the two most flamboyant cuvées are called Génération XIX and Edmond – the latter being the name of Alphonse Senior's father. True artists with Sauvignon – although we should not forget their excellent and supple reds made with Pinot Noir grapes – the Mellot family have constantly sought to raise the level of quality, both in the cultivation of the grapes, where the vines are grown and pruned according to unusually strict rules, and in the winemaking process, where pressing is conducted with extraordinary precision. While never compromising on the quality of their supple and fruity "basic" Sancerres, their worthy aspirations have gradually raised them to the peaks of the great Sauvignons of the world.

VINE VARIETY

99 acres (40 hectares) white: Sauvignon.
20 acres (8 hectares) red: Pinot Noir.

OUR FAVORITE WINES

Alphonse Mellot's white Sancerres are among the most brilliant and pure illustrations of the genius of the Sauvignon grape. The 2000, 2001, and 2002 of the Génération XIX and Edmond cuvées illustrate this mastery with astonishing flair. These wines will age perfectly, as can be seen today with the form of the 1989 wines.

In the Mellot family, the first names Alphonse or Edmond have been handed down from father to son for almost 20 generations of dedicated winemakers.

Clos Rougeard

The wine producers of the Loire region include many of the most colorful characters of the industry. Rigorous in their approach to their daily work, redoubtable when it comes to tasting on account of their caustic and devastating wit, the Foucault brothers (Charly and Nady) are also bon viveurs beloved of all their colleagues, enjoying nothing more than to be at the table eating good food and drinking all that is best in the world of wine, which naturally includes their own wines. Benefiting from biodynamic viticulture – a courageous decision that requires constant vigilance – the grapes from the beautiful terroirs around Varrains-Chacé yield red wines that are perhaps the most satisfying of their appellation. Lively, with considerable depth, and with tannins as complex as those in the finest Médocs, these wines have an extraordinarily long bottle life. Unlike their colleagues, the Foucaults have always used new casks to make their wine, but never allowing the wood to dominate the taste and texture of the wines. The small quantity of very superior and delicious dry white wine produced here has, in a good year, an unrivaled elegance, reminding us that the Brezé terroir is arguably the finest in the Loire region for Chenin grapes.

VINE VARIETY
25 acres (10 hectares): 90% Cabernet Franc, 10% Chenin.

OUR FAVORITE WINES
The youngest vintage that we have tasted, the 2001, is very representative of the wines produced by the Foucault brothers. In the dry white Saumur Brezé cuvée, the sometimes coarse fruitiness of Chenin is suppressed, giving the wine an aristocratic rigor worthy of the finest Champagnes. The red Saumur-Champigny wines are a happy marriage of fullness and delicacy, an excellent example being the superb Cuvée Le Bourg.

Château de Pibarnon

Laid out within the magnificent setting of a natural amphitheater and planted almost exclusively with Mourvèdre grapes, the Pibarnon terroir is archetypical of the Bandol wines. Situated on the coast overlooking the Mediterranean between La Ciotat and Toulon, the vineyard was established in 1978 when the charismatic Henri de Saint-Victor fell in love with the site. His property, where all the delights of Provençal life are to be found, represents an impressive and admirable human adventure, today being carried forward by Henri's son, Eric. This model enterprise is reflected perfectly in the style of the wine produced. Fine Bandol wines such as Pibarnon have a natural class that immediately singles them out from the crowd of other wines produced on the Mediterranean coast. When still young, the red Pibarnons are never very powerful but, in almost every vintage, they present a balance that becomes ever more impressive and striking as they age.

VINE VARIETY

109 acres (44 hectares) red: 90% Mourvèdre, 10% Grenache. 10 acres (4 hectares) white: 50% Clairette, 30% Bourboulenc, 20% other.

OUR FAVORITE WINES

The 1989 and 1990 vintages are today fine, mature Bandol wines. They have a superb, still youthful, complexity of bouquet. The 1998 and 2001 are already very promising, with a refined texture and great depth. They have a highly original range of aromas. Unlike the majority of wine currently available, red or black berries are not the dominant note in a young Pibarnon. Immediately noticeable is a combination of spicy, licorice, peppery, and cocoa notes, together with hints of herbs and an astonishing and delicate vegetative register.

Situated between the hills and the sea, the luxuriant landscape around Bandol is also home to the wonderful Mourvèdre grape variety.

Domaine
Tempier

The post-war period of European reconstruction was also a period marked by the evolution of a number of small, high-quality vineyards. Inspired by the philosophy of the founders of the appellation contrôlée principle, their owners sought to have their region recognized as conforming to demanding standards of quality. The Bandol wines of Provence owe a great debt to the energies and determination of Lucien Peyraud who fought tirelessly during the 1950s to establish his appellation at Tempier, the domaine he ran with his wife. His ambitions were based most notably on the use of a difficult grape with a great pedigree: Mourvèdre. Lucien, and later his children, were to be highly successful in demonstrating the subtleties of which this grape was capable, whether used on its own or in combination with other varieties, in a number of wonderful small vineyards with evocative names such as Cabassaou, Migoua, and Tourtine.

VINE VARIETY

70 acres (28.5 hectares) red: 60% Mourvèdre, 17% Cinsault, 15% Grenache, 5% Carignan, 3% Syrah.
2.5 acres (1 hectare) white: 50% Clairette, 25% Ugni-Blanc, 25% Bourboulenc.

OUR FAVORITE WINES

Of the various cuvées produced from the different plots of the Tempier domaine, the Cabassaous of 2003 and 2001, exceptionally successful vintages from this domaine, have a perfect fullness and depth of expression.

Domaine de Trévallon

The extraordinary jagged profile of the Alpilles massif dominates the picturesque villages of Saint-Rémy and Les Baux-de-Provence, forming a narrow but daunting barrier between the Camargue to the south and Avignon to the north. A number of vineyards of serene beauty lie together at the foot of this limestone wall, Trévallon being the most famous representative. And yet, paradoxically, bureaucratic red tape has seen fit to exclude this wonderful creation from the appellation Baux-de-Provence, using the significant presence of Cabernet-Sauvignon as a pretext. Eloi Dürrbach fell in love with this property before deciding to plant vines there in 1973. The result was an unclassified wine, made from grapes planted among pine trees and rocky outcrops, exposed to the wind and sun, with a masterly rigor of construction combined with a very Mediterranean aromatic liveliness and the velvety texture of a truly great wine. More than 30 years later, Trévallon remains unique in French viticulture – a situation with which Eloi Dürrbach is more than happy.

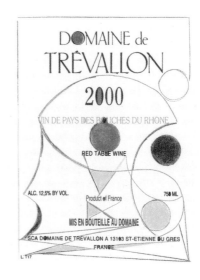

VINE VARIETY
*37 acres (15 hectares) red: 50% Cabernet Sauvignon, 50% Syrah.
5 acres (2 hectares) white: 45% Marsanne, 45% Roussanne,
10% Chardonnay.*

OUR FAVORITE WINES
Of recent vintages, where concentration is combined with refinement, the delicious 2000 and 2003 bring together fullness of body and refinement of texture with a fragrant bouquet suggesting truffles and spices.

Domaine
Antoine Arena

The wines of Corsica are perhaps the least-known French wines. The variety of its terroirs and its countless climatic variations, perfectly adapted to the local grape varieties – Muscat, Niellucciu (equivalent to the Tuscan Sangiovese), Sciacarello (planted only in the Ajaccio region), and Vermentino – yield wines of a much greater subtlety and quality than is generally realized. Established at Patrimonio in the north of the island, with vineyards on a magical hillside fully exposed to the sun, Antoine Arena knows better than anyone how to bring out the best from his vines, creating wines that are both original and captivating. The dry whites produced from Vermentino grapes, the reds, and the delicious but not cloying Muscats are all characterized by aromatic brilliance and airy freshness. Whether it is the delightful Grotte di Sole, or the Carco that Antoine Arena reinvents each vintage year, there are few wines that can, like these, be said to be defined as much by the mind and imagination of their maker as by their terroir and grape variety.

VINE VARIETY
10 acres (4 hectares) red: Niellucciu.
17 acres (7 hectares) white: 60% Vermentino, 40% Muscat.

OUR FAVORITE WINES
The Antoine Arena whites have a delicate refinement and unique personality equally apparent in the Carco and Grotte di Sole cuvées and in the astonishing and refined Muscat du Cap Corse. The reds combine refinement with a well-constructed and full body – particularly in the case of the remarkable 2004 vintage.

Situated near the hill village of Patrimonio in the north of Corsica is one of the most beautiful vineyards in France. Its qualities have been further enhanced by a true artist, Antoine Arena.

M. Chapoutier

Celebrating its bicentenary in 2008, this house is, together with that of Paul Jaboulet Aîné, the ambassador of Hermitage wines throughout the world. That said, its fame was briefly eclipsed during the early 1980s, and it was not until Michel Chapoutier took over the business in 1987 that it saw a return to form and renewed vigor. Determined and passionate about wine-growing, Michel immediately made some drastic choices in a desire to raise the quality of his wines, in particular the Hermitage appellation of which this house is the largest owner. Perhaps the most far-reaching of his decisions was to convert the entire domaine to biodynamic viticulture, a method that is governed by a rigorous respect for the environment and forbids the use of any conventional fertilizers, chemicals, or insecticides. Another fascinating decision was to create, alongside the traditional and refined Monnier de la Sizeranne, wines produced from the best areas of L'Hermitage: Le Pavillon (from Les Bessards), Le Méal, and L'Ermite. These, together with the numerous other crus used by Chapoutier and his team, express with endless subtlety all the variety of the great terroirs of the northern side of the Rhône valley and Châteauneuf-du-Pape.

VINE VARIETY

190 acres (77 hectares – 35 Hermitage and 30 Châteauneuf-du-Pape) red: 70% Syrah, 30% Grenache. 20 acres (8 hectares) white: 90% Marsanne, 10% Viognier.

OUR FAVORITE WINES

The 2000, 2001, and 2003 Hermitage cuvées Le Méal, Le Pavillon and L'Ermite each possess, in their different styles, an astonishing and dazzling depth that is equal to the greatest years of the preceding decade – particularly 1990 and 1995.

Here in the Chapoutier winery the barrels are being topped up (ouillage). This involves adding wine from the same source at regular intervals to compensate for loss through evaporation or absorption into the wood of the barrel.

Domaine
Jean-Louis Chave

Gérard Chave and his son Jean-Louis – the latter named after his grandfather and several other members of this family whose history as wine producers dates back several centuries – represent, alongside Léonard and Olivier Humbrecht, the most talented partnership in French winemaking. Their kingdom is a small but wonderful maze of terroirs on the slopes of the hill known as L'Hermitage. Unlike some of the other famous wine producers of L'Hermitage, the Chaves blend wines produced from different spots that have been grown, harvested, and already pressed. Visiting the cellars with Gérard, as he tastes a sample of that year's wine drawn from the barrels with a pipette, provides a fascinating lesson but, alas, one reserved for the chosen few. The student is taught to appreciate the powerful mineral content of the wines from Les Bessards, that mass of granite overlooking the Rhône, the fleshy, velvety nature of those from Le Méal, the aristocratic silkiness of L'Hermite. In this way, one comes to understand the nuances and complexities of the different parts of the Hermitage hill, perhaps the finest illustration of an appellation d'origine. The lesson concludes by tasting the blend created from these marvels, when the student can only marvel at the artistry of the winemaker and his perfect judgment.

VINE VARIETY

25 acres (10 hectares) red: Syrah.
12 acres (5 hectares) white: 80% Marsanne, 20% Roussanne.

OUR FAVORITE WINES

The wonderfully balanced red of 1990 (as well as the limited production of Cuvée Cathelin) will long be remembered. Both the whites and the reds of 1999, 2001, and 2003 have a near-perfect and astonishing harmoniousness.

Domaine
Auguste Clape

Pressed up against the Massif Central that comes to a sudden end where it meets the Rhône, Cornas is the southernmost of 50 miles (80 kilometers) of vineyards planted on the sloping hillsides in a long, narrow strip of hillsides – that at the northern end being Côte Rôtie. Remote from the main transport routes and lacking any famous wine-producing house in the village, Cornas is the least-known of the great crus of the northern section of the Rhône valley. However, it is an area worth visiting to see the spectacular situation of the vines, in two superimposed cirques, around and above the village. Auguste Clape and his son, Pierre, have devoted much careful labor to this granite-soil terroir. They understand all its subtleties and, like Gérard and Jean-Louis Chave in L'Hermitage, they know better than anyone how to bring out the best from their grapes, now the power, then the refinement, here the spices, there the blackcurrant notes. The result after blending is a splendid Cornas that is harmonious, deep, and ready for a long period in the cellars.

VINE VARIETY
15 acres (6.1 hectares) red: Syrah.
1 acre (0.4 hectares) white: Marsanne.

OUR FAVORITE WINES
The 2000 and 2001 vintages are the equals of the wonderful
1989 and 1990 vintages with their vigor and muscular depth.

Domaine
Jean-Luc Colombo

Had music been his chosen form of expression, Jean-Luc Colombo would by turns (and sometimes at the same time) have been an instrumentalist, a conductor, a sound engineer, and a producer. Sticking to wine, this enthusiast with a thirst for new experiences has long been both a consultant enologist, helping some of the best producers in the Rhône valley to refine the tannic structure of their wine, and a winegrower. However, it was not long before he took on a third role: that of *négociant*, offering under his own signature some good examples of a selection of crus north and south of the town of Valence. Ever since he started out in the wine industry in the 1980s, though, he has constantly drawn his strength and unique personality from the rugged granite slopes of his Cornas vineyard. The wines he makes here with his wife Anne, herself a talented winemaker, have sacrificed nothing of the robust vigor of their terroir but have gained balance and a silkiness of texture. Without any trace of tannic roughness or rusticity, Colombo's various wines, in particular Les Ruchets, testify to the unrivaled quality of this terroir, one of the least-known in the Rhône valley.

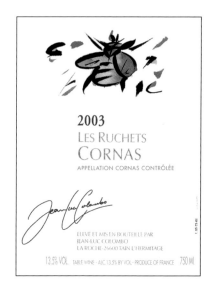

VINE VARIETY
15 acres (6 hectares) red: Syrah.

OUR FAVORITE WINES
Three AC Cornas wines – Terres Brûlées, La Louvée, and Les Ruchets – are made here. The first seduces with its robust generosity, and the second with its velvety texture and silky finesse, while Les Ruchets conveys its harmonious fullness of body with a rare elegance. Of recent vintages, 1999, 2001, 2003, and the promising 2004 stand out for their well-balanced personalities.

Delas

Delas Frères was for a long time a worthy but slightly dusty Rhône *négociant*. Less famous than its Tain l'Hermitage neighbors Jaboulet and Chapoutier (from the other side of the river, as Delas is based on the left bank near Tournon), it used to offer a range of classic wines from almost every site in the northern Rhône area. It was then bought by the champagne house Deutz, on whom the true value of its acquisition gradually dawned – for among the collection of in-part excellent terroirs it brought with it, Delas also possessed a number of extraordinarily well-positioned sites on the Hermitage hill and more specifically in the Bessards sector. Little by little, Deutz began to change things, bringing both precision and passion to bear. Located on a steep slope at the western extremity of the impressive hill, whose enormous mass dominates the Rhône, Les Bessards represents the very quintessence of Hermitage. The soil and subsoil are pure granite, the vestiges of a rocky Massif Central ridge cut in two over time by the raging Rhône, which originally skirted it. Crumbling gradually to form natural drainage into which the roots of the vines penetrate deeply, and facing due south, this uncompromising terroir is one of the most impressive and purest anywhere. Delas has now been pruning and working this rough diamond with all the care it deserves to make a named single-site cuvée of never more than around 6,000 bottles.

VINE VARIETY
Les Bessards cuvée: 15 acres (6 hectares): Syrah.

OUR FAVORITE WINES
Delas only started isolating this particular parcel of vines for a dedicated cuvée in the mid-1990s. Rigorous in structure, and displaying tannic intensity and impressive depth, this is a cathedral among wines. The 1999 is as straight as a spire with unrivaled architectural finesse.

E. Guigal

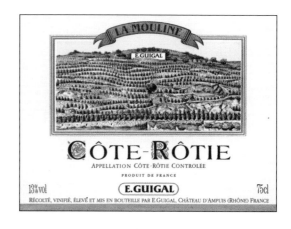

There is no doubt that Marcel Guigal's name will be one of those inscribed in a list of the greatest winemakers of modern times. His achievement has been to oversee the renaissance of a great cru, Côte Rôtie, that had been virtually abandoned, rescuing the wine and viticulture of his region from the somewhat haphazard approach of the past, and making his name an international guarantee of quality for the wines to which it is attached, from the unassuming Côtes-du-Rhône to the mythical Côte Rôtie and Hermitage cuvées. In fewer than 20 years Marcel Guigal has demonstrated unequivocally to the entire world that the Rhône valley is worthy of a place among the most eminent winegrowing regions of the world. The son of Étienne Guigal, the wine producer who, in 1946, created the small house that bears his name, Marcel built his reputation around two exceptional Côte Rôtie cuvées: the beautifully structured Landonne, and the velvety and limpid Mouline. In 1985, the suave and exuberant Turque was introduced, further enhancing the success of this house. Matured in barrels for an unusually long time – 42 months – and subject to the meticulous supervision of Marcel and his son Philippe, year after year these wines continue to be among the very best of the Rhône wines and, in the best vintage years, of any wine in the world.

VINE VARIETY

138 acres (56 hectares; of which half lies in the Côte Rôtie) red: Syrah.
54 acres (22 hectares) white: Marsanne, Viognier, Roussanne.

OUR FAVORITE WINES

Countless legendary cuvées have been produced by Guigal. Of the Côte Rôtie wines, La Landonne and La Mouline reached a peak of perfection in 1978 and 1985. This extraordinary brilliance can also be found in the 1999 and 2001 cuvées, as in the superb Château d'Ampuis of 1995. Both the red and the white Hermitage Cuvée Ex-Voto made a highly promising debut in 2001.

Marcel Guigal and his son Philippe, expert tasters and wonderful ambassadors for the great wines of Côte Rôtie and the entire Rhône valley.

Château Grillet

Château Grillet enjoys an outstanding situation. While the Condrieu slopes are exposed mainly to the east or southeast, the small amphitheater within which the Château Grillet vineyards grow on a fine granite soil faces directly toward the south. These vines and the historic château where Blaise Pascal once stayed, today splendidly restored, overlook the broad waters of the Rhône. This happy combination of geology and position is the reason for the creation of this tiny appellation, in the hands of a single owner. The moment the sun breaks through the clouds, it immediately starts to warm the Château Grillet soil and vines. Owned by the same family for more than a century, the cru naturally seeks to emphasize its uniqueness. Reorganized in the 1970s by André Canet, it is now his daughter, Isabelle, who continues his work with the same scrupulous care and attention. The unique personality of a Château Grillet wine is characterized by its density of constitution and length.

VINE VARIETY

8 acres (3.4 hectares) white: Viognier.

OUR FAVORITE WINES

Often somewhat enigmatic when young, Château Grillet reveals all its finesse and mineral intensity as it ages, and is exceptionally long-lived. The 1981, 1989, 1990, and 1995 are thus perfect examples of a wine with an unique personality. Unlike the neighboring Condrieus, this wine is notable more for its body than its perfume.

Paul Jaboulet Aîné

Born in 1807, Antoine Jaboulet founded the house bearing his name at Tain l'Hermitage, a small town lying between the hill of L'Hermitage and the no less imposing river Rhône. After the Second World War, the Jaboulet family created a cuvée of red Hermitage, La Chapelle, that quickly became the ambassador for this deep and well-structured wine in all parts of the world. Full-bodied like the great Médocs, La Chapelle is a wine that ages wonderfully, developing a bouquet of spices, cedar wood, and berries. The body is velvety, supported by solid but not stiff tannins; the finish is always fresh. As it became ever more difficult over the generations to keep this exceptional domaine within the family, after two centuries of good and loyal service to the wines of L'Hermitage and the Rhône valley, the Jaboulets finally sold their house and vineyard to a businessman from the Champagne region, Jean-Jacques Frey, who already owned Château La Lagune, in Haut-Médoc. It seems scarcely necessary to recommend he continue the fine tradition of the Jaboulets in maintaining the quality of L'Hermitage and Côtes-du-Rhône wines, since he has already made it clear that he intends to do so.

VINE VARIETY

208 acres (84 hectares) red: Syrah.
40 acres (16 hectares) white: 70% Marsanne, 30% Roussanne.

OUR FAVORITE WINES

La Chapelle is without doubt the only great wine produced in the Rhône valley that can boast an uninterrupted level of quality throughout the post-war period. Vintages such as 1949, 1961, 1978, 1989, and 1990 still bear witness to their extraordinary legend. More recently, the 2001 and, particularly, the 2003 are clear indications that the tradition continues.

The Hermitage hill, an isolated outcrop of the granite Massif Central separated from its parent mountains by the fast-flowing waters of the Rhône, provides a wonderful setting for the south-facing Syrah vines.

Domaine
Georges Vernay

Georges Vernay, with his round cheerful face enlivened by a mischievous smile and piercing gaze, is an example of all that is best in the French winegrower. Generous and talkative, passionately devoted to his terroir and his wines, he seeks to produce wines based on finesse and purity of expression. When he decided to give up growing two fruits – grapes and apricots (the latter on the banks of the Rhône) – to devote himself entirely to the family vineyard, Condrieu, there was almost nothing there to work on. Only 15 acres (6 hectares) of vines – of a cru producing one of the most aromatic and original of white wines – had survived into the post-war period. Thanks to his hard work, combined with an unusual degree of charisma, he was able to revive the appellation so that today 100 producers share 247 acres (100 hectares), and, most importantly, to create Coteau de Vernon, most refined of all the Condrieus and made from vines grown on a very steep slope with a magnificent aspect. Today, Georges's daughter Christine has taken over from her father, further developing the quality of the wines and now also producing an excellent Côte Rôtie, Maison Rouge.

PRODUCT OF FRANCE
Coteau de Vernon
CONDRIEU
Appellation Condrieu contrôlée
2004
14% vol.   Mis en bouteille à la Propriété   750ml
EARL Georges VERNAY, Viticulteur à CONDRIEU (Rhône) FRANCE

L.03

VINE VARIETY

17 acres (7 hectares) red: Syrah.
25 acres (10 hectares) white: Viognier.

OUR FAVORITE WINES

With its finesse, delightful aroma, and perfect breadth and balance, the Coteau de Vernon is one of the most perfect examples of Viognier to be found anywhere in the world. Outstanding for their impressive harmony are the vintages of 2001 and 2004. Equally noteworthy is the delicious Côte Rôtie Maison Rouge.

Château de
Beaucastel

Belonging to a single owner, this property lies on a spectacular terroir of rolled pebbles, the subsoil containing a considerable amount of clay (desirable in terms of water supply to the vines). It is situated at the northeastern end of the appellation, a few miles from the town of Orange. Renovated by the Tramier and then the Perrin families from the early 20th century onwards, this has become one of the most innovative and successful wine-producing businesses of Châteauneuf. Surprisingly, in an appellation where white wines make up a minuscule fraction of the total production, the whites produced on this domaine are as excellent as the reds. The full-bodied and perfumed Roussane grape plays a vital role in the white wines, particularly in the Cuvée Vieilles Vignes, produced from this grape only. The red grapes have a similar originality: the intense, pedigree Mourvèdre is grown on almost one-third of the land alongside the smooth Grenache, Syrah, and Cinsault. In addition to these are Counoise and all the other varieties of grapes used in an appellation that allows 13 different kinds to be used in total. The cuvée Hommage à Jacques Perrin is prepared almost exclusively from the grapes of old Mourvèdre vines.

VINE VARIETY
222 acres (90 hectares) red: 30% Grenache, 30% Mourvèdre, 10% Syrah, 10% Counoise, 5% Cinsault, 15% other.
25 acres (10 hectares) white: 80% Roussanne, 15% Grenache, 5% other.

OUR FAVORITE WINES
Beaucastel Rouge is a wine that benefits from several years in the cellar, time being needed to temper its youthful ardor. Fine examples are the wonderful vintages 1989 and 1990. Today, the 2001 shows an even more noticeable elegance of texture. The magnificent 2004 vintage of the white Roussanne Vieilles Vignes has an astonishing velvetiness and delicious freshness.

Clos des Papes

Despite its name, Le Clos des Papes refers to 24 plots of land distributed among almost all the different terroirs of Châteauneuf, although 17 of its 79 acres (7 of 32 hectares) are found in one of the most spectacular areas of the appellation: the Crau plateau. One of the classics of Châteauneuf, there has scarcely been a disappointing vintage for 20 years. This extraordinary reliability owes much to the careful work of Paul and Vincent Avril, the father and son who share the management of a domaine that has been in the family for two centuries. The grapes are cultivated for quality not quantity, to an extent that few producers either in France or elsewhere would find acceptable. Traditional wine-making methods are used, always favoring balance over instant power. The Clos des Papes reds age beautifully, becoming deep, honest and fresh, without any of the heaviness so often encountered in southern French wines.

VINE VARIETY
72 acres (29 hectares) red: 65% Grenache, 20% Mourvèdre, 10% Syrah, 5% other.
7 acres (3 hectares) white: 25% Bourboulenc, 25% Clairette, 25% Grenache, 25% Picpoul.

OUR FAVORITE WINES
The outstandingly harmonious balance of the Clos des Papes reds places them in the top rank of Châteauneuf-du-Pape wines. The vintages of 1978, 1989, 1990 and, more recently, the superb 1998, 2001, and 2003 are outstanding exemplars of their appellation. Of the whites, the 2004 has a dazzling refinement and freshness.

At Châteauneuf-du-Pape, the pebbles (as seen here) or the more frequently encountered large galets *help to retain moisture in the ground, even during the hottest times of year.*

Domaine de la
Janasse

Since the beginning of the 1990s the Sabon family has quietly but radically been transforming this fine Courthézon domaine into one of the benchmarks of Châteauneuf-du-Pape quality. The consistency of the wines is impressive, and this is true for the large volumes of vin de pays as well as the elite vineyard cuvées. Cuvée Chaupin is one such and originates in a truly spectacular terroir to the northeast of the appellation that can be seen from the autoroute south of Orange. This wine is made entirely from Grenache, and is aged in casks (partly new) and large casks. The Vieilles Vignes cuvée combines fruit from the Chaupin vineyard with fruit from three other sites offering different soil types. The vinification and aging techniques are similar, although small amounts of Syrah and Mourvèdre in the blend lend the wine a certain intensity. Modern in style with a dark hue, black fruit nose and generous unctuousness, the wines made by Christophe Sabon lack nothing of classic Châteauneuf character as they are also powerful, good-natured, intense, long on the palate, and eminently well-bred.

VINE VARIETY

115 acres (46.5 hectares) red: Grenache 70%, Carignan 10%, Mourvèdre 10%, Syrah 5%, others 5%.
9 acres (3.5 hectares) white: Grenache Blanc 60%, Clairette 20%, Roussanne 20%.

OUR FAVORITE WINES

Almost every year since 1995 (in particular 1998, 2001, and 2003), this domaine's Chaupin and Vieilles Vignes (old vines) cuvées have combined fullness of body with an admirable elegance of texture. These two superb Châteauneufs are expressive, long on the palate, and age to perfection.

Château
La Nerthe

Although the town of Châteauneuf-du-Pape has been famous since the Middle Ages when the Avignon popes made it their summer residence, its vineyard was not fully appreciated until the 19th century. It owes its discovery to the inventiveness and dynamism of the owner of Château La Nerthe at that time, Commandant Ducos, who established the modern standards for the Châteauneuf appellation. Skillfully managed by Alain Dugas, the cru has belonged to the Richard family (specialists in wines and coffees for restaurants) since 1985. The 222 acres (90 hectares) of vines are situated around the château, mainly in the southern end of the appellation, with almost a quarter on the Crau plateau. Beautifully terraced, with numerous pebbles, the vines are grown according to organic methods, producing fine wines in both white and red. Les Cadettes has great personality with depth and pedigree, making it a very good wine to lay down.

VINE VARIETY
208 acres (84 hectares) red: 54% Grenache, 24% Syrah, 17% Mourvèdre, 4% Cinsault, 1% other.
14 acres (6 hectares) white: 36% Roussanne, 30% Grenache, 21% Clairette, 13% Bourboulenc.

OUR FAVORITE WINES
The fullness of constitution and perfection of tannins in this house's Les Cadettes make it an exemplar of a great Châteauneuf wine – particularly in the wonderful 1990, 1995, 1998, and 2001 vintages. The two white cuvées are also frequently outstanding, notably in 2004.

Château
Rayas

Situated on a sandy terroir, in airy surroundings shaded by pine forests, the Rayas domaine stands apart from others in Châteauneuf. Rejecting the modern methods used by many wine producers, here only old, wine-encrusted concrete vats and wooden barrels are to be found in the château's historic *chai* (storehouse). By contrast, in essential matters, this domaine is ahead of its time: only a few bunches of grapes are grown on each vine plant; harvesting does not take place until the grapes are fully mature; and vinification is natural with only moderate extraction. Without making a mystery of them, Emmanuel Raynaud – who succeeded his uncle in 1997 – applies these methods with great sensitivity. Like those produced at his domaine in Vacqueyras, Château des Tours, the Rayas wines are pale in color when young. Impatient wine connoisseurs should be prepared to wait, since with aging these wines acquire a subtlety of bouquet, delicacy of texture and long freshness that puts them in a class of their own. This is arguably the most refined of any wine from the South of France.

VINE VARIETY

29 acres (11.8 hectares) red: Grenache.
4 acres (1.8 hectares) white: 50% Clairette, 50% Grenache.

OUR FAVORITE WINES

A wine of almost mythical fame, Rayas has produced some unforgettable vintages, including the wonderful 1989, 1990, and 1995. In more recent times, the 2001 and 2003, and what promises to be a fine 2004, are exemplars of the incomparable breeding and finesse of the cru.

Tardieu-Laurent

Michel Tardieu knows more about Rhône wines than anyone we have hitherto encountered. Once the chauffeur of a local politician, he made use of the tedious hours of waiting to visit, one by one, the different crus of the region and to get to know those vignerons who seemed to him the most interesting. His encounter with Dominique Laurent, wine merchant from Burgundy with a magic touch in matters of élevage (the wine-maturing process), was to change his life. Together, they created a small house dedicated to luxury wines, selecting the most exceptional out of all the best Rhône valley appellations and further improving them with élevage in casks, this process being overseen by Dominique Laurent. Launched in 1994, the partnership of Tardieu-Laurent led to the production, from 1995 onwards, of some dazzling wines, notably the Cornas and Hermitage. Gradually, other crus – Côtes-du-Rhône Guy-Louis, Côte Rôtie, Châteauneuf, and Vacqueyras Vieilles Vignes – have been raised to an astonishing level of quality. The noble, woody aromas that are particularly pronounced when the wines are young subsequently disappear, allowing all the subtleties and pedigree of the different crus to emerge in their full glory.

VINE VARIETY

Bought-in wines only.

OUR FAVORITE WINES

With an extensive list featuring many of the great appellations of the Rhône valley, the Cornas, Hermitage, and Côte Rôtie Vieilles Vignes are frequently – particularly in 1999 and 2003 – magnificent examples of their appellations. From the south of the Rhône valley, the Châteauneuf-du-Pape Vieilles Vignes 2003 has an impressive fullness, perfectly brought out by superb élevage.

Domaine du
Vieux Télégraphe

Whereas the majority of domaines in the appellation is made up of many small plots of land, this splendid property in Bédarrides consists of a vineyard with a single owner, entirely situated on the Crau plateau. One of the most famous Châteauneuf terroirs, the sun beats down on the plateau from early in the springtime. The high terraces to the east of the village of Châteauneuf face due east, with views over the majestic landscape of the Rhône valley as far as Mont Ventoux, making this site unique in the appellation. By pursuing the rigorous methods essential to growing and producing wine, the Brunier family – who also own two other important domaines, La Roquette in Châteauneuf and Les Pallières in Gigondas – has, in the last 15 years, crossed the significant barrier marking the difference between a great wine and an outstanding one.

VINE VARIETY
161 acres (65 hectares) red: 65% Grenache, 15% Mourvèdre, 15% Syrah, 5% other.
12 acres (5 hectares) white: 40% Clairette, 30% Grenache, 15% Roussanne, 15% Bourboulenc.

OUR FAVORITE WINES
A memorable vintage, the beautifully balanced 1998 Vieux Télégraphe has vigor combined with fullness of constitution. This lively fullness can also be found in the 2003 vintage.

The traditional method of training vines en gobelet. Requiring neither trellis nor supporting post, the plant is free-standing, the branches trained in a circular manner around a short stem. It is often used for the southern grape variety, Grenache.

Châteaux
Montus et Bouscassé

Lying at the foot of the Pyrenees, the beautiful landscape around Madiran, with its valleys and hills, is divided between corn fields, animal pasture, and, on the open hillsides, vines. Tannat, the main grape variety grown here, was at one time dismissed as unsuitable for fine wines. As its name indicates, it is tannic, giving a wine that was in the past powerful, dark in color, and often horribly astringent. It was not until the early 1980s that a young and ambitious vigneron, Alain Brumont, set about civilizing this rough grape, demonstrating just what could be done on this terroir. To the delight of wine lovers, he produced red wines that are full, deep, and aristocratic, with, above all, a velvety and ripe structure. His two star cuvées, produced from two separate properties – Montus Prestige and Bouscassé Vieilles Vignes – were an almost overnight success. With his unflagging energy and limitless enthusiasm, Brumont was not content to rest on his laurels. Continuing to innovate both in the cultivation of his vines and the élevage of his wines, he was also involved in the renaissance of the wonderful, mellow white wines from the neighboring Pacherenc du Vic-Bilh vineyard. Almost every year, he produces new cuvées and new experiments. Few vineyards owe so much to a single person and few wines have been admitted to the circle of the great wines in such a short space of time.

VINE VARIETY

272 acres (110 hectares) red: 65% Tannat, 20% Cabernet Sauvignon, 10% Cabernet Franc, 5% Fer Servadou.
74 acres (30 hectares) white: 50% Courbu, 40% Petit Manseng, 10% Gros Manseng.

OUR FAVORITE WINES

Always impressive, the Montus Prestige and Bouscasse Vieilles Vignes are Madirans of noble texture and refined taste, the very best being the 1990, 2000, and 2001 vintages. A new cuvée de prestige, Tyre, was added to the list in 2002.

Domaine Cauhapé

Squeezed between two rivers that tumble down from the nearby Pyrenees, the Gave de Pau and the Gave d'Oloron, the Jurançon vineyard clings to the steep slopes of narrow hillsides, separated from one another by small streams. With the imposing massif behind and the ocean about 62 miles (100 kilometers) away, there is no lack of sun or water. The result from this curious mixture of conditions is one of the most original wines in all France: Jurançon. The dry version is made from Gros Manseng grapes, the sunny aspect giving it fullness while the well-watered environment gives it acidity. The sweet wine is made from *passerillé* Petit Manseng grapes, grapes left to dry on the vine, allowing the sugars to become concentrated. *Pourriture noble* (noble rot) cannot become established here, as in the Sauternes area, because the winds are too strong. Jurançon wines are, in fact, very different from Sauternes. They have a wonderful array of aromas: candied citrus, quince paste, honey, and spices. In the mouth, the ever-present acidity harmoniously balances out the sweetness of the sugar. Henri Ramonteu, the innovative and exemplary producer, notes not only the year of his grandes cuvées, but also the harvesting period. From October to January, he picks each grape individually as it matures so that each cuvée has the maximum intensity and richness.

Henri Ramonteu, creator of outstanding Jurançon wines, at a tasting.

VINE VARIETY
99 acres (40 hectares) white: 55% Gros Manseng, 45% Petit Manseng.

OUR FAVORITE WINES
Quintessence, made from Petit Manseng grapes, has all the nobility of the great Jurançon wines. It ages perfectly, as can be seen from the vintages produced in the late 1980s and early 1990s. A superb wine of a more recent vintage is the 1999.

Château
Tirecul La Gravière

The wines of Monbazillac once enjoyed a prestige equal to that of the finest Sauternes, and were served at the grandest occasions. The basic rules of sweet wine viticulture and harvesting were gradually forgotten by the Monbazillac producers, though, and the cru's reputation collapsed. Even today elite winemakers such as Claudie and Bruno Bilancini struggle to achieve recognition for the high quality wine they produce at their superb property. Their vines are located on the best Tirecul slopes and enjoy a microclimate that is extremely well suited to the development of noble rot. Meticulous growers, the Bilancinis are also exceptionally precise and disciplined winemakers. Their cellar could serve as a model for makers of sweet wine all over the planet. Tirecul differs from Sauternes (which is more syrupy, mellow, and often develops faster in the bottle) in its high proportion of Muscadelle. Aging in new oak, thanks to the resulting controlled oxygenation, refines the typical dried fruit (quince, apricot) and noble rot (mango, citrus fruit) aromas, and infinitely prolongs the wine's aromatic length. The wine is at its best at around ten years of age.

VINE VARIETY
23 acres (9.2 hectares) white: 50% Muscadelle, 45% Sémillon, 5% Sauvignon Blanc.

OUR FAVORITE WINES
This property's remarkable sweet wines display the richness and nobility of the finest Sauternes and possess a sumptuous finish all their own. The classic vintage from this producer is the 2001, which will almost certainly be joined at some point by the 2005. In exceptional years, the grapes with the highest sugar content are used to make limited quantities of a special cuvée known as Cuvée Madame.

United Kingdom

England, and to a far lesser extent Wales, are old winegrowing countries. One of the first things the Romans did after invading was to plant vines and systematize the production of wine. During the Middle Ages a large number of the 300 recorded vineyards were cultivated by the religious orders, as they were on the Continent. Nevertheless, English possessions in France up to the Hundred Years' War (throughout the 12th century, England imported about as much Bordeaux wine each year as it did in 1950!), and later British maritime and commercial dynamism, conspired with the rigors of the climate to limit the development of viticulture in the British Isles. Only southern areas have high enough temperatures and adequate sunshine to grow grapes, although these are still significantly lower on average than what are generally considered by the canons of international viticulture to be the minimum levels. Around 80 estates scattered throughout southern England and Wales, below a line that extends from Norwich to Cardiff with a northern extension toward Birmingham, are dedicated to producing mostly white wines either from hybrid or Alsatian or German varieties.

Nyetimber

A delightful manor house in Sussex, to the south of London, Nyetimber was given to Count Godwin by William the Conqueror and was subsequently owned by Thomas Cromwell. This glorious past did not prevent the property from eventually becoming somewhat run down, however. Restored between the wars, it acquired its vocation as a wine estate later still, when bought in 1986 by Chicagoans Stuart and Sandy Moss, who planned to make a high-quality sparkling wine there. They planted its well-exposed sites with the three main Champagne grape varieties and installed a winery that was in keeping with their ambitions. Starting in 1994, the vintages followed in succession and Nyetimber's sparkling wines developed into the most accomplished examples of English fizz. Far from being merely a more or less faithful copy of Champagne, despite adopting many of the same methods and codes, Nyetimber, with its distinct character, has come to define a particularly English type of wine – agile, lively but firm, refreshing, and technically flawless.

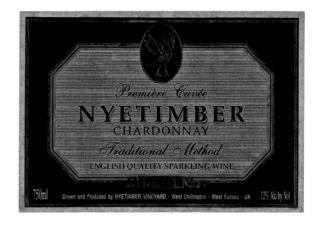

VINE VARIETY
36 acres (14 hectares) white: Pinot Noir, Pinot Meunier, Chardonnay

OUR FAVOURITE WINES
While there is a prestige wine, called Aurora, that is only produced in the best years, production consists essentially of two sparkling wines: the Classic Cuvée (a blend of the three Champagne grape varieties), and the Première Cuvée (made from Chardonnay alone). In 1999 the Classic blend was harmonious and well balanced, displaying a certain acidity but with a deep, rather delicate body, while the Blanc de Blancs revealed itself to be elegant but slightly less firm on the palate

Italy

No other country has so successfully, so radically, and so rapidly – in less than a generation – renewed the basis and form of its wine production. And yet it has been able to remain faithful to the ancient, diverse, and abundant spirit of Italian civilization. In the past, the greater part of Italian wine exported consisted of Chianti – cheerful but rough, in its characteristic straw flask – sparkling Lambrusco, and soft Valpolicella. The only exceptions to this somewhat negative reputation were a few genuinely aristocratic but rather austere wines from Piedmont, such as the best Barolos, and Tuscany, an example being that from the wonderful village of Montalcino.

In the space of just a few years, this restricted picture has entirely changed, revealing new and wonderful wines from every region of Italy, from Campania, the province that was once the cradle of the finest wines of ancient Rome, or from the remotest Alpine valleys. The same impulse has infected several determined and ambitious family businesses in Sicily and the Abruzzi, regions traditionally associated with the production of strong but characterless wines. Meanwhile, in those regions traditionally associated with fine wines, a battle was being waged between the classic methods of winemaking and modern innovations, culminating in the triumph of new styles and new developments in technique.

In Piedmont, a number of younger winemakers were able to refine the harshness of Barolo and Barbaresco wines by carefully controlling the ripeness of the grapes and the length of time taken for making and maturing the wines. In Tuscany, the revolution was even more far-reaching, with some of the aristocratic winemakers demonstrating the potential of the region with the creation of new wines. Quickly dubbed "super-Tuscans" by the American press, and made with the great Bordeaux grape varieties, they were first developed on the Tyrrhenian coast, spreading subsequently even into the Chianti region.

Beginning in the early 1980s, this creative and revolutionary energy shows no signs of flagging; it has, however, become more focused. Italian winemakers have come to realize that the greatest asset of their wines is their authenticity. It is this that makes them not only great, but also a delicious part of a way of life that no one can fail to envy.

Ca' del Bosco

Lombardy and its capital Milan, located at the very center of northern Italy, constitute the country's industrial heartland. In terms of viticulture, however, for a long time the region was known chiefly as a producer of large quantities of very ordinary wine. Only Valtellina, made in the Alpine valleys that feed into Lake Como, provided any relief from the general mediocrity. But in the Brescia area a new quality wine, made using the Champagne method and from similar grapes (Chardonnay, Pinot Noir, and Pinot Blanc instead of Pinot Meunier), has started to draw attention to itself. Franciacorta became an independent DOCG (Denominazione di Origine Controllata e Garantita) in 1995. This official recognition was due primarily to Maurizio Zanella, who took over the family firm Ca' del Bosco after studying enology in Burgundy and Bordeaux. Zanella revolutionized the estate. First, he modernized the vineyard practices, abandoning the traditional low-density cultivation typical of the region and planting 4,000 vinestocks per acre, the greatest European vineyards. He then applied the high standards widely taken for granted in Champagne to the production of his own sparkling wines. In 20 or so years he succeeded in his ambitious plan, and Franciacorta and the wines of Ca' del Bosco are now drunk to celebrate happy events in the lives not just of Italians but of wine lovers all over the world.

VINE VARIETY
363 acres (147 hectares) red: Pinot Noir, Cabernet Sauvignon, Merlot, Carmenère (and others); white: Chardonnay, Pinot Blanc, Pinot Noir.

OUR FAVORITE WINES
Ca' del Bosco makes six Franciacortas and is one of Italy's most interesting producers of sparkling wines. One of them is Annamaria Clementi, a delightful and ambitious millésimé blend. The 1998, with its perfect freshness and notes of crystallized fruit and toast, also shows how well these wines age.

Gaja

"**I** want the wine lover to appreciate the creativity of my work because that is what we Italians excel at. We are disorganized and unruly, but we live to innovate! And everyone should try to be more Italian from time to time!" Angelo Gaja's heartfelt outpouring to the journalist Anne Serres sums up wonderfully the thrilling career of possibly the greatest character on the current Italian winemaking scene. When he took the reins of the family firm in 1970 as the fourth generation of Gaja to be based in Barbaresco, Gaja immediately threw himself into all the debates and developments that have punctuated the transformation in quality of fine wine in Italy over the last 30 years: the importance of discipline in the vineyard and of controlling yields; the quest for the best terroirs and the introduction of international grape varieties (he was the first to plant Cabernet Sauvignon in the region in 1978); refinement of barrique aging; and, at the dawn of the new century, research into the ideal balance between varieties in his best wines, even if this meant flouting the regulations and abandoning official DOC status. This ability to endlessly invent is without doubt an inherent part of the Italian psyche, but Gaja might add that very few Italians have developed it to the same extraordinary extent that he has.

VINE VARIETY
247 acres (100 hectares) red and white: Nebbiolo, Barbera, Chardonnay, Sauvignon Blanc, Cabernet Sauvignon.
Main vineyards: Sori San Lorenzo, Sori Tildin, Costa Russi, Sperss and Conteisa.

OUR FAVORITE WINES
Believing with good reason that the Barbera variety could play an interesting complementary role alongside Nebbiolo in his elite wines, Angelo Gaja chose to make his Sori Lorenzo, Sori Tildin and Costa Russi Barbarescos and Sperss and Conteisa Barolos in the Langhe quality zone, as Nebbiolo is the only variety permitted in the Barbaresco and Barolo DOCGs.

With vineyards enjoying the best exposures and inventive vinification methods, Angelo Gaja has returned Piedmont to the highest level of world viticulture.

Armando Parusso

Four generations of Parusso have gradually developed this estate, located between the villages of Castiglione Falleto and Monforte d'Alba (in other words at the heart of the Barolo zone), into one of the wine's leading producers. With the last few vintages of the 1990s and those of the new century, Armando Parusso has made a name for himself as the most extraordinary of Barolo stylists, combining power and finesse like no other. Admittedly his path to Piedmontese excellence was smoothed by wonderful sites enjoying superb exposures. Other than in the case of his delicious Barbera and Dolcetto, vinified with great care and delicacy, Parusso's success derives from the splendid slopes of Mariondino and above all Bussia. He has, however, played these trump cards with great skill, using all his winemaking talent to bring out the distinctive deep and elegant personality of the sites. The silky texture and highly refined tannins of his wines are of the kind that remain engraved on the memory of wine lovers for a very long time.

VINE VARIETY

49 acres (20 hectares) red: Nebbiolo, Barbera, Dolcetto; white: Sauvignon Blanc.
Main vineyards: Bussia and Mariondino.

OUR FAVORITE WINES

The 2001 Bussia is possibly the finest and deepest Barolo we have tasted from this excellent year. With his highly developed sense of balance and harmony, Armando Parusso has created a full-bodied yet refined masterpiece. Slightly less deep but with a beautiful nose, the 2001 Mariondino is also up there with the very best.

Bruno Giacosa

Bruno Giacosa is without doubt one of the great winemaking figures in Piedmont, where his good sense and the potential of his Barolos and Barbarescos have long been admired. He seems to have gradually refined his production style over the years and his recent wines possess greater delicacy and clarity of expression than those of the 1980s. Traditional-style fermentation takes place in stainless steel tanks and the wines are aged for a relatively long time in large casks (two to three years for the Barolos; 18 to 30 months for the Barbarescos). Little inclined to get dragged into the never-ending debate between traditionalists and modernists but highly respected by the local winemakers, Bruno Giacosa can be seen as a traditionalist without blinkers who seeks to divest Nebbiolo of its youthful infelicities and somewhat rustic tannins – even if this sometimes means sacrificing a little of the fruity zestfulness of the wine in its youth.

VINE VARIETY
45 acres (18 hectares) red: Nebbiolo, Barbera, Dolcetto.
Main vineyard: Falletto di Seralunga.

OUR FAVORITE WINES
Elegant, refined, and reserved, the 2000 Falletto Barolo opens up completely when decanted. Once oxygenated, it reveals itself to be a wine of remarkable breadth and depth. Characterized by the same discreet elegance, the 2000 Barbaresco Riserva is also a fine ambassador for its denomination.

Bruno Rocca

Like many great Piedmontese winemakers, and within the space of a generation, Bruno Rocca has brilliantly transformed a small traditional producer that used to sell wine from the vat to passing customers into a professional winery at which a close eye is kept on every detail in order to maintain the quality of wines that are in demand all over the world. This transformation has been the result of both relentless hard work and undeniable talent. Rocca's wines possess a body, energy, and precise expression of terroir character that make them models of their type. His flagship wine is Rabajà, from vineyards enjoying a southwestern exposure that look down on the family home and winery buildings. Rich yet delicate, it is the result of very low yields and benefits from aging carefully tailored to suit the specific character of the wine, using a high proportion of new French oak barriques. The same degree of perfectionism is applied to his other Barbaresco cuvées – such as Coparossa – as well as to his delicious Barbera and Dolcetto wines. Bruno Rocca has succeeded in preserving the pure, civilized, honest quality of these traditional wines, gradually improving their aromatic definition and precision with a succession of small adjustments.

VINE VARIETY
30 acres (12 hectares) red and white: Nebbiolo, Dolcetto, Barbera, Cabernet Sauvignon, Chardonnay.
Main vineyard: Rabajà.

OUR FAVORITE WINES
The wine that shows off the full extent of Bruno Rocca's talent is his Rabajà, a Barbaresco of brilliant and precise definition. The same artistry and finesse are also to be found in his other wines, in particular the Barbera and his delicious Langhe.

Ceretto

From the founding of their firm in the 1930s to its brilliant development initiated by brothers Bruno and Marcello (the founder's sons) in the 1960s, the Ceretto family has been one of a handful of families that has fundamentally transformed the image and quality of the Barolo and Barbaresco DOCGs. The Cerettos were among the first to develop an in-depth knowledge of the best sites for these two wines from the point of view of exposure and (an even less well-known factor) geographical make-up. This enabled them to acquire first of all some excellent Barbaresco vineyards and then, at the end of the 1960s, a number of plots among the best Barolo crus. The Ceretto estate is therefore dispersed over a large number of sites but these include some of the region's most exciting. While the firm's larger-volume wines are fairly uniform, each of its single-vineyard wines displays a strong personality that comes to the fore over time, particularly where extensive and often rather ambitious barrique aging is employed.

VINE VARIETY

247 acres (100 hectares), of which 27 produce Barolo. Nebbiolo, Dolcetto, Barbera, Arneis, Cabernet Sauvignon, Merlot, Pinot Nero, etc.
Main vineyards: Bricco Rocche, Prapò, Brunate (Barolo), Bricco Asili and Bernardot (Barbaresco).

OUR FAVORITE WINES

The Bricco Asili and Bernardot Barbarescos require a certain length of time to integrate their rather emphatic oak. However, the 2001 examples display an elegance of tannins that is also a feature of the refined Barolo Prapò of the same year. Brunate and above all Bricco Rocche are impressive for their length on the palate and aging potential.

Domenico Clerico

Some wines are difficult to tame. This is truer of Piedmont than of anywhere else. Nebbiolo's acidic structure, even when the fruit has been harvested at the peak of ripeness, can bother some drinkers – as can the impression it creates on the palate of possessing greater length than depth. These characteristics, flaunted by traditional firms and makers as a kind of badge of honor, came up against the incomprehension of a new generation of international consumers in the 1980s. This difficulty, combined with the improvement in vineyard and winery practices during the same period, led to what could be described as all-out war between the traditionalists and the modernists. Domenico Clerico rapidly became one of the most brilliant representatives of the second group. An incredible winemaker, he began to elaborate Nebbiolo wines that were brightly colored and generously oaked but with a depth of texture and quality of nose that were difficult to surpass. More accessible than many others, his wines are certainly not lacking in sap or typicity, however. For this he has his great terroirs to thank, notably the outstanding Ciabot Mentin Ginestra and the famous Pajanà, which he has served with remarkable precision and attention to detail.

Domenico Clerico and the joy of fine wine Italian-style!

VINE VARIETY

52 acres (21 hectares) red: Nebbiolo, Dolcetto, Barbera. Main vineyards: Mentin Ginestra and Pajanà.

OUR FAVORITE WINES

Domenico Clerico's top wine is his Ciabot Mentin Ginestra Barolo. Brilliant and extremely consistent, it is above all impressive (as is the firm's other great wine, Pajanà) for its velvety richness. Arte, a proprietary blend of Nebbiolo and Barbera, can be magnificent, as in 1990.

9

BAROLO

LITRI
6349

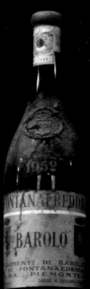

Fontanafredda

Founded almost a century and a half ago, Fontanafredda rapidly became one of Piedmont's most famous producers, developing an extremely wide range of regional wines both sparkling and "still." A number of years ago the firm took its main Barolo crus in hand in order to improve their definition and character. Rigorous work in the vineyard, a rejection of all chemical products, and traditional vinification (albeit conducted with a greater degree of precision than in the past) have enabled Fontanafredda to attain a high level of quality, the potential for which was always present in its fine portfolio of terroirs. With its Barolos La Rosa, Lazzarito, Vigna La Delizia, and Paiagallo Vigna La Villa, and the fine Coste Rubin Barbaresco, Fontanafredda now produces a range of powerful and vigorous wines that have shown remarkable strength of character over recent years.

VINE VARIETY
173 acres (70 hectares) red: Nebbiolo, Barbera, Dolcetto, Moscato.

OUR FAVORITE WINES
Fontanafredda's wines have made great progress over the past few years, gaining in purity of expression without losing anything of their still fairly raw tannic vigor. The 2000 La Rosa is a powerful Barolo, spiritedly combining tannins, spice notes, and acidity. The intense Lazaritto, meanwhile, offers a warmer finish.

Fontanafredda's time-defying casks have accommodated numerous great Barolo vintages.

Elio Altare

For a long time the surly acidity and harsh tannins of many Barolos shocked consumers who did not know what to expect, while connoisseurs regarded these two admittedly not very likable characteristics as a sign of authenticity. This ultra-traditional style was overthrown at the end of the 1980s by a new generation of Barolo winemakers, with Elio Altare quickly becoming one of the leaders. An admirer of the great Burgundian crus, he treated Nebbiolo as he would have done Pinot Noir. A champion of modernity in Barolo and the inventor of extremely short fermentation times, the purpose of which is to refine the tannins of the Nebbiolo grape to the greatest possible extent, Altare created a very personal style. His inimitable wines may not have the power of the DOCG's best terroirs, but they possess an unsurpassable aromatic charm and an unmistakable satiny texture.

VINE VARIETY

22 acres (9 hectares) red: Nebbiolo, Barbera, Dolcetto, Cabernet Sauvignon.
Main vineyards: Arborina and Brunate.

OUR FAVORITE WINES

The year 2001 was when Elio Altare once again succeeded in producing wines of almost perfect brilliance and balance. This is true of his Barolos (in particular the tremendous Arborina) as well as his Langhes, such as Larigi and La Villa. A relatively recent addition is his Barolo from the celebrated Brunate vineyard, which became an immediate cult when production began a dozen or so years ago. All recent vintages have been outstanding.

Aldo Conterno

A classic Barolo producer that became a pioneer in the modernization of the wine in the 1960s, the success of this estate relies on its Cicala, Colonnello, and Bussia crus whose perfect south-southwestern exposure has kept it at the very top of the DOCG seemingly forever. The combination of terroir and supreme winemaking skill was responsible for some of the greatest Barolos of the second half of the 20th century before something of a barren patch occurred at the beginning of the 1990s. Under the efficient guidance of son Stefano, however, the wines (and in particular the sublime Granbussia Riserva) soon recaptured their former finesse, fullness of body, and stylishness – all of which are characteristics of the best Bussia terroirs. Offering finesse rather than power and displaying marvelously silky tannins, this estate's wines have helped to earn Barolo a place among the world's very best reds.

VINE VARIETY

70 acres (28 hectares) red: Nebbiolo, Barbera, Dolcetto, Merlot, Cabernet Sauvignon, Freisa; white: Chardonnay.
Main vineyards: Vigna Cicala, Vigna Colonnello and Bussia.

OUR FAVORITE WINES

The Granbussia Riserva is to Barolo what a well-made Musigny is to the Côte de Nuits. The 1999 shows superb length, while the Bussia and Colonnello demonstrate the ability of this producer to take the superlative finesse of these terroirs to even higher levels.

Luciano Sandrone

Luciano Sandrone describes his simple winemaking philosophy as follows: to endeavor to get the best out of his vines without compromising their quality in any way in the winery. Taking an essentially traditional approach and calling on the power of observation of older generations, Luciano and his brother Luca have also adopted the best aspects of modern viticulture, in particular the harvesting of grapes at the peak of ripeness (both tannins and sugars). While their vinification methods are respectful of both fruit and terroir, they can also be adapted to suit the specific characteristics of a vintage or cru. This constant encounter between old and new can be seen in the aging process, which begins in large 130 to 160 gallon (500 to 600 hundred liter) traditional Barolo casks before continuing in barriques chosen to suit the particular wine in question in terms of the sourcing of the wood (and so on). This attention to detail, made possible by impressive facilities, has enabled Sandrone to make a modern style of Nebbiolo that continues to display the typical Barolo characteristics of austerity and reserve when young.

VINE VARIETY
62 acres (25 hectares) red: Nebbiolo, Barbera, Dolcetto. Main vineyards: Cannubi Boschis and Le Vigne.

OUR FAVORITE WINES
Cannubi Boschis is a legendary Barolo and the brilliant Le Vigne comes a close second. Luciano Sandrone's two famous crus produce wines whose immense aromatic class and elegant textures blossom after a few years of aging. Another wine worth tasting is the straightforward and wonderfully natural Barbera d'Alba.

A meticulous and generous craftsman, Luciano Sandrone has given the classic Barolo style a new lease of life.

Marchesi di Gresy

Barbaresco remains less well known than its neighbor Barolo. While they are both made from the Nebbiolo grape, Barbaresco is generally a less robust wine but has a unique personality that stems largely from its refinement of expression. No other producer has taken this delicacy to greater heights than Alberto di Gresy at Cisa Asinari. Admittedly, no one else in the DOCG can boast such wonderful natural assets. The pride and joy of the estate (which has been in the possession of the Gresy family since 1797) is its 30-acre (12-hectare) Nebbiolo vineyard in Martinenga on Barbaresco's finest slope, a steep amphitheater enjoying a full southern exposure. There is nothing showy about these aristocratic wines. The grape is simply allowed to develop its naturally long and lively structure with delicate tannins underpinning a slender body, and unfurl its eminently distinguished floral nose. Displaying abundant character and depth, they can be seen as "old Europe" at its best.

VINE VARIETY
117 acres (47.5 hectares) red: Nebbiolo, Dolcetto, Barbera, Merlot, Cabernet Sauvignon; white: Muscat (Moscato), Sauvignon Blanc, Chardonnay.
Main vineyards: Martinenga, Camp Gros, Gaiun (Barbaresco).

OUR FAVORITE WINES
The superlative finesse of the 2001 Gaiun testifies to the impressive quality of its terroir. Along with Camp Gros, of which the 1999 is outstanding, these two vineyards form part of the Martinenga hillside whose wonderful exposure is fully expressed in the silkiness of texture and delicacy of what was generally a difficult year, 2002.

Rivetti

The Rivetti family, Piedmontese in origin, left Europe to seek its fortune in Argentina. Having succeeded, it returned to Italy and acquired a fine estate at the heart of the Asti winegrowing region. This was in 1977. In less than 30 years, La Spinetta (the name of the estate) would develop into one of the region's key producers, making a name for itself with its delicious, light Moscato d'Asti of course, but above all with its Barbera d'Asti, its Barbarescos, and (since 2000) its Barolo. This success is based on the firm's loyalty to indigenous varieties and styles but also to the very wide appeal of its wines. Pleasure (for that is indeed the main sensation aroused by Giorgio Rivetti's wines) starts with the very look of the bottles – their shape and color, carefully and subtly chosen by the inveterate perfectionist himself, as well as the design of the labels, from the elegant and original lettering to the firm's emblem: Dürer's engraving of an impressive-looking rhinoceros. Undisputed leader of a select band of brilliant winemakers, Rivetti has radically transformed the Piedmontese wine scene over the past 20 years. His famous Pin, a Barbera–Nebbiolo blend, has proved an enormous hit in chic Italian restaurants, as has his delicious Moscato d'Asti. His best wines, however, are his Starderi and Gallina Barbarescos, while his Campè Barolo is unusually opulent and fruity for this DOCG. Rivetti's latest venture, a Tuscan estate called La Spinetta Casanova, is dedicated to Sangiovese.

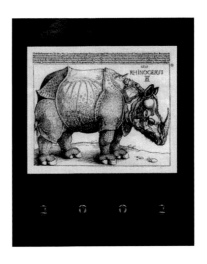

VINE VARIETY

247 acres (100 hectares) plus a further 148 acres (60 hectares) at Spinetta-Casanova in Tuscany. Red: Nebbiolo, Barbera, Sangiovese; white: Muscat (Moscato), Chardonnay, Sauvignon Blanc.

OUR FAVORITE WINES

The 2001 Campè Barolo is impressive for its highly expressive morello cherry nose and dense, classy texture while the 2003 Pin is well-rounded and immediately flavorsome and seduces with its raspberry and strawberry aromas. And who could resist the delicious and refreshing Biancospino Moscato, a frizzante with just 5.5% alcohol.

Roberto Voerzio

Over the past 20 years this young *contadino* (meaning "small farmer" in Italian) passionate about his Barolo has become a great master acclaimed throughout the world. As an unrivaled viticulturist, Roberto Voerzio has had a considerable influence on recent developments in the areas of trellising and yield reduction; as a brilliant winemaker, he knows how to capture the quintessence of the greatest terroirs in La Morra, at the heart of the Barolo zone, in his wines. The sites he cultivates are without doubt the best in the village: Capalot and Brunate, blended to make the Riserva and vinified separately for the classic Brunate, Rocche dell'Annunziata, La Serra, Sarmassa, and the incomparable Cerequio reach a peak of intensity in his hands without detracting from the harmony and finesse of his wines. But Voerzio also knows how to transform a more humble grape such as Barbera into the deliciously deep Posse dell'Annunziata. His estate may be relatively small but he is better than anyone else at expressing the whole range of nuances of his terroirs.

VINE VARIETY

21 acres (8.5 hectares) red: Nebbiolo, Dolcetto, Barbera, Cabernet Sauvignon.
Main vineyards: Brunate, La Serra, Cerequio, Sarmassa, Rocche dell'Annunziata Torriglione and Capalot.

OUR FAVORITE WINES

Roberto Voerzio's Barolos are intensely concentrated wines displaying exquisite definition. Each develops its own subtle nuances, thereby demonstrating the variety of the quality zone's best terroirs.

Sottimano

Founded in the mid-1970s, this fine Barbaresco estate started in Cottá and grew steadily through the acquisition of high-quality sites such as Currá, Fausoni, and Pajorè. In 1990, Rino Sottimano adopted ecological principles in the vineyard, abandoning all use of pesticides, chemical weedkiller, and fertilizer. This gentle approach has borne fruit, bringing about a steady and significant improvement in production quality. Over the last few years, coinciding with the arrival on the scene of Rino's son Andrea, the wines have attained an even higher level of quality, their depth of expression and complexity of nose earning them a very high place in the Barbaresco DOCG hierarchy.

VINE VARIETY
32 acres (13 hectares) red: Nebbiolo, Barbera, Dolcetto.
Main vineyards: Currá, Fausoni, Pajorè.

OUR FAVORITE WINES
Elegant and with a wonderfully long finish, the 2001 Pajoré is a brilliant example of Barbaresco at its best. It is a delicate yet intense wine with an original and complex nose.

Vietti

This firm, founded in the 19th century, was for a long time one of the most traditional producers of Piedmont wines. It has made spectacular progress over the last ten years, its Barolos, Barbaresco, and indeed all its other reds gaining considerable finesse and elegance of structure. This new dimension can be explained by its stringent production standards: it only vinifies its own harvest and boasts a diverse range of sites of unequaled quality. Also impressive are the rigor and precision of these wines' expression of terroir character and the directness of their pure and intense style. The young Luca Currado obtains an astonishing synthesis of the best of both traditional and modern styles and seems to have a perfect understanding of what makes a great wine. Dominated for a long time by theoretical debate concerning the relative merits of these two approaches, Piedmontese winegrowing seems to have achieved a happy balance that is perfectly illustrated by the development of this producer.

VINE VARIETY

74 acres (30 hectares) red: Nebbiolo, Barbera, Dolcetto; white: Arneis, Muscat (Moscato).
Main vineyards: Villero, Rocche, Brunate and Lazzarito.

OUR FAVORITE WINES

This firm's slender, elegant style is evident in its delicious Barbera d'Asti La Crena, an enormously and immediately likable wine of astounding finesse. Wine lovers will enjoy discovering the softness and subtlety of its Barbaresco and delight in its exemplary Barolos. Typical of their respective terroirs (Villero, Lazzarito, Brunate and, above all, Rocche di Castiglione), these are characterized by tannins of rare quality and are simultaneously firm, precise, and devoid of the slightest heaviness. The 2001 offerings will travel a long way over a long time!

Founded over a century ago, Vietti has now been reinvigorated by a young and highly dynamic generation.

Cantina di
Terlano

The Alpine valley of Terlano shelters a collection of vineyards that are well adapted to the production of slender, deep, and subtle whites. This indeed is the main objective of this relatively large producer, which offers a highly consistent range of wines year in, year out. Cantina Terlano adheres to a clear-cut, well-established style featuring fullness of body and aromas, freshness on the palate, little in the way of wood notes (even though the more ambitious offerings are matured in oak), and good aging potential. This cooperative also sells a wide range of older white vintages going back to the 1990s and 1980s. The reds are well structured but do not generally offer the intensity and originality of the whites.

VINE VARIETY
346 acres (140 hectares) red: Lagrein, Merlot, Schiava; white: Gewürztraminer, Sauvignon Blanc, Pinot Bianco, Chardonnay, Pinot Grigio, Müller-Thurgau, Sylvaner, Riesling.

OUR FAVORITE WINES
Whites are definitely the focal point of this estate's production. The single varietals Lunare Gewürztraminer, Quarz Sauvignon Blanc, Vorberg Pinot Bianco, and Terlano Chardonnay combine remarkable richness with a wonderful intensity and real aromatic finesse. It is worth emphasizing the astonishing capacity of these wines to age in the bottle, a relatively rare characteristic for Italian whites.

Cantina di
Termeno

Founded over a century ago, Cantina Termeno is without doubt the most popular of the Alto Adige producers. For many years it has been combining consistent high quality with an extremely competitive pricing policy. Production is supervised by Willi Stürz, a talented and sensitive enologist who strives constantly to achieve the best possible balance in his wines. The winery is extremely well equipped and the technology at his disposal allows Stürz to produce wine of great purity, honesty, and aromatic clarity. On the minus side, Cantina Termeno sometimes goes a little too far in its desire to follow international trends, producing wines with emphatic oak and high levels of alcohol that are out of keeping with the traditional local style. While it is its whites that reach the highest level of quality, its reds also have plenty of drive, especially the dense and fleshy Lagreins, and the simple but wonderfully fruity Pinot Nero.

ROAN₂₀₀₃

KELLEREI · CANTINA · TRAMIN
SÜDTIROL · ALTO ADIGE
ITALIA

VINE VARIETY

568 acres (230 hectares) red: Lagrein, Merlot, Schiava, Cabernet Sauvignon, Cabernet Franc, Pinot Nero; white: Gewürztraminer, Sauvignon Blanc, Pinot Bianco, Chardonnay, Pinot Grigio, Müller-Thurgau, Sylvaner, Riesling.

OUR FAVORITE WINES

The higher-quality range, in particular the Gewürztraminer wines, includes Nussbaumer (the light, fresh, classic version), the late-harvested Roan (richer and more powerful), and Passito Terminum (which is extremely dense and seductive).

Ferrari

The history of this firm, today one of Italy's most interesting producers of sparkling wine, began with the obsessive determination of its founder Giulio Ferrari, born in 1879 in the Trentino region of Alpine valleys, to make a "superior-quality spumante." Driven by this ambition, he went to Montpellier to study, acquiring expertise in the second fermentation that takes place in the bottle, the natural method (as practiced in Champagne) of giving sparkling wine its fizz. At the end of his life he passed on both his firm and his great ambition to a carefully chosen successor, Bruno Lunelli, secure in the knowledge that his work would be continued and perfected. And successive generations of the Lunelli family have done the founder proud. Ferrari Brut, the firm's main cuvée, is upright, pure, long on the palate, and without any trace of heaviness – the very model of a good aperitif. One of Ferrari's main strengths is that it relies on grapes grown in its own vineyards or on estates whose viticulture it is able to supervise. The other is its cellars, which are geared up to long aging in the bottle – ranging from two years for the Brut to as many as ten for the prestige cuvée, which is naturally named Giulio in honor of the firm's determined founder.

VINE VARIETY

Bought-in grapes; Chardonnay, Pinot Noir, Pinot Blanc.

OUR FAVORITE WINES

The three mainstays of Ferrari's focused and classic range are: an excellent Brut which is slender and intense; an attractive Chardonnay named Perle, which makes a delightful aperitif; and the Riserva del Fondatore, which is only released after a long period of cellar-aging. The firm's sparkling wines are all impressive for their consistency and harmony.

The slopes of the Alpine valley shelter magnificent vineyards capable of producing red and white wines of great personality.

Foradori

Long ago, vineyards were planted on the right bank of the river Adige, which carves its way through one of the most captivating of Alpine valleys before flowing into the Po. Many of these vineyards were devoted to Teroldego, a local variety whose wines were praised in the 19th century as "possessing the robustness and body of a Bordeaux" by authors who also noted that it was not without a degree of rusticity. Elisabetta Foradori, who succeeded her prematurely deceased father at a very young age, is proud of the lofty beauty of her mountainous region and is confident of the not yet fully exploited potential of this grape. She has made it a point of honor to research and resurrect the different biotypes of the Teroldego, which she grows on an estate resembling a kind of earthly paradise. Today she celebrates the grape, now tamed and refined, in two wonderful wines: Foradori, which brings out its full fruity freshness; and Granato, which undergoes a longer period of barrique aging and possesses impressive depth and power. These wines testify to the quality of both grape and terroir.

GRANATO

2001

FORADORI

VINE VARIETY

64 acres (26 hectares): Teroldego.

OUR FAVORITE WINES

Although this estate produces other wines made from both local and international varieties, its Teroldego cuvées, made with grapes from the Teroldego Rotaliano DOC, are what make it stand out from the rest. The 2003 Foradori is a wonderful wine with delicate tannins and a distinctive freshness; Granato, more ambitious, possesses a marvelously velvety texture and exudes a generous, well-balanced, delicious charm that is simply irresistible (2001).

Schiopetto

Far removed from the cliché of picture-postcard Italy, Friuli-Venezia Giulia is a region of highly individual character. Rugged and harsh, it is located in the northeastern corner of the country, bordering Slovenia. Ravaged in the past by conflicts of interest with its once-powerful neighbor Austria, it brings a real independence of spirit to its interpretation of what it means to be Italian. The same is true of its wines, which differ greatly in character from those made elsewhere in the country. Its production is predominantly white and even the region's best-known designated quality zone, Collio, offers a range of wines made mainly from varieties of French (e.g. Sauvignon Blanc) and, above all, German origin. The main characteristics of the wine made here are honesty and clarity of aroma. These are wines that are meant to be enjoyed young. What Schiopetto adds to this pleasant but rather limited profile are a greater depth and intensity of expression. Thus the firm's Pinot Blanc and Tocai Friulano display a remarkably sustained nose and astonishing vigor. It also produces reds, the most ambitious of which, Podere dei Blumeri, combines local varieties with those of Bordeaux.

VINE VARIETY
74 acres (30 hectares) red: Merlot, Cabernet Sauvignon, Cabernet Franc, Refosco del Pedonculo Rosso; white: Tocai Friulano, Pinot Bianco, Pinot Grigio, Sauvignon Blanc.

OUR FAVORITE WINES
The whites are direct, subtle, elegant and not without a certain depth. Of the 2004 vintage, the Pinot Blanc seduces with its density, freshness, and diversity of aromas, while the Blanc des Rosis blend possesses good balance. That year's Sauvignon Blanc and Tocai are classic expressions of their respective varieties. Finally, the 2002 Podere dei Blumeri red makes up for a lack of depth with its supple, fruity freshness.

Allegrini

The vineyards of Valpolicella cover the sides of the narrow valleys that descend from the mountains of the Pre-Alps toward Verona and the River Adige. Bordered by the Alps to the north and Lake Garda to the west, this vast and attractive region of sloping and terraced vineyards has an enterprising ambassador in the form of the Allegrini family. The family owned an extensive vineyard in the village of Fumane as far back as the Renaissance and today farms 247 acres (100 hectares) of vineyard in the western part of the denomination. It was the first producer to isolate specific vineyard sites such as its spectacular La Grola vineyard on chalky clay terraces a couple of miles from Lake Garda. One of the areas in which the family's innovatory prowess can be seen is in its mastery of *appassimento*. It dries the grapes in small crates (in which the fruit is also harvested) placed one above the other in vast, well-ventilated cellars. The producer applies the same precise, modern approach to every stage in the growing and winemaking process from trellising to aging. Of its wines, La Grola and the interesting La Poja, made with fruit from a parcel of pure Corvina (the local variety usually used in blends), are brimming with personality.

VINE VARIETY
247 acres (100 hectares) red: Corvina, Rondinella, Molinara, Sangiovese, Syrah, Cabernet Sauvignon, Merlot.

OUR FAVORITE WINES
Allegrini's range starts with Valpolicella wines that are technically well made but of no more than average depth; it culminates with La Poja (made entirely from the local grape Corvina) and La Grola (a blend of Syrah, Sangiovese, Rondinella and Corvina dominated by the latter), which are full but fresh-bodied, possessing a fruity, aromatic charm. The highly seductive Amarone can be drunk relatively young.

Allegrini's trellised vines follow on in an old Veneto tradition.

Masi

Crucial to the history of Masi are a place (Vaio de Masi) and a family (the Boscainis), the latter having chosen the former as the site of a vast and thriving winegrowing estate back in the 19th century. The Boscaini family has gradually developed outward from this central point and has now established itself in Tuscany and even Argentina. Naturally, though, the production of specialties such as Amarone and Valpolicella remains at the heart of the family's activities. Among Masi's vast production, a few select sites have been isolated in order to produce superior-quality wines, in particular highly ambitious Amarones. This large house places a considerable emphasis on research and innovation. It is experimenting with drying techniques, and with the reintroduction of secondary local varieties such as Oseleta and Dindarella in order to complement the classic Corvina and Rondinella varieties.

VINE VARIETY
1,285 acres (520 hectares) red: Corvina, Rondinella, Molinara, Dindarella, Oseleta; white: Trebbiano.

OUR FAVORITE WINES
Masi produces a wide range covering practically all the region's classic and also more modern wines. Campofiorin and Brolo di Campofiorin, made in part from dried grapes, and Amarone wines such as Mazzano and Campolongo di Torbe, stand out in particular.

Dal Forno Romano

East of Verona, the Valpolicella winegrowing region produces an ocean of inexpensive, drinkable wine year in, year out. While it is often very ordinary, in Romano Dal Forno's hands Valpolicella is transformed into a delicious and unforgettable wine exhibiting highly developed flavors and aromas, and a full, generous body. In 1983, when he took over the small family vineyard located on the slopes of the Illasi valley, Romano Dal Forno immediately threw himself into a quest to achieve the highest possible quality not only for his Valpolicella but also for other local specialties, Amarone and Reciotto, made from grapes dried on wicker racks (resulting in a high concentration of sugar). To improve things even further, in 1990 he built a winery and cellars to his own specifications, allowing him the necessary time and space to work his magic. A masterpiece requires patience. This is as true of Valpolicella, made with grapes harvested at the peak of ripeness, aged for three years in barriques and then a further 12 months in the bottle prior to release, as it is of Amarone, whose grapes are pressed in January after many weeks of *appassimento* (drying) and fermented slowly and naturally in barriques for several months, where they likewise remain for three years before being aged for a further two years (!) in the bottle. Romano Dal Forno is one of an extremely select group of inspired winemaking artists inventing a new personality for their region's wines.

VINE VARIETY

37 acres (15 hectares) red: Corvina, Rondinella, Croatina, Oseletta.

OUR FAVORITE WINES

Highly consistent from one year to the next, Romano Dal Forno's Valpolicella is in a class of its own, so extraordinary are its aromatic luxuriance, velvety texture and general richness. Furthermore, long aging in the cellar means his wines are ready to drink as soon as they are released for sale, as is currently the case with the 2001. Boasting a highly concentrated nose and possessing the body of a truly great red wine, his Amarone is a gem with enormous aging potential.

Quintarelli

For many years, Giuseppe Quintarelli, an ultra-famous but extremely publicity-shy Veneto producer, has been producing small volumes of wine (from fruit grown in his Valpolicella vineyard) that are fought over by wine lovers throughout the world. Eccentric, enigmatic, and consistently eschewing all personal contact, this individualistic and highly resolute winemaker applies principles that are all his own to the production of wines of the Valpolicella, Amarone, and Reciotto type. His Amarone is made from late-harvested grapes that are dried until March before being pressed and then aged for several years in old Slovenian oak casks. Though lacking the brilliance of a Dal Forno, the highly traditional results testify wonderfully to the strong personality of an unusual wine that is closely connected with its region, its history, and the men who have contributed to its greatness over the centuries.

VINE VARIETY

30 acres (12 hectares) red: Corvina, Rondinella, Molinara, Cabernet Sauvignon, Nebbiolo, Croatina, Sangiovese, Pelara.

OUR FAVORITE WINES

Quintarelli's Amarone, which commands extremely high prices, is a deep, intense wine that shows few signs of age even after several years in the cask and a few more in the bottle. The Reciotto, with a higher level of residual sugar, comes a close second.

Giuseppe Quintarelli, a legendary producer of great Veneto wines.

Antinori

Antinori is without doubt the best-known name in Italian winemaking. It is also that of a family with a resplendent past whose roots go back to the glory that was Florence in the Middle Ages and the Renaissance. Having arrived in the city from the village of Calenzano in the 13th century, the Antinori family soon became some of Florence's greatest merchants. Their interests extended beyond wine to banking and the silk trade. In the 20th century, under the elegant but efficient leadership of Piero Antinori, this dynasty of aristocratic Florentine merchants became the leading ambassadors of Italian wine. The firm has certainly not forgotten its Tuscan roots but now has a presence in Piedmont and Apulia, too, where it owns some excellent vineyards. In Tuscany, in addition to producing the excellent brand name wine Villa Antinori and the solid Chianti Classico Badia a Passignano, Antinori was one of the first winemakers to develop "super-Tuscans," luxury wines designed to seduce an international public, in the 1980s. He did this first with his cousin Mario Incisa della Rochetta's Sassicaia, which the firm distributed for many years, then with his own Tignanello and Solaia vineyards at the heart of the Chianti DOCG, and ultimately with Antinori's Guado al Tasso estate in the Bolgheri quality zone on the Tuscan coast. Despite their international character, Antinori's wines are perfect expressions (even down to their sophisticated packaging) of the solid but elegant spirit of Tuscany.

VINE VARIETY

This firm boasts almost 3,500 acres (1,400 hectares) of vineyards in Tuscany and Umbria. The most famous are Guado al Tasso (Bolgheri), Tignanello and Peppoli (Chianti), and Pian delle Vigne (Montalcino). Depending on the terroirs and the wines, the varieties from which the firm's wines are made are either classically Tuscan or more international.

OUR FAVORITE WINES

The best of a wide and utterly consistent range is Tignanello, a brilliant and intense super-Tuscan made predominantly from Sangiovese with some Cabernet Sauvignon. We feel the 2000 and 2001 are better balanced than the Solaia (Tignanello's sister-vineyard). Also worthy of attention are the successful Bolgheri Guado al Tasso (2000) and the wonderfully deep Brunello di Montalcino.

Avignonesi

In 1377, when Pope Gregory XI decided to return to Rome after 70 years of the Avignon papacy, a number of Avignon families decided to accompany him. One of these families kept the name of their native town, and some of its descendants settled not in Rome but in the medieval village of Montepulciano. There, in the mid-16th century, it built a winemaking cellar to go with its vineyard and, almost 500 years later, the firm's current winery buildings occupy the same site. Taken over in 1974 by two brothers, the property underwent a rejuvenation through the planting of Cabernet, Merlot, Pinot Nero, and Chardonnay alongside its traditional Montepulciano vineyards. The soul of Avignonesi Montepulciano can be found on the historic Le Capezzine farm at an elevation of nearly 1,000 feet (300 meters): of the estate's 47 acres (19 hectares), 15 are planted with the historic Albarello variety and just 2.5 hectares with 127 different local varieties!

VINE VARIETY
269 acres (109 hectares) spread over four estates: Le Capezzine, I Poggetti, La Selva, and La Lombarda. Red: Sangiovese, Albarello, Cabernet Sauvignon, Merlot, Pinot Nero; white: Chardonnay, Sauvignon Blanc.

OUR FAVORITE WINES
This firm enjoys a deserved reputation as one of the best producers of Vino Nobile di Montepulciano; its Riserva is in a class of its own and 1997 remains a particularly memorable year. The other great local specialty is Vin Santo.

Castello di
Brolio

In Tuscany, where reminders are constantly surfacing of the region's power in the Middle Ages, great families play a vital role. Simultaneously, as guarantors of the traditions and glorious history of the area and contributors to the region's contemporary development, they convey a particular philosophy of life through their demeanor, the character of their surroundings, and the products themselves. Lords of Brolio since 1141, the barons of Ricasoli embody this sense of permanence. From its perch 1,575 feet (480 meters) above sea level the castello looks down on almost 600 acres (about 240 hectares) of vineyard in the southern Chianti region not far from Siena. It was here that Bettino Ricasoli, future prime minister of the newly unified Italy, defined the ideal combination of grape varieties for Chianti wine: Sangiovese, for "aroma and vigor," complemented by Canaiolo and Malvasia. Today, this pride in Chianti has been rediscovered with the creation of Castello di Brolio, a magnificently deep wine of ambitious construction. The same refined and intense structure can be found in the estate's other great wine, Casalferro, made from Sangiovese and Merlot. Dense, vigorous, and benefiting from expert aging, this wine is without doubt one of the most dynamic ambassadors of Tuscan modernity.

VINE VARIETY
593 acres (240 hectares) red: Sangiovese, Merlot, Canaiolo, Cabernet Sauvignon; white: Chardonnay, Malvasia.

OUR FAVORITE WINES
The 2001 Castello di Brolio Chianti Classico is deep and intense. Lavishly aged, it stands out for its fullness of body and length. Just as powerful but displaying a highly sophisticated personality, the Casalferro of the same year, a blend of Merlot and Sangiovese, possesses a rare elegance of texture.

The majestic Castello di Brolio, which has been in the Ricasoli family for more than eight centuries.

Biondi Santi

For at least a century (it was founded in 1840), Biondi Santi has been a symbol of classic Brunello with its intense body, leathery nose, high level of acidity, tannins softened by long aging, and prodigious longevity. Located just below the village of Montalcino, the vines of the Greppo estate are the products of massal selection – in other words, the newest plants are propagated from the oldest. Traditional methods take pride of place in the vinification and aging (almost four years in large oak casks) processes. Franco Biondi Santi and his son Jacopo adhere firmly to these principles and categorically reject the use of barriques (which are becoming increasingly common throughout the region), thereby helping to forge a separate identity within the modern Tuscan winemaking scene for their firm in particular and Montalcino as a whole.

VINE VARIETY

49 acres (20 hectares) red: Sangiovese.

OUR FAVORITE WINES

This estate is understandably proud of some of its historic vintages – the legendary 1945 and 1955, for example. More recent years include a dense, full-bodied Brunello di Montalcino of an aromatic quality far removed from the more modern, fruity Tuscan style.

Fèlsina

Of all the great Italian producers, Giuseppe Mazzocolin is one of those unanimously admired by lovers of Tuscan wine. In addition to his talents as a winemaker, his learning and acuity are also widely praised. The estate reflects the local way of life, combining simplicity with a certain natural refinement. Close to Siena and, like that proud city (nicknamed the "daughter of the road"), a pilgrims' stopping-off place on the route to Rome, which was the port of embarkation for the Crusades during the Middle Ages, Fèlsina once belonged to the Benedictine order. Its vineyards are also notable as the meeting place of two different soil types: the calcareous rock of the Chianti hills, and the sandy terraces of the Siennese country. This duality carries over into the wines, some of which remain true to their local roots while others offer a brilliant interpretation of the new Tuscan horizons. Thus, the Chianti Classico Berardenga (named after the commune in which the vineyard is located) and the Riserva Rancia are fine expressions of the Sangiovese grape, while Maestro Raro is pure Cabernet Sauvignon.

VINE VARIETY
178 acres (72 hectares) red: Sangiovese, Cabernet Sauvignon; white: Chardonnay, Malvasia.

OUR FAVORITE WINES
True expressions of classic Chianti, both Berardenga and Riserva Rancia offer a firm, deep structure – the latter with even more abundant personality. Maestro Raro is a super-Tuscan devoid of the slightest flabbiness.

Castello di
Ama

The charm of the Tuscan landscape derives from its astonishing variety, its mischievous alternation of a succession of hills, narrow valleys, and small woods creating the impression that one has arrived at the end of the world before a sudden bend in the path opens up an immense and sumptuous horizon of gentle slopes punctuated by cypress trees and hilltop villages. The spirit of these parts has been wonderfully captured and celebrated in a superb installation at Ama by the French artist Daniel Buren, one of a number of artists commissioned by proprietors Lorenza Sebasti and Marco Pallanti to create works using the architecture and marvelous site as they see fit. This artistic impulse has also been transmitted to the wines made with great talent and expertise by Marco, a former canoeing champion who has put his Bordeaux enology degree to good use by bridging the divide between the balance and refined textures of great Bordeaux and the elegant and slender vigor of Tuscan wines. Whether one picks up a bottle of the castello's Chianti (with its brilliant expressions of terroir character), La Casuccia and Bella Vista, or the legendary L'Apparit, all these wines convey with supreme elegance the key characteristics of finesse, honesty, and balance.

French artist Daniel Buren celebrates the Tuscan landscape at Castello di Ama with this bold and original interplay of mirrors and windows.

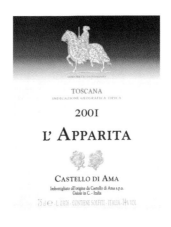

VINE VARIETY

222 acres (90 hectares) red: Sangiovese, Merlot, Malvasia Nera, Canaiolo; white: Chardonnay.
Main vineyards: Bella Vista, La Casuccia, L'Apparita (Merlot) and Il Chiuso (Pinot Noir).

OUR FAVORITE WINES

All Castello di Ama's wines are extremely classy, remarkably pure and devoid of any heaviness. Its 2001 Chianti Classico is flawless and will age beautifully, as has been demonstrated by the estate's other great vintages such as 1990 and 1995. Bella Vista (2001 and 1999) and La Casuccia (2001), originating from specific parcels planted mainly to Sangiovese, are remarkable for their fine tannins and elegant texture. L'Apparita reached a peak of voluptuousness and silkiness in 2001.

Castello di
Fonterutoli

In 1398, Ser Lapo Mazzei, a respectable member of the
Florentine government, drew up the first-ever contract for
the purchase of a quantity of Chianti wine, thereby helping
to see the denomination on its way to a glorious future.
Thirty-seven years later, his granddaughter married a certain
Piero di Agnolo da Fonterutoli, whose vast estate at the heart of
the Chianti zone has remained in the family's possession ever
since. A magnificent property surrounded by a hamlet, Castello
di Fonterutoli remains the focal point of the family's viticultural
interests although a magnificent yet discreet new winery has
been built a few miles away, and the family now owns another
winegrowing estate, Belguardo, in the Maremma region on the
Tuscan coast. On the Chianti side, the vast vineyard, planted
at a very high density rare for the region, is split between four
sites all located to the south of Castellina: Fonterutoli, Siepi,
Badiola, and Belvedere. From this unrivaled patrimony the Mazzei
family created one of the star wines of the super-Tuscan type,
Siepi, before deciding in the mid-1990s to focus their efforts
on Chianti Classico, developing a great wine that, like those of
Bordeaux, is named after the castle. Six centuries after Ser Lapo,
Castello di Fonterutoli has become one of Chianti's best and
most seductive flag bearers.

VINE VARIETY

*171 acres (69 hectares) spread over four sites (Siepi, Badiola,
Belvedere, and Fonterutoli) red: Sangiovese, Merlot, Cabernet
Sauvignon.*

OUR FAVORITE WINES

*Siepi, a brilliant combination of Sangiovese and Merlot,
is a success every year and cannot be accused of being an
international clone. Outstanding examples are 1999, 2001
and 2003. However, these vintage years plus 2000 can be
enjoyed at their best in the very well-balanced and ambitious
Chianti Classico Castello di Fonterutoli, which combines tannic
finesse with great depth.*

Poggio di Sotto

Set on a magnificent *poggio* ("knoll") overlooking the vast Montalcino landscape, Poggio di Sotto is a charming old Tuscan farm that has been carefully restored by Piero Palmucci, who is passionate about the region as well as its wines. He purchased the estate at the end of the 1980s and in these dream surroundings where olive trees occupy even more land than the vines, he has succeeded in creating a unique style of wine that is both representative of the finesse of the denomination while also possessing a definite personality of its own. Indeed, his terroir, located in the Castelnuovo dell'Abate zone, is predisposed to the expression of delicacy rather than brute force. The moderate yields and lack of technical intervention also favor very pure definition. Furthermore, Poggio di Sotto's wines are always pale in color, almost diaphanous and, as a rule, possess the most exquisite nose of all the Brunellos a few hours after decanting.

VINE VARIETY
30 acres (12 hectares) red: Sangiovese.

OUR FAVORITE WINES
The Brunello di Montalcino Riserva (which is only produced in great years) and the "classic" Brunello are highly refined wines. This is evident in every aspect from their pale color to their tannic finesse and delicate nose and body.

Isole e Olena

Once a region of vast estates farmed by humble sharecroppers, until the beginning of the 20th century Tuscany presented a landscape of workers' hamlets huddling in the hollows of hills and often completely isolated from each other. Isole and Olena were two tiny farm and vineyard workers' villages of this sort. Long abandoned, they were united, along with their adjacent vineyards, by Paolo de Marchi, who had developed a passion for the land and its wines. This native of Piedmont, with lively intelligence and a mischievous air, revived the vineyards and brought to the fore the specific character of the terroir, favoring authenticity over flashiness, precision over bombast, and finesse over power. His regular Chianti Classico is thus a model of its type and his premier wine, Ceparello, is on a par with Tuscany's best. De Marchi knows better than anyone else how to tame the rusticity of the grape in order to emphasize its candid, robust aromas and express its full tension, dynamism, and wonderful length. Simultaneously faithful to his terroir and a born experimenter, De Marchi has also planted international varieties that are vinified separately and, like his Chianti, Cabernet Sauvignon, Syrah, and Chardonnay, also offer a simple, honest interpretation of their fundamental varietal character.

VINE VARIETY
123 acres (50 hectares) red: Sangiovese, Canaiolo, Syrah; white: Malvasia, Trebbiano, Chardonnay.

OUR FAVORITE WINES
All this estate's wines, including its non-traditional Chardonnay and Syrah, excel with their sincerity and good balance. However, it is with his Sangiovese that Paolo de Marchi really shows what he is capable of. The Cepparello (1998, 1999, 2001, and 2003), made from the fruit of some of the oldest Sangiovese vines in existence, is the most dazzling expression of this variety and captivates with its slender, intense depth. This is not to say the estate's Chianti Classico is in any way unworthy. On the contrary, its fine texture is equally impressive, and its length and balance have few rivals in its category.

Malvasia grapes destined to be made into wonderful Vin Santo are laid out on traditional reed beds to dry. The grapes will wither and become highly concentrated in sugar.

Frescobaldi

These days, Frescobaldi is one of Italy's most important winegrowers. In addition to its original Tuscan holdings, it now has a presence in Friuli (Attems in the Collio DOC zone) and the Veneto. Over the last few years the company has been busy developing the top end of its viticultural business, going as far as taking control of the celebrated Ornellaia estate on the Tuscan coast. As previously with Luce, a vast property in the Montalcino zone, more or less completely given over to the production of an ambitious Sangiovese–Merlot blend, this purchase was made through the offices of the Mondavi family. Castelgiocondo, already in Brunello di Montalcino, and the modernist Santa Maria vineyard in the Morellino di Scansano DOC were added to Frescobaldi's existing collection of historic estates that included the large Castiglioni estate (whose vineyards were replanted in the 1990s) in the southern Chianti district, Pomino, where the Frescobaldi family planted Chardonnay and Cabernet Sauvignon as long ago as the 19th century, and most importantly Nippozano, an immense property with a superb medieval castello and now the heart of the business. These last two produce two super-Tuscans that share the same well-rounded, full-bodied, and luxuriously well-aged character: Montesodi from Nippozano, and Giramonte from Castiglioni.

VINE VARIETY

2,471 acres (1,000 hectares), 395 (160 acres) of which are dedicated to Nippozano, spread over 9 estates. Red: Sangiovese, Cabernet Sauvignon, Cabernet Franc, Merlot, Syrah.

OUR FAVORITE WINES

While the 2000 Ripe al Convento Riserva from Castelgiocondo displays the full-bodied, sunny and slightly rustic style of the traditional Brunellos, the 2001 Luce IGT, 2003 Giramonte and 2003 Montesodi are luxury modernist examples of the international style.

La Massa

The small village of Panzano (between Greve and Radda), where all this producer's vines are planted, is located at the heart of the Chianti region in a landscape that is wonderfully welcoming in summer but shows a far harsher face in winter and even early spring. Fattoria La Massa has been producing wine since the Middle Ages and is typical of the local vineyards in its simultaneously rustic and aristocratic, austere, and elegant character. The vineyards in this landscape of gentle slopes and rolling hills are situated at an intermediate altitude (around 1,150 feet/350 meters), which affords them some respite from the worst of the scorching summer heat. Taken over in 1992 by its current owner Gianpaolo Motta, La Massa made rapid progress during the closing years of the century and is now one of Tuscany's benchmark producers, renowned for both its star wine, the Giorgio Prima Chianti Classico, and its excellent Sangiovese–Merlot blend.

VINE VARIETY
67 acres (27 hectares) red: Sangiovese, Merlot.

OUR FAVORITE WINES
This estate produces an archetypal Chianti Classico, Giorgio Primo, which shows wonderful depth in good years such as 1997, 2001, and 2003.

Ornellaia

This estate is the perfect symbol of the fabulous revolution that has occurred in Tuscany over the past 20 years, resulting in what the American press have nicknamed the super-Tuscan. It was the product of Ludovico Antinori's imagination and personal ambition, and was created *ex nihilo* at the beginning of the 1980s. Antinori ran the operation along the same lines as many a great Napa Valley winery, combining Sangiovese with Bordeaux varieties that are able to thrive on these alluvial terroirs thanks to a milder climate than in Chianti, building resolutely futuristic cellars, seeking advice from consultant Michel Rolland, and looking to position the wine in the top echelon from the very beginning. Despite producing wines in the first few years that were heavily oaked and slightly dull, Ornellaia eventually took off and began to make rapid progress. Tired of running this pharaonic project alone, Ludovico decided at the beginning of the new century to relinquish the estate to the Californian Mondavi family, who sold it on almost immediately to Frescobaldi, incurring the bitterness of the Antinoris in doing so. Today, the Frescobaldi family are the sole proprietors of this fine vineyard and have had the good sense to continue the work already accomplished – both with the flagship wine named after the property and with Masseto (made from Merlot grown on a specific clay-rich site), a stereotypically chic and impressive wine that we believe lacks the class now being shown by Ornellaia.

VINE VARIETY
225 acres (91 hectares) red: Cabernet Sauvignon, Merlot, Cabernet Franc, Petit Verdot.

OUR FAVORITE WINES
While the 2001 Masseto (100% Merlot) is a wine of ultra-seductive richness and roundness, some might prefer the complexity and balance of the Ornellaia from either the same year (which we consider the most successful in the history of the vineyard) or from 2003, which was rich and brilliant. Far from being an international super-cuvée, Ornellaia is now starting to develop a strong personality of its own.

A sumptuous wine from the coastal area of Tuscany, Ornellaia is one of the most sought-after of the super-Tuscans.

Montevertine

Montevertine is located in the Radda district at the heart of Chianti, more or less equidistant between Siena and Florence. A steel magnate with a passion for this region, in which he used to spend all his vacations, Sergio Manetti began restoring this ancestral property in 1967. For the benefit of his friends and clients, he then bought 5 acres (2 hectares) of vineyard and built his first winery. The success of this wine made for the enjoyment of his friends took its producer by surprise and led him to devote his entire energy to winemaking. Sergio Manetti has now passed away, but the estate he founded continues to pursue the same ideals and to defend a particular idea of how Tuscan wine should be. The property remains firmly attached to the regional typicity of its wines and has always refused to plant international varieties. For example, Pergole Torte, its prestige wine (first made in 1976) has always been made from 100% Sangiovese. Like all the estate's wines, it expresses the intense character of the best Chiantis with great sincerity. It also adds an energy and class that are all its own.

VINE VARIETY
32 acres (13 hectares) red: 85% Sangiovese, 10% Canaiolo, 3% Colorino, 2% Malvasia.

OUR FAVORITE WINES
Le Pergole Torte is a sappy and powerfully structured wine that is at its best after a few years of aging. The 1997 and 1998 vintages, for example, are now drinking well.

At Montevertine in the heart of the Chianti region, the vineyards present a serene Tuscan landscape of rolling hills crowned with cypress trees.

Poliziano

Created in 1961 and taking its name from the Renaissance poet Angelo Ambrogini, who was born in Montepulciano and known by the name of Poliziano, this now vast estate has become a benchmark producer of Vino Nobile di Montepulciano, a Tuscan DOCG of extremely strong character. Frederico Carletti, who succeeded his father at the head of this family estate at the beginning of the 1980s, introduced rigorous methods in the vineyard and has also reinvigorated vinification and aging techniques. Asinone, made with grapes from his best terroirs, is an excellent example of Montepulciano for anyone who wants to sample the complexity of this wine. Naturally, as so often in Tuscany, the challenge of producing Cabernet–Merlot blends has also been taken up, and Le Stanze is among the very best in its category every year. In parallel with his work at Poliziano, Carletti has recently established a new vineyard, christened Lohsa, in the promising coastal district of La Maremma. This is also planted with international varieties and is helping to demonstrate that great wines are sublimely indifferent to the petty argument between traditionalists and modernists.

VINE VARIETY

272 acres (110 hectares) red, of which 35 (14 hectares) are dedicated to the Asinone selection; Sangiovese, Colorino, Merlot, Cabernet Sauvignon.

OUR FAVORITE WINES

In terms of Vino Nobile di Montepulciano, Asinone is a must. The brilliant 1997 remains one of the most successful ever.

Tenuta
San Guido

For a long time Sassicaia was a miraculous exception and remains one of Tuscany's leading wines. The vineyard forms part of a vast estate owned by the Incisa della Rochetta family. Located on the Tyrrhenian coast halfway between Livorno and Grosseto, close to the picturesque village of Bolgheri, it is unusual for two reasons. First, at the time of its creation in 1944, this was a somewhat neglected region that was marshy and cut off from the rest of Tuscany by the impressive Apennine chain that rises up just a few miles inland. Second, conscious of the site's milder, more temperate climate and seduced by the elegance of great Bordeaux, Marchese Mario Incisa de la Rochetta took the astonishing decision to plant these deep alluvial Apennine soils with Cabernet Sauvignon and to a lesser extent Cabernet Franc. This bold course of action bore fruit slowly at first but then with dazzling success in the 1980s under the cool and modest guidance of son Niccolò Incisa della Rochetta. The wine's success is due largely to specific stylistic features far removed from the nouveau-riche caricatures that seem to thrive in this category: the finesse of its nose, which is never dominated by oak; its slender but concentrated body underpinned by a very tight-knit tannic structure sometimes bordering on the harsh in lesser years; delightfully fresh and incisive length. In short, this is a devilishly classy wine.

VINE VARIETY
173 acres (70 hectares) red: 85% Cabernet Sauvignon and 15% Cabernet Franc.

OUR FAVORITE WINES
Sassicaia, San Guido's main wine, has a highly assertive style with a long, clean body devoid of any heaviness of fruit or flesh supported at all times by tight-knit tannins that can verge on the hard-edged in years of only average ripeness. While, in our view, the 1985 remains the estate's most accomplished wine, 1999 and 2001 are also highly successful slender and elegant wines.

San Giusto a Rentennano

Since 1992 two brothers and a sister – Luca, Francesco, and Elisabetta – have devoted their lives to the family estate. This is located at the heart of the Chianti district – in other words, at the heart of a Tuscany that is as warm and generous in summer as it is harsh in winter. Their wines reflect this duality. Well structured, tight-knit, and intense, they open up after breathing in the ambient air in a glass or carafe and gradually reveal their full generosity of spirit. Elisabetta, Luca, and Francesco Martini di Cigala give Sangiovese a leading role in all their reds. And their super-Tuscan, Percarlo, offered up as an IGT Tuscan rather than as a DOCG Chianti, is no less than 100% Sangiovese. Made from fruit from six different zones, Percarlo is a veritable synthesis of the estate's different terroirs. Fermentation takes three weeks and is followed by 22 months' barrique aging. This vigorous handling is also applied to the estate's other top-end cuvées: Le Baroncole, a solid and archetypal Chianti Classico; and the firm Merlot La Ricolma.

VINE VARIETY
77 acres (31 hectares) red: Sangiovese, Canaiolo, Merlot; white: Malvasia, Trebbiano.

OUR FAVORITE WINES
This estate's most ambitious wine is without doubt its Percarlo. The 2001 reveals a distinct personality with impressive tannic richness and good acidity. It is a fine, sincere, mature wine that is proud of its Tuscan origins. In a different category, the 2002 Merlot seduces with its tight-knit texture and splendid fruit.

Siro Pacenti

For a long time, Montalcino was a bastion of tradition. Wines were left to age for lengthy periods in the antique oak casks of the village's cellars where their youthful, fruity aromas and vigorous tannins were gradually replaced by a nose reminiscent of leather, spices, and fruit brandy along with a taut but soft body. This style, fervently championed by producer Biondi Santi, has been all but superceded over the last few years by a number of producers of a more contemporary cast of mind. At the forefront of these modernists is Giancarlo Pacenti who, with a highly developed instinct for what makes a good wine, has taken his inspiration from the growing methods, vinification and aging techniques that are now thriving everywhere else. While remaining perfect ambassadors of their type, his wines display a highly seductive freshness of nose and suppleness of body.

VINE VARIETY
Red: Sangiovese.

OUR FAVORITE WINES
The talent of Siro Pacenti's winemaker is brilliantly expressed even in his entry-level cuvée. The 2004 Rosso di Montalcino is a supple, full-bodied wine with a magnificent nose of red fruit. In another league, though, is the 2001 Brunello di Montalcino, which shares the same freshness and exceptionally velvety tannins while displaying all the class of its terroir – a truly inspired wine.

Cabernet Sauvignon, the Bordeaux variety par excellence, has found a new and fulfilling role in Sassicaia.

Tenuta di
Valgiano

Lucca, like Pisa, is an attractive Tuscan coastal town. Looking down on it from an altitude of 820 feet (250 meters) is Valgiano, which immediately entrances visitors with its civilized Mediterranean landscape and elegant 18th-century villa nestling among the undulating vineyards. Young and enthusiastic, Moreno Petrini and his wife have succeeded in just a few years in turning this charming property into a thrilling laboratory for new Tuscan wines, ignoring the eternal dilemma of whether to choose local or international varieties and focusing on the most important thing – how to achieve the purest possible expression of terroir character. On their slopes of calcareous rock and terraces littered with pebbles deposited here when the Apennines were formed, they grow Sangiovese (the dominant variety in the blend), Merlot, and Syrah using biodynamic methods. Often making drastic decisions during the realization of their main wine, both before and during harvest as well as during the winemaking process itself (which relies on gravity, thereby eliminating the use of harmful pumps and pipes), from their very first vintages in the 1990s they have been producing cheerful, full-bodied and flavorsome wines of outstanding harmony. Valgiano's wines gain in depth and elegance of tannins with each successive year, earning the venture a reputation as one of Tuscany's most promising winemaking experiments.

2003

TENUTA DI VALGIANO

Colline Lucchesi
denominazione di origine controllata

Imbottigliato all'origine da - bottled by
Tenuta di Valgiano snc Capannori, Lucca - Italia

PRODUCT OF ITALY   RED WINE
1500 ML ℮ **ALC.14% BY VOL.**
CONTIENE SOLFITI

VINE VARIETY
40 acres (16 hectares) red: Sangiovese, Merlot, Syrah.

OUR FAVORITE WINES
Each new year adds a further dimension to this still-young wine. The 1999 is admirable for its full body and ripe fruit; the 2000 saw the tannins become more refined; in 2001 the wine added greater elegance to these qualities; this was confirmed in 2003 and even in the suppler 2002.

Masciarelli

Gianni Masciarelli took over the family property, in which vineyards rub shoulders with olive orchards, in 1981. In doing so, he developed an immediate passion for both ancestral crops and embarked on an ambitious program with each. The estate, today spread over 11 different vineyard sites, has become an ambassador for the little-known Abruzzo region that looks out toward the Adriatic. Without seeking to conceal the generous and sunny character of the region and its wines, Masciarelli has tamed some of their power, refined the tannins and emphasized their chocolate and spice aromas, endowing his Montepulciano d'Abruzzo with an individuality far removed from the sad caricatures all too frequently encountered in the region. At the heart of a sizable output, he has isolated a highly ambitious cuvée named Villa Gemma. His wife Marina Cvetic has also been infected with Gianni's passion for the grape – to such an extent that she has created a range of wines in her own name that display a similar stylistic approach.

VINE VARIETY
482 acres (195 hectares) of which 30 are set aside for the firm's Villa Gemma Montepulciano. Red: Montepulciano d'Abruzzo, Cabernet Sauvignon; white: Trebbiano and Chardonnay.

OUR FAVORITE WINES
The Villa Gemma wines, made from Montepulciano d'Abruzzo, are powerful and full-bodied; their depth and character never fail to make an impression. The 1998, 2000, and 2001 are brilliant vintages currently aging to perfection.

Valentini

The magnificent vineyard of this great producer, close to the famous port of Pescara and its fine restaurants, deserves to be protected by the Italian state as a national monument. Rigorous viticultural principles and a winemaking process that involves the very minimum of intervention (no barriques or oak flavors but rather an emphasis on hygiene and strictly controlled élevage in an oxidation-free environment) give his wines an energy and an eternal quality thoroughly in keeping with the world view of this lover of pre-Socratic philosophy. He sees his wine as a powerful and noble expression of the fundamental elements of the universe (water, air, and fire), and has no time whatsoever for the "low tricks" of modern winemaking. His sales policy reflects the same high standards and wisdom: his wine is only released for sale when it is ready for drinking. Both his white (of a vinosity unique in Italy) and his red (which is remarkably spicy and subtle) are absolute musts whenever they appear on restaurant wine lists. Valentini's great vintages include 1997 (red) and 2000 (white).

VINE VARIETY
161 acres (65 hectares) red: Sangiovese (Montepulciano); white: Trebbiano.

OUR FAVORITE WINES
This estate excels at making both red and white wines. Its most surprising wine is its Trebbiano. Whereas this grape generally produces fairly mundane results, in the expert hands of Eduardo Valentini it is transformed into a wine of aromatic complexity, mineral tension and aging potential unique in Italy. In terms of their elegant perfume and nobility of tannins, his red Montepulcianos – in particular the Cerasuolo cuvée – rival Tuscany's greatest Sangiovese-based wines.

Montevetrano

With time and human talent, what started out as a kind of wager or game has developed into one of southern Italy's most charming wines. In the mid-1980s, Sylvia Imparato, carried along by the enthusiasm of a number of wine-connoisseur friends, decided to create a wine of quality on her property, which was divided at the time between orchards and traditional vineyards. The orange, lemon, and apricot trees still stand on this beautiful family owned estate at the heart of the ancient Campagna Romana between Pompeii and the Amalfi Coast, and their fruit is made into delicious preserves that are everyone's pride and joy. Of the original vines, though, only the high-quality local Aglianico variety survives. Under the expert guidance of brilliant enologist Ricardo Cottarella, Cabernet Sauvignon and Merlot were planted alongside it, not with a view to making yet another conventional international wine but, on the contrary, with the aim of making a slender, original, and deep cru of distinct character. From the very first wines produced at the beginning of the last decade to those being made today, this winemaking experiment has taken on very real dimensions without ever losing its charming spirit of friendship and passion.

VINE VARIETY

12 acres (5 hectares) red: 60% Cabernet Sauvignon, 30% Merlot, 10% Aglianico.

OUR FAVORITE WINES

The key characteristics of this wine of abundant personality are smooth tannins and a harmonious structure. Boasting an aromatic palette dominated by licorice and black fruit, the 2003 stands out for its fresh and engaging length. A little more rigid, the 2001 also delivers a long and harmonious finish.

Feudi di
San Gregorio

Campania is the birthplace of quality wine. During the Roman Empire wealthy patricians liked to spend the summer months in the Naples region. They took great delight in the local wines, whose prices soon far exceeded those of anywhere else. Two thousand years later, the region's special status is being revived by an elite group of talented producers assisted by a number of highly skilled and open-minded enologists. Contrary to what has happened in many regions with reawakening viticultural ambitions, Campania's producers have succeeded in exploiting the potential of a local variety, Aglianico. Modernizing growing methods and vinification techniques in order to remove any trace of rusticity, they have revealed in this variety a freshness of fruit, a finesse of texture, and a general balance that are emphasized all the more by the specific Campania terroirs in which it is planted. Spearheading this renaissance is Feudi di San Gregorio. Other indigenous varieties (without the slightest hint of rusticity) also occupy an important place in the firm's wide range of wines, thereby demonstrating what can be lost as a result of the standardization of grape varieties. However, it is its reds (and in particular its Taurasi DOC reds) that earn this estate and its wines a place among the very best.

VINE VARIETY
618 acres (250 hectares) red: Aglianico, Primitivo (Zinfandel); white: Greco di Tufo, Fiano.

OUR FAVORITE WINES
All of this producer's wines, even the most simple, are stylish and refined, developing real character with age. The 2004 Fiano di Avellino Pietracalda, for example, is deliciously fresh, spicy, and harmonious. But it is with its reds that Feudi di San Gregorio really scales the heights. The wonderfully classy 2004 Serpico, made from Aglianico, the brilliant and highly ambitious 2002 Patrimo, and above all two magnificent Taurasi DOC wines of which the classic version is lean, sinewy, and spicy (2002), and the Piano di Montevergine, in a year such as 1999, displays a nobility of tannins and a breeding that make it one of the very best of reds.

Feudi di San Gregorio: vineyards, hills, and hilltop villages – archetypal features of the Campania countryside since time immemorial.

Azienda
Galardi

Campania and its indigenous grape Aglianico were, for a long time, the forgotten members of Europe's fraternity of great wines. What was needed in order to start winning over wine lovers again was for local producers to wake up to the potential of their vineyards and for brilliant enologists to tame the variety's natural vigor. Among those who have helped to transform the region is enologist Ricardo Cotarella, who remains without doubt the best known. Terra di Lavoro, the wine whose production he has supervised from the outset, can be seen as the rare but valiant flag bearer of this renaissance. Founded in 1990 and owned jointly by a number of families, Azienda Galardi may only produce one wine, but it is a wine of power and intensity that made an immediate impact on wine lovers and their palates. The vineyard clings spectacularly to a volcanic slope in the northern part of Campania, a terroir that produces incredibly rich, dense wines that nevertheless display a surprising freshness and tannic finesse. The first two vintages (1994 and 1995) are highly sought after by connoisseurs and command correspondingly high prices (the wine has always been produced in very small volumes).

TERRA DI LAVORO

2004

ROCCAMONFINA
Indicazione Geografica Tipica

Prodotto e imbottigliato da Galardi s.r.l.
Sessa Aurunca - Caserta - Italia

750 ml. **e**   Prodotto in Italia   13% VOL.

VINE VARIETY
25 acres (10 hectares) red: Aglianico, Piedirosso.

OUR FAVORITE WINES
Terra di Lavoro, the one and only wine produced by this estate (its highly evocative name means "land of labor"), impresses initially with its depth and density on the palate. Endowed with a fine but intense tannic structure and lacking any hint of bitterness (which can result from excessively long fermentation), recent vintages have all combined class with a long finish.

Argiolas

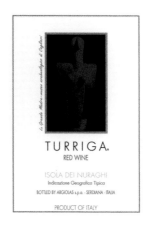

Founded in 1938, Azienda Argiolas has long been one of the leading estates on an island covered with vineyards but suffering from a poor reputation for quality. With the 1980s came the success of Turriga, a blend of several Mediterranean varieties including Cannonau (a local grape of Spanish origin), Bovale, Carignano, and Malvasia Nera. Powerful, fleshy, and velvety, Turriga rapidly won fans both at home and abroad with its seductive, full-bodied style that continues to develop in the bottle. This success was presided over by Francesco and Giuseppe Argiolas, the heads of the family business. They manage the vineyards with model rigor and precision, and also had the perspicacity to engage brilliant enologist Giacomo Tachis to help with the vinification.

VINE VARIETY
544 acres (220 hectares) red: Cannonau, Bovale, Carignano, Malvasia Nera, Monica; white: Vermentino, Malvasia di Cagliari, Nasco, Nuragus.

OUR FAVORITE WINES
Dominated by one of southern Italy's most famous reds, Turriga (generally highly concentrated but also extremely supple, with well-rounded, mature tannins), this producer's range consists predominantly of simpler, more immediately fruity wines.
Two exceptions are the ambitious white Cerdeña (a powerful Vermentino with a high alcoholic content whose warmth verges on the point of heaviness), and Angialis (Nasco and Malvasia), a rich, full, not particularly complex but well-made sweet wine.

Benanti

The region around Etna, one of Europe's biggest volcanoes, is not exactly known for its high-quality vineyards. And yet in many ways it is very well suited to winegrowing. In a number of places the climate is more like that of Switzerland than southern Italy. There is plenty of rain, the temperature is agreeably mild even in summer (when the rest of the island is scorchingly hot), and temperatures at night are significantly cooler than during the day. The Benanti family of wealthy industrialists (pharmaceuticals) invested ambitiously in the area in the 1990s with the explicit intention of capitalizing on this viticultural potential. The estate grows almost exclusively local varieties such as Nerello Mascalese (a kind of southern Pinot Noir, whose lightness of color and delicate aromas it resembles), and the white variety Carricante. It is managed by Salvo Foti, an expert in Etna viticulture and a highly talented winemaker.

VINE VARIETY
96 acres (39 hectares) red: Nerello Mascalese, Nerello Cappuccio, Nero d'Avola, Cabernet Sauvignon; white: Carricante, Minnella Bianca, Chardonnay.

OUR FAVORITE WINES
Benanti's Monovitigno (monovarietal) range is worth exploring for its rigor of expression and capacity to develop interestingly with age. The reds are very well structured with powerful tannins that are rather harsh when young but acquire great depth and complexity over time. The estate also makes a number of wines that are more "predictable" in style. Lamorèmio, an easy-going red displaying extremely mature and supple tannins, is one.

Planeta

It would be impossible to dream up a more fitting name with which to set about conquering the world. But Planeta is not the invention of a team of international marketing experts, it is the surname of the proprietors. The young generation who are now in charge – Alessio, Francesca, and Santi – have transformed the firm into Sicily's most ambitious winemaking venture, skillfully combining a genuinely modern approach with a strong desire to exploit the potential of southern Sicily's vineyards. Almost 500 acres (about 200 hectares) of vines are divided between four main sites: Sambuca and Menfi in the southwest; Vittoria and Noto in the southeast. Some vineyards are given over to indigenous varieties such as Nero d'Avola, others to popular international varieties. The Planeta family has been assisted by the Piedmontese enologist Carlo Corino, who spent a long time working in Australia. The influence of that country can be detected in wines that are well-rounded, candid, simple, and direct, offering generous amounts of immediately seductive fruit.

VINE VARIETY

Noto, 148 acres (60 hectares) red: Nero d'Avola; white: Muscat (Moscato). Vittoria, 42 acres (17 hectares): Nero d'Avola and Frappato. Menfi, 116 acres (46 hectares): Merlot, Syrah, Cabernet Sauvignon. Sambuca, 222 acres (90 hectares): Grecanico, Nero d'Avola, Sauvignon Blanc, Fiano, Syrah, Cabernet Sauvignon and Pinot Noir.

OUR FAVORITE WINES

Planeta's wines offer generous amounts of fresh fruit, often combined with flattering oak, are sprightly and well-rounded and have a soft finish. This producer's range includes delicious wines made from traditional local varieties such as the 2004 Fiano (white), and international varieties such as the 2003 Syrah or 2004 Moscafratta (a blend of Merlot, Cabernet Sauvignon, and Nero d'Avola).

At Menfi, in southern Sicily, Planeta has dragged local winemaking into the modern age without ruining the landscape.

Tasca d'Almerita

Tasca started to make a name for itself as a pioneer of Sicilian quality wine back in the 1960s. The estate is without doubt one of the island's most spectacular. Located at the center of Sicily, it forms a green oasis at the heart of the arid landscape of the Caltanissetta region. This casa vinicola is run by Count Lucio with the help of his sons Alberto and Giuseppe (the firm's enologist). All three are keen to distance themselves from the heavy and extremely concentrated style all too frequently associated with Mediterranean wine in general and Sicilian wine in particular. The climate is relatively mild with a marked difference in temperature between day and night. Extremely hot spells are less common than anywhere else in southern Italy. As a result the whites offer an attractive freshness of aroma and are rich without being heavy. The Tascas also produce a real rarity in this region: a dry sparkling Chardonnay. Two years ago the family bought a new estate on the small Aeolian island of Salina, where it has started to make a very good sweet wine, Tenuta Capofaro, from the traditional Malvasia grape.

VINE VARIETY

855 acres (346 hectares) red: Merlot, Syrah, Alicante, Cabernet Sauvignon, Nero d'Avola, Pinot Nero, Nerello, Perricone, Petit Verdot; white: Catarratto, Chardonnay, Pinot Bianco, Grecanico, Inzolia, Sauvignon Blanc, Traminer, Trebbiano, Moscato.
Also 12 acres (5 hectares) on Salina, Malvasia delle Lipari (white).

OUR FAVORITE WINES

The reds – in particular, the Cabernet Sauvignon – are highly characterful. Far removed from the duller, more routine expressions of the variety, this Cabernet is powerful and highly concentrated but at the same time fresh and full of energy. Since 2003, the Contea di Sclafani Chardonnay, once rich but rather heavy, has grown more slender and refined with a longer finish.

Spain

Spain has the greatest area of vineyards in the world with more than 2.4 million acres (1 million hectares) under production. However, in terms of volume of wine produced it ranks only third. The reason is easily understood: the low density of planting per hectare and the number of semi-abandoned vineyards.

Wine is produced in almost every part of the country but particularly on the vast limestone plains where the altitude means that the vines benefit from the slightly cooler nights. The best red wines are produced in Catalonia and northern Castile, while the best balanced whites come from Galicia and Navarre. Andalusia is known for its inimitable fortified wines, including the skillfully aged *rancio* wines matured in wooden casks.

Some of the finest Mediterranean grape varieties originated in Spain, including Grenache, Mourvèdre (also called Monastrell or Mataro), and Carignan. But, rather surprisingly, the most wonderful of all Spanish varieties and the one that accounts for the greatest volume of fine wines in the Rioja and Ribeira del Duero regions, Tempranillo, is scarcely grown outside Spain. While formerly Spanish red wines were given an over-long period of maturation in oak casks, the last ten years have seen a radical change with wines that now impress with their aromatic fullness and velvety texture, making them more instantly appealing to a wider worldwide clientele.

List of domaines

Descendientes de J. Palacios

The Palacios family has played an important role in the perfection of a type of fine Spanish wine that is simultaneously respectful of a long tradition and particular climate while being modern, intelligent, and generous. The grapes are cultivated along biodynamic lines, resulting in fruit of incomparable quality and balance. The winemaking process, on the other hand, is very modern and scientific. While no artificial corrections or adjustments are used, everything possible is done to ensure that all the flavors accumulated over the year are preserved in the wine. Álvaro Palacios has no objections to rigorously controlled extraction or to the use of new oak casks, maintaining that it is only by using these costly containers that the texture of the wine will develop into its definitive form. Here, in Bierzo – known as the "Oceanic Priorat" in tribute to the wines made by the same family in the Priorat area – the natural elegance of the fruit and tannins of the Mencio grape have been much improved by maturation in new oak, giving a wine that is now arguably even better than the majority of Priorat wines. It is an esthetic wine for those who are knowledgable enough to appreciate its complexity.

VINE VARIETY

67 acres (27 hectares) red: Mencia.

OUR FAVORITE WINES

In recent years, particularly 2001 and 2003, the domaine's prestige wine, Corullón (the result of the remarkable collaboration between Álvaro Palacios and his cousin Ricardo Perez), has reached levels of quality unimaginable until now for an appellation that has hitherto been little known. The Mencia grape retains a lot of its aromatic freshness even when very ripe. When skillfully matured, it will give a wine with a highly polished texture.

Agustí Torelló

Catalonia is the main terroir for the Spanish sparkling wine, Cava. Although produced by the same method as that used in the Champagne region of France, wine connoisseurs often dismiss this wine, judging it by the standards of mass-produced Cavas. It is true that it is frequently an unrefined wine with a certain lingering bitterness. There are, however, a number of true artists in the field of winemaking capable of bringing out the best from their rich and unique heritage of local grape varieties, producing wines with a refinement of expression that is quite astonishing. Such wines are perfectly suited to accompany the most daring dishes of Basque and Catalan cuisine. A great Cava can be recognized by its unique hints of honey and toasted almonds. Light-bodied, its alcoholic strength is frequently no more than 11%. It has a highly aperitif finish, preserved by minimal or zero dosage. Important producers in the Rioja region, in Catalonia the Torelló Mata company makes only high quality sparkling wines, remaining faithful to the true local style – which is to say without the addition of Chardonnay or Pinot grapes that might give a more Champagne-like touch. It also produces some of the most exciting white wines in the whole of Spain. Particularly to be recommended is the Reserva Barrica made from pure Macabeo grapes and matured for four months in wooden casks. Drunk with one of the exotic culinary creations of the El Bulli restaurant (based in Roses, on the Costa Brava), you might believe you had died and gone to heaven!

VINE VARIETY

69 acres (28 hectares) white: Macabeo, Parellada, Xarello; red: Trepat.

OUR FAVORITE WINES

The entire range of wines from this Cava producer – making minuscule amounts compared to the big companies, but standing head and shoulders above them in terms of quality – is highly impressive. The Gran Reserva Mata wines have a purity of definition, with hints of toasted almonds and citron that will surely win round any lovers of sparkling wine. Rivaling the very best of champagnes in complexity of taste and refinement of bubbles, though, is the famous prestige cuvée, Kripta, presented in a curious but magnificent glass amphora. Another impressive wine is a pure Macabeo, matured in casks and (in this sparkling form) perhaps the most elegant wine produced anywhere from this grape.

Codorníu

Because of its enormous output, the product of a company regarded as almost a national Spanish institution are shunned by connoisseurs of rare wines. The tourist, on the other hand, should not miss a visit to the ultra-modern production plant designed by the Catalan architect Joseph Puig i Cadafalch, which makes the sparkling wines and their total lack of presumption seem decidedly down to earth. Nineteen miles (30 kilometers) of cellars are required to house more than 100 million carefully quality-controlled bottles, so a visit involves riding on a small train. Unlike Champagne, Cava is not confined to any particular region, which means that grapes are supplied from all over Spain (Rioja, Aragon, Navarre, and Estramadura) to Catalonia, where the wine is generally produced. Spanish grape varieties give a particular quality to the bouquet, more reminiscent of toasted almonds than the toasted bread of champagne. Increasingly, however, Chardonnay grapes are used, thus avoiding the possible bitterness produced by the local varieties when they are not properly looked after. Codorníu makes much use of Chardonnay for its prestige cuvées, Anna and Jaume. Local color is sacrificed in the interests of a greater purity.

VINE VARIETY
7,413 acres (3,000 hectares) white: Chardonnay, Parellada, Macabeo, Xarel-lo.

OUR FAVORITE WINES
Rather like Moët in France, this huge Spanish firm produces something of everything. Worthy of note is its prestige cuvée, the Jaume de Codorníu, sold in magnums. Using mainly Chardonnay grapes for their aromatic freshness and pure, mineral-rich length, this Cava has much less local character than some of the others made by smaller houses such as Gramona.

Even with a supportive belt, this grape harvester's back will be aching by the end of the day.

Finca Sandoval

The famous Spanish journalist Victor de la Serna is, like his father, one of the world's greatest connoisseurs of wine. His encyclopedic knowledge not only of Spanish vineyards but of vineyards worldwide is not just theoretical. He is quite prepared to get his hands dirty and, together with a group of friends, came up with the idea of making a good, and possibly great, wine from the grapes grown on his family's land in Manchuela, an area that until then had only produced table wines of no great distinction. His intuition led him to the belief that his beloved Syrah grapes could thrive on the high limestone plateaus (600–700 yards/ meters) of the province of Cuenca in southeastern Spain, and that the traditional local variety, Bobal, used to produce an everyday rosé, was undervalued. His ambitions to produce a high-quality wine were aided by the free hand allowed to innovative winemakers by Spanish law. The first wines to appear were immediately acclaimed for their full body and aromatic charm. Their maturation in oak has the effect of refining the bouquet which, as it develops, further brings out the characteristics of the terroir. A great wine is born.

VINE VARIETY
28 acres (11 hectares) red: Syrah, Bobal, Grenache.

OUR FAVORITE WINES
This fine wine, made mainly from Syrah grapes produced by this new winery (established in 2000) is already regarded as a classic. Arguably one of the most successful wines from northern Spain, its rich color, velvety texture, and beautifully smooth tannins make it an example of the best modern-style wines. While it will be readily appreciated by wine-lovers from all over the world, it remains true to its origins.

Gramona

Jaume Gramona Martí, the enologist of this small family business, can be proud of the guidance he has given, earning the respect of the most important wine experts of his country. Using local grape varieties that have a balance of sugar and acidity that is ideal for the fizziness, he produces sparkling wines with perfect bubbles. As in the case of the French Crémants, this is combined with a less frequently encountered aromatic originality that does not involve any sacrifice of purity and elegance, and a back taste that, as they say in the Champagne region, leaves a trace of its origins. The wonderful thing about the La Plana soils is that they preserve purity in the minerality of the finish. The autolysis of the yeasts, the basis of the complex bouquet of this type of sparkling wine, does not make it heavy, but instead transforms it, as in the great Champagne crus. The limited quantities of Reserva produced (40,000–50,000 bottles) allows the dosage, reduced to a minimum, to be strictly controlled. By way of comparison, taste some III Lustros and then a good non-vintage brut champagne. The heaviness of the dosage in the latter will seem quite unnecessary.

VINE VARIETY

124 acres (50 hectares) white: Xarello, Macabeo, Chardonnay; red: Pinot Noir.

OUR FAVORITE WINES

The best cuvées are those based on the Catalan grape varieties grown on the clay-limestone soils of La Plana, and are the most admired for this type of wine. They include the Celler Batlle Gran Reserva 1998 and the III Lustros 1999, wines that for refinement and originality are every bit a good as those of Augusti Torello. They should not be missed when they appear on the wine lists of the best Catalonian restaurants.

Barbadillo

Still run by the original family, Barbadillo is the most famous business in Sanlúcar de Barrameda on the Atlantic coast. The sea spray gives the Palomino grapes grown near the coast saline hints that are typical of a Manzanilla. We, personally, preferred the dry Manzanillas, young wines with strongly marked notes of flor yeast aldehydes that develop in the many casks (an astonishing 50,000) stored in the cathedral-like Barbadillo cellars. These are, of course, fortified wines, the alcohol being added during the winemaking process. They are then matured according to the solera system: barrels are placed one upon the other in four stages, the youngest wines being gradually moved down by gravity as they age from the top stage to the bottom (on the ground, or *solera*); meanwhile, the barrels at the bottom, containing perfectly mature wine ready for bottling, are emptied and filled by the wine from the level above. To understand how this slow and complex maturing process produces such original and accomplished wines – still little known in other parts of Europe – we recommend a visit to the wonderful cellars near the castle of Santiago.

A bull watches over the treasures in the cellars.

VINE VARIETY
1,234 acres (500 hectares) white: Palomino.

OUR FAVORITE WINES
This firm produces all the usual range of sherries, but, in addition, its most original product is Manzanilla with its hints of the sea coast, iodine, and salt. The Solear is the easiest to obtain and is highly reliable in quality. If not won over by this, you will be convinced by the more exclusive Muy Fina, or the even more interesting En Rama, should you should be lucky enough to find a bottle. The old reserves of the Reliquias collection, marketed in a beautiful carafe, are some of the very best examples of this type of wine, particularly the sublime Amontillado, a blend of the fabled soleras Soberana and Hindemburg.

Pedro Domecq

With very few exceptions, the largest of the wine-producing businesses in Andalusia have become so enormous that they can no longer be run by the individual Spanish families that created them. The Domecq family, whose name will be familiar to anyone interested in bullfighting, sold their business to Allied Lyons. It passed subsequently to Pernod Ricard, and will very likely become part of the Fortune Brands group. That said, a member of the Domecq family still runs the soleras and makes decisions about the house style. This is no small task, since it involves overseeing more than 100,000 barrels and the production of 18–20 million bottles a year. There are, perhaps, Fino sherries with more individual personality than La Ina, but they rarely have such refined aromas or reliability. Their airy lightness is due in great part to the manner in which they are produced. It is perhaps a pity that the law decrees that wines to be exported must be more fortified than those sold in the home market. A Fino drawn straight from the barrel, such as can be sampled in the sherry wineries, has a unique freshness and delicacy. Equally admirable is the skill with which the long pipette drawing off the sherry is handled.

VINE VARIETY

2,718 acres (1,100 hectares) white: Palomino, Pedro Ximenes.

OUR FAVORITE WINES

Known throughout the world, the great classic produced by this house is La Ina, a Fino sherry of admirable cleanness and reliability, modern in style but very pure. Of the range of wines given a further aging in soleras, the Sibarita Reservas such as Palo Cortado develop a delightful bouquet of walnut with an extraordinarily long finish.

Emilio Lustau

The best known ambassador for sherries in the world of wine, the Emilio Lustau company is still owned by the original family and remains faithful to the traditional and complex soleras production method. Its specialty is Amontillado, a Fino sherry that has been aged to become more oxidative and to which no younger wine has been added. Its darker, amber color and more pronounced rancio, giving a delicious bouquet of baked apples, makes it suitable to accompany hot dishes that do not go well with the more delicate Fino. Perhaps even more exciting in aromatic terms than the Palomino is the company's other specialty, a solera Muscatel (the Iberian version of Muscat). The oldest Muscats are used in the making of Las Cruces as they are also in that of the "single cask" wines, and have a caramel bouquet that is truly remarkable. These wines make a perfect ending to a meal, perhaps with a mild Havana cigar.

VINE VARIETY

Bought-in grapes: Palomino, Moscatel, Pedro Ximenez, in quantities sufficient for around 5 million bottles.

OUR FAVORITE WINES

Just as the name of the more recently founded Barbadillo company has become identified with Manzanilla, so has that of Emilio Lustau with Amontillado sherry from Jerez. The limestone soil (albariza) on which the grapes, purchased from a large number of different suppliers, are cultivated is ideal for this inimitable aperitif wine, itself a delicious accompaniment to Spanish ham and tapas. The Reserva Escuadrilla, with its delicate rancio, is the most sophisticated of the wines, but more original are the "single cask" wines made in traditional soleras. Available all over Spain, these are strictly selected.

Andalusia: the strange lunar landscape of these limestone hills is perfect for vines.

Bodegas
Julian Chivite

Established in the 19th century, and still run with great success by descendants of the original family, this large bodega has recently been expanded at Arinzano by the construction of some of the most beautiful buildings in the world for wine producing, designed by the architect Rafael Moneo. These buildings provide a perfect backdrop for the prestige wines of the house, the Coleccion 125, created for the bodega's 125th anniversary. Many different grape varieties thrive and mature in the soil and microclimate of this important vineyard, without, however, acquiring a particularly distinctive character. The outstanding quality of the Chardonnays and the red wine (an unusual combination of 60% Tempranillo and 40% Bordeaux varieties) is due to skillful blending and very careful cultivation. The Muscat is in a different category altogether, and is unrivaled in Europe. The delicately mellow Gran Feudo, fresh and fruity, is a very fine wine, but the 20,000 bottles of the unforgettable Coleccion cuvée, worthy of the very best of the world's *grains nobles* varieties, represent a kind of apotheosis of *petit grain* Muscats.

VINE VARIETY
1,458 acres (590 hectares) white and red: Chardonnay, Muscat, Tempranillo, Cabernet Sauvignon, Merlot, Grenache.

OUR FAVORITE WINES
All the wines produced by this bodega are of high quality, culminating with the red and white series, Coleccion 125. The Chardonnays are notable for their lightness, finesse, and cleanness of expression. However, like the reds, they are somewhat lacking in character. By contrast, the El Candelero vineyard, planted with Muscat grapes that are harvested late in the season when some of the grapes have become botrytized (with "noble rot"), produces a sublime sweet wine of great finesse that is arguably the most delicious example of this grape variety anywhere in the world. The 2003 has already become legendary.

Safe from fatal attack by the phylloxera insect, the first bud of a grafted vine stock emerges from its waxy covering.

Miguel Torres

The Torres family has been the most innovative and enterprising of any in Spanish viticulture since the Second World War. Its Catalan origins led it to turn to France – and the Bordeaux region in particular – for technical information. With regard to marketing, it looked to California and Chile where it has not only established its wines, but also successfully created and developed local vineyards. In each case the guiding philosophy has been to produce quality wines that are, nevertheless, of the style demanded by consumers seeking wines that are immediately accessible and easily identifiable, remaining similar from one vintage to the next. To do this, Miguel Torres has shaken up Catalan traditions favoring oxidative wines given a long maturation in oak casks, making significant innovations to winemaking methods and wine type. He has also introduced and established in the terroir some of the most famous European grape varieties. The French quickly took to his particular favorite, the Gran Coronas, and the rest of Europe followed. It is elsewhere among his list, though, that the most precious of his wines are to be found. Still clearly revealing their Catalan roots, they have a strong personality, characteristic particularly of the Conca de Barbera and Penedès wines.

VINE VARIETY

4,571 acres (1850 hectares) white: Chardonnay, Sauvignon, Muscat, Gewürztraminer, Riesling, Parellada, Macabeo, and others; red: Cabernet Sauvignon, Cabernet Franc, Merlot, Tempranillo, Pinot Noir, and others.

OUR FAVORITE WINES

This group produces an enormous quantity of wines, with an easily accessible style, from all the great grapes, either blended or single variety. Mireia Torres's remarkable enological abilities ensure their reliability and undeniable seductiveness. Our favorites are the Waltraud cuvée, a pure Riesling with a light mineral aroma, and, particularly, the red Grans Muralles from the Conca de Barbera appellation. The latter is a skillful blend of Catalan grapes, always unique and especially delicious in the 2001 vintage.

Álvaro Palacios

There are few more romantic and spectacular vineyards than those on the volcanic terraces of Priorat, an hour's drive inland from the Mediterranean coast. Here time seems to have stood still, with nothing to remind us of the contemporary world except perhaps the ultra-modern equipment of the major wine producers. A large family, the Palacios come originally from Rioja but only fully realized their dreams when they moved to their "new world" at Gratallops where they perfected a combination of tradition with modern methods in a dynamic balance that resulted immediately in wines of impressive personality. Pioneering the revival of Priorat wines with René Barbier of Clos Mogador in the same village, Álvaro Palacios has proved himself ever more determined to perfect his wines, controlling their rougher aspects and natural strength through skillful processing. Similarly, for his prestige cuvées he has sought to limit the influence of the Carignan grapes that can give a wine that is appealing when young but that does not age well. Instead, he gives higher importance to the marvelously intense Grenache grape, to which he adds a small quantity of Bordeaux varieties and some Syrah to refine the tannins. Some purists may disapprove, but the enthusiastic approval of both Spanish and foreign connoisseurs for Ermita and Finca Dofi would seem to show that his efforts have been entirely justified.

VINE VARIETY

62 acres (25 hectares) red: Grenache, Cabernet Sauvignon, Merlot, Syrah, Carignan.

OUR FAVORITE WINES

All the wines produced on the small-scale domaine reveal the hand of a master, the Ermita having a formal perfection that is most evident in the 1999 and 2000 vintages, and, to a lesser extent, in the 2003 (of which only 2,300 bottles were produced). This quality is also reflected in the Finca Dofi (a combination of four "noble" grape varieties) and Terrasses (mainly Carignan and Grenache grapes).

It would be hard to imagine any better way of cultivating the ancient hillsides of Priorat than by the traditional use of a man and a horse.

Bodegas
Gerardo Méndez Lázaro

Too much sun is the enemy of white wines that need to preserve freshness and acidity. It is not surprising, then, to find that the most suitable Spanish vineyards for making them are in the more temperate regions near the Atlantic coasts in the north of the country. The Rías Baixas zone produces large quantities of wines that are technically well made but should be drunk young. Very few producers dare leave the grapes to ripen fully lest the levels of acidity drop too far. Yet this degree of ripeness is necessary if the essence of an appellation and a particular terroir is to be fully expressed. Gerardo Méndez has fully understood this at his small vineyard in Val do Salnes, situated to the north of the appellation. By limiting the yield, he condenses the essence of the terroir, producing a wine that is fat, full-bodied, and harmonious. A good Albarino is best when drunk with a meal, since it does not have the aperitif and flowery aromas of a good Muscat or Sauvignon. Instead, in combination with the iodine of the wonderfully fresh Atlantic fish and seafood, it undergoes a metamorphosis, gaining in length and intensity, with a remarkable harmonious texture that Spanish sommeliers will not hesitate to recommend.

VINE VARIETY
12 acres (5 hectares) white: Albarino.

OUR FAVORITE WINES
Each time a tasting has been held of wines of this currently very fashionable appellation (one of the very few in Spain to produce exclusively white wines), the Cepas Vellas Do Ferreiro from this small, traditional domaine has been judged the best. The grapes used are harvested when fully ripe and processed in such a way that they avoid being overwhelmed by primary fermentation aromas. With perfect density, complexity and finish, everything is in place to make this a great wine, revealing all the potential of the Albarino grape.

Bodegas y Viñedos
Aalto

Aalto is the fruit of the association between two major figures in Ribera del Duero: Mariano García (a winemaker of many years' experience and for a long time in charge of production at Vega Sicilia), and Javier Zaccagnini (one-time director of the regulating council of the Ribera del Duero DO [*Denominación de Origen*], and someone who knows the local terroirs better than any). Choosing land near Roa, Quemada, and Gumiel, they established an ultra-sophisticated winery at Quintanilla de Arriba, opting for a deliberately "modern" style rather different from the wines made elsewhere by García. Nevertheless, beneath the first intensely oaky and toasty impression it is possible to distinguish the aromas of the great Tempranillos, and particularly the hints of balsam, leather, and berries that take over from the oak after about four or five years. Its clearly pronounced style requires it to be decanted a few hours before drinking, allowing the character of the terroir to develop fully. Only then can we properly appreciate the monumental nature of the body and texture, and the remarkably persistent aromas. This five-year-long experiment has already established itself as one of the most aristocratic wines of Spain.

VINE VARIETY

104 acres (42 hectares) red: Tinto Fino (Tempranillo).

OUR FAVORITE WINES

The first great wine from this property, established in 1999, was the 2000, a vintage with an astonishingly intense personality, clearly made with the greatest care and skill. The 2001, made from old vines (the already famous Aalto PS) repeated this first success, and the 2003 looks highly promising. Aalto is one of the most impressive examples of the prestige wines of this appellation, with their sumptuous bouquet, owing much to the high quality of the oak casks, but with something more that will ensure a great future.

Bodegas
Arzuaga Navarro

Quintanilla de Onésimo, lying along the road to Valladolid, is one of the most admired Ribera zones, particularly since the fabled Pingus began to be produced here. The wines are typically refined in texture, developing rapidly in the bottle. Florentino Arzuaga, enchanted by the beauty and serenity of the landscape of this appellation area, established the bodega in the early 1990s with the intention of producing modern-style wines. Although a business of considerable size, with cellars holding up to 3,000 casks and 200,000–250,000 bottles of reserve wine, the quality remains constant. A particularly attractive feature is that the somewhat bitter, chocolatey note characteristic of Tempranillo is softened by hints of spices resulting from the use of 5–10% Bordeaux grape varieties. For everyday drinking, Arzuaga produces La Planta, a fruity, supple wine made from young vines, with the hints of balsam and toast characteristic of this appellation. There is a luxurious hotel on the estate, making it an ideal place for a visit.

VINE VARIETY
371 acres (150 hectares) red: over 90% Tempranillo.

OUR FAVORITE WINES
The bodega's Tinto Crianza is one of the best examples of the new style now being produced in Ribera del Duero that brings out the elegance of the tannin. The grapes are harvested when very ripe and the wine matured in American oak casks. The Reserva has even greater definition and complexity, the 2000 being a notable example.

Tinto
Pesquera

Pesquera takes its name from the small village in the Ribera region where its bodega and vineyards are situated. The characteristic soils of the area give body, color, and tannin to the wines, together with a hint of spice in the bouquet. It comes as no surprise to learn that visionary winemakers such as Alejandro Fernandez and Emilio Mauro chose this as the area in which to produce their wines. An ardent devotee of the Tempranillo grape and local winemaking traditions, Dom Alejandro (as he is affectionately known locally) is the father of the movement to give new life to Ribera wines. Endowed with a unique understanding of commercial opportunities and public relations, he has successfully attracted an enthusiastic following from a number of international wine experts, establishing the Ribera appellation as the most prestigious Spanish wine in the world market. His Reserva has an unusually natural quality, avoiding the heaviness and excessiveness of many stereotypical modern-style wines that frequently have too great a level of alcohol. His wines retain a freshness combined with firm and flavorsome tannins; they can be enjoyed to best advantage with food rather than on their own. However, serious competition from a number of wine producers who are even more rigorous in terms of cultivation and winemaking is beginning to make itself felt.

VINE VARIETY

297 acres (120 hectares) red: Tempranillo.

OUR FAVORITE WINES

The wines produced by the Alejandro Fernandez bodega celebrate the Tempranillo grape traditional to the Ribera region. This variety gives a wine that is powerful but austere, because the level of acidity has not dropped too far. Those cuvées that have matured longest in wood are the most refined and sought-after. The special selection Millennium produces at least 20,000 bottles, but only in the best vintage years. Now rightly regarded as something of a cult wine, it is unusually successful in balancing a combination of robustness and refinement. The 2002 will be a worthy member in the ranks of this range.

Bodegas
Vega Sicilia

Vega Sicilia is one of the most important wine-producing houses in the world. Its fame is equal to the environment in which it is produced, with a terroir and a microclimate that are unique and unmatched in all Spain. It is owned by members of the Alvares family, perfectionists who are aware not only of their good fortune but also, more acutely, of their duties. A visit to the bodega makes clear that, when aiming for this degree of quality and fame, the magnificent surroundings alone are not enough. There is also a need for technical installations of the highest quality, and one can only marvel at the care taken as the grapes arrive and are processed by gravity over the vats; meanwhile the purity of the atmosphere in the chambers where the Unico is slowly aged is astonishing. Sometimes in spotless casks of French oak, sometimes in new barrels, the air is scented with an unforgettable odor of heather honey and spices, aromas that will also be found in the wine. The most recent and pet venture of the technical team at the bodega is white wine. Unlikely as it might seem, until recently the limestone soils of the upper zone of the vineyard, so favorable to white grapes, were planted with nothing but red varieties. If the resulting white wines come up to the owners' expectations, Spain will soon have its first truly great dry white wine.

Beloved by gods, this bodega is also a place of pilgrimage for wine lovers.

VINE VARIETY
*346 acres (140 hectares) red: 90% Tempranillo,
10% Cabernet Sauvignon, Merlot, and others.*

OUR FAVORITE WINES
*Everything produced by this bodega is unique and essential.
The Valbuena No. 5 takes its name from the village where it is produced and from the fact that it is not presented for sale until five years after the harvest. It is a perfect expression of a great terroir. However, the supreme example is the Unico – a wine not as exclusive as might be thought from its name, since more than 80,000 bottles are produced. The unique aging method, using alternating sizes and shapes of wooden containers, gives the wine a magical fullness and velvety smoothness, as well as an unusually long finish for a red wine. Forthcoming vintages promise to be superb, made better by recent improvements in production methods, and benefiting from the high standards of hygiene in the new winery.*

Dominio de
Pingus

The Pingus story is very much of our time. Peter Sisseck, nephew of the great Danish enologist Peter Vinding and a specialist on the fine wines of the Libournais and Burgundy regions, fell in love with the vine-covered landscape of the Ribera area and the quality of the grapes produced there. Identifying historic vines from the most esteemed plots, Sisseck turns the grapes into wine according to the principles of his "garagiste" friends in Saint-Émilion and of their mentor Alain Vauthier, owner of Château Ausone. The skill used in the preparation of these wines has not escaped the notice of Robert Parker, who has given the highest score ever awarded to a Spanish wine to the house's first vintage. Produced in minuscule quantities, a bottle can cost a king's ransom. All that Sisseck needed was to find an ideal spot where he could pursue his dream. His eye fell on a building on the banks of the Duero river, by Quintanilla, and it was here that he constructed a small but perfect fermenting room. With its rich texture and soft tannins, Pingus rises to heights previously unknown in Spanish wine. Equally deserving of its worldwide success is a second cuvée, Flor de Pingus, which more obviously expresses the character of the terroir, being made of grapes harvested from soils rich in manganese, giving a taste that is more mineral-rich.

RIBERA DEL DUERO · DENOMINACIÓN DE ORIGEN

PINGUS
2003

Embotellado por Dominio de Pingus, S.L.R.E.: 7268-VA
Quintanilla de Onesimo. (Valladolid)
Alc. 14% Vol.   PRODUCE OF SPAIN   750 ml

VINE VARIETY
12 acres (5 hectares) red: Tempranillo.

OUR FAVORITE WINES
Pingus and Flor de Pingus are two so-called "garage" wines (luxury wines produced on a small scale), produced in minute quantities but of spectacular quality. Quickly becoming cult items, with prices to match, they offer, not surprisingly, an explosion of aromas and an accompanying silky oakiness. Here we sense the presence of a great terroir and the hand of a great winemaker, and, concealed beneath the spectacular appearance of the young wine, is astonishing finesse of texture and perfection of form that has never before been known in this region of Spain. The 2003, marked by the stifling heat of summer, will shock the purist, but no one could resist the elegance of the 2000 and 2001 vintages.

Compañia de vinos
Telmo Rodriguez

The company, created in 1994 by the enologists Telmo Rodriguez and Pablo Eguzniza, is one of the most interesting ventures in European viticulture in recent years. Rodriguez, a gifted winemaker, was beginning to feel the limitations of the family vineyard at Remelluri in the Rioja region. Aware of the wonderful grape and wine heritage of his country, but also of changes in the public's tastes and expectations, he decided to produce modern wines in all his favorite appellations. Working closely with his grape suppliers, he created a technical team that shared his vision. His style is very different from two all too frequently encountered tendencies: the conservatism of producers with an almost religious regard for the terroir who will justify any faults in their wines as being the authentic expression of their origin; and the excesses of over-enthusiastic modernizers who overwhelm this same terroir with oak and technology. His preference is for clean, elegant, and harmonious wines that have immediately found favor with the public.

VINE VARIETY

No vineyard; grapes of a large number of appellations are bought in.

OUR FAVORITE WINES

All the wines produced by this small and innovative company are notable for their sense of balance, mouthfeel, and fidelity to the expression of the terroir. Of the Riojas, the Altos de Lanzaga is one of the most harmonious examples of the new, non-oxidative style of the appellation; the same is true of the Ribera del Duero Matallana. Our particular favorite, though, is the astonishing sweet Muscat of Malaga, Molino Real, which for aromatic splendor is as good as that produced by the Bodega Julian Chivite.

Marqués de Griñón

A member of the Spanish aristocracy and, more importantly, a major winemaker, Carlos Falco is also an agronomist, enologist, and connoisseur. The owner of a magnificent but arid estate near Toledo, a visit to Israel to see the vineyards and their sophisticated irrigation systems proved a revelation. If it was possible to ripen grapes in the desert, then it would certainly be possible to do the same in Spain. The results exceeded all expectations. Falco has been able to adapt Bordeaux varieties and, using a clever system of drip-irrigation, a Petit Verdot with even riper tannins than those found in Médoc. The chalky soil proved to be a further advantage, adding quality and complexity to the bouquet and structure of all the grape varieties. Today, Falco's exemplary methods have resulted in Emeritus, one of the most original and refined red wines to be found in Spain. The Syrah grapes contribute an intensely balsamic bouquet and a touch of voluptuousness – something that, because of an outdated regulation, modern Bordeaux wines have to forgo (although this was not the case in the past). The single-variety Petit Verdot wines can sometimes be astonishingly successful – richly vigorous with smooth tannins. The 1999 is now fully mature, with a magnificent bouquet.

VINE VARIETY
111 acres (45 hectares) red: Cabernet Sauvignon, Petit Verdot, Syrah.

OUR FAVORITE WINES
Carlos Falco likes to make unblended, single-variety wines, some being more successful than others. That made with Petit Verdot grapes is outstanding (not least for its remarkable fullness), as is the more fruity, supple Syrah. Greatest of all, however, is the Emeritus, a blend of the best cuvées of the three varieties. While the 2002 is slightly disappointing, the 1998 and 1999 are sensational.

The planting of rows of free-standing bush vines has only become popular in the last hundred years.

Bodegas Fernando
Remírez de Ganuza

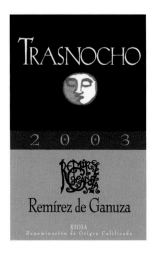

In the past, winemaking in the Rioja Alavesa concentrated on producing wines to be drunk very young from the fruity grapes for which the area was famous. It took a visionary mind and outstanding vine cultivator, Fernando Remírez de Ganuza, to understand that the clay-limestone soil of Alava could produce grapes of a much more refined quality. In a similar way to Álvaro Palacios, he took what was best from both traditional and modern methods to produce a unique style. His Riojas are characterized by their deep color, the lack of any hint of oxidation, and an indication of a perfectly judged period of maturation in oak casks. The finest aromas of Tempranillo, black cherry, blackberry, and spice reveal themselves from the first with an unsuspected suaveness and distinction. While not perhaps as intense as that found in the best Ribera del Duero wines, the full and generous structure of this wine surpasses them in pure refinement and well-integrated oakiness. The Tinto Joven, Erre Punto, produced by the carbonic maceration method, has a very pure fruitiness, very different from the oaky and strongly vanilla-flavored decoctions still favored, unfortunately, by many local producers.

VINE VARIETY
131 acres (53 hectares) red: 90% Tempranillo,
10% others (Graciano, Grenache, Cabernet Sauvignon).

OUR FAVORITE WINES
In the last few years, Trasnoccho, the domaine's prestige cuvée, has arguably represented the pinnacle of Rioja wines. Few can rival the density, naturalness, and beautiful finish of the 2001 and 2003 vintages. Standing alongside these is the equally fine Reserva 1998 Remírez de Ganuza, a masterpiece of harmony, and triumph of modern methods in this appellation.

Vinos de los Herederos del
Marqués de Riscal

Awarded many medals in the great international fairs held in the 19th century, this famous and long-established name has marked the beginning of a new millennium with the construction of a spectacular winery designed by the architect Frank Gehry, who was also responsible for the celebrated Guggenheim Museum. The high plateaus of the Rioja Alta and Rioja Alaves, with their clay-limestone soils, have a semi-continental microclimate with chilly nights that give the Tempranillo grapes an unequaled finesse. The wines produced in the 1990s display this to its best advantage. After too many vintages that can best be described as pedestrian, the house has currently rediscovered the secrets of these complex and almost immortal wines, adding a small proportion of Mazuelo and Graciano grapes, and perhaps even a discrete quantity of Bordeaux varieties. This would explain the longer finish and the subtlety of the tannins of recent vintages of the Baron de Chirel, the bodega's special cuvée. This wine, though, represents only a tiny proportion of what is made here. Five million bottles are produced annually, half of which will be exported, using 37,000 American oak casks.

VINE VARIETY
544 acres (220 hectares) red: over 90% Tempranillo.

OUR FAVORITE WINES
The quality of the classic wines (Reserva and Gran Reserva) in the current range from this estate is somewhat variable, although their oakiness is more straightforward and better integrated than in the past. By contrast, the new Baron de Chirel cuvée has equaled the success of the Dalmau made by the Marqués de Murrieta bodega, and in much larger quantities (200,000 bottles). A combination of refined bouquet and texture, precision of fruit tastes, and long finish make this a modern classic of the Rioja region. The 2001 looks set to rival the remarkable 1996 vintage.

The traditional Médoc vat as used in the heart of the Rioja region: a symbol of the longstanding links between the two vineyards.

Bodegas
Marqués de Murrieta

This long-established business in the Rioja region was the first to introduce the idea of the Bordeaux-style château to Spain with the creation of its "Château Ygay," now called "Castello Ygay." The Tempranillo grapes produced on the family's vast domaine have long been known for their finesse and delicacy. Local tradition and the Spanish taste for very oaky wines mean that they are matured for a long time in wooden casks. Non-Spaniards will always find the Reserva and Gran Reserva wines somewhat strange and exotic, the wood having the effect of over-drying the tannins and even dominating the natural refinement of the terroir. This is why Vincente Dalmau Cebrian, one of the estate's owners, took on the challenge of creating a new and more modern-style wine, where the characteristics of the grape variety and the initial style of the wine are better preserved even after fermentation. The cuvée bearing his name immediately met with the approval of local connoisseurs. It marks an irreversible evolution in the best of the Rioja wines where we now see a greater intensity of color and depth combined with a velvety texture. The period of maturation in wooden casks is now shorter than previously (19 months). Another specialty of this estate is a curious and original white wine made from Viura grapes. It has the classic Spanish hints of dried fruit, cinnamon, and nutmeg, but again it is apparent that this is a wine that is beginning to make concessions to the "modern style."

VINE VARIETY

741 acres (300 hectares) red: over 90% Tempranillo.

OUR FAVORITE WINES

The most important wine in a long list produced by this great and ancient house is the Dalmau cuvée. Despite very limited quantities (20,000 bottles), it marks a high point in the winemaker's skill. It uses 10% Cabernet Sauvignon grapes to give greater complexity to the tannins. However, it is mainly the Tempranillo grapes that dominate the taste of the blend and dictate the style of the wine – majestic, with a generous bouquet of black olives and hints of toast. The superb 2000 and 2001 point the way toward the development of the famous Ygay cuvée, a classic of this house and one with the driest of tannins.

Bodegas y Viñedos
Pintia

In a desire to diversify its holdings of vineyards, Vega Sicilia did not have to travel far to find a terroir worthy of its interest. The sandy-clay soils between Valladolid and Zamora are remarkably well suited to the Tempranillo grape, allowing it to develop all the rich potential of its aromatic range. The winemaker Xavier Ausas has applied the same principles as at Valbueno, including harvesting only optimally mature grapes, carefully handling the grapes using gravity (free run), plus a slow and carefully controlled maturation in barrels that are 70% French wood and 30% American – the first bringing the delicate finesse of its tannins, the second the sugars that soften the natural robustness of this grape variety. As is common practice in Spain, in addition to its own grapes the bodega also buys those harvested from well-established local vineyards. The first vintage to go on sale, the 2001, has an impressive authority and openness with notable density and form. The 2002 and 2003 are further milestones along the route toward an even greater finesse of tannin extraction, bringing out increasingly complex aromatic subtleties. A very stylish product has been born, confirming the hopes invested in this new project. It will not be long before its true value is recognized by the connoisseur.

VINE VARIETY
222 acres (90 hectares) red: Tinta di Toro (Tempranillo).

OUR FAVORITE WINES
Following the Bordeaux model, this bodega makes just one wine, Pintia, made entirely of Tempranillo grapes. From the first, this wine impressed connoisseurs with its power and the strong personality of its terroir. Noticeable are the balsamic notes characteristic of Ribera del Duero wines, together with a similar hint of bitter chocolate. It is beautifully smooth, although the technical team at Vega Sicilia maintains it is still a little rough. The 2003 vintage (134,000 bottles) is remarkable.

Portugal

Portugal's position on the Atlantic coast is of great benefit to its viticulture, tempering the violent summer heat and lengthening the maturation cycle of the grapes. Nevertheless, in the past the average quality of Portuguese wines left much to be desired, and the red wines produced from the vast vineyards of Alentejo and Ribatejo lacked distinction. This situation has changed, though, and today many attractive, fruity, and expressive table wines are beginning to appear, and deserve to be better known internationally. Inland from the coast, we see the same phenomenon with the famous Dão vineyards producing increasingly good wines.

Outside Portugal, the most famous Portuguese wine is, of course, port. The two finest versions of this fortified wine are vintage port (bottled young to preserve all the vigor of the grapes), and tawny port (aged in wooden casks for a long period to give a smoother texture and inimitable aromas of dried fruits and walnuts). Recently, new red wines have been developed by the large companies of the Douro region using the best grape varieties such as Touriga Nacional and Tinta Roriz. The body and aromatic complexity of these wines immediately places them among the very best in the country.

List of domaines

Porto
Adriano Ramos Pinto

The champagne house Roederer acquired this firm in 1880, relatively recently in terms of the history of the port-producing houses of Portugal. The size of the task of managing the many properties – particularly the superb and unusual Quinta da Ermavoira in the Douro valley, and its fascinating archeological museum – proved to be, perhaps, bigger than anticipated. Nevertheless, Jean-Claude Rouzaud and his teams set about the task with characteristic perfectionism. Today the marque is well-respected for its stylish ports which emphasize refinement over power. The smooth red wines are a carefully blended mixture of grapes from hot climates combined with others from vines grown at higher altitudes and cooler temperatures – from the Quintas Bom Retiro and Bons Ares (hence the name Duas Quintas, "two quintas"). The smoother, more civilized tannins of these Bordeaux-inspired wines distinguish them from others of the Douro region. The remarkable technical director of the company, João Nicolau de Almeida, established the broad lines of the house's philosophy early on. He realized that it was important to control supplies by having a large house vineyard, while emphasizing the historical aspects of the house and the estates of the Douro valley to underline the marque's pedigree.

VINE VARIETY

Quinta Bom Retiro: 153 acres (62 hectares) red: 25% Tinta Barroca, 20% Touriga Nacional, 15% Touriga Francesa, 20% Tinta Roriz, 20% mixed.
Quinta da Ermavoira: 371 acres (150 hectares) white: 10% (various); red: 16% Tinta Barroca, 23% Touriga Nacional, 13% Touriga Francesa, 13% Tinta Roriz, 10% Tinta da Barca, 15% mixed.
Quinta Bons Ares: 49 acres (20 hectares) white: 35% Viozinho and Riesling; red: 30% Cabernet-Sauvignon, 10% Touriga Nacional, 25% other.
Quinta da Urtiga: 10 acres (4 hectares) mixed.

OUR FAVORITE WINES

Although the vintage ports have, in recent years, much improved in character, the traditional strength of the house lies in its old tawnies. Ten, 20, and 30 years old, they are increasingly produced from a single quinta, the fruit and rancio being well balanced and giving a long finish. Also popular is Adriano, a younger wine that has been cleverly blended to give a fine and long finish.

Chryseia

The Symington family, producers of some of the greatest vintage port wines, are also admirers of Bordeaux wines. Thus it was natural for them to get together with Bruno Prats to create a new and fine red wine in the Douro valley, attempting what many others had tried but failed to do. They had no hesitation in agreeing that the grapes to be selected from the many local vineyards should be Touriga Nacional and Touriga Francesa, varieties with a balance that would adapt well to this type of wine, coming from areas where the fruit generally matures late in the season. To this would be added a certain quantity of Tinto Roriz. The wine is made according to the principles of the Bordeaux school. Rather than striving for immediate impact, the makers seek to bring out the best tannins from the grapes and to give the wine a high quality finish. Chryseia immediately distinguished itself from other locally produced wines with its superior harmony and smoother, less aggressive texture. While some connoisseurs continued to prefer the more traditional style of Douro wines, many others were converted. Today, demand has outstripped production. The 2003 can only further enhance the reputation of this generous wine, which makes a fine accompaniment to a meal.

The sublime Douro Valley is one of the most spectacular vine-covered landscapes in the world and part of our human heritage.

VINE VARIETY

In the Symington vineyards in the Douro valley, red: Touriga Nacional, Touriga Francesa, Tinto Roriz.

OUR FAVORITE WINES

Since its creation, Chryseia has consistently been one of the most harmonious and reliable Portuguese wines available. While the choice of grapes used can vary from one vintage to another, the philosophy remains unchanged: to produce a red wine from the best grapes of the Douro valley with the qualities of elegance, balance, and complexity of the greatest European wines. The 2003, which has rather more body than the previous vintages, is a perfect example of this ambition.

Croft Port

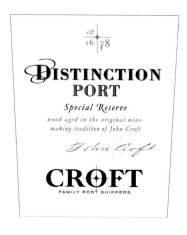

Established in the 17th century, the house became known as John Croft in 1736. After a number of changes of ownership, it is now part of the small empire formed by descendents of the Yeatman and Flatgate families, as are Taylor's and Fonseca. The Guimaraens family, who now run the business, have cleverly maintained the different characters and styles of each of the houses, these being related – in the case of the vintage and single-quinta ports, at least – to the grapes available to them. Here, the style of the wine is determined by those produced at the famous Quinta de Roeda, described by the 19th-century Portuguese poet Vega Cabral as the diamond in the crown of Douro wines. The natural vigor of the terroirs of the central Douro valley found in some other grapes, often giving wines that when young are somewhat too aggressive, is less apparent in the Quinta de Roeda grapes. They have, on the other hand, an impressive fruitiness evoking liqueur cherries and blackcurrants, with tannins that are never too dominant. The single-quinta, non-vintage ports made here are given a slightly abbreviated maturation, although even here we are talking about a period of more than a human generation. As is often the case with English companies, wines like the tawny ports that are aged to develop the rancio quality are less memorable.

VINE VARIETY

Quinta de Roeda, red: Touriga Nacional, Touriga Francesa, Tinto Roriz, Tinto Barroco.

OUR FAVORITE WINES

The evidence of recent vintage ports produced by this historic house seems to show that they have continued to improve under the intelligent management of Bruce Guimaraens. The magnificent grapes from the Quinta de Roeda play an important part in this success. The perfect timing determining when to add the fortifying spirit to arrest fermentation gives a smoothness such as that found in Taylor's ports but with slightly less heaviness. The result is a perfect compromise, with an impressive fruitiness. The tawny ports have less personality.

Dow's Port

The history of the great port-making houses of Oporto is complicated, with interlinked vineyards and families. In 1877, the name Dow replaced the earlier names of Silva (1798) and Cosens (1862). Today, the firm belongs to the Symington family, who have demonstrated their affection for this house with the construction of an imposing new and modern winery at Quinta do Sol. This quinta has several vineyards planted on cleverly reconstructed terraces with an open southerly aspect. Advantage is taken of differences in soil types and rainfall – ranging from 15 to 30 inches (400 to 800 millimeters) – to create a vintage of unique complexity. From Bomfim come depth and a velvety smoothness, the pink schist of Ribeira gives a unique perfume of violets (reminiscent of a Latour), while Quinta do Santinho contributes to the robustness and power characteristic of a very dry microclimate. The style of the grapes is also very suitable for making crusted (or crusting) ports. These blends of wines from three or four years are fermented in the bottle, and often have a more expressive character than vintage port.

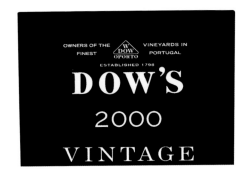

VINE VARIETY

Quinta do Bomfim: 121 acres (49 hectares):
22% Touriga Francesa, 12% Touriga Nacional, 12% Tinta Roriz,
11% Tinta Barroca, 40% various very old vine varieties.
Quinta do Santinho: 35 acres (14 hectares).
Quinta Senhora da Ribeira: 52 acres (21 hectares).

OUR FAVORITE WINES

The vintage ports made by the Symington family for this company are admirable. In style they appear somewhat drier – not because of any lack of untransformed sugar, but because of the pronounced character of the terroirs of the Bomfim and Santinho quintas. This is characterized by firm, mineral-like tannins that give an uprightness of impact reminiscent of a Château Latour. The 2000 and 2003 are excellent and perhaps more complete than the astonishing 1994 and 1997 vintages. Unusually for an English-style company, the old tawny ports are also very good.

Ferreira Port

An integral part of the huge international group Sogrape, this old Portuguese firm, established in 1751, has lost nothing of its prestige in Portugal. Its inheritance of first-class vineyards, found in many different areas of the Douro valley, ensures a constant supply of high-quality grapes – those from Quinta do Porto contributing elegance, and those from Quinta do Caedo robustness. As is often the case with Portuguese firms, attention is also paid to first impressions, since they are designed for consumption on the spot. White port, often a rather insipid wine, here has a remarkable mellowness, due to the selection of clay rather than schist soils. The tawny ports retain a fresh and clear rancio with unusual aromas of mandarin and citrus. It should not be forgotten that Ferreira also produces the most prestigious of all Portuguese red wines, a blend of grapes from many sources. Some very old vintages of the Barca Velha have a finesse of bouquet – recalling that of the very best Burgundies – that might almost induce the wine lover to weep tears of joy.

VINE VARIETY

Quinta da Leda, Quinta do Seixo, Quinta do Porto, Quinta do Caedo: 371 acres (150 hectares): Tinta Roriz.

OUR FAVORITE WINES

This house is not famous for its vintage ports, and since they are not much sought after, it concentrates on marketing many non-vintage wines. As they mature, their quality can be remarkable, with a finesse and fruity youthfulness that will come as a pleasant surprise to those who find port wines too heavy. The tawny ports are remarkable, particularly the single-quinta tawnies, Quinta do Porto (10 years old) and Duque de Bragança (20 years old).

Fonseca Port

The Guimaraens family bought the Fonseca business in 1822, and have been in charge of this much respected firm – part of the Taylor group – ever since. It is currently run by David Guimaraens, who seems to be as talented as his father, Bruce, before him. The firm specializes in vintage ports, produced mainly from grapes from the Quinta do Panascal that are still trodden in the traditional way in a *lagar*, a low-sided cement or stone trough. These ports are notable for their velvety robustness. The young wine is fiery, demanding a long aging period. The name Guimaraens is used only relatively rarely for the vintage ports, about three times every decade. The great vintages of the 1990s have continued to gain in refinement of texture without losing any of their legendary fullness of body. As for the other types of port, there seems to have been a slight move in the last ten years towards more supple wines that have less of the strong and even violent minerality (the famous taste of sun-warmed volcanic rock) for which they were previously celebrated. The firm has recently installed specially designed mechanical vats, nicknamed "port-toes," that punch down the cap of grape and other solids (*pigeage*), an innovation that has certainly contributed to this subtle change in style.

VINE VARIETY

Quinta do Panascal and Quinta do Val do Muros: 109 acres (44 hectares) red: Tinta Roriz, Tinta Barroca, Touriga Nacional, Touriga Francesa, Tinto Cao.

OUR FAVORITE WINES

As is usual with the English firms in Portugal, this house concentrates on producing vintage port. Robust and rich in style, sometimes verging on heavy, it ages very well. The year 1994 was outstanding, giving a very high quality wine, other equally good years were 1966, 1970, and 1997. While the tawny ports are less impressive, the late bottled vintage and non-vintage ports (labeled Guimaraens rather than Fonseca) are among the best available.

W. & J. Graham's Port

It was not until 1970 that the Symington family, Scottish in origin, bought the long-established company of Graham's, also founded by a Scot, merging it with Croft and Dow's. The modern winery at Malvedos and, in particular, an ingenious system with mechanical *lagar* enabling the temperature to be carefully controlled have made it possible to improve the quality while still respecting the wine's style to produce an almost ideal balance of power and amiability. While at one time the fruitiness of some of the vintage ports lacked subtlety, today it offers a new type of Douro classicism, with a perfect balance of the mineral notes of the volcanic soil and the red and black (ripe blackcurrant) berry aromas of grapes that are ripe, but not too ripe. One of the reasons for this success seems to be the complementary nature of the quintas: the very sunny, south-facing Malvedos and the cooler Vila Velha. Equally admirable is the quality of the mutage, thanks to the purity of the alcohol used to arrest fermentation. Another wine produced here that is worthy of note is the lively and classy crusted port, bottled when still quite young and aged in the bottle for three or four years.

VINE VARIETY

Quinta dos Malvedos: 173 acres (70 hectares) red: Tinta Roriz, Tinta Barroca, Touriga Nacional, Touriga Francesa, Quinta da Vila Velha, Quinta do Vale de Malhadas.

OUR FAVORITE WINES

In recent years, the reliability of quality of the wines made by this firm has much improved. Modern but beautifully crafted, their production is supervised by Charles Symington. The 2000 and 2003 vintages are models of harmony, the crusted port is full of character, and the tawnies have charm, depth, and freshness.

A large number of casks are needed to age the best tawny ports for 30 years or more. The cool and damp cellars at Vila Nova with their beaten earth floors are ideal for this long process of maturation.
The soil and grapevines are damaged less when horses are used for ploughing.

Niepoort Port

Dick Niepoort has raised his old family business (founded in 1842) to a hitherto unimaginable level of quality and fame. Initially, he devoted his energies to producing highly original red wines – first Redoma in 1991, then Elegance (made from the best grapes of the Vale Mendiz vineyards) and Batuta ("conductor's baton"). The latter was the most characteristic of its terroir, being produced from old vines grown in the heart of Cima Cargo. This is not to suggest that he neglected port wines. The vintage ports are uniquely refined yet, at the same time, are capable of delivering the volcanic notes so characteristic of the type of wine. The 2000 and 2003 vintages are perhaps the most accomplished. Nor are the more modest categories forgotten. The simple ruby port, quite light in color but with a youthful liveliness, cannot be bettered. Its bouquet of red berries is evidence of the care taken in its production. All Nogueira's skill and artistry is revealed in the magnificent tawnies. The current ten-year-old is the most subtle and aristocratic of any that we have tried, but there is not one that is not successful, as is proved by an astonishing 40-year-old. It only remains now for this important house to come up with a really great white port. Dick Niepoort and associates have, furthermore, taken over the management of the vineyards of Quinta do Passadouro. Here, independently of the mother house but with the same philosophy, he produces magnificent ports.

VINE VARIETY

*Quinta de Napoles: 86 acres (35 hectares) red,
of all the appellation varieties.
Quinta do Carril: 22 acres (9 hectares) red,
of all the appellation varieties.*

OUR FAVORITE WINES

Dick Niepoort and his trusted colleague José Nogueira can be numbered among the ranks of the best tasters and connoisseurs of this appellation. Every type of wine produced here reveals both their passion and their skill, having a finesse and accuracy in the expression of the terroir that sets a standard by which all others can be judged. Although one of the last firms to produce them, we have a particular soft spot for their Garrafeiras. These sometime sublime single-vintage wines are aged for as long as possible in large glass demijohns holding 17–21 pints (8–10 liters). The tawnies are no less impressive.

The soil and the grapevines are damaged less, when horses are used for ploughing.

Warre's Port

Founded in 1670, this is the oldest house in Oporto. It has been part of the Symington empire since a member of that family went into business with the owners of the marque in 1882. Although currently lagging a little behind the more successful Graham marque, the products of this house have retained all their style and quality. These owe much to the relatively late harvested grapes of the Quinta da Cavadinha, where production takes place in a very modern winery. The range of late bottled vintages is particularly attractive with a striking, almost exotic, bouquet with refined hints of tobacco and violets. Somewhat unusually for a British firm, it has sought to make tawny ports of a more delicate style that appeals more to the Portuguese who like a light color and ester-rich bouquets. Of the young blends, Warrior is a classic of its kind, with a good color, spicy aroma, and attractive taste that make it suitable for drinking both with food and on its own.

VINE VARIETY

Quinta de Cavadinha: area and grape varieties not given, probably on account of the changes being carried out at this partly experimental vineyard.

OUR FAVORITE WINES

This English firm specializes in the production of rich, mellow vintage ports that are often better balanced than other more famous brands. Recently, improvements have been made in the elegant and complex Otima range of tawny ports. Another impressive product here is the late bottled vintage 1992, a sumptuous and well-developed wine.

Taylor's Port

T aylor's is the flagship of the group of companies owned by the Guimaraens family and their relatives. It benefits from having a vast vineyard situated in an ideal spot in the heart of Cima Corgo, with mainly northern and western aspects that prevent the grapes from exposure to too much sun. Here, the producers have perfected a style of vintage port that has earned the admiration of English and American customers for its spectacular power in which mutage plays a vital role. The high tannin content ensures a slow and reliable aging. With age, the great classic vintages of the 1960s and 1970s acquire aristocratic aromas of tobacco and spices so reminiscent of the great Hermitages that, if one did not known better, one would imagine that Syrah grapes were included in the blend. Today, the strong personality of the vintage ports seems to have been tempered somewhat, even if the essential richness still impresses. Another strength of this house's wines – and a type pioneered here – is the late bottled vintage that manages to retain all its vigor and density, together with a clearly stated aromatic complexity. These qualities are linked to the excellence of the grapes varieties used, including – we are delighted to find – a small quantity of the too-little used Tinta Cão.

VINE VARIETY

590 acres (235 hectares) consisting of:
Quinta de Vargellas: 287 acres (116 hectares) red: 25% Touriga Nacional, 25% Touriga Francesa, 22% Tinta Roriz, 6% Tinta Cao, 7% Tinta Amarela, 7% Tinta Barroca, 8% others.
Quinta de Terra Freita: 151 acres (61 hectares): 13% Touriga Nacional, 27% Touriga Francesa, 22% Tinta Roriz, 4% Tinta Cao, 13% Tinta Barroca, 7% Tinta Amarela, 14% others.
Quinta do Junco: 119 acres (48 hectares): 20% Touriga Nacional, 15% Touriga Francesa, 20% Tinta Roriz, 10% Tinta Cao, 20% Tinta Baroca, 15% Tinta Amarela.

OUR FAVORITE WINES

A firm bearing the stamp of English tastes in port, Taylor's is known particularly for its imposing vintage ports from the Vargellas and Terra Freita quintas. Certainly the most powerful, rich, and sugary of any on the market, these ports become much more refined with age. The bottom-of-the-range wines lack character, and the tawnies are not the firm's strong point.

The grapes are tread in lagars, which are broad, shallow vats of cement that preserve the must at a constant and ideal temperature until it is fortified.

Quinta de la
Rosa

The Bergquist family has been linked with Quinta de la Rosa since 1905. One of Philip Bergquist's ancestors was the first to lay claim to the production of a single-quinta vintage port that appeared under his name in 1924 and 1927. The vicissitudes of history have meant that this property fell into decline and was not renewed until 1988. Major work to reconstruct the terraces increased the vineyard from 15 to 136 acres (6 to 55 hectares), and today the domaine is a little Eden with tidy *patamares* (modern-style terraces) and a luxurious hotel. It produces olive oil and some excellent table wines. For the production of the vintage wines, the traditional method of treading the grapes in granite *lagars* continues, although *pigeage* vats, where the grapes are automatically punched down, are also used. Philip Bergquist personally supervises the winemaking process, assisted by one of the most brilliant enologists of the younger generation, Jorge Moreira. They deserve praise for the consistency of style and quality of all the wines made at the quinta, produced exclusively from the quinta's own grapes. The dynamism of this firm has, almost certainly, contributed to the increased production of quinta wines, a phenomenon that can only delight wine lovers everywhere.

VINE VARIETY
Quinta de la Rosa, Quinta das Laemalas: 136 acres (55 hectares) red: Tinta Roriz, Tinta Barroca, Tinta Cao, Touriga Nacional, Touriga Francesa.

OUR FAVORITE WINES
The old vines of this quinta were still in production in 2000, giving an exceptionally dense and elegant vintage. The other specialty of this house is the Finest Reserve "Vintage Character," a wine of exemplary cleanness and complexity that can compare favorably with equivalents produced by more famous marques.

Quinta do
Infantado

The Roseira family bought the property at the end of the 19th century but, for a long time, confined themselves to growing grapes for sale to the big houses. It was not until 1986 that they began to export wines from grapes grown on the spot because until then only wines stored at Vila Nova de Gaia were granted the Port Wine Institute's (IVP) seal of authenticity. Since that time, João Roseira has been convinced that he can pursue his vision of port wine, creating a counterpoint to the larger houses with a restricted production of hand-crafted wines, similar to those created by his vigneron friends in France such as Emmanuel Raynaud of Château Rayas and Jean-Paul Brun in Beaujolais. The adoption of organic cultivation methods, continued use of the traditional *lagar* fermentation, and a very slow and progressive mutago for grapes that naturally contain a high level of sugar, has led to the production of a wine with a marked and unique personality. The complexity of its taste is due also to the use of several different and mixed grape varieties with different maturing patterns. The late bottled vintage is also to be recommended, while Roseira's version of ruby port, rather than being second-best, is a wine that is a complete expression of the fruit of the best grapes from high quality vineyards.

VINE VARIETY
Quinta do Infantado: approximately 62 acres (25 hectares) red: 15 varieties, including Tinta Roriz, Touriga Nacional, and Touriga Francesa.

OUR FAVORITE WINES
This firm is proud of its vintage ports, produced since 1990 without compromising on quality from organically produced grapes. Mutage is carried out very slowly, allowing the wines to retain all the strength of expression of their terroir. The 1997 is remarkable. The superior ruby port, a blend of two or three different vintages but with all the character of a vintage port, has the same strong personality.

Quinta do
Monte d'Oiro

José Bento dos Santos is one of the most charming personalities in Portuguese viticulture. An unapologetic bon viveur, his cellar contains a wonderful collection of old Portuguese wines – including gems such as the sublime Barca Velhas from the 1940s and some very old Setubal Muscats. An innate estheticism has led him to create a perfect little vineyard on the clay-limestone soil of Estremadura. Here the most stringent rules for the production of fine wines are applied, following the methods he studied and admired in France. His decision to rely on Syrah grapes proved a wise one: combined with a small amount of Viognier or Cinsault grapes, the immediate result was a wine of great character with a vigorous but harmonious bouquet of blackcurrants and red berries, and with tannins that are much more civilized than those generally found in the local Portuguese grape varieties that are better adapted to the schist soil of the Douro valley than to the microclimate found around Salenquer. José's good communication skills have made it possible for him to bring his wine to the attention of the best restaurants in his own country, and it seems astonishing that it is still not all that well known in France or the rest of Europe.

VINE VARIETY

37 acres (15 hectares) red: Syrah, Touriga Nacional, Touriga Francesa, Tinto Roriz, Cinsault, Petit-Verdot; white: Viognier.

OUR FAVORITE WINES

In just a few years, the quinta's Reserva cuvée made from Syrah grapes with the addition of a small quantity of Viognier has become established as one of the best, if not the best, reds from the Lisbon region. The 2000 is extraordinarily good and succeeding vintages even better.

Quinta do
Noval

Twelve years ago, both the historic domaine and the company of Marquis de Pombal were taken over by the giant insurance company AXA, which has invested considerable funds – and all the experience acquired through its foray into winegrowing in Bordeaux – to fully realize the qualities of this Portuguese vineyard and its wines. Founded by the Rebella family in 1715, it is now reaching heights never before attained in its long history. The superb Noval vineyard, the first to have given its name to a firm, is situated in the heart of Cima Corgo, the finest zone in the Douro valley, with vines planted on beautifully constructed terraces, well exposed to the sun and perfectly maintained. Here, the grapes can reach an ideal level of ripeness, and have a pronounced aroma of red berries and aromatic herbs that develops with age toward tobacco and tertiary hints evoking those of the great Pauillacs and Hermitages. While, unsurprisingly, the majority of wine production is modern and mechanized, for the vintage wines the traditional *lagar* is still used – the only method that can successfully extract all the intensity of flesh and fruitiness from the grapes. The domaine's legendary fame was born with the magical 1931 and 1963 vintages, but the 2000 and 2003 are likely to be equally fine.

This historic illustration shows the care taken by female harvesters with the grapes, placing them gently in their wicker baskets.

VINE VARIETY
Quinta do Noval, Quinta do Silval: 358 acres (145 hectares) of red: this includes 6 acres (2.5 hectares) of ungrafted vines used for the Vintage Nacional.

OUR FAVORITE WINES
The first to market late-bottled vintages, this firm is hard to beat for wines of this style – powerful, complex, and very redolent of their terroir. The jewel in its crown is, however, the small production of Vintage Nacional (3,000 bottles) from ungrafted vines, a wine of truly unique density and aromatic impact.

Germany

Germany is Europe's white wine paradise! Over recent years, global warming has led to an increase in the frequency of great vintages while a new generation of winemakers, showing greater respect for terroir and good viticultural practice, is drawing fresh attention to a historic patrimony of the utmost interest to lovers of great wine. Wines of enormous accomplishment and originality continue to be made on the steep slopes of the Mosel and the Rhine, benefiting from slate soils that enhance the aromatic character of Riesling. The classic type of German wine, characterized by low alcohol and exquisite fruit supported by residual sugar, seems to be the type still best suited to the majority of terroirs, but it would be a mistake to overlook the progress shown by dry wines made from harvests that are considerably more mature than before, the best of which are now officially classified as premiers or grands crus. The German public is being seduced by wines made from white Burgundian varieties (Chardonnay, Pinot Gris, Pinot Blanc) vinified in barriques, but these wines do not yet seem capable of competing with the best results being achieved with these grapes elsewhere. On the other hand, significant progress has been made with Pinot Noir reds from an elite group of perfectionist producers, and it is now only their low volume that is holding them back.

Weingut
Fritz Haag

Under its old name of Dusemond, the Juffer hillside was considered to be the Mosel's greatest vineyard as long ago as the beginning of the 19th century. Although it has a number of rivals today, the perfection of the site and above all its uniformity of exposure (uniquely, the Mosel follows a straight course here without meandering) gives rise to wines of great finesse. Wilhelm Haag and his son Oliver are two of the district's best stylists and have developed an incomparably elegant, pure, and subtly perfumed style of wine. The grapes are vinified by lot in separate vats, as these great winemakers refuse to blend either different batches of fruit or fruit from different parcels of vineyard, thereby preserving the micro-differences that make up the unique charm of each vintage. This explains the individual barrel numbers printed on the labels. They also produce tiny quantities of Beerenauslese and Trockenbeerenauslese wines. These sell for astronomical prices, but rarely have we tasted examples as accomplished and magical in their aromatic refinement.

VINE VARIETY
19 acres (7.5 hectares) white: Riesling.

MAIN VINEYARD SITES
Brauneberger Juffer, Brauneberger Juffer Sonnenuhr.

OUR FAVORITE WINES
All this property's vineyard holdings are located on the Brauneberger Juffer slope. As is common in the Mosel region, a sundial has been placed in the part of the vineyard that enjoys the best exposure, and this core area has attached the suffix "sonnenuhr" to its name. This grower excels at producing classic-type wines, particularly those of the Spätlese variety, all the recent vintages of which are distinguished by a marvelous crystalline purity. The 2004 and 2005 will no doubt rival the prestigious 1997 and 1999.

Weingut
Dr. Loosen

The main secret behind the unmatched quality of this estate's wines lies in the vines themselves. Many of the vineyards are planted with old, ungrafted Riesling vines that are meticulously identified, preserved, and reproduced for new planting. Their small grapes have an inimitable flavor that expresses the character of the central Mosel's best slopes (which Loosen had the good fortune to inherit) with maximum intensity. Ambitious, determined, an inveterate lover of fine food (and an accomplished chef) – who could have been better positioned to become the world's most heeded ambassador of German wines, and the champion of Riesling's greatness? Comparing his wines with those of his best colleagues, Dr. Loosen's generally display greater immediate elegance on the nose and greater concentration, without sacrificing anything of their longevity. A recently tasted 1993 Erderner Prälat Auslese had lost none of its youthful brilliance.

VINE VARIETY
30 acres (12 hectares) white: Riesling.

MAIN VINEYARD SITES
Wehlener Sonnenuhr, Berkasteler Lay, Erdener Prälat and Treppchen, Ürziger Würzgarten.

OUR FAVORITE WINES
We consider Ernst Loosen and his faithful cellar master Bernhard Schug to be the greatest makers of Riesling in the Mosel. From Kabinett (the first category in the QmP system) upwards, their wines display a density, brilliance, finesse, and fidelity to terroir character that are impossible to imagine for anyone who has not tasted them. The most elegantly perfumed of their wines is Wehlener Sonnenuhr, but we have a weakness for the unique opulence of Erdener Pralät and the spiciness of Würzgarten. The 2004 offerings are miraculously elegant and full-bodied.

Vine plants lined up like toy soldiers on the steep slopes of slippery slate in the central Mosel region.

Weingut
Heymann-Löwenstein

It takes a heroic caliber of winemaker to cultivate vines on Winningen's 70°-plus slopes! These good-quality schist soils have been rescued from neglect by the installation of a system of monorails and small wagons. Reinhard Löwenstein is a visionary winemaker who appreciates the value of his natural heritage and who has taken considerable risks to grow extremely high-quality grapes in a rather cooler microclimate than at the heart of the Mosel region. Following the example of the region's best winemakers, the fruit from each parcel of land is vinified separately. These parcels differ in terms of soil type, featuring schist of different colors (blue-black, red) and degrees of hardness that produce subtly differentiated minerally wines of great distinction. Löwenstein is credited with having been the first in the area to produce great dry wines sought after by Germany's best restaurants. Where he has trodden, others have followed, but few of his fellow winemakers dare to reduce their yields to 30 hectoliters/hectare and sometimes below in order to obtain fruit of sufficient ripeness and concentration!

VINE VARIETY
35 acres (14 hectares) white: 99% Riesling.

MAIN VINEYARD SITES
Winninger Uhlen, Röttgen.

OUR FAVORITE WINES
For many years, the Koblenz section of the Mosel was overlooked but over the last 20 years Reinhard Löwenstein has succeeded magnificently in rehabilitating Winningen's slopes – in particular the incredibly steep Uhlen. Although he specializes in dry wines of wonderful finesse made from grapes picked at the point of perfect ripeness, he also makes exemplary rich, sweet wines with grapes affected by botrytis (noble rot). His 2004 offerings are outstanding.

Weingut
Joh. Jos. Prüm

In Wehlen, first names are essential in order to distinguish between the various members of this extensive family and their estates (the result of successive inheritances). The most renowned Weingut bears the initials of ancestor Johann Joseph and has been run for more than a generation by Dr. Manfred Prüm, one of Europe's most engaging winemakers. Beneath his wise and benevolent exterior lurks a will of steel and winemaking expertise as accomplished as it is enigmatic. In his hands the delicate, feminine wine of Wehlener Sonnenuhr reveals an uncommon vigor and develops a pervasive bouquet that combines strong minerality with daring acerbity. His Beerenauslese and richer Auslese wines slowly take on a yellowy-amber hue and seem almost immortal. The only precaution that needs to be taken with wines of such individuality is to give them at least five or six years in the bottle and to decant them half a day before drinking! The estate's other great wine, its Graacher Himmelreich, starts life a touch more austere but ages just as majestically as the Sonnenuhr.

VINE VARIETY
47 acres (19 hectares) white: Riesling.

MAIN VINEYARD SITES
Wehlener Sonnenuhr.

OUR FAVORITE WINES
Many people consider this estate to be the leading producer of Wehlener Sonnenuhr wines. It possesses numerous parcels of vines at different altitudes within the vineyard, allowing it to excel in all categories. Its Kabinett and above all Spätlese wines are unusually sinewy and long-lived, but Manfred Prüm succeeds even more brilliantly with his noble rot wines. These are highly sought after by collectors and command exorbitant prices. Even at 20 years of age they retain an astounding, spicy freshness and no one has yet discovered the secret of how they are made.

Weingut
Wwe. Dr. H. Thanisch –
Erben Thanisch

Konrad Adenauer, who knew what he was talking about, regarded Doctor, from a tiny slope of very hard Bernkastel slate with a magnificent southern exposure, as Germany's greatest wine and liked to serve it to visiting statesmen. Although a number of German critics consider the vineyard's reputation to be somewhat exaggerated, we fully share the verdict of the former German chancellor. This estate, whose current proprietor is Sofia Thanisch-Spier, owns the oldest portions of the vineyard, which are planted with ungrafted vines. The wine made here is the most perfect expression we know of this great terroir. Rather than pandering to lovers of originality and new techniques, the methods employed here are simple and follow a fine family tradition. In good years, the wine stands out for its own natural qualities. Displaying a character that is barely less forceful, Bernkasteler Badstube is made from sites bordering the Doctor vineyard (although enjoying a slightly less ideal exposure) and bears a strong resemblance to it. Both wines need seven or eight years in order to unfold their full personality.

VINE VARIETY
16 acres (6.5 hectares) white: Riesling.

MAIN VINEYARD SITES
Bernkasteler (under its old spelling, Berncasteler) Doctor, Lay, Graben (the last two are blended under the label Badstube).

OUR FAVORITE WINES
The pinnacle of this estate's production is its incomparable Doctor, which has all the richness of a Spätlese from the moment it is harvested. Its refined aromas continue to develop over time, and provide an astonishing and interminable cinnamon and bitter orange finish. The 1998 and 2001 vintages show it at its most eloquent, while the 2004 seems set to join them.

Weingut
Sankt Urbans-Hof

In just two generations, Sankt Urbans-Hof has become one of Germany's most thriving and respected estates. The dynamic Weis family has placed its faith in high-quality viticulture and purchased outstanding but extremely difficult-to-work parcels of Saar and Mosel vineyard – notably sections of the famous but somewhat over-large Goldtröpfchen vineyard. The winery employs precise modern methods to produce wines that are somewhat closed at first but that open out over time to reveal the individual character of the terroir. Nik Weis, who has many winemaking friends in France, has continued to work on the vines and soil. Indeed, this has been reflected in his most recent vintages, featuring wonderfully well-defined Kabinett and Spätlese offerings (even in the difficult year 2000), opulent Auslese wines, and impressive *Eiswein*s. Prices remain reasonable for such good quality, with a wide range of vineyards and vintages available.

VINE VARIETY
94 acres (38 hectares) white: 95% Riesling.

MAIN VINEYARD SITES
Leiwener Laurentiuslay, Piesporter Goldtröpfchen, Ockfener Bockstein, Wiltinger Schlangengraben.

OUR FAVORITE WINES
This vast estate, superbly managed by Nik Weis, produces wines of pure and radiant fruit that add considerable charm to the often rather austere wine of the Saar valley. The wine that dominates this firm's cellars nearly every year thanks to its almost uncanny sophistication is the Ockfener Bockstein. Its mildly saline finish means it makes a marvelous aperitif – especially the Spätlese, which possessed perfect poise in 2001 and 2004.

The magic ring of the Piesport "little drop of gold" (the Goldtröpfchen), where one can imagine the water nymphs from the Mosel River resting. The vines grow right down to the water's edge and can only be harvested by boat.

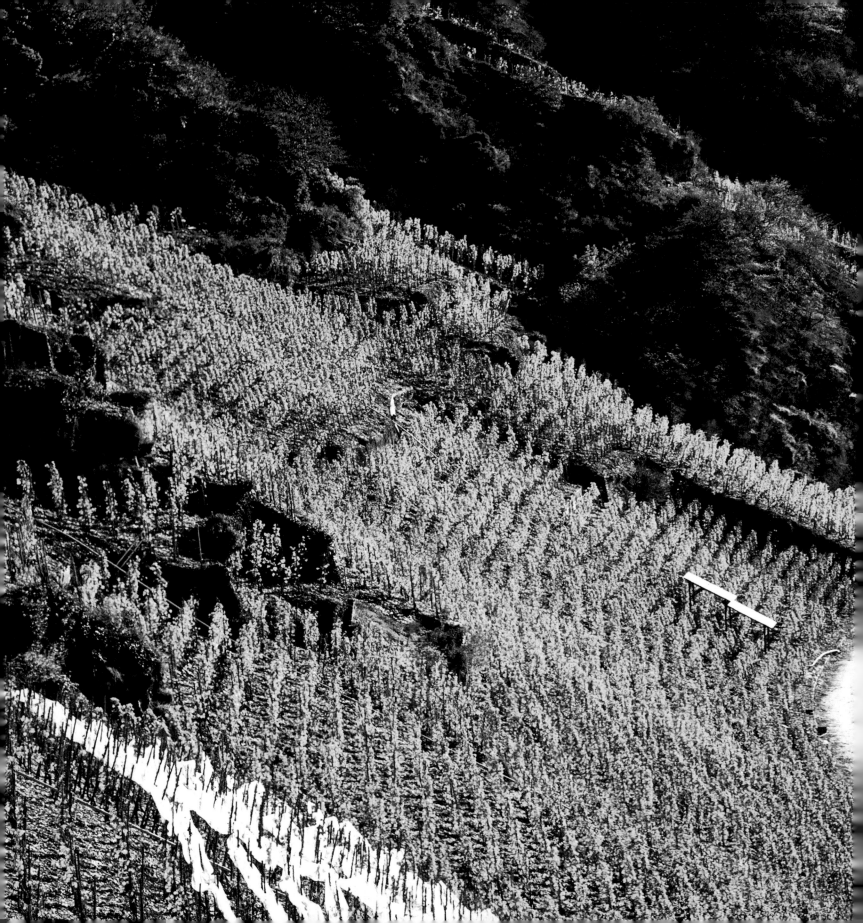

Weingut
Reichsgraf von Kesselstatt

The Reh family made its fortune producing mass-market sparkling wine. This allowed it to invest in high-quality vineyards in Burgundy (Domaine Bertagna) and Germany. The vineyards of the vast and historic Kesselstatt estate (formerly owned by aristocrats of Austrian origin) are now run by Annegret Reh, who made the sensible decision only to work the best sites herself – those capable of justifying the extremely expensive viticulture they require. With the help of her husband Gerhard Gartner, the first German chef to be awarded two Michelin stars, this strong-willed perfectionist produces restrained and subtle wines of great finesse. But she also makes sure they can hold their own at the table. The softest are from Kaseler Nies'chen, the most minerally from the famous Scharzhofberg vineyard (in which she owns a number of fine parcels of vines adjoining those of Egon Müller), and the most opulent and spicy from the distinguished Goldtröpfchen and Josephshof vineyards. The estate excels at making classic-style wines that are low in alcohol with plenty of syrup to preserve the delicate bouquet. In terms of price, they are among the most reasonable in the region.

VINE VARIETY
99 acres (40 hectares) white: Riesling.

MAIN VINEYARD SITES
Kaseler Nies'chen, Scharzhofberg, Piesporter Goldtröpfchen, Josephshof.

OUR FAVORITE WINES
This estate excels in each of the areas in which it has vines. Its most emblematic wine, however, is Josephshöfer, as it is the sole owner of this vineyard which enjoys an ideal site on the banks of the Mosel beneath Graacher Himmelreich and next to Wehlener Sonnenuhr. The Josephshof's vines are now sufficiently mature to express the full quality of this excellent terroir and enjoy a microclimate that favors the development of noble rot. The very refined 2004 raises high expectations for the sumptuous 2005, surely the best vintage since 1971 (and before that 1959).

Weingut
Van Volxem

Roman Niewodniczanski, the young heir to a major German brewing family, took over this historic Saar estate in 1999 with a very clear idea about the style of wine he wanted to make: as dry as possible from grapes that are as ripe as possible (following the example of Reinhard Löwenstein in the Lower Mosel). He soon achieved success, producing wines that emphasize the virtues of a valuable legacy of old vines in the best of Wiltingen and the surrounding area's vineyards. The yields are ridiculously low (30–35 hectoliters/hectare), but the brilliance and purity with which his wines express the minerality of the local schist soils immediately attracted the attention of even the most discriminating of Riesling aficionados. The exceptional, extremely rich 2003 vintage gave rise to wines of greater mellowness, slightly less unusual perhaps but magnificent nevertheless. We expect great things from a parcel of vines recently acquired by the estate in the Altenberg vineyard at Kanzem, an excellent site that has been somewhat neglected by the religious institutions that own most of it.

VINE VARIETY
49 acres (20 hectares) white: 96% Riesling.

MAIN VINEYARD SITES
Scharzhofberg, Wiltinger Gottesfuss, Kanzemer Altenberg.

OUR FAVORITE WINES
The type of wine we like the most from this estate and which seems best adapted to its particular soil type is rather different to that produced in the Mosel region, with a higher alcohol content and less residual sugar. Good examples are the best of its 2000 and 2001 vintages from the old vines (Alte Reben) of the Gottesfuss vineyard.

Weingut
Egon Müller Scharzhof

The name Egon has been passed down from father to son for five generations of the Müller family and each of its bearers has devoted his talents to the prestigious Scharzhofberg vineyard, a fine schist slope above the river Saar with a cool microclimate ideally suited to slow-maturing Riesling. Egon IV has inherited his family's winemaking skills and in our opinion raised them to an even higher level. Everything possible is done here to foster the development of noble rot, and chemical intervention in the vineyard is therefore kept to a minimum. The yields are low, generally below 50 hectoliters/hectare, and harvesting is carried out with great care. Vinification follows traditional lines, the main objective being to protect the wine from oxidation and any deterioration in the purity of its aromas. A good Scharzhofberger from this estate is without equal anywhere in the world in terms of the finesse and delicacy of its aromas. The wine's strong acidity is balanced to perfection by an energetic minerality. This stems from the terroir and, compared to the best wines originating from schist soils in France, is saline rather than bitter. The extremely rare wines made from the richest selection of grapes, which sell at local auctions for astronomical prices (often ten times as expensive as Château d'Yquem), are more deserving than any others of the term "extravagant perfection."

Scharzhof, home of the Müller family, where the most deservedly famous wines of the Saar can be sampled. These include sweet wines made in very limited quantities, probably the most expensive wines anywhere in the world.

VINE VARIETY
20 acres (8 hectares) white: 98% Riesling.

ONLY VINEYARD SITE
Scharzhofberg.

OUR FAVORITE WINES
This estate's only vineyard is as legendary as the quality of its wine, which explains the difficulty of tracking it down and the very high prices it commands – another good reason for choosing the superior Spätlese and, above all, Auslese categories made from the best grapes. These are wonderfully elegant wines that need time to develop. The 2003 examples are magnificent and will hopefully age as well as the 1971 vintage.

Weingut
Hermann Dönnhoff

This cult estate owes its excellent reputation to the highly engaging personality of Helmut Dönnhoff, an accomplished and modest winemaker who remains attached to the best aspects of the local tradition. His wines sparkle with a kind of natural self-confidence. Their balance, fruit, and faithful expression of the character of some of the Nahe region's greatest sites (whose soils are more metamorphic and volcanic than those of the Mosel, accentuating Riesling's spicy side), have won them a faithful international clientele that strips the estate of every last bottle as soon as each new vintage goes on sale. A good wine from this producer offers the best possible introduction to the world of German white wine, a world still far too little known outside the German-speaking nations. The first impression is of a magical alliance between white fruit, cinnamon, and nutmeg, the traditional spices of central European cuisine, and mineral and even petrol notes after a number of years bound to the soil. Acidity, sometimes rather strong in the young wine while at the same time serving as a framework for the uninhibited expression of the fruit, is balanced by sugar. And all this without any sense of alcohol and without the help of oak. This is a wine that brings its drinker into direct contact with sun, soil, and yeast!

VINE VARIETY

40 acres (16 hectares) white: 75% Riesling and 25% Pinot Blanc (Weissburgunder).

MAIN VINEYARD SITES

Niederhäuser Hermannshöhle, Oberhäuser Brücke, Schlossböckelheimer Kupfergrube.

OUR FAVORITE WINES

Helmut Dönnhoff is a great stylist of classic Rhine-type wines – low in alcohol, rich in residual sugar and as far as possible made from overripe grapes or grapes wizened by noble rot. The microclimate best suited to this style is that of Brücke, on the northern side of the river, which produces wonderful Auslese. However, the most minerally and refined of Dönnhoff's wines is Hermannshöhle. The best of the recent vintages is without doubt the 2002.

This vineyard in the heart of the Nahe region is situated on the steepest slopes in Europe. Here, in the burning heat, the grapes take on all the violence of the volcanic soil in which they grow, yet retain the natural elegance that we can expect from a Riesling.

Weingut
Emrich-Schönleber

Reserved but determined, Werner Schönleber has become one of Germany's most admired wine producers almost despite himself. Fully aware of the quality of the slopes around the little village of Monzingen, he has attended to the tiniest of details in order to bring these wines to the highest imaginable level of expression. His wines redefine the word "purity." From their earliest youth onwards they display all the crystalline clarity of a mountain stream. The rigor and precision of Werner Schönleber's vinification methods are wonderfully well suited to the nature of Riesling, which in his hands develops floral notes of infinite subtlety (with secondary nuances of cinnamon and quina) reminiscent of the finest Bernkasteler Doctor. In general the Frühlingsplätzchen, despite its complicated name, is the most floral and the earliest to open up, but from around five years of age the Halenberg expresses the qualities of the estate even more forcefully and eloquently, adding a increased mineral tonality and sharper acidity. Over the last few years, the firm's noble rot wines have continued to improve and the many producers not yet as skilled in such a careful and precise selection of grapes could learn much from them.

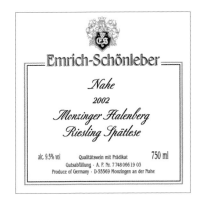

VINE VARIETY
30 acres (12 hectares) white: 76% Riesling, 9% Pinot Gris (Grauburgunder), 5% Pinot Blanc (Weissburgunder), 10% various.

MAIN VINEYARD SITES
Monzinger Halenberg, Frühlingsplätzchen.

OUR FAVORITE WINES
This meticulous winemaker makes Eiswein (a difficult category of wine to succeed with) like no other. In terms of its density, vibrant aromas, and finish, his Halenberg 2002 surpasses anything we have tasted. And the classic wines from this same, little known site, rival the very best, thanks to their internal energy and aromatic refinement.

Assmannshausen, at the northwestern end of the Rheingau, is one of the areas famous for sumptuous Rhine Valley Pinot Noirs.

Weingut
Georg Breuer

The premature death of Bernhard Breuer, the intellectual leader of German viticulture and the unifying force behind its elite producers, came as a severe blow to his family and many friends. Life has to go on, however, and his work was carried on faithfully by his brother Heinrich and daughter Theresa. The estate specializes in wines from the town of Rüdesheim (the tourist capital of the Rheingau region), where it owns a highly respected hotel and restaurant. The soils of the splendid Berg slope are composed of slate and Taunus quartzite, producing wines that are more slender, more refined, and firmer than those from any of the area's other vineyards. Harvested at 55°F (13°C) and vinified dry, the Rieslings have a truly memorable charm, often revealing elegant bitter orange notes. The estate's noble rot sweet wines are produced in other sites not far away – Bischofsberg, whose microclimate is better suited to this style of wine, and Nonnenberg in the village of Rauenthal, set back further from the river, a touch colder though protected from the wind. Bernhard Breuer used to make these sweet wines only in particularly propitious years – but to perfection. Their style, featuring a somewhat higher than normal level of transformed alcohol, perplexed some people but in 2003 the estate's sumptuous Beerenauslese and Trockenbeerenauslese wines rediscovered a more familiar balance.

VINE VARIETY

74 acres (30 hectares) white: 80% Riesling, 18% Pinot Blanc (Weissburgunder) and Pinot Gris (Grauburgunder), 2% Orleaner.

MAIN VINEYARD SITES

Rüdesheim Berg Schlossberg, Berg Rottland, Rauenthaler Nonnenberg.

OUR FAVORITE WINES

The vines of Berg Schlossberg are admirably well suited to the production of dry white wine, displaying unsurpassable class and a firmness that offers remarkable aging potential. The 1994, 1998, and 1999 vintages are now sufficiently mature to be enjoyed with the finest-quality cuisine.

Schloss
Johannisberg

The famous Baroque castle of the princes of Metternich, monumental rather than elegant, dominates the Rhine valley from its hilltop perch. Its real wealth lies in the unique quality of its terroir and the warm microclimate that gives its Riesling its entrancing perfume. The story goes that sweet wines made from rotten grapes were invented here. What is beyond dispute, however, is that the grapes are selected with an unrivaled degree of care and expertise. The extraordinary botrytis wines of the last few vintages leave no doubt as to why the rot affecting the grapes from which they are made is called "noble." The light hue of the richest wines and the brilliance of their fruit flavors are perfectly preserved as the wine ages thanks to a gracious rather than aggressive acidity that also makes for an uncommonly refreshing sweet wine. There is no trace of iodine or mushroom, simply the purest imaginable expression of white and exotic fruit aromas and above all a body of heavenly lightness relative to the wine's richness. Christian Witte, the estate's new technical director, has now set his heart on producing wines of enormous style and character in the less sweet categories, too.

VINE VARIETY
86 acres (35 hectares) white: Riesling.

MAIN VINEYARD SITE
The practice at this estate is to blend wine from different sites and to market the results under the prestigious "château" name, as in Bordeaux.

OUR FAVORITE WINES
The true personality of this excellent terroir is only revealed in its special Rosalack and Goldlack selections, which take their names from their respectively pink, and pink and gold seals, and in the wonderful historical wines of the Bibliotheca Subterranea, Schloss Johannisberg's private cellar. This is white wine at its most perfect, displaying an aromatic refinement unique in the Rhine valley.

Weingut
Robert Weil

The mighty Japanese firm Suntory has provided Wilhelm Weil with the means to create a winemaking facility unique in Germany. The well-planned state-of-the-art cellars enable the whole range of white wines, from the driest to the sweetest, to be made here with unrivaled precision. No expense is spared in the vineyard, where the growing and harvesting of the grapes is exemplary. The results were not long in coming. In just a few years, the estate's famous blue label has come to symbolize both German wine of the very highest quality and the legitimate pride of the winemaker. Kiedrich's best slopes have always had the reputation of producing the most harmoniously fruity wines in the Rhine valley. Indeed, their soil contains a little less schist than most, with more surface stones and gravel, and more clay. This gives fruit the upper hand over minerality. Noble rot occurs regularly and, as in 2003, a truly exceptional vintage, produces must with an enormously high sugar content (more than 300° Oechsle). The combination of these two factors results in a wine of unique charm.

VINE VARIETY
161 acres (65 hectares) white: 98% Riesling.

MAIN VINEYARD SITE
Kiedricher Gräfenberg.

OUR FAVORITE WINES
Few estates of this size attain the degree of across-the-board success that Weingut Robert Weil has achieved, and consequently its richest wines are snapped up by avid collectors. The Spätlese category also reaches its most perfect expression here, revealing perhaps even more terroir character than the estate's sweet wines.

Weingut
Dr. Bürklin-Wolf

The sheer size of this estate makes it impossible to overlook but also means getting to grips with a very wide range of wines. Christian von Guradze, Dr. Bürklin's son-in-law, has both tenacity and a willingness to innovate. In the vineyard, he has gradually converted to biodynamic methods, the only approach capable of producing grapes worthy of the great sites he is fortunate enough to farm. Conscious of the highly complex nature of the traditional German labeling system, he has decided to imitate the more logical hierarchy used in Burgundy by distinguishing between four levels of dry wine: a basic wine bearing the name of the grape variety; a "Village" wine; premiers crus (denoted by the initials PC); and finally a selection of grands crus. The estate's sweet wines, meanwhile, continue to specify the category of sweetness in the usual way (Auslese, Beerenauslese, etc.). The average level of quality of the last few vintages has been impressive across the range, from highly complex, flavorsome dry wines to sweet wines of a freshness and dynamism rare in the Pfalz region (where they can sometimes tend towards the heavy). A tiny volume of Muscat (Muskateller) from specially selected grapes is also made here, rivaling the Riesling in the extravagant beauty of its fruit.

VINE VARIETY
222 acres (90 hectares) white: 72% Riesling, 12% Pinot Noir (Spätburgunder) and Pinot Blanc (Weissburgunder), 16% various.

MAIN VINEYARD SITES
Forster Kirchenstück, Jesuitengarten, Pechstein, Ungeheuer, Ruppertsberger Gaisböhl, Deidesheimer Hohenmorgen, Wachenheimer Rechbächel.

OUR FAVORITE WINES
This estate is Germany's great specialist in truly monumental dry wines. Its clutch of 2003 grands crus, dominated by a majestic Forster Kirchenstück, is the most impressive in the property's long history.

Weingut Geheimer Rat
Dr. von Bassermann-Jordan

This large historic property no longer belongs to the Bassermann-Jordan family. It has, however, retained its impressive collection of vineyards and its talented winemaker Ulrich Mell, and pursues the same aim of producing great terroir wines. Forst's basalt soils and Deidesheim's sand have always been considered among the most prestigious in the Pfalz region as they are ideally suited to Riesling. Here the grape achieves greater ripeness than anywhere else in Germany thanks to a warm microclimate that favors the production of dry wines. The new "grand cru" legislation is another factor pushing wine producers in this direction – one greatly appreciated by the catering and tourist industries. The Forst wines – in particular, those from the famous Jesuitengarten vineyard (also the source of sweet wines of great richness) – are fuller-bodied and more spicy, while those from Deidesheim are suppler with more expressive fruit when young. Ulrich Mell's main priority is the precise expression of individual vineyard character, and the general success of his 2002 and 2003 offerings derives from the pronounced individuality of each of his wines at every level of sweetness.

VINE VARIETY
114 (46 hectares) white: 90% Riesling.

MAIN VINEYARD SITES
Forster Jesuitengarten, Kirchenstück, Ungeheuer, Deidesheimer Kalkofen, Kieselberg, Hohenmorgen.

OUR FAVORITE WINES
This estate specializes in wines from the Jesuitengarten vineyard in Forst at the heart of the area's basalt deposits. This is a site with abundant personality that produces every category of wine from full-bodied dry to the most voluptuous of sweet wines.

The domaine's bottle with its Art Nouveau label provides a magnificent container for these wines, the most aristocratic and flavorsome of the Pfalz (Palatinate) region, a land where the generosity of the climate matches that of its people.

Weingut
Müller-Catoir

The great minerally, spicy Rieslings from the Forst district are actually an exception in the Pfalz. The soil type most frequently encountered is loess of varying thickness that favors swift ripening and endows the Rieslings with opulent fruit. It can also sometimes be better suited to Pinot Blanc and Pinot Gris. The model on which these fine fruity wines are based was perfected at Weingut Müller-Catoir by Hans-Günter Schwarz, one of the leading personalities in the German wine industry. Now retired, Schwarz was a perfectionist in the vineyard, extremely well informed in the cellar, and an outstanding · communicator. He exerted a considerable influence over a new generation of producers who were seduced by the naturalness and rigor of his approach. Additionally, he achieved considerable worldwide success with highly perfumed wines, although vineyard character was sometimes relegated to second place. His most spectacular wines, moreover, came from voluptuous noble rot Rieslaner and Scheurebe varieties that were less influenced by the soils in which they were grown. His successor, Martin Franzen, appears to have taken a new direction with the full consent of the Catoir family towards a more delicate style, although this development seems to have been held slightly in check by the enormous richness of the 2003 vintage.

VINE VARIETY
49 acres (20 hectares) white: 60% Riesling, 12% Rieslaner, 12% Pinot Blanc (Weissburgunder), 7% Pinot Gris (Grauburgunder), 5% Muscat (Muskateller), 4% Scheurebe.

MAIN VINEYARD SITES
Gimmeldingen Mandelgarten, Mussbacher Eselshaut, Haardter Bürgergarten.

OUR FAVORITE WINES
While this estate is particularly proud of its hybrid varieties, Rieslaner and Scheurebe, we by far prefer its best Rieslings, which are rich, velvety, and almost exotically exuberant (those from the Mandelgarten vineyard for example), and Muscats, which are marvelously perfumed but produced in all too small volumes.

Weingut
Friedrich Becker

For a long time now, the area of the Pfalz near the French border has suffered from a lesser reputation than that of the core Haardt valley area. Because they are not as well suited to Riesling, its vineyards held less interest for wine lovers. But then a new generation of winemakers who saw the potential of these sites came along and started to make great wines from the Burgundian grape varieties. Friedrich Becker has made a name for himself perfecting the cultivation and vinification of Pinot Noir, taking it to a level of quality previously unseen in the region. His marly, kaolin-rich soils proved ideally suited to this approach, yielding brightly colored wines that are tannic but with a voluptuous texture that makes them immediately seductive. In terms of its balance of alcohol and purity of aromatic definition, Becker's admirable 1996 Reserve is no doubt capable of beating many a recent-vintage Burgundy in a blind tasting. The estate's Chardonnays boast a similar richness, but their flattering oak, adapted to local tastes, makes them somewhat stereotypical. The Sonnenberg vineyard also produces quality Rieslings of Alsace-like body and character. This is entirely logical as there is no difference between the soils and microclimate of these winegrowing districts which straddle the border just a couple of miles apart.

VINE VARIETY
36 acres (14.5 hectares) white and red: 60% Pinot Noir (Spätburgunder), 22% Riesling, 18% various.

MAIN VINEYARD SITES
Schweigener Sonnenberg, Kammerberg.

OUR FAVORITE WINES
This estate is first and foremost a brilliant producer of Pinot Noirs that, in our opinion, have been Germany's most accomplished reds for some years. Its 2001 and 2002 Reserve wines rival the great Burgundies in terms of body while presenting a more immediate floral nose.

Weingut
Gunderloch

The vineyards fronting the Rhine between Nierstein and Nackenheim, with their steep slopes and dense, impeccably maintained rows of vines, are among Europe's most impressive. Everything seems to have conspired to produce perfect winegrowing conditions, above all the slate soils rich in iron oxide (particularly in the Rothenberg vineyard) and a microclimate strongly influenced by the river and therefore favoring the early development of noble rot. What is more, the wines made by this highly regarded estate certainly will not dash the hopes raised by the perfection of these conditions – from the Spätlese upwards, that is. The dry wines are too brusque and lacking in refinement and flavor due to insufficient residual sugar to carry the fruit. The Spätlese wines, on the other hand, impress with their density, tension, and aromatic exuberance, while the special selections, which are richer and fuller-bodied than those of the Mosel and more openly fruity than those of the Rheingau, are nothing short of captivating. One might imagine that the Hasselbachs would rest on their laurels given the fame they have achieved and the current quality of their wines. Not so! They believe there is further progress to be made in terms of expression of vineyard character and in finding the ideal balance for the Rothenberg vineyard. Passionate tasters, they are always delighted to involve wine lovers in their research. Their 2005 bottlings, having benefited from exceptionally propitious weather, bear brilliant witness to their efforts.

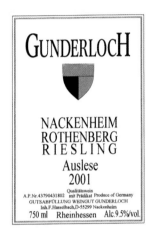

VINE VARIETY
35 acres (14 hectares) white: 80% Riesling.

MAIN VINEYARD SITES
Nackenheimer Rothenberg.

OUR FAVORITE WINES
Fritz and Agnes Hasselbach's vinification methods are geared mainly toward producing the superior categories of Riesling. After a few years in the bottle, the sensational bouquet of spices and cinnamon and emphatic minerality are capable of winning over any Riesling fan. Particularly admirable are the rigor of the grape selection and the aging of the Hasselbach's Rothenberg. The Goldkapsel 2001 Auslese offers a prime example of their style.

Weingut
Wittmann

Who would have guessed just 20 years ago that some of Germany's most remarkable wines would soon be produced in an obscure corner of Rheinhessen away from the great river on soils boasting neither slate nor granite sand? The Wittmann family has played a significant role in the discovery and exploitation of its priceless natural assets. First of all it took the trouble to analyze its soils and microclimate, and plant the most suitable varieties. The adoption many years ago of organic methods enables the estate to harvest grapes of exceptional ripeness and aroma which are then brilliantly vinified by son Philipp, a remarkable taster and expert on wines from all over the world. Philipp knows the importance of restricting intervention to a minimum, but is also well aware of the limits of a laissez-faire approach. The degree of precision he brings to the pressing and fermentation processes produces stunning wines of depth and complexity. We had never tasted dry wines as wonderfully expressive as his Morstein 1999 – and then came the 2001, 2002, and 2004, which were, if anything, even purer and more refined! The rare botrytis wines, especially the 2002 Auslese "S," share the same qualities. They are marvelously suave, long in the mouth, and exceptionally elegant.

VINE VARIETY
62 acres (25 hectares) white: 47% Riesling, 30% Pinot, 10% Sylvaner, 13% various.

MAIN VINEYARD SITES
Westhofener Morstein, Kirchspiel, Aulerde.

OUR FAVORITE WINES
This estate's entire production is remarkable and benefits from many years of organic viticulture but inevitably the Rieslings rule the roost, particularly their dry incarnation. Those from Westhofen's three main vineyards verge on perfection (the Morstein perhaps has the edge).

Weingut
Keller

In just 20 years, this traditional small-scale estate in a long-forgotten corner of Rheinhessen has become one of the best known and most highly respected producers in Germany. It owes its success to the sound principles it employs in vineyard and cellar alike, but above all to the exceptional passion and perfectionism it brings to everyday tasks. A meticulously managed vineyard is not in itself enough to produce world-class wines. It is also important to have a personal vision of how a great wine should be. This vision initially involved emphasizing the Riesling fruit, and the wines produced by the estate in the 1990s drove German wine waiters wild. But Klaus-Peter Keller was too talented a taster not to notice that the wine needed greater depth in order to express more of the minerality and complexity of the terroir even at the expense of some of its immediate seductiveness. Ultimately, the quality of his terroirs and work in the vineyard allowed Keller to progress on both fronts. His wines improved enormously up to the point where in 2004 his three main "crus" rivaled the nobility and perfection of those of Weingut Wittmann. And to judge by his 2003 Morstein Goldkapsel Auslese, a wonderful expression of a great vineyard and example of a remarkable vintage, his sweet wines have taken the same route. All lovers of Riesling should know about this prodigiously talented winemaker.

VINE VARIETY

31 acres (12.5 hectares) white: 60% Riesling, 30% Pinot and Sylvaner, 10% various.

MAIN VINEYARD SITES

Dalsheimer Hubacker, Westhofener Morstein, Kirchspiel.

OUR FAVORITE WINES

Weingut Keller has only been producing truly outstanding wines for 20 years or so. Until recently they struck us as brilliantly made but rather too "technical." Young Klaus-Peter Keller has taken a critical look at the estate's methods and concentrated on making wines that express a greater degree of vineyard character. These monumental wines of crystalline purity are nothing short of extraordinary.

Weingut
Andreas Laible

This small, traditional estate is something of an anomaly in Baden. Most of the region's winemakers specialize in the Burgundian varieties, producing an oak-rich style of wine that is very popular locally but lacks any real personality. The restaurant trade in this busy tourist region adores them and as a result they command improbably high prices. At Weingut Andreas Laible, on the other hand, price is justified by quality – all the more so as the estate remains faithful to Riesling, which is delicate and refined with all the classic suppleness to be expected from granite soils. The Burgundian varieties are not completely neglected, however, and are also made here with considerable flair. Furthermore, they also display the same charm and freshness of expression, a considerable winemaking achievement. A visit to the vineyard helps to explain the estate's success. The Plauelrain slopes are among the most difficult in the region to work, forcing those who tend them to bring a degree of discipline to the task that favors the ripening of the noble grape varieties. In addition to wine, the estate also distils excellent schnapps from its own fruit. Andreas Laible's two sons work alongside him in the winery. It now remains for them to improve the quality of their reds, which are still somewhat lacking in personality.

VINE VARIETY
17 acres (7 hectares) white and red: 58% Riesling, 15% Pinot Noir (Spätburgunder), 12% Traminer, 15% various.

MAIN VINEYARD SITES
Durbacher Plauelrain.

OUR FAVORITE WINES
Durbach's granite soils produce the most refined Rieslings in Baden, and Laible father and sons are particularly skilled at making them into both dry (the best are denoted by the initials S.L.) and dessert wines. Another strong point in 2003 was the estate's Gewürztraminer Auslese, one of the best in Germany.

Weingut
Rudolf Fürst

Rudolf Fürst created from nothing the idea of a noble red wine in Franconia – a region unfortunately better known for its acidic and modestly fruity Sylvaners. Admittedly, his predecessors had already planted Pinot Noir on Bürgstadt's slopes but they did not attempt to make them into wines for keeping. He was therefore the first to reduce yields drastically enough to produce ripe grapes with good tannins and to adopt vinification techniques that would ensure both maximum immediate aroma and long, even aging. He also had the necessary flair to understand the nature of each vintage and express it in all its individuality. This is demonstrated by a comparison between 2002 and 2003. His Parzival blend and the famous Centgrafenberg "R" Reserve freely express the aromatic subtlety of 2002 and the warmer, more southern tones of 2003 while sharing the same sense of balance and tannic precision. The estate's white wines – the Rieslings as well as the Pinot Blancs – also have abundant charm.

VINE VARIETY
42 acres (17 hectares) red and white: 40% Pinot Noir (Spätburgunder), 18% Riesling, 14% Pinot Blanc (Weissburgunder), 28% various.

MAIN VINEYARD SITES
Bürgstadter Centgrafenberg, Klingenberg.

OUR FAVORITE WINES
As far as Riesling is concerned, Rudolf Fürst cannot compete with the big names of the Mosel or Rhine, but there are few winemakers who can match his Pinot Noir reds. His style is deliberately inspired by the greatest modern Burgundies with lavish aging in oak and is unlikely to please lovers of "natural" wines. But lovers of sophistication, complexity, and aristocratic textures will fall for his Centgrafenberg wines. The best bear the initial R on their labels.

Austria

Austria's winegrowing industry showed great intelligence in the way it recovered from the adulterated wine scandal of the early 1980s, which left the country's reputation for wine in tatters. It owes its swift rehabilitation as much to the diversity of its terroirs as to the courage and discipline of its winemakers, but the latter would not have been able to summon up the necessary energy without the unconditional support of their fellow citizens and the Austrian state. This support could serve as a model to other European countries. The Austrians love their wines and are proud of them – with good reason as their natural character and aromatic finesse make them the perfect accompaniment for food. The great tradition of Rhine Rieslings is pursued on the banks of the Danube with wines that are even more minerally and rich in natural alcohol. These sites enable the local variety Grüner Veltliner to attain a perfection of expression unknown anywhere else while the vast expanse of Lake Neusiedl promotes the – sometimes dazzlingly fast – development of botrytis (noble rot) and hence the production of extremely rich though occasionally impersonal sweet wines. A more recent development is the amazing progress made by the country's reds. Local varieties such as Blauer Portugieser, Blaufränkisch, Zweigelt, and Saint Laurent produce wines that are rich in color and have peppery aromas, while global warming favors the planting of classic Bordeaux varieties such as Merlot and Cabernet Sauvignon.

List of domaines

Weingut
Bründlmayer

This property, which is very large for Austria, is masterfully run by Willi Bründlmayer, one of Europe's most enterprising but also most thoughtful and idealistic winegrowers. In his quest to optimize the harvest, Bründlmayer works tirelessly at improving cultivation methods on his beautiful estate. In particular, he has adopted the lyre training system – a method devised and developed in France, though not greatly esteemed there – in order to increase the grapes' exposure to sunshine, thereby assisting the ripening process and development of aromas. The Lamm site is admirably well suited to Grüner Veltliner, an authentic Austrian variety with a peculiarly spicy aroma and velvety texture that makes it rather smoother in its youth than the fuller-flavored Rieslings from the same sites. The Austrians and sometimes their central European neighbors seem to regard it as the highest expression of Austrian viticulture, and it is difficult to find any Grüner Veltliner wines that are better balanced or more seductive than those made here. Particularly after some aging, however, we find superior integrity and complexity in the Rieslings, especially those from Heiligenstein's old vines, which are the equal of Wachau's best (which they also resemble in style).

VINE VARIETY

124 acres (50 hectares) in the Kamp Valley, 45 miles (70 kilometers) northwest of Vienna. Vineyard sites include Zöbinger Heiligenstein, Lamm (the lower portion of Heiligenstein) and Käferberg.

OUR FAVORITE WINES

The Heiligenstein Rieslings have power, panache, and abundant terroir character. Grapes grown on lyre trellises seem to develop greater ripeness and aromatic complexity.

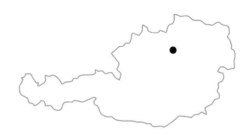

Weingut
Franz Hirtzberger

Franz Hirtzberger is a star among Wachau winegrowers and has done more than anyone else to restore Austrian wine to the highest level of quality. The wines from his fairly cool vineyards bordering the Danube (neatly terraced because of their steepness) have made a name for themselves with their pronounced minerality and aromatic refinement. The Singerriedel slope bordering the village of Spitz benefits from an ideal south–southeastern exposure. The lower half (Honigvogl) is planted with Grüner Veltliner, and the upper half with Riesling. Hirtzberger's wines perform extremely well in Riesling tastings in America and elsewhere. He stands out from his Wachau colleagues for the extreme purity and aromatic transparency of his wines, the result of his technical mastery of the winemaking process. Although modesty prevents him from admitting that this expertise is responsible for the excellence of his wines (instead he cites small yields and the quality of the grapes), it is blindingly obvious in tastings. Only extremely precise pressing produces juice of such clarity, purity, and delicacy of perfume and, in the case of Riesling (where any clumsiness in the pressing process can produce over-prominent tannins), the estate's "modern" style has worked wonders. All that remains to be seen now is how well these wines age.

The tints of the fine Grüner Veltliner wines in the Wachau are echoed in the yellows and greens of the painted houses.

VINE VARIETY

30 acres (12 hectares) white: 45% Grüner Veltliner, 40% Riesling, 15% Chardonnay and Pinot Blanc (Weissburgunder).

OUR FAVORITE WINES

Despite the popularity of Grüner Veltliner, the Wachau region's Rieslings display greater finesse, purity, and aromatic assurance. We were particularly impressed by the Smaragd (a style of dry wine with a minimum alcohol content of 13%) made from grapes from the superb Singerriedel slope. The estate's 2000 offerings are remarkable, especially given the unevenness of that year in central Europe.

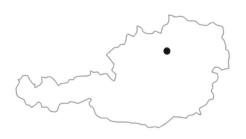

Weingut
Aloïs Kracher

This highly talented winemaker, who attracts an absurd amount of media coverage, has developed a way of exploiting the very special microclimate of Lake Neusiedl in the Seewinkel region close to the border with Hungary. High levels of humidity give rise to the general onset of noble rot every year, affecting even delicate-skinned varieties such as Chardonnay and the Pinot. Despite the fact that the rot is occasionally less than noble, producing mildly caramelized wines or wines with a faint taste of mushroom, the public shows enormous enthusiasm for these sumptuous products. Thanks to the no-expense-spared vinification methods and aging in new oak, Kracher has succeeded with great skill in making very sweet dessert wines in a modern style with the widest possible appeal. His "new wave" style proved an immediate hit in Austria. The lover of great dessert wines will find this style worthy of admiration rather than affection, however. This is because the perfect balance between alcohol, acidity, and sweetness lacks the sustaining, supporting minerality provided by the granite of Wachau or the slate of the great German terroirs. Instead, the local sand and gravel soils emphasize the "primary" aromas, and favor an immediate suppleness and unctuousness. This is not to say these wines do not age well: a 1991 Traminer Beerenauslese tasted last year showed extraordinary depth of flavor!

VINE VARIETY

*52 acres (21 hectares) white: 30% Chardonnay,
40% Welschriesling, 10% Scheurebe, 10% Traminer, 10% Muscat.*

OUR FAVORITE WINES

*This estate specializes in making noble rot wines from all
its grape varieties. The one that surprises us most is the
Chardonnay, because in France at least the grape does not
respond well to the onset of noble rot. Kracher's "new wave"
Traminer Beerenauslese impresses with its richness and length
on the palate, but presupposes a sweet tooth!*

Weingut
F. X. Pichler

Great terroirs do not always have the good fortune to be managed by winemakers who appreciate their value and possess the necessary skill to take them to their highest level of expressiveness. Some of Dürnstein's slopes are lucky enough to be under the care of a man of great sensitivity, whose knowledge and expertise follow in the best Austrian tradition. Franz Xavier Pichler's wines, made in the simplest and most natural manner in the world but with great rigor and precision, attract immediate attention with their power and density, though they can be a trifle severe when young. That said, it is this upright quality that enables them to age reliably and magnificently. They display a strong link with their terroir, amplified by Riesling's propensity to transmit its information with an energy that stems not least from its wonderful acidity. The best Smaragd bottlings from the excellent 1990s vintages were designated by the letter M. Thanks to the generosity of a great collector we have been able to taste the Kellerberg 1992 M, a wine of intense aromatic richness and remarkable nobility of bouquet. It is a shame this wine is not easier to find in wine merchants, which have always preferred the very rich and woody dessert wines of Burgenland. In addition to Riesling, Pichler is very well known for its Sauvignon, which comes as no surprise, so close are the two in style and responsiveness to terroir.

VINE VARIETY

30 acres (12 hectares) white: 50% Grüner Veltliner, 47% Riesling, 3% Sauvignon.

OUR FAVORITE WINES

This estate produces some of Austria's most uncompromising and long-lasting Rieslings with a slightly more pronounced minerality and spiciness than those from the best-known German or Alsatian vineyards. The Kellerberg Smaragds fully deserve their worldwide reputation. We are less familiar with the Grüner Veltliners.

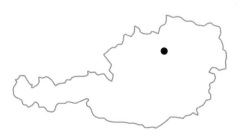

Weingut
Prager

Under the guidance of Ilse and Toni Bodenstein, an extremely high quality of viticulture is practiced at this historic property, which has been in the possession of the Prager family for more than three centuries. In terms of production methods, it is worth pointing out to our Alsatian friends in particular that chaptalization is never employed here, that the Smaragds are fermented completely dry, without the slightest hint of (inexcusable) residual sugar, and that malolactic fermentation is avoided in order to preserve the freshness and purity of the aromas. The mere sight of the magnificent Dürnstein and Wessenkirchen slopes will immediately convince visitors of the potential for quality of the best Wachau vineyards. The wines made by this estate, which stand out for their precision and honesty, confirm this impression and justify Prager's worldwide reputation. Occasionally, the Smaragd Rieslings may be found somewhat too pungent or full-bodied in their youth, with a minerality as abrupt as the slopes they are grown on, but with age their concentration and aromatic complexity come wonderfully to the fore. Wines under five years of age should be decanted two or three hours before drinking.

VINE VARIETY
32 acres (13 hectares) on wonderful terraced slopes (the Klaus, Steinriegl, Achleiten, Weitenberg, Wachstum Bodenstein, Kaiserberg and Hollerin sites) white: 50% Riesling, 25% Grüner Veltliner.

OUR FAVORITE WINES
The class of this estate's Rieslings speaks for itself, sometimes with finesse (Achleiten) and sometimes with an emphatic minerality (Klaus).

Typical of the viticulture of the Rhineland and central Europe, these vines are grown on terraced hillsides. The energy of this soil comes out in the strong mineral accents of the wines.

Weingut
Schloss Halbturn

The owners of the magnificent Schloss Halbturn in Burgenland, the Waldbott-Bassenheims, belong to one of the oldest families of the Austrian nobility. It was an inspired decision on their part to appoint the remarkable Karl-Heinz Wolf as manager of their vineyards. This well-known gourmet and skilled professional chef is an unrivaled expert on the world's finest wines. He has brought together a brilliant team, transforming the property's vines and wine. The vines are cultivated along biodynamic lines, but with strict regard for the disciplined work that this method involves, rather than the more typical hands-off approach. As is apparent from the diversity of vines grown here, both the geological make-up of the chalky soil (Muschelkalk) on the slopes of the Joiser-Jungenberg and the climate are equally suitable for Bordeaux and Burgundy grape varieties. The most successful wine, the Imperial, is a blend of the two Cabernet varieties with Blaufränkisch, giving a wine that is very rich in the style currently fashionable but with a sufficiently refined texture to balance the oakiness. The Pinot Noir, "Carlo", Wolf's particular favorite, has improved a lot and the forthcoming vintages promise great things.

SCHLOSS HALBTURN
BARON WALDBOTT-BASSENHEIM

VINE VARIETY

99 acres (40 hectares) at the Joiser Jungenberg vineyard, red: Cabernet Sauvignon, Cabernet Franc, Merlot, Pinot Noir, Zweigelt, Blaufränkisch; white: Sauvignon, Chardonnay, Gruner-Veltliner.

OUR FAVORITE WINES

The pick of the crop is used for the production of the highly aromatic Imperial cuvées. Their intense color and flavor make Imperial one of the most promising Austrian wines, ensuring certain international success.

Baroque buildings where age-old wine flavors have been reproduced for centuries. Austrian vineyards have a long history and their present revival is a matter for celebration for lovers of white wine.

Luxembourg

Luxembourg's small winegrowing area, tucked between the French and German borders, shares something of both its larger neighbors' winemaking cultures. Its minerally Riesling, naturally lively and low in alcohol, is strongly influenced by the nearby Saar. Logically, however, the country's best slopes are an extension of the geology of the French Moselle, featuring clay-marl formations that differ considerably from the ancient German schist. With the help of the global warming that has been making itself felt over the last ten years, Luxembourg's winemakers are understandably convinced that the Burgundian varieties – Chardonnay, Pinot Blanc, Auxerrois, and even Pinot Noir – are capable of ripening on the local south- and southeast-facing sites. In terms of style, the best of these wines are starting to resemble their Alsatian equivalents.

Domaine Aly Duhr et fils

Luxembourg's vineyards, very little known beyond its own borders, closely resemble those of the adjacent German Mosel region, except that in geological terms the area is an extension of the Parisian Bassin and is dominated by Triassic limestone soils – which explains why the Burgundian varieties have adapted so well here. The Duhr family realized very early on that good quality levels could be achieved with high-density planting, and Leo Duhr started to make brilliant wines from the best northern varieties. His son Abi shares the same gift, emphasizing both the aromatic potential of these varieties and the delicate minerality of the terroir. He has gradually introduced more natural methods into the vinification process (the use of indigenous yeasts, for example) and has also refined barrique aging techniques. His excellent 2000 vintage has set new quality standards for Luxembourg producers, and restaurants throughout northern Europe could do far worse than include his wines on their lists.

VINE VARIETY

22 acres (9 hectares) red: Pinot Noir; white: 6% Elbling, 27% Pinot Gris, 20% Rivaner, 20% Riesling, 14% Pinot Blanc and Auxerrois, 5% Gewürztraminer.

OUR FAVORITE WINES

Abi Duhr, the son of Leo and Aly, is without doubt Luxembourg's most talented winemaker and has come closer than anyone to achieving the quality of the great French and German wines he admires so much. His prestige cuvée Le Clos du Paradis, a Burgundy-type wine, and above all his Wormeldange Riesling, possess wonderful finesse and purity. However, his most astonishing wine is his Elbling, an ancient Mosel variety with a noble floral nose.

Switzerland

Swiss wine has never achieved the international fame it deserves. There are two reasons for this: first, its entire production is consumed at home and second, most of the wine is light, fruity, and designed to be drunk within the year. Until very recently the only exception was the Valais region, whose magnificent sites favor the production of full-bodied wines with aging potential made from local white varieties such as Petite Arvine, Humagne and Païen (known as Savagnin in Franche-Comté), and Syrah reds. Now Ticino is waking up and refining its Pinot Noirs and, above, all Merlots, while the impressive terraces that border Lake Geneva, where Chasselas has traditionally reigned supreme, are opening up to Chardonnay and other classic French varieties, leading to a diversification of production methods. The latest generation of producers is dominated by an abundance of forceful personalities who are rediscovering smaller yields and vinification methods designed to convey terroir character and who are even dreaming up new styles of wine, such as sweet Valais and expressive Sauvignon Blancs from the Canton of Geneva.

List of domaines

Domaine
La Colombe

Over the years, Raymond and Violaine Paccot have become a point of reference for wine producers in the canton of Vaud. Their vines are grown on sunny slopes near the villages of Féchy, Mont sur Rolle, Saint-Livres, and Gilly. They are cultivated with exemplary precision using methods that are as natural as possible, yet consistent with the production of the best quality grapes. The wine is made by simple, straightforward techniques that are, nevertheless, always very precise. The owners' long-standing friendship with chef Freddy Girardet has led to an interest in the production of wines that are light but not watery, suitable for drinking with the local specialty, lake fish. One cuvée inspired by him, and bearing his name, is a blend of white grape varieties that makes the perfect accompaniment for risotto with cep mushrooms or cream of asparagus with morels. The wines from Chasselas grapes have a forceful character unusual in Europe. The small Mont sur Rolle vineyard gives the most mineral-rich wine, while the brown earth of the Brez vineyard at Féchy gives the most elegant wine. The most original wine is arguably that from the vineyard called Vigne en Bayel, both for its refinement and for its extraordinary development in the bottle. The reserve red wines, particularly the Colombe Noire (a blend of Pinot Noir and Gamaret), are improving with every new vintage.

A perfect landscape of lake and vine-covered land. Easy on the eye, but its upkeep represents endless hard work.

LE BREZ

2004

DOMAINE LA COLOMBE
RAYMOND PACCOT

VINE VARIETY
25 acres (10 hectares) red: Pinot Noir, Gamay, Gamaret, Garanoir; white: Chasselas, Chardonnay, Pinot Gris.

OUR FAVORITE WINES
Raymond Paccot is particularly skilled in the production of white Chasselas wines with a Féchy appellation. One of his best terroirs, Vigne en Bayel, gives wines of unrivaled energy and freshness. Experiments with different red grape varieties, including a new hybrid, Gamaret, are promising but do not yet match the refinement and originality of the white wines.

Simon Maye et fils

The reason that the suitability of the beautiful slopes of the Valais for producing great wines is so little known is simple: the Swiss drink all the wine produced there themselves. The Chamoson alluvial cone is one such area, producing highly accomplished red and white wines. The geography and climate here make it possible to bring the grapes to full maturity and even, in the case of Petite Arvine, to harvest late in the year. The grapes retain their acidity, guaranteeing a freshness and aromatic refinement that are becoming increasingly rare in Europe. Simon's sons, Axel and Jean-François Maye, have proved to be not only remarkable grape growers but also winemakers without equal. With great skill, they have identified the grape varieties best suited to each of their properties. The most chalky soil is planted with Humagne, Pinot Noir, and Syrah vines, while the dry and gravelly areas support the white grape varieties. The red wines from this domaine made great progress in the 1990s, and now almost eclipse classic white varietals. The result of limiting the yield from the Syrah vines grown in the Chamoson area has been wines of a refinement and complexity worthy of a fine Côte Rôtie. Although the Pinot Noir has an admirable personality, our preference is for the red Humagne on account of its originality, density, and rarity. The family's long-standing friendship with Freddy Girardet has contributed much to the preservation of a quality that is of paramount importance in wine intended for drinking with a meal.

VINE VARIETY

28 acres (11.5 hectares) red: Gamay, Pinot Noir, Syrah, Humagne Rouge; white: Sylvaner (Johannisberg), Chasselas, Petite Arvine, Savagnin (local name Païen or Heida).

OUR FAVORITE WINES

Although the white wines are very good (especially the Petite Arvine and the Savagnin), it is the reds produced by this respected winemaker that really excel. The old vine Syrah, in particular, from the magnificent terroir of Prés des Pierres near Chamoson in the upper Rhône valley, has a refinement of texture that would be hard to better. The Humagne, from grapes grown on the chalky soil of La Tzoumaz, has an admirable rectitude.

Louis Bovard

This skilled and dynamic producer is the owner of one of the most beautiful estates on the shores of Lake Geneva with vineyards in the well-respected areas of Epesse, Villette, Saint-Saphorin and, most importantly, 12 acres (5 hectares) of a Grand Cru, Dézaley. One of the most extraordinary creations in European viticulture, it is situated on a magnificent slope directly over the lake. The vines are grown on hundreds of tiny terraces called *charmus*, the majority of which still belong to the city of Lausanne. In addition to the harvest from his own vines, Louis Bovard buys in extra grapes, allowing him to produce 200,000 bottles a year. He exports some of his wine – unusual for Switzerland where almost all wine produced is sold on the home market. Assisted by the French enologist Jean-Luc Colombo, Bovard is now producing wines that have an even greater precision and rigor, the style having gained in structure and naturalness. Recent experiments with the use of casks for the Collection Louis-Philippe Bovard look very promising. The house's Dézaley may surprise some connoisseurs with its delicately spicy aromas and, as it ages, the developing notes of honey, lime-blossom, and hazelnut that recall some of the best Marsannes produced from the characteristic terroirs of gravelly soil over chalk marl found in the northern Rhône Valley.

The steep slopes of the Valais, the mist over the terraces perhaps an indication of the beginnings of noble rot.

VINE VARIETY

42 acres (17 hectares) red: Pinot Noir, Gamay, Gamaret, Merlot, Syrah; white: Chasselas with some Sauvignon, Chenin Blanc.

OUR FAVORITE WINES

This domaine specializes in the production of Dézaley appellation white wines. The most prestigious vineyard on the lake, it is beautifully laid out on sunny terraces. The Chasselas wines produced here are the most complex and vinous in all Switzerland. The most expressive of the cuvées has the delightful name of Médinette.

Cave la Liaudisaz,
Marie-Thérèse Chappaz

Marie-Thérèse Chappaz is the true artist of viticulture in the Valais. Her meticulously cultivated vines can stand as a model for all would-be biodynamic growers (who seem sometimes to be more interested in the soil than the vines). She knows better than anyone when the grapes are completely mature and ready for harvesting, and she has an unerring feel for winemaking, producing sweet wines of a quality on a par with the very greatest successes from France and Germany. She makes three cuvées: Malvoisie (with Pinot Gris), superbly unctuous; Hermitage (Marsanne), more aristocratic but more austere; and, best of all, a delicious Petite Arvine which, for balance of acidity and sugar, can only be matched by the very finest Jurançons. Even her simplest wines, sold in 1-pint (50-centiliter) containers that she calls *pots*, have a rare freshness and honesty. It is best to start with the wines from the different terroirs: Fendant is from Martigny, where the limestone soil gives the Chasselas grapes an unusually solid structure; the white Marsannes comes from grapes grown on a granite soil. The reds produced here have been very fine in recent years – notably an original blend of Bordeaux grape varieties called Grain Noir, reminiscent of the Loire in its heyday.

VINE VARIETY
16 acres (6.5 hectares) divided between five villages.
Red: Pinot Noir, Gamay (Dôle), Cabernet Sauvignon, Cabernet Franc, Merlot; white: Petite Arvine, Marsanne (Hermitage), Pinot Gris (Malvoisie), Chasselas (Fendant).

OUR FAVORITE WINES
All the cuvées from this tiny and traditional domaine are exceptional, with the sweet wines made from grapes affected by noble rot standing out in particular. Astonishingly vigorous, pure, and elegant, they can be said to represent the peak of Swiss viticulture at the present time.

Denis Mercier

The vines of this family-owned domaine, run since 1982 by Denis Mercier and his wife, grow on a very pretty site on the slopes of the Crêt-Goubing. Careful viticulture (the soil being enriched by compost prepared on the site) and a deep respect for the environment result in grapes of the highest quality. These are processed with the precision that is characteristic of the best Swiss winemakers. Of the white wines, the Hermitage is preferable to the popular Fendant, particularly the cuvées made with grapes that have been allowed to shrivel and dry on the vine, giving a wonderful aromatic richness. The reds have the strong personality of the best Valais terroirs. The most frequently encountered of these is Dôle, a light but very attractive blend of Pinot Noir and Gamay. However, the domaine's two great specialties are the Cornalin made from the rare and very high-quality grape of the same name (a variety that is more vinous and refined than the Valais Pinot Noir), and a marvelous Syrah, admired by Swiss sommeliers for its refinement and noble tannins.

VINE VARIETY

12 acres (5 hectares) red: Pinot Noir, Gamay, Cornalin, Syrah; white: Chasselas, Pinot Blanc, Marsanne, Riesling.

OUR FAVORITE WINES

The red wines from this domaine are even more successful than the whites. The unusual Cornalin is particularly good, with a remarkable refinement and velvetiness of texture. The Syrah, one of the most well-rounded of this category of Valais wines, has all the characteristic elegance of this grape.

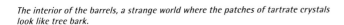

The interior of the barrels, a strange world where the patches of tartrate crystals look like tree bark.

Maurice Zufferey

Nicolas Zufferey is one of the most respected wine producers in the Valais. The winery at Muraz, established by his uncle Charles Caloz, was one of the first to rediscover Cornalin, a red grape variety native to the Valais that invariably gives a wine of strong personality and which would appear to be even better adapted to the terroir and climate than Pinot Noir. The vines are cultivated using environmentally friendly integrated pest management (IPM) methods, where the use of chemical products to protect the vines is limited to the minimum. The partial grassing of the land limits erosion and encourages biological processes that help to nourish the vines. The style of the wines produced here is unique, being characterized by a wonderful aromatic purity and an almost infallible precision in the expression of the wine's origin, combined with a deliciously refreshing taste. This last characteristic is also found in the prestige cuvées matured in wood such as the Chardonnay Les Glariers and the red Clos de la Combettaz. The red Humagne will appeal to those who like a vigorous country wine; it goes particularly well with the Alpine cuisine. While its tannins are less elegant than those in the Cornalin, its cheerful energy and its highly expressive bouquet of red berries make it ideal for a winter evening.

The tally stick is not only a trophy, but also a reminder of the preceding vintage and a promise for the next.

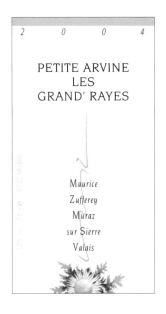

VINE VARIETY
21 acres (8.5 hectares) red: Humagne, Cornalin, Pinot Noir (60% of the domaine's total production); white: Petite Arvine, Chardonnay, Riesling, Sylvaner.

OUR FAVORITE WINES
While the white wines produced here are notable for their expression and class – particularly Les Grand' Rayes made from Petite Arvine grapes – the domaine is chiefly famous for its Pinot Noir red wines. The most successful is the Clos de la Combettaz, made with grapes from the oldest vines.

Hungary

When the Médoc was no more than a wild and desolate strip of land between water and forest, the imperial vineyards of Tokay (or Tokaj under the Hungarian spelling generally adopted today) had already been meticulously classified and benefited from highly sophisticated vinification methods that produced fermented sweet wines of unique renown. During the brief communist interlude, when the vineyards were extended into the Great Plain, quality suffered and the wine was often characterless and mediocre; it is wonderful to witness its current revival and see it gradually regain its international reputation. The arrival of French, Spanish, Danish, English, and German viticulturists and wine experts, encouraged by the local authorities, has played an important part in this process, creating a spirit of competition that favors quality. Recent vintages have been spectacularly successful but should not be allowed to eclipse the efforts of other Hungarian winegrowing regions such as Villany, with its excellent red wines made from the Bordeaux varieties, and even more importantly the area north of Lake Balaton whose basalt soils produce highly expressive minerally whites that rival the greatest Austrian or German crus.

List of domaines

Attila Gere

Attila Gere is, with Szepsy, the most famous wine-maker in Hungary, and he deserves to be just as well known outside his country. The vineyards of Villany date from Roman times when the favorable conditions were quickly recognized. The climate, Mediterranean levels of sunshine, and numerous underground geothermal springs mean that the soil does not cool down too much at night, while the limestone subsoil gives energy to the wine made from grapes grown here. Over a period of 20 years' hard work, Gere has been able to satisfy himself that the Kopar terroir's reputation for the highest quality is fully justified. It is here that his greatest red wines are produced. His other vineyards have excellent situations in the terroirs of Konkoly, and particularly on the dolomitic limestone soils of Ordőgárők. It comes as something of a surprise to discover how much the tannins of the Cabernets and Merlots grown here develop their potential in the wooden casks. Once everything was in place, Gere could give free rein to his ambitions. The result was two superb prestige wines: Kopar (a blend of 60% Cabernet Sauvignon and Cabernet Franc, and 40% Merlot that makes a very aristocratic wine); and the sumptuous and baroque Solus, made of 100% Merlot. Gere's other products deserve more investigation, particularly the style of wines made from old, little-known Hungarian grape varieties such as Bakator, Purcsin, Csoka, and others.

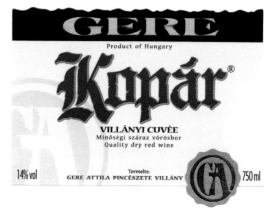

VINE VARIETY

124 acres (50 hectares) red: Cabernet Sauvignon, Cabernet Franc, Merlot, Kekfrankos, Kekoporto, and others including Syrah, Pinot Noir, and historic Hungarian varieties.
Crus Kopar, Konkoly, Ordogarok.

OUR FAVORITE WINES

One of the most exciting discoveries of recent decades in the field of European red wines has been Kopar, this producer's blend of Bordeaux varieties. An aristocratic wine of great completeness, in our view it stands among the very best of European wines. Solus, a wine made of pure Merlot, is destined to make a mark.

A striking feature here is the intelligent leaf removal that allows the clusters of grapes to receive the maximum amount of sunshine.

Hétszőlő

The French company GMF is a large insurance group that invested considerably in Tokaj at the time of denationalization. It chose its vines well, taking over the imperial domaine established in the 17th century by the Rakoczy family, together with their house. The wine produced here is the authentic Tokaj of Tokaj, because it is made from grapes grown on the southern slope of Mount Tokaj, overlooking the Tiszra river. The microclimate of this site is perfect for the development of botrytis, or noble rot, while the soil gives the wine a bouquet of the greatest velvety refinement. The company's choice of personnel has been similarly astute, particularly with the appointment of Tibor Kovács, one of the best enologists in Hungary. He had the courage to defend the "new" winemaking techniques, challenging the backward-looking conservatism of his colleagues who refused to allow the new Tokaj the right to an appellation. The highly floral aromas of the young 5-*puttonyos* wines are the most elegant we have encountered. They benefit from all the advantages of a complete fermentation, giving the wine stability and, most importantly, a perfect balance of acidity, sugar, and alcohol. These are true works of art, and it is a shame that their production still needs to depend on foreign subsidy.

VINE VARIETY
30 acres (45 hectares) white: 67% Furmint, 30% Harslevelu, 3% Muscat Crus Hétszőlő (literally "seven vines") and Nagyszölo.

OUR FAVORITE WINES
The company's specialties are the recently fashionable Forditas and, particularly, the Aszús. The wines benefit from the wonderful microclimate of the imperial vineyards, and while their refinement and purity are perhaps not currently fully appreciated, a day will come when it will be acknowledged that the imperial classification awarded in 1700 is as apt today as it ever was.

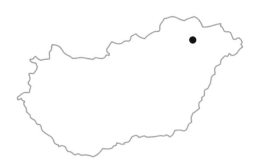

Disznókő

Given the substantial financial backing at AXA's disposal, the insurance company regarded it as its duty to participate in the "renaissance" of Tokaj. Planting, overseen by Jean-Michel Cazes from Bordeaux, has taken place over the entire surface of Disznókő (literally, "Pig's Hill"), just outside the town of Mad, an area classified as premier cru in 1700. Winemaking and retail buildings open to the public have also been installed. Daniel Llose, the energetic technical director of AXA's properties, made it clear from the outset that he would move away from traditional local winemaking methods which, between 1950 and 1990, had resulted in an increasingly pedestrian version of the sweet wine. Instead of pasteurizing the musts and adding sweetening agents, the Aszú grapes were henceforth fermented in the musts or in the current year's wine, while the casks were topped up (*ouillage*) to prevent any oxidation. This new type of sweet wine is cleaner, fresher, and more fruity. Local experts were initially scandalized, and furious arguments ensued. A ceremonial tasting was arranged and relayed on local television to demonstrate that the great vintages of the pre-Communist period were similarly un-oxidized. The result has been that the new style is now increasingly being imitated. The Disznókő team has also begun to produce a dry wine made of Furmint grapes, though this has only started to be of interest since the late 1990s.

VINE VARIETY

62 acres (100 hectares) white: 60% Furmint, 28% Harslevelu, 10% Zeta, 2% Muscat.

OUR FAVORITE WINES

The 1993 and 1995 vintages, the first to be produced in the new style, have come on remarkably to give 5- and 6-puttonyos wines, their aroma of mandarins and spices unaffected by oxidation. They have a very long finish, but without the flinty or fiery hints associated with volcanic soils, found in many other wines from this area.

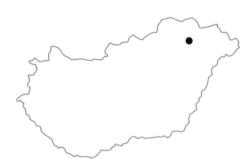

Királyudvar

István Szepsy is synonymous with Tokaj. Descended from a family owning vineyards for several centuries, he was obliged to bide his time during the Communist period, frustrated by the neglect of the country's wine heritage. The end of this period gave him a new freedom to develop. He understands better than anyone the terroirs, the techniques of viticulture, and the quality of all the Furmint clones. What's more, his 1993 wines were able to demonstrate an ideal synthesis between tradition and modernity. He subsequently went into business with the wealthy Chinese wine enthusiast Anthony Hwang (who has also taken over the Huet domaine in Vouvray), setting up Királyudvar with the intention of making it the major producer of Tokaj. Vines in the best terroirs of Tarcal and Mad have been purchased, and a magnificent winery constructed. The exceptionally good 1999 vintage allowed the partnership to demonstrate what it was capable of, establishing criteria of quality for the region with which it would be difficult to compete. Everything is done to ensure that the sweet wines produced are the richest and most natural possible. They concentrate uniquely on 6-*puttonyos*, blending grapes from these fine terroirs. The extraordinary Lapis is made separately.

In the small, humid, and mysterious cellars of Tokaj, a curious fungus develops on the bottles (stored upright), which may contribute to the bouquet of the very old wines.

VINE VARIETY
68 acres (110 hectares) white: mainly Furmint and Harslevelo. Crus Lapis, Betsek, Szent Tamás, Nyulaszo, etc.

OUR FAVORITE WINES
István Szepsy is the undisputed champion of 6-puttonyos Aszú. He is uniquely skilled in bringing out the spicy notes of the volcanic soil and blending these with the noble rot-induced notes of mango, citrus fruits, and quince, and the perfectly defined hints of dried fruit (true Aszú) to produce wines of astonishing aromatic complexity. His 1999 Lapis, made from grapes planted on a very steep slope, is superb, while the dry Furmint of 1999 is perhaps the best Hungarian white wine we have ever tasted.

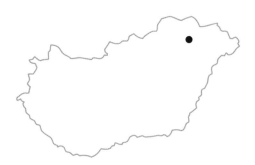

Oremus

The Alvarez family, owners of the wonderful Vega Sicilia house in Spain, had no vineyards for white wines. And so it was that they were receptive to a proposal made to them by a young Hungarian enologist, Andréas Bacso, appointed by the Hungarian government to oversee the denationalization of the wine industry – a job he carried out brilliantly. Impressed, the Alvarez family appointed him to run their new property in the very promising Tolcsva area. The great Hungarian families, including the famous Rakoczys, who once owned properties there could never have imagined that viticulture and winemaking would one day reach such heights of refinement. Bacso has designed and built a wonderful fermenting room, with gravity-fed vats arranged on three levels. An ingenious system is used to add the Aszú grapes to the must, and the wines are aged in cellars that, though they extend for 3 miles (5 kilometers), have a healthy atmosphere throughout – something not always the case in Tokaj. The cultivation of the vines, overseen by Sandor Szurki, is a model of good practice: missing root stocks are replaced immediately, and meticulous training of the vines allows the grapes to reach an advanced stage of maturity. The still wines, the Forditas (obtained from a second pressing of the pomace – grape skins, pips, pulp, and stalks – of Aszú grapes), and the Aszú wines are models of their kind.

VINE VARIETY

284 acres (115 hectares) white: 55% Furmint, 40% Harslevelo, 5% Muscat de Lunel.
Crus Mandulas, Kutpaka, Budelazi, Peto.

OUR FAVORITE WINES

Oremus produces what is perhaps the most homogenous range of wines in Tokaj. Particularly fine is the dry white made from late-harvested Furmint grapes (14.5%), which have only a low yield in order to give the wine the necessary lipids. The Aszús are among the most complex and are the grapes that best reveal the character of the volcanic soil on which they are grown. The 5- and 6-puttonyos of 1995 and 1999 are masterpieces of their kind.

The golden treasure of the Tokaj cellars: a testament to some fine vintages and talented men.

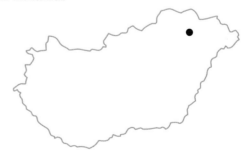

Royal Tokay Company

This English company was inspired by the visionary spirit of the Danish enologist Peter Vinding who was an unconditional admirer of the terroir, history, and wines of Tokaj. He dreamed of restoring the terroirs – and, in particular, those placed in the first category in the famous classification of 1700 – to their former and individual glory. With the willing assistance of the Hungarian state, he was able to buy or take out long-term contracts for the grapes harvested from plots of land in the most famous vineyards of the Mad area, such as Birsalmás and Szent Tamás. He was the first to shorten the time taken to mature the wines in wood, and to top up the casks (*ouillage*) in order to reduce the amount of oxidation in the wines. Although he realized that he would not make his fortune by doing so, he specialized in wines at the top of the range, the sweetest and richest of all being the 5- and 6-*puttonyos* (a 6-*puttonyos* wine must contain 150 grams/liter residual sugar and 45 grams/liter sugar-free extract), sold under the name of each terroir. Tasting several vintages, it is possible to define the personality of the best of these wines: those from Betzek are the most masculine, with a marked acidity; Szent Tamas is the most elegant; Nyulaszo is the most complex and perhaps most aristocratic.

VINE VARIETY

198 acres (80 hectares) white: mainly Furmint.
54 acres (22 hectares) Cru Nyulaszo; 40 acres (16 hectares)
Cru Betzek; 27 acres (11 hectares) Cru Szent Tamás;
22 acres (9 hectares) Cru Sarkad; 25 acres (10 hectares)
Cru Mezesmaly; 25 acres (10 hectares) Cru Danczka.

OUR FAVORITE WINES

The wines of the 1993 vintage are very refined, but the splendid 1995 wines are even better. We have not tasted any of the more recent vintages.

Ideal misty conditions for Aszú grapes, which give the syrupy wines of Tokaj their incomparable bouquet.

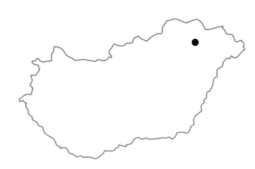

Vylyan

This pioneering property was the result of the efforts and vision of Pál Debreczeni, a wealthy businessman and wine connoisseur. Appalled by the mediocrity of Hungarian red wines of the 1980s, he planted his first vines in 1992 in an area with a very warm climate where the soil has a deep layer of silt over limestone. He decided to use traditional varieties combined with some Bordeaux varieties that had given promising results when planted by pioneers like Attila Gere. He sought the advice of a number of expert consultants, including the Hungarian Tibor Kovács of Hétszőlő and Jean-Pierre Confuron of Vosne-Romanée in Burgundy (to make the Pinot Noir wine that he is so fond of). With his wife Monica, Pál Debreczeni established a domaine that quickly became noticed for its perfectionism and daring. He died in 2004, but Monica continues to run the enterprise with similar energy. Villany is a terroir best suited to the production of full-bodied red wines, enjoying a highly favorable sub-Mediterranean microclimate. Varieties that particularly suit these conditions are Portugieser (Kekoporto), Blaufränkish (Kekfrankos), and its hybrid, Zweigelt. However, the Cabernet Sauvignon gives more complex wines with an excellent maturity of tannins. Its refined character plays an important role in the original style of the Cuvée Duennium, a wine that gives eloquent expression to the characteristics of the local terroir while still meeting international criteria.

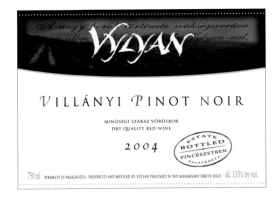

VINE VARIETY

309 acres (125 hectares) white: Chardonnay; red: Cabernet Sauvignon, Pinot Noir, Merlot, Zweigelt, Kekporto, Kekfranko.

OUR FAVORITE WINES

This enterprising property makes clever use of a combination of international and traditional local grape varieties. The Pinot Noir has become one of the finest in Europe, while the Duennium cuvée, a blend of Cabernet and local varieties, is gaining in complexity with each year that passes. Those who like a full-bodied wine will choose the Zweigelt, an intense and convincing wine of great originality.

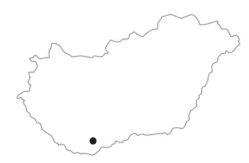

Mediterranean

From the land of biblical Canaan, where the tribes of Israel refreshed themselves with the grapes that grew there in abundance, to the Phoenicians, whose dynamic commerce took them from one end of the region to the other, wine was at the heart of human activity in the eastern Mediterranean for two thousand years. These days, the region's vines produce mainly table grapes. A number of groundbreaking winemakers have nevertheless taken up the challenge of producing fine wine, and in some cases have been doing so for several decades. Success has been achieved in Lebanon, where winegrowers have benefited from the relative coolness and fertility of the Bekaa Valley, and more recently at the heart of Israel. Over the last ten years, the style of Greek wine has been significantly modernized by winemakers who are gradually revealing the diversity and strong personality of the country's terroirs and indigenous varieties. The Peloponnese favors the production of full-bodied, flavorsome reds, while Naoussa and Macedonia can claim an even higher level of quality. The country's white wines are still more accomplished, particularly the extremely aromatic dry whites made from Assyrtico grapes grown in the volcanic soils of Santorini and Malgousia.

List of domaines

Château
Musar

In an era when taste in wine has become internationalized, prizing strength and immediacy of flavor above subtlety, Château Musar offers a wonderful and refined contrast. The ancient vineyard in the Bekaa plain reveals its somewhat old-fashioned but utterly bewitching charm through its wines – not just red, but white and even rosé – which are frequently allowed to mature in the bottle for several years. Château Musar expresses in a uniquely personal way the idea of a civilization with a tradition of winemaking and drinking, based as much on its complex mixture of influences as on its elegance. Founded in 1930 and taking its name from the 18th-century castle of M'zar, Musar is the creation of the Hochar family, and particularly Gaston. It was he who initially decided to create the wine, taking advice from his friend Ronald Barton, who was then the owner of the famous Château Léoville-Barton vineyard at Saint-Julien in France. The Hochar family was drawn into the project and, under the guidance of Serge, Gaston's son, Château Musar was to become the most famous wine in the Middle East. Spread over the Bekaa plain, this huge estate rises to an altitude of 3,281 feet (1,000 meters).

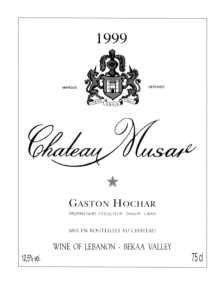

VINE VARIETY
44 acres (180 hectares) red: Cabernet Sauvignon, Carignan, Cinsault; white: Obeideh, Merwah.

OUR FAVORITE WINES
The white 1999 vintage is an original and generous wine, marked by a full-bodied nobility, elegance, and honeyed bouquet reminiscent of an earlier epoch. The red Château Musar has charm and refinement – notably the 1998 and 1999 vintages, which have subtlety and a very refined finish.

Domaine du
Castel

Although the first person to plant vines in Israel in modern times was Baron Edmond de Rothschild in the 19th century, it was not until the 1970s that there was a serious interest in producing fine wines. Today, the Israeli wine business is thriving, run by a mixture of large firms concentrating on everyday table wines and small producers dedicated to the making of quality wines. Standing out among the latter and quickly drawing ahead of them was Domaine du Castel. In 1988, Eli Ben Zaken, at the time the owner of an Italian restaurant in Jerusalem and a lover of fine wines, planted a few vines of Cabernet and Merlot in the hills overlooking his home situated to the west of Jerusalem. After the first vintage harvested in 1992, the wine immediately attracted attention. The vineyard expanded, cultivated according to the most up-to-date methods of viticulture, and favoring in particular a relatively high density of planting. The altitude (2,297 feet/700 meters above sea level) means that the grapes are protected from the worst of the summer heat. Now assisted by his son and son-in-law, Eli Ben Zaken can be proud of the progress he has made in a relatively short time. Both the red Castel Grand Vin and the white C du Castel have a fullness and, above all, a balance that are the hallmarks of a great wine.

VINE VARIETY

32 acres (13 hectares) red: 39% Cabernet Sauvignon, 29% Merlot, 1% Cabernet Franc and 5% Petit Verdot; white: 26% Chardonnay.

OUR FAVORITE WINES

The 2003 white Chardonnay is a powerful and honest wine with a bouquet that combines hints of oak and fresh butter with astonishingly floral notes. It has an impressive density of structure with no flabbiness. As for red wines, along with the very pleasant (mainly Merlot) Petit Castel, the 2003 Cabernet Sauvignon has rich fullness and charm of body combined with a delicate velvetiness. The variety and vigor of the grape variety is very evident, making this a fine wine that deserves to be well known.

Gerovassiliou

Just a couple of miles from the sea and not far from Thessaloniki, the estate is located in an area of great beauty (and particularly mild winters) named Kalimeria by the Byzantines. In 1983, Evangelos Gerovassiliou, who had been involved in the creation of Château Carras, Greece's first world-class wine of modern times, planted a fine sloping vineyard here on calcareous marl rich in marine fossils, a very good subsoil for white grapes. In addition to the two best traditional Greek grapes, Assyrtico and Malagousia, Gerovassiliou also grows French varieties, bringing enormous skill and precision to the winemaking process. His influence on the young generation of Greek producers currently regenerating Greek viticulture is considerable. In terms of red, his Syrah-dominated blends are no doubt extremely well adapted to Epanomi's microclimate, but it would be fascinating to see what the talented Gerovassiliou could achieve with indigenous Greek red varieties. His ability to gauge the right level of tannic extraction, a skill he learned from Professor Peynaud in Bordeaux, would no doubt produce some highly memorable results.

VINE VARIETY
101 acres (41 hectares) red: Syrah, Merlot, Grenache; white: Assyrtico, Malagousia, Sauvignon Blanc, Chardonnay, Viognier.

OUR FAVORITE WINES
Evangelos Gerovassiliou has shown great talent in combining indigenous varieties with the best French varieties (in both his reds and his whites), but his most original wines are his Assyrtico and Malagousia whites, which are fresh and sinewy with delicious citrus notes.

Gaia

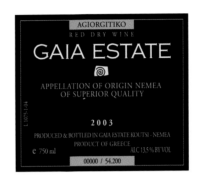

Gaia is the fruit of an association between two of the biggest winemaking talents in Greece today: agronomist Leon Karatsolas, and enologist Yannis Paraskevopoulos. They started out making wine in Santorini, rejecting traditional techniques in order to give the astonishing range of aromas of the Assyrtico variety a more modern dimension (particularly in the Thalassitis cuvée). They subsequently planted Agiorgitico on its "home ground" in Nemea. There they applied the most intelligent principles of modern winemaking to achieving maximum terroir definition and succeeded in making what we believe to be Greece's most balanced and harmonious wine today: the 2000 Gaia Estate, whose tannic refinement and well-integrated oak could serve as a model to winemakers throughout the entire Mediterranean region. And what a relief to find that it is no mere imitation (even a successful one) of decent Bordeaux!

OUR FAVORITE WINES

This estate's Santorini appellation Assyrtico whites, made in the French style, achieve a remarkable aromatic purity that should make it eminently exportable. The red Gaia Estate cuvée (made from the excellent indigenous grape Agiorgitico) frequently overshadows its Nemea AO competitors with its density and harmony. Gaia's most original wine, however, is its Retsina, whose freshness and subtlety will come as a revelation to those who associate the name with the mediocre examples of the style that are all too common.

North America

The United States of America is on the way to becoming the country consuming the most wine in the world. Despite the fact that wine production continues to expand, only a small proportion is exported. Although grapes are grown in many central and East-Coast American states, it is the West Coast that produces by far the most wine and the most esteemed crus. As elsewhere in the world, its success owes much both to the quality of the soil and the climate, and to human skill and effort. Seeking out the most suitable sites for vine growing – generally volcanic slopes weathered by erosion, or enriched by silt deposited by river or sea – producers found that the climate suited many of the European varieties. These produce fruit here of a quality as good as, or even better than, that of their native land.

Bordeaux varieties and Chardonnay reach a perfect maturity in northern California, while Pinot Noir thrives in the cooler parts of southern California, with Rhône and Spanish varieties enjoying the warmer areas. Oregon specializes in Burgundy varieties, while Washington State is gradually revealing its great potential for growing a wide range of different grape varieties. In California, and particularly in the small Napa Valley region, financial investment and enological know-how have perfected the production of luxury wines, eagerly sought after by connoisseurs. They are rich in natural alcohols and have a powerful bouquet. The quality of the ordinary wines from the huge vineyards of the central coastal area is gradually improving, but has not yet reached a high enough standard for export. The wines produced in Oregon and Washington are still made by traditional methods, and the enthusiast will often find examples that have a greater subtlety and elegance.

Canada, too, is beginning to produce quality wines, especially in Ontario and British Columbia (Okanagan valley), but the only one to become well known internationally is ice wine (*Eiswein*), a specialty from Niagara made from grapes with juices concentrated by the first frosts of winter. This wine is sweet but full of vitality thanks to its high levels of acidity.

List of domaines

CALIFORNIA

OREGON

WASHINGTON

CANADA

Alban Vineyards

John Alban was a pioneering "Rhône Ranger," a fan of Rhône Valley wines who rightly believed that the soils and climate of the numerous vineyards to the south of San Francisco were better suited to the Rhône varieties than to those of Bordeaux. Having tired of stereotypical oaky, buttery Chardonnays, he soon realized that the Viognier grape produced wines that were equally rich and fat but more fruity. He was able to put his ideas to the test as early as 1989 with fruit from a very good site in San Luis Obispo County and later in his own Edna Valley vineyard. His Viognier caused an immediate sensation thanks to the honesty and generosity of its fruit, which made for a wine every bit as distinctive as that of Condrieu in the Rhône Valley; it has since become a cult in wine bars and among wine lovers in the know. The estate's Syrahs are perhaps even more surprising and original, and constitute a sumptuous trilogy: harmonious Reva, classic Lorraine (by virtue of its fruit), and best of all Seymour, in which the collective power of all the vineyards in the valley seems to have been concentrated. The current trend is for Syrahs from Walla Walla in the state of Washington, but in our opinion none of these has yet equaled the individuality of Alban's 1999 or 2000 vintages.

VINE VARIETY

*69 acres (28 hectares) red: Syrah, Grenache;
white: Roussanne, Viognier.
Grapes also bought in from the Central Coast area.*

OUR FAVORITE WINES

Alban is without doubt the most consistent of the Viognier producers, conjuring up fat and magnificently perfumed wines on a regular basis. Some years we prefer the Central Coast wines to the Edna Valley. The estate's trio of Syrahs (Lorraine, Reva, and Seymour) are America's best!

Araujo Estate Wines

The Eisele vineyard, which takes its name from its first owner, is the object of a cult like no other among Californian wine lovers. Planted with Cabernet Sauvignon in 1964, it soon started to produce wines of extraordinary body that acquired exceptional firmness with age. Thanks to very careful aging, Joseph Phelps gave them more polish in 1978 and 1985 but was not always able to avoid excessive alcohol, the drawback of a very warm microclimate. Bart Araujo bought the vineyard in 1990 and decided to furnish the winery with the best possible equipment in order to take it to an even higher level of quality. Ambitious, determined, and assisted by Françoise Peschon (an enologist from Luxembourg), he adopted organic methods in the vineyard. With the advice of Michel Rolland, whose flair he had admired at Harlan Estate, he started to harvest with greater precision, obtaining astonishingly dense and harmonious wines which are sure to become tomorrow's classics. A lover of white wines, he opted for Sauvignon Blanc and planted the best clones. The results, opposite in style to that adopted by Mondavi, have been thrilling. Deeper, more complex, and made from riper berries, it has become the new benchmark for this varietal in California.

If it were not for the vines, the poor, volcanic soil of the Napa Hills would support nothing but rattle snakes.

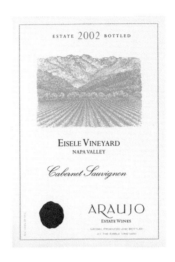

VINE VARIETY

40 acres (16 hectares), red: Cabernet Sauvignon, Syrah; white: Sauvignon.

OUR FAVORITE WINES

Naturally this estate's flagship wine is its Cabernet Sauvignon from the Eisele vineyard, a typically monumental, slow-aging (and remarkably well-made) northern Napa Valley red. We are just as impressed, however, with the first Syrah vintages from this property. These are astonishingly deep and complex – marvelous vehicles for conveying the individual character of this great terroir.

Au Bon Climat

Resembling a kind of Viking *bon viveur*, Jim Clendenen is one of those winemakers who it's impossible to forget, and his *joie de vivre* and generosity are reflected in his wines. These are colorful and flavorsome, overtly sensual but also full of the firmness and energy that derive from terroirs of strong personality. An ardent fan of Burgundy, of which he possesses one of the finest private collections on the planet, he concentrates exclusively on the Burgundian varieties and has deliberately established his winery in the area of California (the Bien Nacido district in Santa Barbara County) best suited to them. He buys his grapes from estates that share his passion and brings to their vinification an artisanal approach nevertheless far removed from the routine or obscurantist tendencies that are widespread throughout the region. Do not expect his Pinot Noirs to display the aromatic finesse this varietal obtains from certain Oregon terroirs; the emphasis here is on powerful red and black fruit and rich textures worthy of a Châteauneuf-du-Pape. The same power is shared by his best Chardonnays, such as the Reserve and Mount Carmel. However, they are never heavy, as their aromatic range is based on citrus and even tropical fruit rather than vanilla, caramel, or confectionery flavors. It would be wonderful to see a winemaker like Clendenen given responsibility for a leading Burgundy cru!

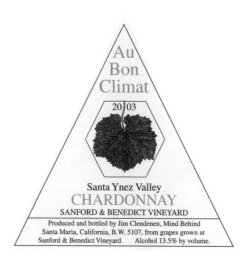

VINE VARIETY
No vineyard of its own but regular purchase of grapes (Pinot Noir, Pinot Blanc, Chardonnay) from the Bien Nacido, Sanford & Benedict, Talley, and Mount Carmel vineyards.

OUR FAVORITE WINES
The most accomplished Pinot Noir is Isabelle – the most dense and complex, and generally the best-aging. The most promising Chardonnays come from the Santa Rita district, whose grapes produce the most sinewy and minerally wines.

Bonny Doon

Anyone wishing to sample the off-the-wall humor and inventiveness of Randall Grahm, California's wackiest but certainly not its least efficient winemaker, need do no more than visit its website. A non-conformist and sworn enemy of the "enologically correct," he has spent the last 30 years making wine his own way, frequently varying his style while displaying at all times the desire to fully explore his convictions as an esthete and an individual. He has recently developed a passion for Riesling and the Italian grape varieties, but has staked his reputation on the Rhône Valley varieties he was the first to commercially exploit. He was quick to understand that the warm, dry soils of Paso Robles and Monterey were better suited to Grenache, Cinsault, and Mourvèdre than the Bordeaux varieties, and his love of great Châteauneuf-du-Pape inspired him to create two superb and extremely skillful blends for which he invented two puns (he shows a particular aptitude for wordplay) and which have made his fortune: Old Telegram refers to his affection for the wine made by the Brunier family and for his own grandfather (Old Grahm); Le Cigare Volant is inspired by the famous decree passed by the municipality of Châteauneuf in 1956 prohibiting any unidentified objects from flying through its airspace. In each case, however, it is the Santa Cruz sunshine that has been captured and bottled.

2003

LE CIGARE VOLANT
RED WINE
CALIFORNIA

VINE VARIETY
62 acres (25 hectares), red: Grenache, Syrah, Mourvèdre, Nebbiolo, Barbera, Cinsault; white: Roussanne, Muscat, Pinot Gris.

OUR FAVORITE WINES
All this estate's wines have something to say and are highly individual – and that includes their names! Currently, the most accomplished are: Le Cigare Volant, a wonderfully unctuous red; Old Telegram, a tauter, fuller-bodied wine dominated by Mourvèdre; Le Sophiste, a honeyed but far from sickly Roussanne white; and the fabulously fruity Muscat de Glacière, one of California's most consistent dessert wines.

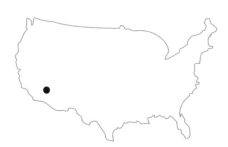

Calera

Calera was one of the craziest but at the same time boldest and most intelligent ventures undertaken by any member of the 1980s generation in California. After investigating every one of California's rare limestone slopes, military map in hand, Josh Jensen, who was completely smitten by the Pinot Noirs of Burgundy, settled on an isolated spot on the slopes of Mount Harlan. The place had neither electricity nor running water (and still hasn't), but at great cost and effort, he planted a vineyard that has repaid all the hard work a hundred-fold. Here, the Burgundy miracle is reproduced with a diversity of exposures and microclimates that give closely neighboring sites a distinct and consistent personality. Josh Jansen is an extremely well informed winemaker with an in-depth knowledge of Europe's winemaking history. His chosen vinification methods run counter to the current trend for spectacular wines, and his results are sometimes misunderstood by highly influential critics. His own clientele, on the other hand, has been extremely loyal and time has proved him (and them) right. In our view the refinement of body and texture and aromatic individuality of his wines are unparalleled in California. His estate's Viognier, almost certainly the first to be planted south of San Francisco, shares the same stylistic qualities, as does its Chardonnay, the latter with a certain additional heaviness.

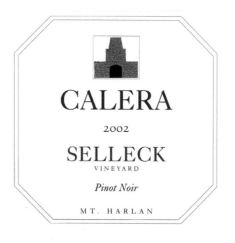

VINE VARIETY

49 acres (20 hectares): 80% Pinot Noir, 12% Chardonnay, 8% Viognier.
Pinot Noir vineyards: Selleck (5 acres/2 hectares),
Jensen (13 acres/5 hectares), Reed (4.5 acres/2 hectares),
Mills (15 acres/6 hectares).
Grapes bought in from the entire Central Coast region.

OUR FAVORITE WINES

This estate's Pinot Noirs are California's most distinguished and best aging, and sometimes bear an astonishing resemblance to the great Côte de Nuits reds. Selleck is the most reserved, while Reed boasts the greatest aromatic richness. Calera's Viognier will surprise many with its individuality and charm.

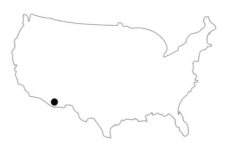

Château
Montelena

With its renowned 1973 Chardonnay, which beat a number of Burgundy grands crus to first place in the famous Paris tasting of 1976, this estate gave the reputation of Californian wines a significant boost. Of course, those were the days of Croatian magician Mike Grgich, who subsequently left to set up his own firm, taking his secrets with him. After Grgich came Jerry Luper, now forgotten but once one of his country's most intelligent winemakers and very close in sensibility to the current crop of European *terroiristes*. Luper made magnificent reds which, like those he made at Diamond Creek with his friend Al Brounstein, defined the most noble type of wine produced in Calistoga: deep, virile, and full of mineral character. Today Bo Barrett, owner of the property and a renowned enologist in his own right, makes wine in a more spectacular Californian style that nevertheless needs time to develop in the bottle as the estate's terroir is of the highest order. While not perhaps achieving the exceptional harmony or gradations of Martha's Vineyard, this terroir features three different soil types (volcanic, sedimentary, and alluvial) which help to vary the character of the grapes and produce complex tannins.

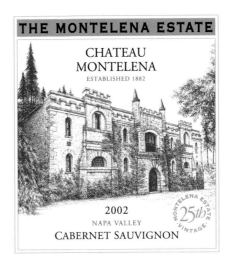

VINE VARIETY
116 acres (47 hectares) red: 80% Cabernet Sauvignon, 20% various (Zinfandel, Merlot, Cabernet Franc).

OUR FAVORITE WINES
This estate's Chardonnays currently lag some way behind its reds, which are dark, extremely well-structured, somewhat brusque in their youth, but capable of aging magnificently in the case of great years (such as 1978 or 1987) or acquiring weight and dryness in the case of numerous more recent vintages.

Caymus Vineyards

The Wagner family, originally from Alsace, can pride itself on being one of the oldest farming families still working the land in the Napa Valley. One of the Wagners' descendants started a winery in 1915 – in other words before Prohibition – and in 1940 Chuck Wagner's grandfather acquired the magnificent Rutherford property where a number of classic Californian wines have been made for more than 30 years. On the alluvium-rich soils of the Rutherford Bench, the estate's rigorously trellised vines produce spectacularly colored grapes that are extremely rich in sugar and tannins. Following the example of his father, Chuck Wagner understood that this natural vigor had to be tamed by extended aging in wood and ultimately reached the same conclusions as his friend Jo Heitz. Controlled oxygenation gave the wine a groundbreaking velvety smooth, sensual texture and, most important, helped it to avoid uncontrolled reduction during the first few years in the bottle. Its roundness, sweetness, and velvety texture are sometimes barriers to finesse and elegance. But these latter qualities are not what fans of Caymus wine are looking for, and it has to be said that great acidic vintages such as 1979 or 1986 have developed superbly in the bottle.

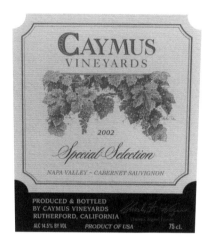

VINE VARIETY
62 acres (25 hectares), red: Cabernet Sauvignon; white: Sauvignon Blanc plus bought-in grapes.

OUR FAVORITE WINES
Other than price, there is little difference between this estate's regular wine and its famous Special Selection wine, which sees more oak. Caymus makes archetypal spicy Napa Valley wines – regarded as velvety by some and as overwhelmed or transfigured by oak by others.

Chuck Wagner, one of the great pioneering vine growers of the Napa Valley, wearing his beloved straw hat.

Clos du Val

Owner John Goelet, a rich New Yorker, entrusted the estate's technical direction to Frenchman Bernard Portet from the outset, Portet's father had been the steward of Château Lafite and the *château* spirit served as a model for the creation of the estate in 1972. It has remained a point of reference ever since. History has endorsed the Frenchman's choice of Stag's Leap as a suitable location for planting. Nowhere else in the Napa Valley does Cabernet Sauvignon attain such aromatic finesse or achieve such an elegant natural balance in its tannins and texture. Therefore, it comes as no surprise to learn that this area was the first to be officially recognized as an appellation. The same flair and intuition led Portet to select Carneros to the south of Sonoma and Napa counties for the estate's Chardonnay (fundamentally important to the business because of its popularity). This area is cooler and allows the fruit to retain higher levels of acidity. The terroir is not quite up to the standard of the microclimate, however, and it is rare that these wines, often delicious in their youth, develop greater depth or complexity with age. Portet courageously refuses to make dense, concentrated "monsters," favoring instead a balance compatible with food, thereby guaranteeing the popularity of his wines with restaurateurs.

The moisture of transpiration that is visible on the grapes in the early morning is an indication that the ripening of the fruit, and particularly of the skin, is determined principally in the coolness of night. The healthy appearance of these grapes is typical of this area.

VINE VARIETY
173 acres (70 hectares) on Stag's Leap. Red: Cabernet Sauvignon, Cabernet Franc, Merlot, Zinfandel; white: Sémillon.
272 acres (110 hectares) on Carneros. Red: Pinot Noir; white: Chardonnay.

OUR FAVORITE WINES
This estate's wines are never extrovert; they do not display strong, unique personalities. Their strength lies instead in their harmony and they are more enjoyable with food than on their own. The Reserve wines, and in particular the Cabernet Sauvignon, have bags of charm and reveal intelligent use of oak. The Zinfandels (the excellent 1999, for example) are far better balanced than most.

Dalla Valle

This small piece of paradise was dreamed up and designed by Gustav Dalla Valle at a time when a number of wealthy industrialists were embarking on second careers as winemakers in heavenly Napa Valley locations. He planted a small model vineyard in the hills to the west of Oakville and constructed a delightful Tuscan-style winery (he was of Italian descent), but could not at this early stage have imagined the site's huge potential. Gradually the exquisite flavors and refined tannins of his wines – particularly his Maya blend (from the best five acres in the vineyard) in which the black cherry and dark chocolate notes of the regular Cabernet Sauvignon are supplemented by hints of cedar – earned him a place in the wine aficionados' list of favorites. His 1992 was one of the Napa Valley's great wines, and his success has continued ever since. It remains to be seen if their aging potential will equal those of the Calistoga wines, until now the best structured and slowest developing in the bottle. The arrival on the scene of new cult wines such as Harlan Estate will no doubt encourage Naoko Dalla Valle not to rest on her laurels.

VINE VARIETY
25 acres (10 hectares) red: Cabernet Sauvignon, Cabernet Franc.

OUR FAVORITE WINES
This "garage" winery produces two cult wines: regular Cabernet Sauvignon, and the Maya blend from old vines. The 1998, 1999, and 2000 form a remarkable trio of vintages whose highly complex wines boast textures of far greater refinement than is usual among the Napa Valley's "luxury" wines.

Rows of gently undulating vines follow the natural contours of the land.

Diamond Creek

We are among the ardent fans of Diamond Creek who hope a statue of Al Brounstein will one day be erected in honor of his planting the first vines here in 1968. Brounstein had a significant headstart on anyone else with his initial faith in a wild, unknown territory and then in taming and civilizing it according to the most enlightened rules of historical European viticulture. It would take a novelist to describe the incredible adventures of the early days, including the arrival of the first vine cuttings and the artisanal but brilliant vinification of the first vintages in the open air with makeshift equipment and the assistance of partner Jerry Luper. But nature generously repaid the work that was put into it, providing three truly great vineyards and three distinct personalities within a few hundred feet of each other. For those skeptical of the notion of the importance of terroir and microclimate, a comparative tasting of Volcanic Hill (a warm site with volcanic soil) and Gravelly Meadow (a cool site requiring late harvesting) will come as a revelation. The intensity of character and nobility of flavor of each drop of juice produced here (now vinified in a modern, exemplary winery) should serve as a model to every young winegrower in America and beyond. The last few vintages are all highly recommended, although they need to age for ten years or more to allow their full quality to unfold.

VINE VARIETY

22 acres (9 hectares) divided between the Volcanic Hill, Gravelly Meadow, Red Rock Terrace and Lake parcels: Cabernet Sauvignon, Merlot, Cabernet Franc, Petit Verdot – just over an acre (0.5 hectare) above Lake.

OUR FAVORITE WINES

All this estate's Cabernet Sauvignons show unforgettable character and are consistent from one vintage to the next. Gravelly Meadow is without doubt the most civilized, and Volcanic Hill the boldest and most original in terms of flavor and structure.

Harlan Estate

Harlan Estate was established by the third wave of grands crus growers in the Napa Valley and has benefited from the experience of the other two! Bob Harlan, a well-known Napa Valley entrepreneur and owner of the luxury Meadowood hotel complex, cleared a number of magnificent Oakville slopes overlooking Martha's Vineyard at the end of the 1980s. With the assistance of David Abreu, the Napa Valley's best-known agronomist, and star French enologist Michel Rolland, he created a pilot winery which was the best planted and best cultivated in the region while also employing the most intelligent winemaking methods. Harlan wine stunned critics with the power and harmony of its very first vintages, and became a favorite of Robert Parker, with all the success that entails. What makes this wine so seductive is that in addition to its majestic structure, which is the norm for Californian wine of this standard, it is also distinguished by a rare formal perfection, boasting a velvety texture, ultra-ripe, almost melting tannins, a radiant finish, and sensational length. One is immediately aware of both the high-quality fruit and a vinification process that does it full justice. What is not yet present is the overriding originality of character (even if controversial) of a Martha's Vineyard or Diamond Creek (thanks to its special microclimate), or the finesse of the greatest Walla Walla Cabernets such as Leonetti.

VINE VARIETY

40 acres (16 hectares): 70% Cabernet Sauvignon, 20% Merlot, 8% Cabernet Franc, 2% Petit Verdot.

OUR FAVORITE WINES

As in Bordeaux, this estate makes a flagship wine (Harlan) and a second wine (The Maiden). The flagship wine is one of California's richest and most unctuous with the most refined tannins. The 2001 has all the monumentality of 1997 with additional aromatic precision.

More like a work of art than mere rows of vines, the magical atmosphere is reflected in the rich bouquet of the wine produced on this estate.

Heitz Cellar

Everything at this legendary winery is redolent of the traditional Napa Valley way of life before the advent of tourism but this has not prevented the business from growing and thriving. David Heitz, who has been in charge of winemaking for 15 years, possesses the same gift as his father. He has a unique ability to judge when the grapes have reached peak maturity and continues to construct his famous Cabernet Sauvignons during the course of long, careful aging, first in large Californian oak casks and then in French oak barrels. His wines are only bottled in their fourth year and seem more polished and highly evolved than others, and admirable for their unchanging aromatic complexity, refinement and aging capacity. In remaining faithful to Heitz the May family, owner of Martha's Vineyard and partners in the firm, made the right decision, as the 1999 and 2001 vintages will go down in history alongside the sublime 1974 and 1975. In addition to this exceptional vineyard (which produces 40,000–50,000 bottles a year) and its two other prestige vineyards, Heitz also produces a Grignolino that is deliciously fruity and a very special Chardonnay at the opposite extreme to the aromatic, oaked style so popular at the moment. This wine bears a closer resemblance to an extremely rich Hermitage in the Chapoutier style, creating a false sense of oxidation and only revealing its true character at the table, where it also gains significantly in length.

VINE VARIETY

358 acres (145 hectares) red: Cabernet Sauvignon, Merlot, Zinfandel, Grignolino; white: Chardonnay. Purchase of harvests from the Bella Oaks Vineyard and Martha's Vineyard (37 acres/15 hectares).

OUR FAVORITE WINES

Heitz is the Napa Valley's ultimate winery, having developed the most original and consistent Cabernet Sauvignon style in California. This style features a spicy eucalyptus and mint nose that finds its most perfect expression in the Martha's Vineyard wine. Having been replanted following an outbreak of phylloxera, we are delighted to see that this site has immediately rediscovered its inherent qualities. Bella Oaks and Trail Side also produce wines of remarkable power and complexity.

When the leaves begin to turn red, the grapes are almost ripe. Well-spaced bunches allow the fruit to take advantage of the sun's rays and the cooling breezes.

Dominus Estate

Yountville takes its name from George Yount, one of the pioneers of Californian viticulture, who planted the first vines here back in 1838. One of the district's best sites, Napanook, belonged to John Daniel, who used its harvest for the famous Inglenook wine of the 1940s and 1950s. An associate of the family since 1982, Christian Moueix became the vineyard's sole owner in 1995. Supported by his French team, he applies the principles of viticulture and winemaking that have been tried and tested in Pomerol over a long period of time, and the general balance of Dominus recalls that of the great Libournais crus, with soft and supple textures and slightly less body than most Napa Valley wines. However, the toasted and chocolate notes of the 1997 vintage bear the unmistakable stamp of its terroir and origins. This wine has a tendency to age rather more quickly than the great wines of Bordeaux and the 1991 that Christian Moueix generously sent to Paris displayed nothing like the freshness of a Château Latour. Since 1996 a second wine, the delicious and refined Napanook, has been made here. The winery, wonderfully designed and constructed by Swiss architects Herzog & de Meuron, is worth a visit not only for the quality of its wines but also for the intelligent way in which it has been integrated into the viticultural landscape.

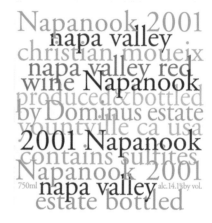

VINE VARIETY

124 acres (50 hectares): Cabernet Sauvignon, Merlot, Cabernet Franc, Petit Verdot, Malbec.

OUR FAVORITE WINES

Like Harlan Estate, this property produces two wines: Napanook, designed for earlier drinking, made from the suppler, fruitier vineyard lots; and Dominus, which offers a balance between power and finesse which is rare for the Napa Valley, but with the sleek, slightly impersonal aspect characteristic of a "luxury" product.

Iron Horse

Barry Sterling became a wine lover during a long stint as a commercial attorney in France. On his return to California, he settled with his family in a heavenly spot in Sonoma County, and founded a winery in partnership with a young and extremely talented local winemaker by the name of Forrest Tancer (who married Barry's daughter Joy, every bit as much of a francophile as her father). It will come as no surprise that they decided to focus on sparkling wine (that most French of styles) on these slightly cooler-than-average sites. What's more, they made sure they had the necessary tools to make it as well as possible. Their first vintages produced a wine that stands out for its individuality of character and refinement of flavor. This sparkling wine laid the foundations for the winery's success and Iron Horse's list of regular customers now includes the White House. With fruit from his family's vineyard in Alexander Valley, which is warmer than Green Valley but less oppressively hot than some districts, Forrest also makes a fine, expressive Sauvignon Blanc and Cabernet Sauvignon reds that are elegant rather than powerful. The family continued to dream of producing a great Pinot Noir of the type they knew could be made in Sonoma's famous Russian River district not far away. They have now achieved this with the last few vintages. The best sparkling wines of recent years are the 1996, the 2000 and, it would seem, the 2002.

VINE VARIETY

259 acres (105 hectares)
185 acres (75 hectares) in Green Valley: Pinot Noir, Chardonnay.
74 acres (30 hectares) in Alexander Valley: Cabernet Sauvignon, Merlot, Cabernet Franc, Sangiovese, Viognier, Sauvignon Blanc.

OUR FAVORITE WINES

This firm's great specialty is its sparkling wine made in the best Champagne tradition and initially inspired by Laurent Perrier's idea to establish his Californian vineyard in Green Valley. The estate's best wines have a personality and complexity of flavor unrivaled in California.

J. Rochioli Vineyards

If there is any Californian Pinot Noir of a certain age capable of being mistaken for a top Burgundy grand cru, it is surely the 1988 made by Ed Selyem with fruit from the Rochioli Vineyard, its magnificent nose and style recalling DRC at its best. In contrast to the methods commonly employed by the Californian school, Selyem was an intuitive winemaker who experimented with whole-cluster vinification and was not afraid of extended aging on the lees without racking. A new generation of the Rochioli family, which was among the pioneers of quality grape growing in Sonoma, now prefers, quite understandably, to make its own wine from its magnificent Russian Valley vineyard, the family having shown astonishing intuition in planting it with Pinot Noir and Sauvignon Blanc 20 years before anyone else thought of doing so. But the family has never really surpassed its own 1991 – no doubt as a result of the inexorable increase in alcoholic strength that has caused such havoc in Europe too. The whites, on the other hand, show plenty of individuality and charm, and really do justice to the terroir: a Chardonnay Reserve that is intense, impeccably well balanced but somewhat stereotypical, and most importantly a Sauvignon Blanc with a real gunflint nose and palate that deserves a place on the wine lists of the world's best restaurants.

VINE VARIETY

161 acres (65 hectares) in the Russian River Valley.
Red: Pinot Noir; white: Chardonnay, Sauvignon Blanc.

OUR FAVORITE WINES

Of its whites, we prefer this estate's Sauvignon Blanc (one of the rare Californian Sauvignons to do full justice to the grape's finesse) to its Chardonnay, which is well made but stereotypical. The extremely fruity and seductive Pinot Noirs do not attain the complexity William and Selyem gave them when they were buying and vinifying the grapes.

For some of the best wines, the grapes are sorted out by hand in order to ensure the utmost quality.

Schramsberg

Modern California, which embodies the dreams – realistic or otherwise – of immigrants from all over the world, was constructed through enormous effort. Schramsberg's extensive underground cellars in the hills overlooking the Napa Valley were dug over a period of several years by anonymous Chinese laborers whose only surviving traces are the pickaxe marks left in the rock. These marks also symbolize the ambitions of another industrious immigrant, Jacob Schram, who in 1862 created the Napa Valley's second winery and the first in the hills rather than on flat terrain. The Schramsberg winery had its moments of glory, but Prohibition put an end to this first chapter in its history. In 1965, Jack and Jamie Davies, a young Californian couple passionate about wine, bought the house and cellars with the intention of creating a great sparkling wine. The methods employed here are similar to those used by the best Champagne houses: a large-scale blending process involving 120 base wines (some originating from the cool, oceanic Marin sector, which imparts a welcome acidity to the wine), fermentation in small barrels (for much of the production), and even traditional hand riddling. Sadly, Jack Davies died a few years ago but his family is still at the helm of this producer of surely some of the most characterful sparkling wines in the New World.

VINE VARIETY

42 acres (17 hectares) belonging to the property, plus bought-in grapes from 80 different Napa vineyards (at Carneros, Mendocino, Sonoma and Marin) covering a total of 255 acres (103 hectares). Pinot Noir and Chardonnay only (white).

OUR FAVORITE WINES

Schramsberg produces a wide range of sparkling wines of consistently high quality which are elegant, deep, and naturally vivacious, without any hint of heaviness or flabbiness. The Brut Rosé seduces with its freshness and fruit but the real stars are the Reserve 2000, which is rich, generous, and honest, and the extremely pure and harmonious J. Schram 1999, which boasts a complex toasty bouquet with notes of fresh butter and white flowers.

Kistler Vineyards

Few Californian producers have had as much praise heaped on them (both by wine writers and the public) as Steve Kistler. His success derives chiefly from the simplicity and precision of his vineyard and cellar practices, from knowing and respecting his terroirs and vines (including the genetic characteristics of each clone, which is extremely rare) in order to be able to farm and harvest them properly and from vinifying with the least possible intervention but with a rigor learned from Bill Bonetti, the Kistler family's brilliant predecessor at Sonoma Cutrer. Californian wine lovers were naturally delighted by these exceedingly well made wines, by the generosity of their structure, the restrained use of oak, and the absence of artificial aromas. Admittedly, we in Europe have some difficulty detecting the minerality American critics have noticed in their bouquet. At the table, though, we have often experienced how well they go with the splendid cuisine of Sonoma County. Kistler could have no better ambassador in France than his prestige blend Cathleen, made from a selection of the best grapes.

VINE VARIETY

62 acres (25 hectares) of Chardonnay, plus grapes bought in from the McCrea, Dutton Ranch, Durell, and Hirsch vineyards, and also from the Hudson and Hyde vineyards in Carneros.

OUR FAVORITE WINES

The most consistent of Kistler's numerous "terroir" wines (and also the one that has been in production the longest) is no doubt the McCrea, but a wine with a far more personal feel is obtained from the estate's own vineyard (and its special clone) on the slopes of the Mayacamas Mountains. These opulent Chardonnays are at their best after two to three years of aging in the bottle.

Marcassin

This estate merits its status as a cult producer. Helen Turley and her husband John Wetlaufer are winegrowers who have taken the growing, harvesting, and vinification of the Burgundy varieties in America to a degree of perfection as high as that achieved in their native land. As a trained enologist with a detailed knowledge of wine microbiology, Turley knows that in addition to grapes of perfect ripeness, the flavor of a great Chardonnay depends on something called yeast autolysis, a complex process whereby the yeasts release molecules that give off noble aromas. This is what led her away from the grape's habitually rather banal aromas to a discovery of how the greatest Burgundies (to which her wines now bear such a resemblance – with additional Californian body!) are made. She has exerted considerable influence over the small circle of producers (Peter Michael and others) wanting to give their work an "artistic" dimension. But, somewhat like Lalou Bize-Leroy in Burgundy, she is the only one who has succeeded in consistently making wines of the highest quality from one vintage to the next. We would have liked to have tasted Marcassin's reds, but Turley clearly doesn't like to be bothered by journalists, least of all French ones!

VINE VARIETY

9 acres (3.5 hectares) near the ocean. Chardonnay.
20 acres (8 hectares) co-owned with the Martinelli family:
Pinot Noir and Chardonnay (Blue Slide Ridge and Three Sisters).

OUR FAVORITE WINES

Our knowledge of this estate is limited by its small production and the rarity of its wines. We have never tasted the Blue Slide Ridge Pinot Noirs, but the Chardonnays have always astonished us with their power, length, and complexity. They are the only Californian wines we are aware of that have achieved such refined flavors from aging on the lees.

The wide open spaces of the Sonoma Valley in the light of an Indian summer.

Newton Winery

Newton is an extremely well-appointed vineyard established in 1977 by Peter Newton and his wife Su Hua. Although the winery now belongs to the LVMH group, the Newtons remain in charge. Wonderful terraced slopes, a meticulously maintained English garden, and impeccable winery buildings make this a model estate. Its wine had just started to find its definitive form at the end of the 1980s when Michel Rolland, working at that time as consultant to the Simi Winery in Healdsburg, was brought in by Su Hua to fine-tune the harvesting and vinification. No one could have imagined how amazing the results would be! Rolland metamorphosed the Merlots into something more mature and refined and then proceeded to transform all the other wines too, coming up with a very attractive Pinot Noir at the same time. John Kongsgaard, the estate's winemaker, had simultaneously discovered the secret of making a Chardonnay (from fruit grown in his family's vineyard) that was infinitely more complex and subtle than anything then being made in the Napa Valley. When he left Newton, Su Hua started to source grapes from the Carneros region and the resulting wines made up in freshness for what they had lost in complexity. Recent vintages can be expected to match and even surpass the standards that thrust the estate into the Napa Valley's front rank.

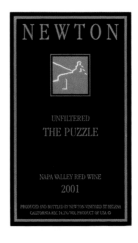

VINE VARIETY

124 acres (50 hectares) on the magnificent terraced slopes of Spring Mountain. Red: Cabernet Sauvignon, Merlot, Cabernet Franc, Petit Verdot; white: Chardonnay vineyards farmed in the Carneros region.

OUR FAVORITE WINES

This estate currently has two prestige wines, which are highly accomplished blends: the Cabernet-Sauvignon-dominated "Puzzle" and "Le Grand Vin" (highly successful in 1999), a classic Bordeaux-style blend. The Chardonnays do not have quite the power they had a dozen years ago.

Opus One

Opus One was the fruit of a collaboration between the most visionary of Bordeaux producers, Philippe de Rothschild, and the most entrepreneurial of Californian winegrowers, Robert Mondavi. Putting their technical and considerable communications expertise to good use, their aim was to unite the complementary strengths of the two continents. Originally conceived as a brand to be attached to Oakville's best produce, Opus One has become a "*château* wine" with its own vineyard at the heart of the district's best terroirs and a spectacular winery that is an architectural and functional masterpiece. Mondavi and Mouton-Rothschild's winemakers worked hand in hand to define the wine's style. Opus One's early, full-bodied vintages with slightly overpowering oak and alcohol have developed via the very luxurious but somewhat impersonal bottlings of the 1990s into a wine of far greater nuance and subtlety over the last three years, confirming Oakville's status as a Napa Valley terroir capable of endowing its wine with the most aristocratic flavors, forging close links with the great Pauillacs and ultimately realizing the dream of the old Californian patriarch. Constellation has revived the partnership with Philippe de Rothschild, and intends to protect the autonomy and imagination of those in charge of this highly distinctive wine.

VINE VARIETY
111 acres (45 hectares) red: Cabernet Sauvignon, Cabernet Franc, and Merlot on ancient block Q of To Kalon Vineyard.

OUR FAVORITE WINES
Opus One has developed greatly since 1979 and benefits from a showcase winery where it has been made since 1991. The most recent vintages retain all the vigor and richness of the early years but show substantial progress in terms of finesse, integration of wood and harmony of the tannins. They may not please fans of wines of very well-defined character, but they compare well with the most cultured European wines.

An exercise in architectural design: a winery where the form reflects and is integrated into the contour lines of the landscape.

Peter Michael

After making his fortune, the English computer scientist Sir Peter Michael found a peaceful haven in a beautiful Sonoma setting which he transformed into one of California's most admired wine estates. An ardent francophile, Michael has always run his winery according to the principles of artisanal winemaking – the style that produces the wines he loves – and has always called on the services of consultants who abound in this field, including Helen Turley. His approach is simple: respect the individual terroir, vinify separately, and intervene as little as possible in the vinification process (which does not mean do nothing!). The current winemaker is Luc Morlet from Burgundy, and since 2000 we have noticed a move away from "tropical" flavors towards greater complexity. With fruit from the famous Gauer vineyard he even produces a micro-wine called Indigène, which is closer to the Marcassin style, accentuating the toasted notes that come from aging on "indigenous" lees. In the same spirit, a separate bottling of the best *barriques* called Point Rouge could even pass for a Bâtard-Montrachet, so reminiscent are its vine flower, pine honey, and citrus notes of that great appellation's most mature Chardonnays. Our greatest surprise, though, has been the enormous success of the most recent blends of Bordeaux varieties called "Les Pavots," which combine power and style like few others – even among California's most celebrated wines.

VINE VARIETY
111 acres (45 hectares) farmed, red and white: all the Burgundy and Bordeaux varieties.

OUR FAVORITE WINES
This estate's Chardonnays are the very opposite of what the Californian style used to be. Instead of heavy caramel, coconut or confectionery notes, they display an attractive floral purity that by no means excludes generosity of body or the inevitable tropical fruits. Our favorite bears the French name "La Carrière."

Ridge

Ridge was created on a historic but forgotten terroir to the south of San Francisco by a group of Stanford University physicists who wanted to make wine for pleasure. The Cupertino slope possesses outstanding natural characteristics: very thin soil, and an elevation (2,625 feet/800 meters) at which the grape's growing cycle is extended favoring the development of fine, complex aromas. The presence of the ocean just 12 miles (20 kilometers) away provides humidity and a cool breeze that are essential for a non-irrigated vineyard. The arrival of Paul Draper in 1967 changed everything. This philosophy professor was to become the most skillful and meticulous viticulturist the American winemaking industry had ever known. With the help of its new owner, wealthy Japanese investor Akiko Otsuka, the winery became an institution admired the world over. The secret of Ridge's quality is based on a close correlation between what they say and what they do. Winemaking at Ridge employs intelligent methods that are individually adapted to each vineyard site. It is based on an approach that is rustic in its simplicity but controlled by sophisticated technology made possible by significant investment. Having embarked on his quest for quality at an early stage, Paul Draper was able to choose the locations best suited to expressing the characteristics of the grape when purchasing vineyard sites and now has the luxury of very old vines (average age 40 years) in the Monte Bello Vineyard.

Vineyard Production:
83 tons from 62 acres
Selection: 25%

95 Monte Bello Vineyard, bottled May 97
In the Santa Cruz Mountains, welcome spring rains delayed the start of our growing season. We thinned the already moderate crop, and warm October weather brought the fruit to ideal ripeness. Fifteen of the twenty-five parcels were chosen in February as most intense and most typical of the vineyard's character. They were assembled in three stages over the following months. Tannins are the biggest to date in the nineties, yet the fullness and complexity of the wine render them supple. Aged almost entirely in new, air-dried american oak, this is classic Monte Bello. Though approachable now, the great '95 vintage will develop fully over the next fifteen to twenty years. PD (3/97)

In 1892, the newly completed Monte Bello Winery produced its first vintage from this distinctive mountain site. In 1962, Ridge made its first Monte Bello from the same ground. This is one of those rare vineyards where time has proven climate, soil, and varietal to be perfectly matched. So that the site's unique character will define the wine, we use the minimal handling typical of traditional winemaking. The world's great wines have always been determined by the vineyard—by nature, not by man. L 1/97 ®REGISTERED TRADEMARK

RIDGE 1995
CALIFORNIA
MONTE BELLO®

69% CABERNET IN A VINEYARD BLEND
GROWN, PRODUCED & BOTTLED BY RIDGE VINEYARDS
17100 MONTE BELLO ROAD, CUPERTINO, CALIFORNIA
12.5% VOL.   PRODUCE OF U.S.A.   750 ML

VINE VARIETY
161 acres (65 hectares), of which 62 acres (25 hectares) are at Monte Bello and the rest are distributed throughout Sonoma in Dry Creek Valley. Red: Cabernet Sauvignon, Petit Verdot, Merlot, Zinfandel, Petite Syrah, Grenache, Carignan; white: Chardonnay.

OUR FAVORITE WINES
The jewel of this estate is its famous Monte Bello wine, whose noble and complex nose (worthy of the best Bordeaux) and longevity have been demonstrating the exceptional quality of the terroir for 40 years. Its Geyserville and Lytton Springs Zinfandels are also classics of their type, consistently offering a rich but never jammy or overpowering nose. For a little while now a wonderfully noble Monte Bello Chardonnay has been responsible for the reappraisal of a number of overvalued Napa Valley and Sonoma wines.

Robert Mondavi Winery

The Californian wine industry was stunned when patriarch Robert Mondavi, the American winemaker with the biggest overseas reputation and certainly the US wine industry's most fascinating 20th-century figure, sold his shares in the company he founded 40 years before to Constellation. In doing so, he handed the wine giant not just an empire but an institution too. The empire consists primarily of an extraordinary winegrowing estate split between three beautiful districts of the Napa Valley: the To Kalon Vineyard in Oakville, which produces the most polished Cabernet Sauvignons and occasionally (block I for the firm, block Q for Opus One) those closest to the Pauillac style, with inimitable cedarwood and pencil lead notes; Carneros for Chardonnay, which ripens slightly more slowly here than elsewhere; finally Stag's Leap, which is well suited to near enough everything. Meanwhile, the institution consists of an ultra-efficient winery with wooden casks and a magnificent cellar, as well as a unique public relations center and venue for cultural events. Mondavi followed the example of his mentor Baron Philippe de Rothschild and did all in his power to boost the cultural standing of his own wines and the Californian wine industry as a whole. The new owners have kept everything as it was, retaining a brilliant technical team led by the talented French enologist Geneviève Janssens and resurrecting the Opus One joint venture with Philippine de Rothschild.

VINE VARIETY

Three wonderful vineyards:
To Kalon Vineyard, Oakville, 556 acres (225 hectares):
mainly Cabernet Sauvignon and Sauvignon Blanc.
Wappo Hill Vineyard, Stag's Leap, 395 acres (160 hectares).
Huichica Hills Vineyard, Carneros, 445 acres (180 hectares):
Chardonnay, Pinot Noir.

OUR FAVORITE WINES

This firm makes all the common white and red varieties but despite their technical excellence, produces few wines of real personality. Exceptions include the Cabernet Sauvignon Reserve, which is extremely suave and polished, and a brilliantly vinified Chardonnay Reserve. These two wines are at their best between two and five years old but do not age as well as certain others. We have never been convinced by the Sauvignon known here as Fumé Blanc.

Despite a series of dramatic disputes and ruptures within the Mondavi family, Robert remains the unchallenged head of the unique estate that he designed and built up.

Shafer Vineyards

Doug Shafer has spent a generation at his Stag's Leap winery perfecting what is sure to be classed one day as a Californian grand cru. All the elements of a great wine are present here: consistently high-quality grapes from a precise, well-defined terroir with good natural drainage and a microclimate that is more even than most of the neighboring vineyards, and vinification that involves taking necessary risks in order to bring out the originality of the terroir but controlled with a degree of precision and discipline that ensure loyalty to the grape's potential. The Shafer terroir accentuates neither eucalyptus nor mint notes but instead the classic aromas of cedar, graphite, and blackcurrant – akin to those from the heart of Médoc. These aromas are accompanied by greater body, greater richness, and also at times greater alcoholic strength than the norm. Aging for a dozen years or so softens the wine while also toning down the sometimes rather cumbersome and unnecessary oak. We have no reservations about the finish, however, which is that of a truly great wine. The estate's Chardonnay has made considerable progress in terms of purity and aromatic distinction over the last few years, while avoiding the heavy butter and lactic aromas common in Napa Valley wine as well as the aromatic vehemence of so-called handcrafted wines.

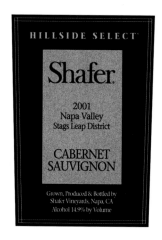

VINE VARIETY
198 acres (80 hectares): Cabernet Sauvignon, Merlot, Cabernet Franc, Syrah, Sangiovese, Chardonnay, Petite Syrah.

OUR FAVORITE WINES
The Hillside Select Cabernet Sauvignon is this model winery's best wine by far, and, along with Cask 23 from the neighboring Stag's Leap Wine Cellar, is perhaps the region's most accomplished Cabernet. Power, finesse, and a degree of tannic refinement rare for the Napa Valley are qualities that deserve to be fully appreciated in Europe. This wine can be seen at its best in the 1996 and 1997 vintages.

Rubicon Estate

In 2005, Francis Ford and Eleanor Coppola decided to simplify the name of their famous Rutherford property from the Niebaum-Coppola Estate Winery to Rubicon Estate after the name of its best wine, which had been made since 1978. Originally Rubicon, along with Beaulieu, had been the first great wine regularly produced in the Napa Valley (by exceptionally talented winemaker John Daniel) under the name Inglenook. The 1941 we tasted in 2004 was superbly preserved with extremely noble cedar aromas worthy of a premier grand cru. The astonishing quality of these old vintages is explained by the nature of the terroir, the extremely good microclimate at the foot of Mount St John at the heart of Rutherford Bench and a very special Cabernet Sauvignon clone (clone 29) that is ideally suited to these conditions. By reuniting all the original Inglenook vineyards and also acquiring a neighboring vineyard from the Cohn family in 2002, Francis Ford Coppola has created what is perhaps an even better stock of vines, bringing together warm, early sites with slightly cooler sites. In charge of the estate is Larry Stone, America's most famous sommelier, who will no doubt restore a touch more regularity to the quality. A good Rubicon is one of California's most expressive wines, offering an extremely noble spice, resin, cedar nose, and an impressively long finish.

VINE VARIETY
272 acres (110 hectares) red: Cabernet Sauvignon, Cabernet Franc, Merlot, Zinfandel. The best sites are Gio, Garden, and Cask.

OUR FAVORITE WINES
The wines that do most justice to this estate's terroir are its Cabernet Sauvignons (always blended with a small proportion of other Bordeaux varieties). These are powerful and spicy (the 2002 is a good example). A small, separate bottling of Cabernet Franc in 2003 shows that this grape is capable of producing finer-textured wines with more refined tannins.

Left
The climate of the Rutherford Bench area is influenced partly by the cool forest immediately behind, more reminiscent of Germany than the United States.

Right
The film director and winemaker Francis Ford Coppola is first and foremost an Italian with a relaxed and instinctive rapport with grapes.

Stag's Leap Wine Cellar

Perhaps predestined by his surname (Polish for "vintner's son"), Warren Winiarski decided 30 years ago to quit his job as a political science teacher and start a new and thrilling (albeit hard) life as a winemaker. After learning the trade from Lee Stewart, a pioneer of quality wine in the Napa Valley, he decided to establish a vineyard adjacent to the one he admired most (which he bought from Nathan Fay in 1986) and put his ideas, the longest pondered and most coherent of any producer of his generation, into practice in a wine that was Californian in origin but followed the criteria laid down by the European grand crus where balance, complexity, and compatibility with food are concerned. His best bottlings, sold under the name Cask 23, rapidly assumed benchmark status – thanks to their assured style and aromatic distinction. At the famous Paris Tasting of 1976, his 1973 beat a handful of leading Bordeaux crus in a blind tasting and became legendary. But this wine pales alongside those currently being made by the estate! After analyzing every acre of vineyard and optimizing production methods, Warren Winiarski has infinitely improved the quality of everything he produces: his Chardonnay shows a better balance of alcohol, acidity, and oak, and his reds are richer and purer while retaining the same noble aromas of cedar and graphite – key characteristics of the rich Fay terroir.

VINE VARIETY

124 acres (50 hectares) in the district of the same name split between two neighboring vineyards, SLV (the initials of the winery) and the famous vineyard previously owned by Nathan Fay: Cabernet Sauvignon, Merlot, Chardonnay, Sauvignon Blanc.

OUR FAVORITE WINES

The wine that made the estate famous remains its best by far. The blend of the best Cabernet Sauvignons from the two sites is known as Cask 23, by Californian standards a slender, sinewy wine that is often misjudged in its youth as it is rather coy about its body and aromas. The last few vintages have been outstanding.

Viader

To judge by the quality of her wines, Delia Viader, born in Argentina and a polyglot with a string of degrees, is one of Napa Valley's most talented and imaginative viticulturalists. Her wonderful little vineyard in the Howell Mountains, audaciously and densely planted on a very steep slope overlooking a small lake providing an important reserve water supply, could serve as a model of good vineyard practice to many a French or European grower. This is a great terroir producing wines that, despite their alcoholic strength, possess an exuberance and aromatic vivacity devoid of any heaviness. Their bouquet, spicier, more complex, and varied than that of wines from the heart of Napa Valley, is softened by the use in the blend of a significant proportion of Cabernet Franc. This spicy aroma is the difference between the "mountain" wines, as they are known here, and those from the lower slopes and plains whose very rich (sometimes over-rich) alluvial soils reduce the aromatic expression of their wines to something banal, even at a high level of quality. It nevertheless took a very special intuition to believe in this very low-yield and therefore relatively unprofitable grape variety. It makes a significant contribution here to a wine whose texture strongly recalls that of Cheval Blanc – high praise indeed! The same intuition can be seen in the planting of a small block of Syrah with Australian and French clones whose very first years showed up the heaviness of the stereotypes being pursued by all too many of Viader's colleagues.

VINE VARIETY

30 acres (12 hectares): 50% Cabernet Sauvignon, 25% Cabernet Franc, 20% Syrah, 5% various.

OUR FAVORITE WINES

We are not going to hide our weakness for this estate's flagship wine: an intelligent blend of 60% Cabernet Sauvignon and 40% Cabernet Franc, and one of California's most refined and individual wines. All the recent vintages have been admirable. The same qualities are shared by an astonishing Syrah produced from a mixture of French and Australian clones.

Cristom

This is without doubt Oregon's most impressive estate at the present time. The single sweep of the vineyard covers a magnificent slope in the Eola Hills district, where the pioneering Bethel Heights vineyard made a name for itself long ago with its supremely well-defined terroir character. The soil is essentially made up of basalt mother rock (of the Jory and Nekia types) as in the Chehalem Mountains district. Owner Paul Gerrie is a fan of Burgundy wines and a close friend of Aubert de Villaine and Jacques Seysses, from whom he acquired his excellent planting technique. Gerrie has named his individual parcels of land – which differ from one another in exposure, altitude, and topsoil – after various female ancestors and, in one case, his wife. His winemaker Steve Doerner possesses an innate understanding (less common than might be thought) of the great Pinot Noir styles, and knows that beyond immediate aroma his priorities are form, texture, and expression of terroir character. Adopting the principle (so simple but at the same time so demanding in terms of necessary grape quality) of whole-cluster vinification without destemming has paid dividends on every front – in particular where the quality of the tannins is concerned. For many, "Marjorie" and "Jessie" will come as a revelation: it is no exaggeration to claim that these two wines achieve the level of complexity of a Bonnes Mares or a Clos de la Roche!

VINE VARIETY

62 acres (25 hectares) split between the Marjorie (10 acres), Louise (11 acres), Jessie (15 acres), Eileen (16 acres), Emilia (5 acres) and Germaine (5 acres) sites. Red: Pinot Noir, Syrah; white: Viognier.

OUR FAVORITE WINES

This estate's Pinot Noirs have frequently struck us as Oregon's most distinguished, reminding us of all the things we like about the Romanée Conti style. This should come as no surprise as whole-cluster vinification is employed here. The wonderful finesse and complexity of the Cristom range culminate in "Marjorie." Dedicated Pinot Noir lovers will no doubt regard these wines as among the best on the planet.

Beaux Frères Vineyards

Beaux Frères is the result of a partnership between Michael Etzel, his brother-in-law the illustrious American wine writer Robert Parker, and Robert Roy. The two brothers-in-law were fans of Dick Ponzi's great Pinot Noirs. Having become convinced back in the early 1980s of the Willamette Valley's great potential, they cleared a superb slope in the Chehalem Valley and began to put into practice everything they had learned in the great vineyards of Burgundy. Michael Etzel soon developed into a remarkable grower and unrivaled winemaker. The viticulture practiced here is largely inspired by biodynamic principles, and for the last three years the estate has incorporated into its daily routines the use of preparations similar to those employed by Lalou Bize Leroy in Vosne-Romanée. The wholesome natural environment makes this kind of approach easier than in Burgundy but credit should nevertheless be given for the additional work involved. Fortunately the benefit (grapes of greater flavor that convey more terroir information) outweigh the risks. The wine style centers on a velvety texture, harmonious tannins, and intelligently integrated wood. This sensual style of wine immediately encountered great success and sells out within a few weeks of release. Success has not robbed Etzel of his good humor, and the winery retains something of the bohemian and artisanal character of its early days. His son has the best teacher and will no doubt relish the opportunity to make wine from a more mature vineyard.

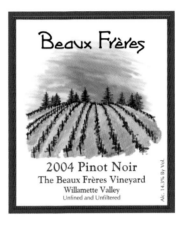

VINE VARIETY
35 acres (14 hectares) red: Pinot Noir.

OUR FAVORITE WINES
This estate ensures that its best grapes go into its Beaux Frères Pinot Noir. The late, low-yield 2004 harvest produced an exceptional wine whose finesse and refinement of texture are very much in keeping with the preceding vintages. The estate's second wine, known as Belles Sœurs ("sisters-in-law"), is made from bought-in grapes and the fruit from younger vines, and is of less predictable quality. However, the young vines of the new Upper Terrace vineyard are already producing wine of considerable style and character.

Ponzi Vineyards

Dick Ponzi was a great Pinot Noir pioneer in Oregon. At Eyrie, David Lett achieved a certain finesse – but with grapes that were not properly ripe. Ponzi was the first to understand the notion of tannin maturity, and to produce wines with voluptuous texture and rich red-fruit bouquet. His success amazed many, including Robert Parker and his brother-in-law Michael Etzel, who entrusted the crop from their Beaux Frères winery to the Ponzis in the early years. While the basalt-rich soils of the Chehalem Mountains give their wines a strong structure, the secret of this style lies in the quality of the viticulture (sustainable methods were adopted at the outset and have now been appropriately certified) and the intelligent use of new oak in the aging process. This said, to make the leap from well made wine to wine of truly great expressiveness requires both talent and selflessness. Dick Ponzi lacks neither and his daughter is demonstrating that neither does she. Their numerous qualities also include an appreciation of the gastronomic value of their wines and it should come as no surprise to learn that the Ponzis are also gifted gourmets who have created one of the Willamette Valley's best restaurants in Dundee. A visit to Beaverton is indispensable to an understanding of the depth of Oregon's contribution to world viticulture.

VINE VARIETY

99 acres (40 hectares), including Aurora (62 acres/25 hectares), Madrona (11 acres/4 hectares) and Abetina (2.5 acres/1 hectare), red: Pinot Noir; whites: Pinot Gris, Pinot Blanc, Riesling.

OUR FAVORITE WINES

The high quality of this estate's Pinot Gris whites (which have infinitely more personality than Oregon's Chardonnays) continued in 2004. Its Pinot Noir, however, revealing a winemaking flair that has been passed down from father to daughter, definitely rules the roost, and Luisa Ponzi achieved remarkable success with the 2003. In particular her Reserve and Abetina (the vineyard with the oldest vines) reached a level that year that will be difficult to surpass.

A luxury Pinot Noir produced in natural country surroundings, epitomizing the good life in Oregon.

Adelsheim Vineyards

David Adelsheim is on his third and best-appointed winery. We knew him initially as a "garage" winemaker, working with plenty of passion and talent at Quarter Mile Lane. However, his talents as a communicator created such a demand for his wines in the US that he was forced to team up with wealthy backers (the Loacker family) in order to ease the strain on both vineyard and cellar. His new estate in Newberg is a model winery. A large, intelligently planted vineyard benefits from the local iron-oxide-rich soils, while the winemaking and aging facilities are of an impressive scale and standard. Like all great winemakers, David is first and foremost a great taster. His role as the quasi-official spokesman for Oregon's winemaking industry has enabled him to acquire an intimate knowledge of the region's different terroirs and their characteristics. He knows that his wines have to go well with food, and he has imposed a style of white wine that is fresh, slender, and minerally without the slightest hint of oak flavors or confectionery aromas. The viticulturist in him inspired a desire to give full expression to the individuality of the local microclimate and soils rather than imitating the Burgundy style in his Pinot Noirs. This new "classicism" has much in common with the vision of winemakers such as Ken Wright and is sure to be widely emulated.

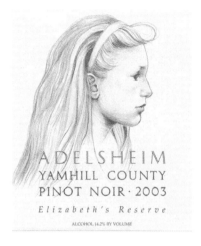

VINE VARIETY
161 acres (65 hectares) split between Quarter Mile Lane (the original vineyard) and the Calkins Lane, Ribbon Springs, and Ellis vineyards in the Chehalem Valley. Red: Pinot Noir; white: Pinot Blanc, Pinot Gris, Auxerrois, Chardonnay.

OUR FAVORITE WINES
All the wines made by this pioneer of characterful wine display abundant personality. The non-barrique-aged whites (Pinot Blanc and even Chardonnay) have, from the very beginning, been wonderfully dry with an astonishing and rare minerality while the Pinot Noirs have shown considerable progress over the years, displaying tannins of greater sophistication than the earlier rustic kind, and boasting superbly developed fruit in the Elizabeth Reserve and Single-Vineyard wines. The most accomplished in 2003, we feel, was the Calkins Lane.

Domaine
Drouhin

Domaine Drouhin in Oregon: Burgundian expertise in a region of the United States of America devoted to Pinot Noir and Chardonnay. Ever since the winery was established in 1986, the work of this entrepreneurial family from Beaune in France has served as inspiration for the entire local winegrowing industry, even if its system of very dense planting, one of the great secrets behind the quality of the family's wines, has been insufficiently copied. Everything here has been designed with enormous intelligence: the single sweep of impeccably cultivated and maintained vines (on red Dundee soil) extending from the winery buildings, the (universally imitated) ultra-modern gravity-flow vathouse, and thanks to the absence of a complex classification system, a range of clearly labeled wines. Véronique Drouhin has proved her worth in charge of winemaking here and we strongly hope that she will soon be officiating in Beaune. Drouhin has respected her father's Pinot Noir esthetic (elegant textures and emphasis on the fruit) while accentuating body and broadening the range of textures. The Dundee vineyards, which bear the closest resemblance to those of the Côte d'Or in terms of slope, exposure and light, have fully lived up to their potential, and the wines being made here are Oregon classics that should not be missed.

VINE VARIETY
86 acres (35 hectares)
71 acres (29 hectares) red: Pinot Noir.
15 acres (6 hectares) white: Chardonnay.

OUR FAVORITE WINES
This firm's expertise is encapsulated in its Laurène Pinot Noir (named after Véronique Drouhin's daughter), which displays a great purity of mulberry and raspberry coulis fruit and refined tannins. The last few vintages have shown considerably more body and a higher alcohol content.

Ken Wright Cellars

No one knows or can explain the complexity of the geological formations of the Willamette Valley better than Ken Wright. After making the most brilliant wines of the 1990s for other people, notably at Panther Creek, he has finally realized his dream of making wine in his own name, surpassing even his own previous achievements. A tasting from the barrel provides an unforgettable lesson in the nuances that differentiate wines grown in basalt soils (of the Jory and Nekia types), those grown in sedimentary soils (Willakenzie), and those grown in Carlton's low-acidity sand. What is impressive in each case is the precision of the vinification process and the flair that ensures the grape's best virtues flow into the wine. All Wright's peers concur in praising the talent of this local master whose meticulous attention to everyday detail borders on the obsessive. But he also knows how to make his grape suppliers apply the requisite high standards of discipline in their viticulture and ensure that they pick exactly the right day for harvesting. All this explains the high general level of quality that pertains at his winery. This consummate professional has thrown himself heart and soul into another venture in Washington's famous Walla Walla Valley, this time with Rhône varieties. Ken Wright's wines can be tasted in Carlton's brilliantly restored and converted former railroad station whose inimitable colonial architecture exudes abundant "western" style.

VINE VARIETY

15 acres (6 hectares) in the Abott Claim and Savoya sites, plus bought-in grapes from the Nysa vineyard in the Dundee Hills, Canary Hill, Carter, and Elton in the Eola Hills (on Nekia soils), McCrone, Guadalupe, and Wahle in the Yamhill district, and also from fruit grown on sedimentary soils in the Coastal Range area.

OUR FAVORITE WINES

This winery has not been established long, but its first few vintages were remarkable for their personality and complexity and well above the average quality of the best of the 1990s. We particularly admire the powerful expression of vineyard character in the Eola Hills wines. The 2004 vintage promises to be very special.

WillaKenzie Estate

Silicon Valley, it would seem, can lead anyone (even an engineer from Burgundy) anywhere! Bernard Lacroute wanted to give his American wife Ronni a wonderful present. What he came up with was a vineyard at the heart of the Yamhill district boasting soil rich in ocean sediments deposited when this whole area was covered by the ocean. It is from this soil that the estate takes its name. Persistent, entrepreneurial, and blessed with a highly logical mind, Bernard Lacroute has created a pilot estate fitted out at great expense that demonstrates the greatest possible respect for the environment (as is not uncommon in Oregon). The deep WillaKenzie soils produce emphatically full-bodied wines that have to be held in check. Careful observation has enabled the individual potential of each site to be fully understood: the lowest (but well-drained) sites produce wine with unusual citrus fruit notes; Aliette's very deep soil enables the grapes to attain the advanced state of ripeness that makes for a highly accomplished wine; Pierre Léon, the estate's classic bottling, is remarkable for its spice and violet notes. Our 2002 favorite, however, is Kiana, which from its earliest youth is the most open of the range and reveals the aromatic finesse of its Burgundy clones. A great future beckons for this pilot estate that represents another step closer to modernity for local winemaking.

This is just the beginning. One day the whole hillside will be covered with vines.

VINE VARIETY

101 acres (41 hectares) red: 75% Pinot Noir, 15% Pinot Gris, 6% Pinot Blanc, 4% various.

OUR FAVORITE WINES

This young estate shows progress with every vintage but apparently only the Pinot Noir from its best sites is capable of producing great wines. These are rich in color, alcohol, and tannins, and exemplify the modern Pinot Noir style. They also betray the influence of talented Greek-Burgundian wine consultant Kyriakos Kinigopoulos. The Emery vineyard is the estate's highest at 700 feet (213 meters) and generally produces the finest wine, but the hierarchy can change from one vintage to the next. The Kiana 2003 is excellent.

Château Sainte Michelle

For the astonishing level of quality achieved by its Ste Michelle wine business, which stands as a symbol of the efficiency of the American viticulture industry, one is prepared to forgive the US Tobacco Company many things. Worthy of admiration is the skill with which it obtains this quality using semi-industrial processes whose results are of a regularity and consistency of character often superior to those achieved on a very small scale with artisanal methods. The diversity of Columbia Valley's microclimates, which ranges from very warm to very cool, has enabled the producer to identify vineyards suitable for every great European grape variety. The basalt soils of Canoe Ridge give white varieties a minerality lacking in California and the cooler areas offer perfect conditions for Riesling, which is so difficult to ripen with any degree of finesse in the Golden State. Chateau Ste Michelle's late-harvest wines have often surprised us with their finesse, but a new threshold has been crossed with Eroica Riesling, whose perfect balance and 12.5% alcohol are ideal for the restaurant trade. The same could be said of the Chardonnay, for which winemaker Bob Bertheau seems to have found exactly the right approach, avoiding both bombast and tartness. As for the reds, the Artist Series 2001 "meritage" (an official generic name for this type of blend in the United States) is also up there with the best.

VINE VARIETY

2,965 acres (1,200 hectares) spread over a number of districts including Canoe Ridge (where the winery is located), Cold Creek, and Yakima Valley. All the usual red and white varieties.

OUR FAVORITE WINES

Thanks to the enormous output of this producer, well-made wines are available in every price bracket. The whites are more distinctive than the reds, however. This is especially true of the Rieslings, the grape on which Washington's reputation was originally founded and which is now coming back into fashion. Eroica Riesling, created in association with the great Mosel stylist Ernst Loosen, is possibly the best of its kind in America.

DeLille Cellars

DeLille refers to the family of Charles Lill, co-founder of this Woodinville "boutique winery" in 1992. Originally from Bohemia, where they were brewers, the Lills emigrated to America in the 1950s, made their fortune, and established a cultural link with their past by planting vines. Their associate in the venture was Chris Upchurch, who gradually revealed remarkable gifts as a winemaker. They shared the same production philosophy as all the "garage" winemakers of the American west: an absolute control over the quality of the harvest necessitated by the small volumes at their disposal, respect for the grape, as natural a vinification process as possible (in contrast with the interventionism taught in the American universities), careful *barrique* aging inspired by the Burgundian tradition, and bottling without pumping or filtration. This promotes smooth textures and a pleasing mouthfeel, and encourages the aromas to open up immediately thanks to a strong oxygenation in the new barrels. In addition to the Bordeaux varieties, the winery also anticipated the popularity of Syrah with the prettily named Doyenne, a highly perfumed and voluptuous wine (possibly a touch too self-evident) that is long on the palate and destined for great success thanks to its deliberate all round appeal.

VINE VARIETY

6 acres (2.5 hectares), red: Cabernet Sauvignon, Merlot, Cabernet Franc, Syrah; white: Sauvignon, Sémillon. Purchase of grapes from the Yakima Valley.

OUR FAVORITE WINES

We have only tasted the astonishing 2003 Chaleur Estate and Harrison Hill reds. These are powerful, polished, and highly concentrated blends more in the Napa Valley than the Washington mold, which explains Robert Parker's high praise and the fully merited commercial success that followed.

Woodward Canyon Winery

Rick Small, along with his colleague Gary Figgins, is one of the founding fathers of winegrowing in the state of Washington and belongs to a generation that preferred the Bordelais varieties to Syrah, which is far more fashionable today. Time has proved them right as the spectacular and modish Syrahs possess neither the refinement nor the aging potential of the region's best Cabernet Sauvignons. Born into a farming family from Lowden, a small village in the extreme west of Walla Walla, Small led a long campaign for recognition of the special qualities of this winegrowing region and ultimately succeeded in getting the formidable US Bureau of Alcohol, Tobacco, and Firearms to grant it AVA status. From the outset, his knowledge of the locality and its people enabled him to source grapes from the best growers but he also developed his own, meticulously cultivated, vineyard, specializing in Chardonnay. This he makes better than anyone else in the state, creating a wine of aromatic complexity that liberates the grape from its superficial and tiresome lactic aromas. Another wine that is a gastronomic delight and can be enjoyed in Seattle's best restaurants is his Sauvignon-Sémillon from the Charbonneau Vineyard; it is fresh, complex, spicy, and not unlike a very good Graves.

Artist Series #12

WOODWARD CANYON

2003

Columbia Valley Cabernet Sauvignon

VINE VARIETY
32 acres (13 hectares) around the winery.
Red: Cabernet Sauvignon, Merlot, Cabernet Franc, Barbera;
white: Sauvignon, Chardonnay.
Significant quantities of grapes bought in from the Sagemoor, Pepper Bridge, DuBrul, Charbonneau and Champoux vineyards.

OUR FAVORITE WINES
This winery's best line is without doubt its Columbia Valley old vines Cabernet Sauvignon. The 2001 presents outstanding aromas and structure, and possesses the customary inherent distinction of Washington wines, which are far closer in spirit to the best Bordeaux expressions of the same grape varieties. Another remarkable Cabernet Sauvignon is its 2003 Artist Series.

Deliciously retro but effective: a "garage" wine as conceived by pioneers in Washington State.

L'Ecole N°41 Winery

The small rural community of Lowden was subject to a strong French influence. French Canadians worked in the area in the 19th century and planted vines there, almost certainly the first. This small, highly regarded winery has taken over the attractive white wooden house that was once the "French" school, which explains its curious name. The love of France and French wines was passed on by its founder Jean Ferguson, owner of the state's oldest bank, to his daughter and son-in-law, Megan and Martin Clubb. There is indeed something French in the sense of balance between acidity and alcohol in the whites that marks them out from other whites more inclined to immediate aromatic expression. The close friendships between the valley's best producers are reflected in a certain similarity of style and quality in their reds, influenced no doubt by the work of the Figgins family at Leonetti. The refined textures and integrated oak of this estate's 2002 Perigee and Apogee reds is similar to Leonetti's style without the latter's exceptional mellowness. These wines of rare natural elegance nevertheless deserve to be considered benchmark wines in their own right.

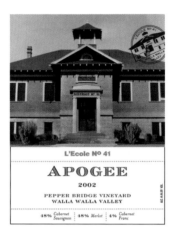

VINE VARIETY

2.5 acres (1 hectare): Cabernet Sauvignon.
An area of the Seven Hills Vineyard co-managed with Leonetti.
Purchase of grapes in the valley.

OUR FAVORITE WINES

This winery is famous mainly for its white wines. These include one of the region's rare high-quality Chenins (medium dry and fruity) and, most importantly, its highly expressive Sémillons such as the barrel-fermented Reserve or the Seven Hills. Its reds have improved, thanks to the progress shown by the Apogee (from the loess soils of Pepper Bridge) and Perigee (from the alluvial Seven Hills) blends in 2002.

Quilceda

The Napa Valley's supremacy would start to fade if wines in the style of those made at Quilceda by Paul Golitzin (the son of the estate's founder Alex) were to proliferate throughout Washington State. Winemaking skills certainly run in the family. Paul's father is the nephew of the famous Russian enologist André Tchelistcheff, who, after training in France, helped perfect the legendary Inglenook, Beaulieu, and Souverain wines in the 1960s, and trained the most talented winemakers of the following generation. Alex Golitzin, who was born in France, trained as a chemist and was the first to spot the viticultural potential of the thin soils of sites just outside Seattle along with the quality of their microclimate. One of his first vintages, the 1979 (we had the opportunity to taste it at the beginning of the 1990s, and it was still magnificently fresh and elegant), attracted the attention of wine lovers, enabling him to continue his "reconversion" to winegrowing. Like Leonetti, the estate is currently the object of a veritable cult but remains safe from the wheeler-dealers and speculators of all sorts who pollute the Californian landscape. This allows the producers to carry on peacefully making wine that conveys the character of an outstanding terroir destined sooner or later to achieve global fame.

VINE VARIETY

32 acres (13 hectares) red: Cabernet Sauvignon, Cabernet Franc, Merlot.

OUR FAVORITE WINES

This estate's small production volume precludes wide distribution of its wines but both our tastings of the 1998 have impressed us greatly. Few American Cabernet Sauvignons and, indeed, few from Bordeaux can rival the refined fruit and tannins of this exceptional wine.

Leonetti Cellar

It would be pointless for us to try to conceal our admiration for Gary Figgins, the most overlooked (by the media) of the great American wine stylists. Like many other offspring of Italian immigrants of his generation, he started off (40 years ago) as a "home winemaker," making small quantities of wine for domestic consumption. The last few vintages have shown that he is currently at his best ever, thanks no doubt to his new winemaking facilities. The wines he produces exhibit a refinement of flavor and texture superior even to California's most famous offerings. Walla Walla's basalt soils are no doubt responsible for the nobility of the tannins, but what has surprised us is the perfect poise and sublime Château-Lafite-like mouthfeel.

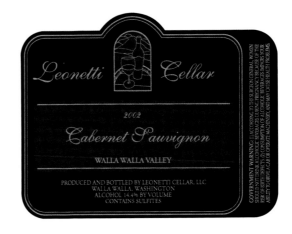

VINE VARIETY

22 acres (9 hectares) red: Cabernet Sauvignon, Merlot, Petit Verdot and Sangiovese plus a Seven Hills vineyard shared with L'Ecole No 41 and just over 2.5 acres (1 hectare) next to the new winery.

OUR FAVORITE WINES

Figgins' 2003 Merlot Reserve, with its delicate truffle notes, silky tannins, and absence of the slightest pungency or hint of chocolate, could be mistaken for a very attractive Pomerol. His 2003 Cabernet Sauvignon goes even further in terms of complexity, and we would happily swap ten bottles of over-praised super-Tuscans for a glass of this supremely civilized wine. Its simultaneous fullness and fluidity is a work of art and surely no one but Figgins could obtain such harmony.

American wine in French wood: no doubt a better combination than the other way around!

Inniskillin

Resulting from an accident of nature (the first frosts of fall must coincide with the moment at which the grapes have reached maximum maturity) and human patience, ice wine (*Eiswein*) originated in Germany and central Europe. Not surprisingly, this exceptional wine can only be produced in very limited quantities. At Inniskillin, the very favorable microclimate of the area around the Niagara river has made it possible to increase and improve production. The grapes are harvested when the temperature falls to –50/–53°F (–10/–12°C). The frozen and concentrated juice ferments slowly to give wines with a pronounced taste of exotic fruits (mango, lychee, passion fruit), which have become an instant success in the Asian and American markets. The European wine lover will find the Cabernet rosé, with its rhubarb-like aromas, novel but unconvincing. The expressive, fat, sensual, and long sparkling wine with its delightful yeasty taste is reminiscent of the rich ciders and perries of Normandy. The Riesling is a little heavy, lacking the purity found in the great *Eiswein*s of the Saar or Nahe regions of Germany, but the lusciousness of the Vidal, and particularly of the "oak aged" cuvée, are not readily forgotten. The company also produces still wines in both red and white. These are well made but, so far, lacking in character.

Frost develops on the grapes more or less in proportion to the initial sugar content of the berries. The ripest berries will often yield juice of two or three times normal acidity when pressed.

VINE VARIETY
247 acres (100 hectares) red: Cabernet Franc, Cabernet Sauvignon, Pinot Noir; white: Vidal, Riesling, Chardonnay.

OUR FAVORITE WINES
This large Ontario-based company has become famous worldwide for its ice wines – sweet wines with a wonderful bouquet, the sugar nicely balanced by a high acidity. It is produced in four types: an unusual rosé from Cabernet Franc grapes; an astonishing sparkling wine; a Riesling; and a Vidal – the last two having great appeal.

Chile

At the end of the 1980s, Chile suddenly appeared on the international scene as a wine-producing country to be reckoned with. With an astounding dynamism, its red Cabernet Sauvignon wines quickly established a reputation, today joined by Merlot. Benefiting from the remarkable potential of the central Chilean plain, sheltered between the towering Andes and the lower cordillera running along the coast, these reasonably priced easy-drinking wines are dark red in color, bursting with fruit, and have a warm and ripe mouthfeel. Protected as they are from the extremes and variations of the climate, and also from other threats (the dreaded phylloxera insect never reached this area), the vineyards in the Aconcagua, Maipo, and Rapel valleys in central Chile require nothing more than water, obtained either from the streams falling down from the Andes or from drip irrigation, to benefit to the full from the advantages of these near-ideal conditions. Developing almost simultaneously with this burgeoning and highly successful wine industry was the production of more ambitious fine wines. At first taking their inspiration from famous international models, today these Chilean wines have acquired a personality of their own, combining exuberance and power with an excellent structure.

List of domaines

Altaïr

Laurent Dassault, a winemaker belonging to the famous family of aircraft manufacturers, is passionate about South America, its landscapes, its way of life, and its produce. When he needs to recharge his batteries, he finds that nothing can beat a long ride through the hills on horseback. At Altaïr he has joined forces with the San Pedro estate to apply the most advanced Bordeaux vineyard and winery techniques to the production of a luxury wine that nevertheless remains a powerful expression of its Chilean terroir. The unique luminosity of the Andes foothills emphasizes the natural fruit of these Bordelais varieties while endowing them with additional notes of red pepper, very ripe, spicy tomatoes, and even the occasional hint of metal that can also be detected in wine from the warmer parts of California. Here, however, this brute aromatic power is tamed and harmonized by means of carefully managed oxygenation. The naturally high glycerol content of grapes that are harvested as late as possible translates into an extremely voluptuous mouthfeel that brought immediate success for this style of wine (where it is not taken too far). The 2002 vintage is already fully developed.

VINE VARIETY
173 acres (70 hectares) at elevations between 1,968 and 2,625 feet (600 and 800 meters). Red: Cabernet Sauvignon, Merlot, Syrah, Cabernet Franc, Petit Verdot, Carmenère.

OUR FAVORITE WINES
The two red wines Altaïr and Sideral (the latter a blend of fruit from the Maipo and Colchacua zones), both dominated by Bordeaux varieties, are modern-style wines boasting a high alcohol content (approaching 15%), opulent oak, and rich, immediately accessible flavors.

The gentle slopes of Errazuriz's prestige vineyard, Dan Maximiano, is in the heart of the valley of Aconcagua.

Casa Lapostolle

Founded in 1994 by Alexandra Marnier-Lapostolle and her husband Cyril de Bournet, Casa Lapostolle has achieved success with the lightning speed that is only possible with an exceptional wine. With the help of Bordeaux enologist Michel Rolland, they built a modern winery offering a brilliant range of high-quality wines – including a veritable Chilean "grand cru," Clos Apalta, made with fruit from carefully selected terroirs. The grapes for this wine come from ungrafted, non-irrigated vines – a rarity in this country. The clay-rich vineyard nestles below the foothills of the Andes, which rise up majestically at the end of the vineyard, forming an L-shape that protects the vines from the strong sunshine during much of the morning and early evening. The Merlot planted here many years ago differs considerably from the French variety. It is actually a cross between Merlot and Carmenère, an ancient Bordeaux variety now almost forgotten in France but which has retained a certain importance in South America. Brilliantly robust, rich, and exuberant, this extremely mature wine is enhanced by 20 months' aging in new oak.

VINE VARIETY

The Casa Apalta vineyard (247 acres/100 hectares) is planted to Merlot (80%) and Cabernet Sauvignon (20%). The fruit for the firm's other wines is sourced from two vineyards located a little further north, at Requinoa (289 acres/117 hectares) and Casablanca (for Chardonnay, 99 acres/40 hectares).

OUR FAVORITE WINES

Exuberant, extremely rich, and full-bodied, Clos Apalta is a wine that leaves no one indifferent. Its enormous unctuousness and nose of ripe black fruit are highly seductive. Recent years have all been extremely convincing.

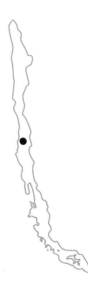

Errazuriz

Many observers seem to regard Chile as a symbol or flag bearer for New World wine, which they see as the fruit of a trend as fleeting as it is enterprising. Errazuriz stands as a serious antidote to this attitude that relegates Chilean wine to the status of mere industrial product or marketing creation. The firm's founder was Maximiano Errazuriz, who was born in Santiago in 1832 into a family of Spanish Basque immigrants. He planted the first vines on the estate in 1870, adopting the ambitious credo "The best of wines for the best of countries!" Located in the Aconcagua Valley north of Santiago, this vineyard remains at the heart of the firm's activities and is run today by a descendant of Don Maximiano, Eduardo Chadwick. In homage to the founder, Chadwick has created a prestige wine that bears Don Maximiano's name. This has now been joined by other reserve wines made from great international varieties such as Cabernet Sauvignon, Syrah, and Merlot.

VINE VARIETY

Red: Cabernet Sauvignon, Merlot, Syrah, Cabernet Franc.

OUR FAVORITE WINES

The Cabernet Sauvignon Reserva, a wine full of verve and vigor, is by far the most interesting of this firm's varietals. The one it is most proud of, though, is Don Maximiano, named after the founder. Luxuriously aged, this is an intense, deep, fleshy wine with a spicy nose and a surprisingly light finish.

Founded in the 19th century, Errazuriz is the longest-established producer in Chile.

Seña

The Spanish word *Seña* translates into English as "sign." Here it means a distinctive mark or signature, and that is indeed what its creators have attempted to achieve with this wine. As previously with Philippe de Rothschild in his own country, Californian producer Robert Mondavi wanted to create an exceptional wine in Chile in collaboration with a local producer. Seña was therefore founded in 1995 by Mondavi in partnership with the head of Errazuriz, Eduardo Chadwick. Made in the Aconcagua Valley, the blend includes a far from negligible proportion of Carmenère alongside the more classic Cabernet Sauvignon and Merlot. Today, after the sale of all the Mondavi vineyards to the Constellation conglomerate, the Chadwicks run the operation themselves, displaying the same ambition to turn the wine into a South American icon.

VINE VARIETY
40 acres (16 hectares) red: Cabernet Sauvignon and Merlot.

OUR FAVORITE WINES
For a number of years, Seña has been one of Chile's most notable wines. A vintage such as 1997 is a good reminder of the dazzling early potential shown by this rich, silky cru. More recent years have continued the momentum and seen the wine developing a eucalyptus and red fruit nose allied with ambitious oak and a mellow but deep body.

Los Vascos

Éric de Rothschild, the proprietor of Château Lafite, was one of the first Europeans to take an interest in Chile's winegrowing potential. In 1988 he purchased a vast estate in the Cañeten Valley, a region with a long viticultural history closely associated with a number of families of Basque origin (hence the name "Los Vascos"). The Rothschild team carried out a major program of refurbishment in both vineyard and winery. Inspired by Lafite, in 1994 the new owners started making a Cabernet Sauvignon monovarietal. On the technical side, vinification and aging facilities were rapidly upgraded in order to allow the firm to achieve its ambitions. Part of the enormous vineyard was very young (the other part was over 50 years old) and quality gradually improved. The Grande Réserve was the first major success. This was followed by Le Dix, made from stringently selected grapes. While the rich, full-bodied style of this wine is indisputably Chilean, its balance and aromatic brilliance are reminders of its kinship with Lafite and Éric de Rothschild's other French properties.

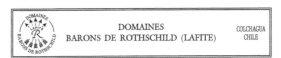

VINE VARIETY
1,433 acres (580 hectares):
red: 95% Cabernet Sauvignon,
white: 5% Chardonnay.

OUR FAVORITE WINES
This bodega produces two Cabernet Sauvignons: under its own name a Chardonnay and a Sauvignon Blanc made from grapes bought from other producers. All are elegant and consistent, but it is above all the cuvée Le Dix de Los Vascos that offers the highest level of quality – as testified by the 2000 vintage, which is extremely harmonious, deep, devoid of heaviness, and boasting ultra-fine tannins.

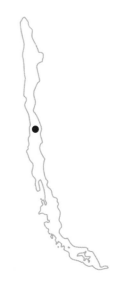

Aquitania

Like Argentina, Chile has benefited enormously from the interest of major international producers who were quick to identify the country's potential for great wine. Thus as early as 1984, Bruno Prats (then in charge of the family property Cos d'Estournel) and Paul Pontalier (director of Château Margaux) decided to explore the country with a view to embarking on an ambitious winemaking project there. Assisted by a Chilean, Felipe de Solminhac, they eventually settled on La Quebrada de Macul, in the Maipo Valley at the foot of the Andes just outside Santiago. As good *Médocains*, their planting of the vineyard gave pride of place to Cabernet Sauvignon. This was soon complemented by Chardonnay from the Traiguén site, which lies considerably further south and benefits from a cooler climate. In 2003 the three friends were joined by a fourth – Ghislain de Montgolfier (of Bollinger) – who contributed to the enterprise his knowledge of great white wines. Lazuli, the most ambitious wine in a range that is gradually gaining in substance, possesses a slender, forthright character strongly reminiscent of the style wines made by Prats, Pontalier, and Montgolfier in Europe.

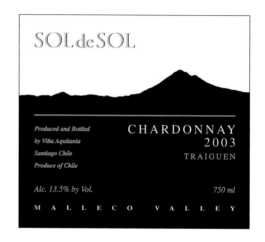

VINE VARIETY
*45 acres (18 hectares)
red: Cabernet Sauvignon;
white: Chardonnay.*

OUR FAVORITE WINES
*Lazuli, made from 100% Cabernet
Sauvignon, is a rigorous and deep
wine that unfolds in the mouth
without any trace of heaviness,
exhibiting a charming freshness that
immediately sets it apart from the
more classic type of Chilean red.
Of the whites, Sol de Sol also stands
out for its freshness while displaying a
remarkably elegant minerality.*

Almaviva

The Comte d'Almaviva, the flamboyant character dreamed up by Beaumarchais for his *Marriage of Figaro*, would no doubt have been delighted by this magnificent wine named after him, which was conceived and created by Philippine de Rothschild in collaboration with one of Chile's main producers, Concha y Toro. The latter's contribution to this alliance formed in the mid-1980s was 99 acres (40 hectares) of vineyard in the Maipo Valley, one of the country's most renowned fine wine regions. Further vineyards have been added since, always showing the same respect for the classic Bordeaux mix of varieties – the only difference being that Merlot has been replaced by Carmenère. The influence of Bordeaux is unquestionably present in this rich, deep, luxurious, and fruity wine that also displays an extremely elegant balance and velvety tannins. Tod Mostero, the property's Chilean winemaker, also has strong Bordeaux links, having studied enology there and worked in a number of the region's grands crus before moving to Baron Philippe de Rothschild's Languedoc property.

VINE VARIETY

210 acres (85 hectares)
red: 70% Cabernet Sauvignon,
27% Carmenère, 3% Cabernet Franc.

OUR FAVORITE WINES

Almaviva has gradually taken flight since it was founded in 1996 and since 2000 in particular has made significant gains in terms of balance and refinement of texture. Recent vintages have been sumptuous.

The futuristic winery of Almaviva, a joint project by the most important Chilean producer and the French Baron Philippe de Rothschild.

Argentina

Wine is nothing new in Argentina, a country where the eating and drinking traditions of southern Europe still largely survive. Nevertheless, for a long time Argentinians were prepared to settle for inferior and badly made wines where quantity was more important than quality. The first generation to produce quality wines, the present winemakers have been influenced by Californian and, more recently, French methods since the recent arrival of many producers from Bordeaux. But to make fine wines in the climatic conditions of the Andean foothills, high-altitude grape varieties were needed, these being the only type to yield well-balanced and well-flavored grapes despite the cold night temperatures.

The vines in the much-favored Mendoza area grow quite happily at altitudes of over 3,281 feet (1,000 meters) and interesting white wines, both still and sparkling, are beginning to be produced. Nevertheless, the production of white wine is likely to remain a sideline since the climate is much better suited to the red Bordeaux grape varieties, particularly Malbec, a variety that does spectacularly well here. Deeper in color, warmer, and more aromatic than in Cahors, it has a strong personality that combines well in blends with Merlot, Cabernet Sauvignon, and Cabernet Franc. It is less successful when used to make single-variety wines, particularly if produced in over-large quantities or when subjected to unnecessary interventions.

List of domaines

Catena Zapata

Italian in origin, the Catena family emigrated to Argentina at the end of the 19th century and became rich landowners, eventually enabling Nicolás Catena to build a state-of-the-art winemaking empire in the Californian mold. The amazing Mayan temple that houses the winery has to be seen to be believed. Also worthy of unmitigated admiration is the extraordinary work carried out in the vineyard in matching terroir with grape variety. This has focused mainly on using the different elevations to their best advantage and on working out in the shortest possible time which vines and cultivation methods are best suited to producing the style of wine demanded by the market. Technique is almost a religion here. This may sometimes mean that terroir plays a secondary role, but it does at least ensure that the winemaking process is carried out with a degree of mastery and precision undreamed of by the venerable old producers. This strategy is perfectly reflected in the wines themselves. They are supple, full-bodied expressions of their respective noble grape varieties, offering an abundance of immediate, characteristic aromas. These are wines of a style that is easy to memorize and enjoy, at least by newcomers to the world of wine. However, the next stage – the quest for more individual, complex expressions of a wonderfully diverse collection of terroirs – is already looming. And this we await with bated breath.

A Mayan temple guarding a wine from the most revolutionary of Argentinian producers: a perfect symbol of an ancient culture, the art of living, and boundless ambition.

VINE VARIETY
Numerous vineyards in Mendoza's best winegrowing districts. Cabernet Sauvignon, Malbec, Merlot, Syrah, Chardonnay, Pinot Noir.

OUR FAVORITE WINES
The wines sold locally are of far less interest than those that are exported – a phenomenon all too common in Argentina. The only truly wonderful wine, which at least shows what they are capable of here, is the Nicolas Catena Zapata, with 20,000 or so bottles produced each year. This is a powerful and sophisticated blend of Cabernet and Malbec, and it will be interesting to track its progress as it ages. The Catena Alta varietals show considerable technical virtue but lack any strong personality.

Cheval des Andes

Cheval des Andes is an ambitious collaboration between the owners of Château Cheval Blanc (Bernard Arnault and Albert Frère) and Terrazas. It started with a desire inspired, understandably, by the beauty of the winegrowing sites in the foothills of the Andes, to produce a South American wine of grand cru quality. The next stage was to choose the men and the means. Las Compuertas, one of Terrazas' gems, planted with old Malbec vines, was selected as the site and the winery was then staffed and equipped in such a way as to enable it to make wine of the very highest quality based on the skill and experience accumulated at the illustrious Saint-Émilion property. Pierre Lurton is responsible for choosing the basic vinification style and supervises the blending process with all the suppleness and taste for a pure and natural end product that are his trademarks. The honest and upright 2002 vintage clearly owes much to his involvement. The Cheval des Andes has a livelier, more spirited temperament than its Saint-Émilion cousin, but ultimately there is little difference between them. Their character and style can be expected to grow even closer as Cabernet Franc plantings taken directly from the Cheval Blanc vineyard are gradually brought into production. The wines should also gain in tannic and aromatic refinement, as has been seen with Morgenster in South Africa.

The cordillera shelters the wines and inspires the skill of the grower. The air, full of the scent of the mountain tops, imbues the grapes and wines with the "taste of the place."

VINE VARIETY

294 acres (38 hectares) red: old Malbec, 40 acres (16 hectares); Cabernet Sauvignon, 49 acres (20 hectares); Petit Verdot, 5 acres (2 hectares); Cabernet Franc (to be planted), 12 acres (5 hectares).

OUR FAVORITE WINES

The 2002 vintage lived up to the owners' expectations and should do extremely well in America. It is opulent but with a firm, uncompromising tannic base, and a powerful nose of ripe fruit. Only time will tell how it will age.

Norton

The beginnings of viticulture in Argentina go back to the 19th century. While the early pioneers included a number of adventurous British settlers such as Sir Edmund James Palmer Norton, the notions of quality and expression of individual style are far more recent. It was not until the wealthy Austrian Langes-Swarowski family took over at Norton that all the stops were pulled out to produce wine – in every price category and across a wide range of grape varieties – that is easy to drink, technically perfect, and occasionally rather more ambitious but always well-balanced, less baroque, and more refined than top wines from other producers. Another point in Norton's favor is that the wines made available for domestic consumption are often the same ones that are exported, and when they appear on the wine lists of Mendoza restaurants, diners can order them with confidence. In Argentina, style is more a matter of altitude (which determines the maturity and aromatic quality of the grape) than terroir, at least for the time being. Norton, like other wineries, has planted vines at elevations of above 3,280 feet (1,000 meters) not only in order to produce well-balanced whites but also in order to produce reds with a greater refinement of tannins and flavors. Its recent vintages have reaped the benefits of this strategy, and there is every indication that those to come will continue along the same route.

The sun beats down on grapes and harvesters alike, but Argentinian modesty makes the men reluctant to bare their legs. Theirs is a very different style from the scruffy casualness of the harvesters in the French countryside.

VINE VARIETY

Approximately 1,433 acres (580 hectares), split between five farms at altitudes of between 2,790 and 3,280 feet (850 and 1,000 meters), red and white, all the classic Bordeaux varieties plus Chardonnay.

OUR FAVORITE WINES

This bodega's wines are always well made and less heady than most in terms of alcohol and flavors, but they lack strong personality. Great character is, however, displayed by Privada, a low-volume blend of Cabernet Sauvignon, Malbec, and Merlot from the De la Colonia vineyard. This is a full-bodied, velvety, and chocolatey – in other words, very Argentinian – wine.

Clos de los Siete

French winemakers hesitated for a long time before investing in the vineyards of the New World and exporting their *savoir-faire* and particular vision of good wine. The current French economic crisis and a desire to protect their heritage by relocating it abroad have finally succeeded. At the head of this movement are winemakers from Bordeaux, many of whom have chosen to establish vineyards in South America, primarily in Argentina and Chile. The most spectacular enterprise of this kind is set in a dream landscape at the foot of the Andes at the heart of Argentina's Mendoza winegrowing area. Originally the idea of Jean-Michel Arcaute, seven Bordeaux grand-cru-owning families got together to buy almost 2,000 acres (about 800 hectares) of virgin land (the surface area of the Pomerol appellation) whose altitude is conducive to even ripening. Michel Rolland, one of the "gang of seven," advises the others at every stage of the vinification process. The plan is for all the members to vinify their own wine in future, and also to devote a proportion of their production to the development of a common brand, a blend called Clos de los Siete. Their aim was to create a high-quality Argentinian wine to be distributed throughout the world by the Bordeaux network. This aim was achieved from the outset, and the first independently produced wine, made by Catherine Péré Vergé under the name Linda Flor, is already competing with the very best Argentinian offerings.

VINE VARIETY

1,483 acres (600 hectares) soon to be increased to almost 2,000 acres (800 hectares), divided into seven zones managed by Michel Rolland, Catherine Péré Vergé, and the Dassault, Rothschild (Benjamin), Cuvelier, Bonnie and Arcaute families. Red: Malbec, Merlot, Cabernet Sauvignon, Petit Verdot.

OUR FAVORITE WINES

The different owners will gradually start making their own wine on their own premises, but so far all the grapes have been vinified at Monteviejo (owned by Catherine Péré Vergé), the first winery to have been completed. The wine made here bears the symbolic name Clos de los Siete, and from its very first vintages has displayed a remarkable fullness of body and flavors infinitely more closely associated with the relevant grape and terroir than is the case with other top-end Argentinian wines.

Poesia

The Garcin family, owners of the famous Clos l'Église in Pomerol (as well as a number of other Bordeaux properties), was initially involved in the Clos de los Siete project. Following differences of opinion with the other partners, it pulled out and developed a smaller estate of its own with the intention of producing a wine that would reflect the microclimate as closely as possible. They succeeded within two years. "Patou" Lévêque, Hélène Garcin's husband and one of the most talented of the younger generation of Bordeaux viticulturists, has handcrafted a great wine from excellent old vines. Everything here has been thought through with the same careful attention to detail on which the success of the new generation of Saint-Émilion and Pomerol wines is based – from work in the vineyard to harvesting and vinification. The Garcins' main aim is to endow wines that are naturally very powerful and sunny with a greater elegance of expression. The 2002, with its velvety texture and the remarkable quality of its tannins (hitherto unknown in Mendoza, where Californian-inspired vinification techniques had always produced wines that were impressive rather than truly seductive) was a great success. In partnership with their friend and advisor Alain Raynaud, the Garcins have just created a new brand called Pasodoble, a Malbec–Cabernet–Syrah blend that looks set to attract a great deal of attention.

VINE VARIETY

32 acres (13 hectares) of old vines: 60% Malbec, 40% Cabernet Sauvignon. Managed by Vignobles Garcin, Haut-Bergey, Léognan, France.

OUR FAVORITE WINES

This small estate produces two reds: Clos des Andes, and the superior Poesia, whose uncommon refinement of texture and aroma makes it one of Argentina's most ambitious and successful wines.

These cathedral-like brick buildings are worthy places in which to make wine. Pride in good winemaking seems to go hand in hand with an appreciation of beauty, a worldwide tendency that can only be welcomed.

Terrazas de los Andes

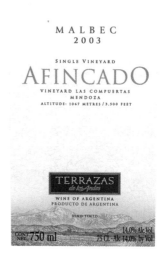

This large modern winery belongs to LVMH and its sheer dynamism drags along the rest of Argentinian winegrowing in its wake. As at Catena, the most significant achievement of the last few years has been the optimization of planting as each variety shows its best qualities at a different elevation. It proved necessary to raise the whites to nearly 4,000 feet (about 1,200 meters) in order to obtain sufficiently well-balanced fruit, yet the reds remain distinctly more representative of their respective varieties, especially the Malbec, which is ideally suited to the climate and soil – although a certain amount of irrigation is necessary. The Malbec has remarkable body, texture, and aromatic complexity, and 2002 proved to be a near-perfect vintage. Another prestige wine, Afincado, offers a more precise expression of the character of a specific terroir (the Los Aromos vineyard located at the heart of the Perdriel terraces on the high Luján de Cuyo plateau). Naturally the company's technical expertise and its Champagne connections have enabled it to develop high-quality sparkling wines that have become almost an institution in Buenos Aires. These wines are made at Agrelo and a prestige blend named Eternum, which is aged for a long time on its lees prior to *dégorgement*, strikes us as the best wine made by Moët et Chandon or its subsidiaries in South America or indeed anywhere else in the Southern Hemisphere.

VINE VARIETY

Total area not known. Vineyards at: Perdriel (Los Aromos) 3,215 feet (980 meters), Cabernet Sauvignon; Vistalba 3,500 feet (1,067 meters), Malbec; Tupungato 3,937 feet (1,200 meters), Chardonnay; Cruz de Piedra 2,625 feet (800 meters), Syrah.

OUR FAVORITE WINES

The Malbec Reserva is the most original wine in a very elaborate range subject to ongoing development. It is the product of particularly well maintained vines benefiting from a superb site. It is complex, long on the palate, and powerful, though not heavy. The 2002 vintage was outstanding.

Yacochuya

This small estate is the pride and joy of a remarkable tribe of great Argentinian viticulturalists, the Etchart family, whose forceful personality has for many years been playing an important role in shaping the development of the country's wines. Circumstances caused the family to quit the large Cafayate bodega that bears its name (now owned by Pernod-Ricard) and establish itself in a dream landscape in the small village of Yacochuya. Here it runs a small pilot vineyard in which all the rich ambient aromas seem to be concentrated in the skins of the grapes. The estate is a joint venture between the Etchart family, and its old friends Michel and Dany Rolland, the stars of Pomerol winemaking. The Etcharts look after the vineyard, while the Rollands make the wine – as only they know how – in the model winery they built themselves and which they own. Of all their involvements in vineyards all over the world, this is without doubt the one closest to their hearts. This is reflected in wines that convey terroir character with a perfect blend of strength and precision. Cafayate's Malbec crop attains such a peak of ripeness that its grapes display even greater tannic complexity than Cabernet or Merlot. This causes us to wonder at the disappearance of the variety from the vineyards of Bordeaux as well as at the banality of its recent expression in the wines of Cahors. Here, however, the vines are cultivated with biblical simplicity and utmost respect for the environment – a permanent source of inspiration.

VINE VARIETY

40 acres (16 hectares) red: 55% Malbec, 25% Cabernet Sauvignon, 8% Tannat; white: 12% Torrontes.

OUR FAVORITE WINES

Naturally, this property's cult wine is its red, which boasts richness, naturalness, depth, and sensuality which to our mind are unrivalled in Argentina. Given the opportunity to taste its white, wine lovers will nevertheless be astonished by the intensity of its fruit, which recalls Muscat and Gewürztraminer. The grapes are harvested at a far greater level of ripeness here than elsewhere in Cafayate.

South Africa

South Africa's earliest vines were planted by French or Dutch Huguenots way back in the late 17th century. This makes them at least as old as many vineyards commonly referred to as "historic." Over the last 20 years, however, numerous structural changes and changes in mentality have turned the country's viticultural scene on its head, and the resulting commotion is far from over! Traditional varieties such as Pinotage (a cross between Cinsaut and Pinot Noir), chosen for their ability to withstand the lack of water in the bush, have given way to the usual range of "international" varieties with the now firmly established intention of adapting them as closely as possible to both public taste and local conditions. Stellenbosch and the Sinonsberg slopes opted for the white and red Bordeaux varieties, Walker Bay chose Pinot Noir, and Paarl turned to Shiraz and the more southerly varieties. A brilliant tasting school established under the auspices of the Cape Wine Masters has had a positive influence on the development of the style of South African wine, as has replanting with healthy vines after a succession of diseases damaged the country's best vines and prevented the production of high-quality red wines.

List of domaines

Bouchard Finlayson

Fans of the Pinot Noir grape are always on the lookout for a microclimate and suitable soils that will allow this variety to ripen well and respect the aromatic glories of the grapes. Peter Finlayson has found just such a place in Walker Bay, in the small valley of Hemel-en-Aarde, sheltered by the heights of Galpin Peak (after which the Pinot Noir is named) and the 3,937 feet (1,200 meter) high Tower of Babel. The climate here is cool, less dry than in the Paarl region, with well-draining argillaceous-gravel soil over a layer of shale that, by contrast, is able to retain moisture. Careful viticulture and skillful winemaking techniques, combining German rigor (Finlayson trained in Geisenheim) and Burgundian empiricism, resulted immediately in reds of great character, similar to those produced by the first person to have made good Cape Pinot Noirs: Anthony Hamilton-Russell. The wine lover should not expect to find in this wine the charm and aromatic complexity of a Vosne-Romanée, but rather the firmness and chewy mouthfeel of a good Pommard. Finlayson is equally enthusiastic about great Tuscan and Piedmontese grape varieties that he had the inspired idea to combine in a wine that is even more faithful in its expression of terroir. Significantly he named it Hannibal, after the great African general who sought to conquer Europe!

VINE VARIETY

47 acres (19 hectares) at the Hemel-en-Aarde ("sky and earth") farm in Walker Bay.
Red: Pinot Noir, Sangiovese, Nebbiolo, Barbera, Mourvèdre.
White: Sauvignon and Chardonnay, plus bought-in grapes.

OUR FAVORITE WINES

The Pinot Noir Galpin Peak is perhaps the best-known South African wine, particularly the very rare (2,000 bottles) selected cuvée, made in the best casks. The style of this deep-colored wine is decisive, powerful, and energetic, but nevertheless very expressive of the terroir. Perhaps the most original wine produced here is the astonishing blended Hannibal, a successful marriage of one-third Pinot Noir combined with the great Italian varieties (Sangiovese, Nebbiolo, and Barbera) plus a little Mourvèdre. The 2002 vintage is excellent.

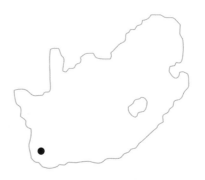

Bredell Wines

The Bredell family was on to a good thing when, in 1932, it decided to make fortified wines in the Portuguese style from the very concentrated grapes of the old, "wild," and often ungrafted vines growing on the slopes of the Helderberg. Here, the hot sun and good natural drainage of the sandy soil over a deep layer of clay yields grapes that are rich in aromas and tannins, qualities that are magnified tenfold in a fortified wine. Anton Bredell does not use the traditional Portuguese low, flat stone (*lagar*) in the production of his wines, preferring instead open concrete vats that give identical results in terms of style and constitution. It is easy to understand the popularity of fortified wines in the southern hemisphere: they are easier to keep and do not vary markedly in character from one year to the next. The style of the wine will, therefore, depend more on decisions made by the maker as to when to stop the fermenting process, so determining how much sugar to leave in the wine. This is done by adding alcohol or sulfur dioxide to the grape must (a process called *mutage* in French). Bredell wines contain 20% alcohol, this high level having the effect of reducing the sensation of sweetness. The other wines produced by this house are more run of the mill.

VINE VARIETY

272 acres (110 hectares) under ownership at the Helderzicht farm situated at the foot of the Helderberg, and also on unirrigated bush terrain.
Red: Tinta Barocca, Touriga Nacional, Touriga Francesca, Souzao, Syrah, Pinotage.

OUR FAVORITE WINES

The ruling wines here are fortified port-style wines, which are often magnificent. The Cape Vintage Reserve Port, in particular, would be hard to tell from the best Portuguese ports. The monumental 1998 is perhaps the greatest South African wine of any kind that we have ever tasted.

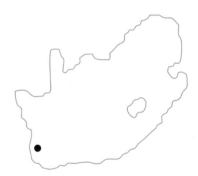

Klein Constantia

It was in the late 17th century that Simon Van der Stel, governor of the Cape and father of Willem Adriaan Van der Stel (who went on to found the Vergelegen estate), chose Constantia as the ideal spot in which to create the first Cape vineyard. Constantia was conveniently placed near Cape Town. Additionally, its proximity to the coast at False Bay meant it enjoyed a mild, damp microclimate that was perfect for the production of dessert wines which could easily be kept for a long time. The granitic soil of the area gave the wine a perfume of refinement that cannot be matched at Stellenbosch. Known as Vin de Constance, it soon became legendary and was favored by many famous world figures – including the French emperor, Napoleon I. It seemed that it had disappeared entirely but, 20 years ago, it resurfaced at Klein Constantia, thanks to the efforts of the new owners, Duggie and Lowell Jooste. They make two types of sweet wine: the first, a very powerful, refined, and elegant wine, made from late-harvest Sauvignon grapes made richer by noble rot; the second, a Muscat made from grapes that are similarly late-harvested, and bottled in a flask of the original 19th-century shape. The richness and aromatic diversity of this last wine even exceed those of the Sauvignon. The best red wine from this domaine is Marlbrook, a wine that well deserves its success: full-bodied, fruity, and velvety, it would certainly be worth exporting.

VINE VARIETY

185 acres (75 hectares) in the foothills of the Constantiaberg. Red: Pinot Noir, Cabernet Sauvignon, Merlot. White: Sauvignon, Semillon, Chardonnay, Riesling, Muscat de Frontignan.

OUR FAVORITE WINES

The winery's specialty is a dry white wine, and more particularly its legendary sweet, unfortified Muscat, Vin de Constance. Today, this wine has regained all the body and nobility that once gave it a place of honor in the cellars of the great and famous. It can be found in many of the top European restaurants.

The imposing mass of the Simonsberg, home to vines and gods.

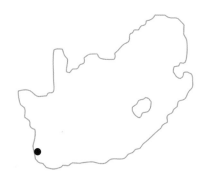

Ken Forrester Vineyards

The Chenin grape was one of the earliest varieties to be planted in South Africa, as it was in California. In both countries, it was later to be overtaken in popularity by Chardonnay. Ken Forrester has remained loyal to the Chenin variety, understanding that this variety is well suited to the microclimate because it is better able to withstand drought. Also an excellent restaurateur with the best wine list in Stellenbosch, Forrester realized that the public would easily tire of the unsubtle oakiness of Chardonnays in the "Australian" style. Provided the grapes are harvested when fully ripe and the wine is carefully made, a Chenin is more suitable for drinking with a meal than a Chardonnay. Forrester spent some time in Anjou, returning intent on creating a fine white wine made from the very best of each year's grapes (including a small proportion made more concentrated by noble rot) fermented in the barrel. The lees are stirred up with the wine resting on them (a process known as *bâtonnage* in French, because the lees are stirred with a *bâton* or stick), but malolactic fermentation is not encouraged. The resultant wine is complex and stylish. However, the most miraculous thing about it is the complete absence of bitterness often encountered in Chenin wines. It would seem that only very healthy grapes are used, with just a small amount of sulfur dioxide.

2004

THE

F M C

FORRESTER MEINERT CHENIN

CHENIN BLANC

KEN FORRESTER WINES SOUTH AFRICA

VINE VARIETY

Bought-in grapes and also from "bush" vines growing on plots of land in the Helderberg Mountains. These are generally not trained onto trellises or irrigated. Mainly white Chenin.

OUR FAVORITE WINES

When it comes to white Chenin grapes, Ken Forrester is the specialist. He makes wines of every type: gentle, fruity and dry, dry and lively, oaky and long lasting, or sweet as a result of noble rot. The most impressive of all (and one that should make the winemakers of the Loire Valley sit up and take notice) is the prestige cuvée FMC (Forrester, Meinert (the winemaker here), Chenin). Fat, long, and aristocratic, it would be hard to find anything better than this splendid and complex dry wine.

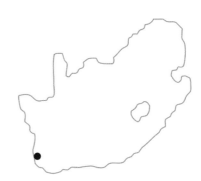

Morgenhof

Despite the German sounding name, Morgenhof was founded in the 17th century by French Huguenots. Today, its owners are once again French, a branch of the Cointreau family. Anne Cointreau has lived here since 1993, and has done much to revive this historic firm which, when she arrived, was in something of a decline. As is often the case in South Africa, the winery is also a training center and tourist attraction, with a well-known and admired restaurant often used for wedding receptions and similar events. An excellent team is on hand to conduct wine tastings and guide the ever-increasing number of curious visitors. Anne Cointreau's French origins are reflected in the style of the wines produced here, placing the emphasis more on refinement and restraint than trying to bring out the intensity and violence of the terroir. The company produces a complete range of red and white wines that are cleanly and precisely made, suitable for easy drinking with a meal. More ambitious wines are produced in smaller quantities, dependent on the gradual maturation of the vines planted on the surrounding hillsides. One of the unusual things about this estate is the presence of two Portuguese grape varieties. These are used in the making of a number of fortified wines of a very classic style.

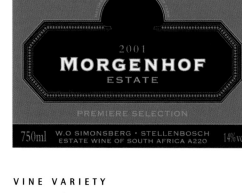

VINE VARIETY
166 acres (67 hectares) on the slopes of the Simonsberg.
Red: Cabernet Sauvignon, Cabernet Franc, Merlot, Pinot Noir, Pinotage, Touriga Nacional, Tinta Barocca.
White: Sauvignon, Chenin, Chardonnay.

OUR FAVORITE WINES
The skill of this winery is well represented by its prestige red which goes by the rather uninspired name of Premiere Selection. The 2001 has well-balanced alcohols and a beautifully clean aroma with the spicy notes typical of the Simonsberg region. Also worthy of note is the sparkling wine, made from Pinot Noir and Chardonnay grapes, where the influence and methods of Gosset champagne are detectable.

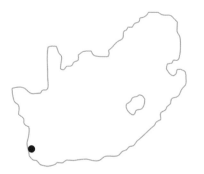

The best harvesting method: the bunches of grapes are lovingly cut by hand with small scissors.

Morgenster

Morgenster split from the Van der Stel family's Vergelegen estates when Jacques Malan, a Huguenot in origin, inherited the property. Keen to make wine, he had to wait until 1992 to replant the estate when Giulio Bertrand (an industrialist with a background in the Piedmontese textile industry) arrived on the scene. The property is wonderfully located close to the ocean, and produces both grapes and olives. Our most recent visit was made unforgettable by the beauty of the restored buildings and the idyllic surrounding countryside, its hills recalling the landscape of the Italian owner's birthplace. The olive oils have acquired a reputation among Cape restaurateurs for their unmatched quality, and visitors come here as much for the oil as for the wine. Judging the 2001 and 2002 red Morgenster (which benefited from specialist advice from Pierre Lurton, director of the French houses of Cheval Blanc and Yquem), this wine is likely to become one of the most famous in South Africa. Made according to traditional rules in a small and architecturally exquisite winery, it is chiefly inspired by wines of the Bordeaux school, seeking above all to bring out tannins that are as noble as possible. We find here the same qualities of complexity and elegance as at Vergelegen, but with even more assurance, something that can only be accounted for by the excellence of the terroir. It would appear that South Africa has found its first grand cru.

VINE VARIETY
99 acres (40 hectares) planted with Cabernet Sauvignon, Cabernet Franc, Merlot, Petit Verdot.

OUR FAVORITE WINES
Imitating the practice followed in Bordeaux, just one wine is produced here from a skillfully balanced mixture of grape varieties, of which Cabernet Franc represents one-third. Its unrivaled aromatic refinement and natural elegance of constitution give full credit to one of the finest terroirs in South Africa.

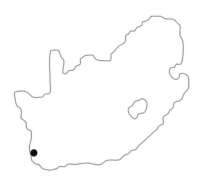

Rupert & Rothschild

Two families, famous in their respective countries of origin, have come together here to create a high-quality vineyard and company that is poised to realize all its founders' ambitions. The South African Ruperts are wealthy international magnates, while Edmond de Rothschild's, and now his son Benjamin's, links with Bordeaux and winemaking are known worldwide. Together, they acquired one of the historic farms of the region – Fredericksburg, founded around 1700 – restoring and extending it with great skill. The decision to consult Michel Rolland from Bordeaux on matters of winemaking technique and to create the style of wines was to bear fruit. In the first few years, the grapes were affected by several vine diseases and did not reach full maturity. These days, the diseased vines have been, or will soon be, replanted. The grapes are harvested when they reach optimal ripeness, sometimes resulting in levels of alcohol as high as 15%. The art of the winemaker lies in embedding this alcoholic richness in a texture as silky and velvety as possible, at the same time preserving the fresh character of the tannins but avoiding astringency. The winemaking process is thus of the greatest importance. Here, it is carried out according to traditional rules, using prime quality casks. For anyone who appreciates the spicy and smoky aromas of Cabernet Sauvignon, the version produced by this estate, one of the most expressive of the Franschoek region, is a must.

VINE VARIETY

173 acres (70 hectares) in various vineyards in Stellenbosch, Durbanville, Walker Bay, and at the farm in Fredericksburg.
Red: Cabernet Sauvignon and Merlot.
White: Chardonnay.

OUR FAVORITE WINES

The fame of the top of the range from this winery relies in great part on the legendary Rothschild name: the white Chardonnay Baroness Nadine de Rothschild, and the red Cabernet Sauvignon Baron Edmond de Rothschild. The red has more personality than the white, with an impressive body and very spicy tannins. As the quantity of grapes from the domaine (recently replanted after an outbreak of disease) used in the blend is increased, this wine gains increasingly in expression. The 2001 and 2002 vintages are excellent.

Rustenberg

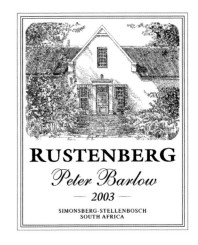

Dating back to 1682, the historic Rustenberg farm has, under the ownership of the two most recent generations of the Barlow family, very successfully concentrated on grape production. The range of wines currently being made here is without doubt the best and most worthy of export that the house has ever produced. Each level of quality within this homogenous range has a matching price, a situation very different from the confusion that reigns in the European market. The Schoongezicht estate, where the visitors' center is situated, is well worth a visit, not only to taste the wines but also to see the building, its immaculate white exterior typical of Cape architecture, but with a modern interior that is perfectly integrated into the whole. The granitic soil of the higher parts of the estate are planted with white grape varieties, the area called Five Soldiers producing a Chardonnay of very high quality. However, the most complex wines produced here are the Cabernet Sauvignons which express subtle nuances of cedar and spices, often resembling those from the heart of the Médoc appellation in France.

VINE VARIETY
408 acres (165 hectares) on the slopes of the Simonsberg and the Helderberg.
All the main red and white grape varieties, including the Provençal trio: Syrah, Grenache, and Mourvèdre.

OUR FAVORITE WINES
Since the restoration of the vineyard, the Cabernet Sauvignons have recovered all their brilliance and grandeur of style, notably in the case of the Peter Barlow cuvée. Adi Badenhorst also produces some nice Sauvignons and Chardonnays, although these are rather less original.

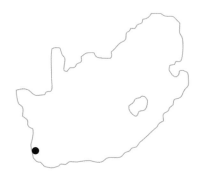

The inimitable architecture of the Cape, reflecting a centuries-old way of living that is becoming increasingly attractive to French winemakers.

Thelema Mountain
Vineyards

This estate is named after Thélème, the abbey in François Rabelais' epic French tale of monastic life *Gargantua*. Thélème's famous rule was *fay ce que vouldras* (meaning "Do what you will"), which is exactly what Gyles Webb did – resulting in the success of his venture. In fact, he was very fortunate to have planted his vines in the 1970s, and on a piece of virgin land. They escaped attack by disease and produced very fine grapes from the start. The slopes of Helshoogte Pass below the Simonsberg rise up to 2,100 feet (640 meters), making it one of the highest and coolest vineyards in the Stellenbosch region. This results in an increase in the aromatic quality of the grapes, and also in the tannins in the red varieties. A subtle aroma of mint, a little like that found in wine from Martha's Vineyard in Napa Valley, gives just the right touch of exoticism to the bouquet of the Cabernet Sauvignons. The Merlot goes even further in the development of differences between the vintages and in its perfection of form. We can be grateful to Gyles Webb for his wise decision to avoid the heavy chocolate notes of Merlots from the Mediterranean area, settling for firm tannins that are fresh without astringency. He also produces some very successful dessert wines, including a complex Muscat made without the need for mutage in a style very similar to that which has made the Constantia wines so famous.

VINE VARIETY
99 acres (40 hectares) red: Cabernet Sauvignon, Merlot; white: Sauvignon, Chardonnay, Riesling.

OUR FAVORITE WINES
This estate was one of the first to produce red wines from fully ripe healthy grapes, anticipating the trend that has swept the Libournais in the last decade. The Cabernets and Merlots from this domaine have a remarkably velvety texture and long finish. The late-harvest Muscat is as good as the famous Klein Constantia.

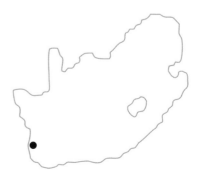

Vergelegen

Today, the beautiful architecture and estates of Vergelegen (meaning "distant land") are preserved as a historical monument. It was built in 1700 by the governor of the Cape Willem Adriaan Van der Stel, whose intention was to create a palace equal in magnificence to Louis XIV's Versailles. The present-day owners, clearly people of considerable means, look after the buildings and wonderful gardens with great skill. For the new winery here they have designed and constructed one of the most beautiful buildings of this type anywhere in the world. The appointment of André van Rensburg – a man combining all the energy and directness of a Didier Dagueneau with the instinct and ambition of a Marcel Guigal – as chief winemaker has resulted in an uninterrupted series of wines that have set widely acknowledged standards of quality for the whole country. The grapes, growing up to 984 feet (300 meters) above sea level on the slopes of the Schaapenberg, benefit from the sea breezes from the nearby ocean, a microclimate that gives the white grape varieties a unique aromatic refinement. André van Rensburg's flair for winemaking is instantly noticeable in the quality of the balance and, particularly, the integration of the alcohol. Furthermore, these wines have a remarkably long life. A fan of red wines of Syrah grapes, Van Rensburg did not rush into the production of his own version. When it did appear, it proved to be a masterpiece which, despite the name on the label, is much more French in style than South African.

VINE VARIETY

Vineyards on the slopes of the Schaapenberg and Rondekop mountains, on granitic soil.
Red: 82 acres (33 hectares) Cabernet Sauvignon;
57 acres (23 hectares) Merlot; 15 acres (6 hectares)
Cabernet Franc; 15 acres (6 hectares) Shiraz.
White: 36 acres (14 hectares) Sauvignon; 32 acres (13 hectares)
Chardonnay; 22 acres (9 hectares) Semillon.

OUR FAVORITE WINES

All Van Rensburg's wines are outstanding for their elegance and precision, but two cuvées are notable for their character: the white Vergelegen, a delicious blend of Semillon with Sauvignon; and a marvelous Shiraz with an aromatic flair worthy of a Mount Edelstone, despite the youthfulness of the vines.

Designed by architects Patrick Dillon and Jean de Gastines, the grand entrance to the Vergelegen estate looks over a dramatic landscape that stretches as far as the Pacific Ocean.

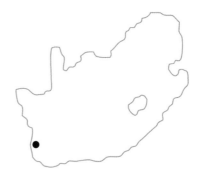

Australia

The sudden emergence of Australian wine over the last 20 years, a consequence of the dynamism of the local viticultural scene and the benevolent complicity of the British wine merchants, is without doubt the most significant event to have occurred in the world of wine in recent times despite the country's modest overall production level (barely 4% of the world total). Australia has succeeded in establishing a new style of wine (far more immediately fruity than that of old Europe) by means of innovative and revolutionary vinification methods, but thanks also to the specific properties of its microclimates and terroirs, whose value intelligent pioneers had intuited in the middle of the 19th century. With regard to white wine, producers have skillfully exploited the comfortable lactic, buttery aromas of Chardonnay and Sémillon. As for red, they have capitalized on the spiciness and natural velvety texture of Syrah, which, with some justification – so original is the wine made from this grape grown in some cases on centenarian vines – they rechristened Shiraz. The historic heart of the Australian vineyards remains southern South Australia and Victoria, but new zones have been brilliantly developed over recent years. These include Margaret River in the extreme west of the country, which is ideally suited to Chardonnay and the white and red Bordeaux varieties, and Tasmania with its distinguished Pinot Noirs. The search for suitable locations continues near Orange, to the north of Sydney, as well as in the Yara Valley just outside Melbourne.

List of domaines

Cape Mentelle

Cape Mentelle was one of the pioneering wine-producing estates in the Margaret River region. During the 1960s, avant-garde agronomists became interested in finding wetter microclimates where vines could be grown without the need for irrigation. The Margaret River area has annual rainfall of over 39 inches (1,000 millimeters), and a microclimate similar to that of Bordeaux so it was decided to plant Bordeaux grapes. The first wines produced confirmed that the varieties had adapted well to the climate. They had neither the heaviness nor the hints of mint and eucalyptus characteristic of grapes from hotter areas of Australia. On the other hand, as is normal for young vines, they lacked body and complexity. The technical skill of the daring pioneers who established vineyards in the area led to further ventures. The production of red wines was now complemented by that of white Chardonnay and Sauvignon wines of an intense aromatic purity and balance. It was not long before these promising terroirs were acquired by the Veuve Clicquot group, which was able to supply the technical and human resources that would enable an increase in production while still ensuring high-quality wines. The Cape Mentelle model of expansion was imitated by Cloudy Bay in New Zealand, and the Cabernet reds produced by these twin properties have become reference points. The white wines still lack personality to some extent, but they are reliable.

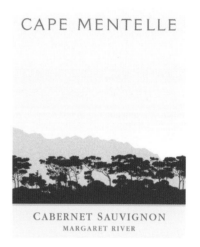

VINE VARIETY

445 acres (180 hectares) red: mainly Cabernet Sauvignon; white: Sauvignon, Semillon.
Grapes also bought from other vineyards in the same area.

OUR FAVORITE WINES

The red Cabernet Sauvignon wines are deservedly the most famous. From the outset, they have always been of a type less like a Coonewarra and more like a Bordeaux, although with vegetable tannins. Under the present management of Tony Jordan, the grapes are harvested later, resulting in a wine that now has not only its previous refinement but also a greater fullness of body and depth of texture.

Château
Tahbilk

Tahbilk, along with Penfolds, is one of the oldest wine companies in Australia. Established in the mid-19th century by a Swiss family it has (unlike Penfolds) remained a family business. The wonderful original vineyard has plots of 140-year-old Syrah vines that miraculously escaped attack by the phylloxera aphid. As a winemaker, Alister Purbrick, whose family has owned the house since 1925, believes strongly in the importance of the terroir and so intervenes very little in the winemaking process. Anxious to preserve this exceptional environment, he devotes much care to the old vines, which date from 1860, propagating the strongest rootstocks to preserve the same Syrah variety. The resulting wine has a unique and unmatched body, texture, and honesty of taste, combined with healthily invigorating tannins. Alister Purbrick takes equal pains with the various Rhône grape varieties, grown in tribute to the Swiss founders of the house and because they adapt so well to the climate of this area. Nowhere else in Australia is it possible to find 86 acres (35 hectares) of Marsanne grapes, one of the varieties used for Hermitage wines, nor the necessary complement of Viognier and Roussanne grapes. The strength of this very individual terroir is perhaps best expressed in the private bins containing Cabernet Sauvignon wines selected from the best vintages years. In 1980, a disappointing year in Bordeaux, we tasted this house's Bin No. 67 with its astonishing intensity and smoothness. It was then that our eyes were first opened to the potential of the Australian terroirs.

VINE VARIETY

415 acres (168 hectares) in the Nagambie Lakes zone, on the banks of the Goulburn river.
Red: Syrah, Cabernet Sauvignon, Cabernet Franc, Merlot.
White: Marsanne, Roussane, Viognier, Semillon, Chardonnay, Riesling.

OUR FAVORITE WINES

The most original wine found in Australia is white Marsanne. Produced in large quantities, it has oxidative characters and is powerful and very distinctive. Connoisseurs, though, will seek out the very rare cuvée from ungrafted Syrah vines which are more than 100 years old. This is a massive but gentle wine. The best casks of Cabernet Sauvignon are bottled separately and given a special bin number – something for the serious collector.

Clarendon Hills

Clarendon was planted with Grenache and Syrah grapes at the beginning of the 20th century. Today the plants produce wonderful grapes that are highly concentrated and rich with aromas. Roman Bratasiuk, the owner and winemaker at Clarendon Hills, was an immediate convert. A fan of the famous grape varieties of the Rhone region, he is able to grow and convert them into wine with an artistic flair that is rarely found in the southern hemisphere. Particularly recommended are the excellent Grenache and Syrah cuvées. Astralis, grown on an iron-rich soil, and Brookman give the most complete Syrahs, with powerful, complex aromas of mint and balsamic aromatic oils. Aromas of eucalyptus and spices can be found in the Grenaches produced from the heavy soil of Hickingbotham. The Clarendon Syrah has greater freshness, and the Liandra has hints of smokiness. For those who like a big wine, the massively constructed Romas vineyard Grenache is to be recommended. Made from grapes grown at Blewitt Springs, a warm and steeply sloping terroir, it has an unforgettably long finish. Roman Bratasiuk is to be congratulated for his courage as a winemaker in making only minor adjustments to the acidity of his wines (very unusual in Australia) yet managing to avoid the aromatic deviations to which fragile wines are subject.

VINE VARIETY

Area unknown.
Purchase contracts for grapes from the following vineyards:
Astralis, Pigott Range, Hickingbotham, Clarendon, Brookman,
Kangarilla, Liandra, Moritz, Blewitt Springs.
Red: mainly Syrah, Grenache, Cabernet Sauvignon.

OUR FAVORITE WINES

This remarkable producer's finest wine is the Syrah Astralis,
made from 70-year-old vines grown on an iron-rich soil.
It has a sumptuous body and bouquet, and is perfectly made.
Both the Grenache from the Romas vineyard and the Syrah from
the Brookman vineyards have frequently impressed us with their
class, density without heaviness, and skillful integration
of oakiness.

The wide rows disguise the low-density planting, perhaps in a less than successful attempt to hide the baldness of the soil.

Cullen

Of all the pioneering winemakers of Margaret River, Diana and Kevin Cullen must be the most delightful. Both doctors, the couple approached this new venture with great seriousness and a deep respect for the environment. They have been able to inspire their daughter, Vanya, with the same passion for excellence in work and for wine that is as faithful as possible to the grapes from which it is made. In the Margaret River region it is possible to ripen the best of the French grape varieties without excessive intervention or correction. Today, the Cullen vineyards are models of intelligent biodynamic viticulture, with vines that are carefully trained (using the lyre or Scott Henry systems) to ensure their exposure to the ideal amount of sun. Winemaking methods are highly accurate and controlled. Respect for nature extends to a respect for the consumers. They have the choice of a large range of modest but well-made wines (which can mature in the bottle into truly impressive wines after four or five years), and a limited production of cuvées that have a much greater richness of aromas and expression of the mineral-rich terroir of Cowaramup with its poor granite soil. As is often the case in Australia, one of the most remarkable qualities of this winery is its desire to educate the public about wine. To further this aim, the family has created not only a highly informative tasting room, but also a restaurant on the site where the public can learn which wines and foods complement each other.

VINE VARIETY

69 acres (28 hectares) red: Cabernet Sauvignon (28 acres/11.5 hectares), Pinot Noir (2.5 acres/1 hectare), Merlot (3 acres/1.3 hectares), Cabernet Franc (1 acres/0.5 hectare); white: Sauvignon (13.5 acres/5.5 hectares), Chardonnay (18.5 acres/7.5 hectares), Semillon (3 acres/1.14 hectares).

OUR FAVORITE WINES

The most attractive cuvée produced by the Cullen family, using biodynamic methods, is the red Diana Madeline, a highly successful blend of Cabernet and Merlot grapes whose ripeness contributes to a wine of rare quality. While visiting the winery, we also tasted some remarkable Sauvignon-Semillon white wines, but the more fragile recent vintages do not travel well.

De Bortoli

De Bortoli is probably the most dynamic and visionary family business in Australia. Originally established in the vast irrigated Riverina plain, known for its good table wines, the company gradually expanded into some of the best sectors in the Melbourne and Sydney regions, ceaselessly seeking to improve its viticulture, winemaking, and educative role in giving new consumers an understanding of wine. Training sessions have even been undertaken in Gevrey-Chambertin in order to understand better how to make Pinot Noir. Steve Webber (who oversees the winemaking here) and his wife Leanne de Bortoli have chosen to concentrate on the upper end of the range, seeking to make wines expressive of the terroir with all the effectiveness that the preceding generation applied to the production of their more modest table wines. One of the strengths of the Australian wine industry is that Australian legislation is more than ready to open its doors to those who wish to "get on." The 2004 Hunter Valley Semillon and the 2003 Reserve Release Yarra Pinot Noir are remarkable for their style and definition of terroir. Rarely in Europe are we lucky enough to encounter table wines with the fruity attractiveness and fine texture of De Bortoli's Cabernet Merlot Sacred Hill.

Morning mist, a factor in the development of noble rot, although here the results are unique to Riverina.

VINE VARIETY

Four large production centers with their own vineyards. Riverina in New South Wales, the firm's original estate, 741 acres (300 hectares), to which large quantities of bought-in grapes of all varieties are added. Yarra Valley, 445 acres (180 hectares). Hunter Valley, 89 acres (36 hectares). King Valley, 445 acres (180 hectares). All the major European varieties, both red and white.

OUR FAVORITE WINES

This producer's great specialty is a sweet wine, Noble One. It is made of Semillon grapes affected by noble rot, similar to that produced in Sauternes. Sometimes tending to heaviness when young, after eight to ten years it develops a delightful bouquet of citrus fruits or apricots. The 1998 and 2000 are excellent. Major changes currently underway indicate that their red wines will better express the character of the local terroir, especially in the Yarra Valley.

Hardy's Wine Company

The second largest wine-producing company in Australia, Hardy's produces every type of wine, from its fruity, predictable but honest and clean table wines to its prestige cuvée. There is no attempt to express a particular terroir, the wines being made as in the Champagne region, where cuvées are composed of complementary combinations of grapes from many different types of soil and microclimate. The first prestige cuvées of Eileen Hardy Chardonnay wines were produced from vines at Padthaway. Gradually, further terroirs with even cooler temperatures were established, successfully producing grapes with a more refined bouquet. Eventually the company extended its estates into the Yarra Valley, then Tasmania, and then to the hills around Adelaide. The two most recent vintages are thus a complex blend of grapes grown in vineyards often thousands of kilometers apart. The excellent results fully justify the company's methods, giving a full wine of great delicacy with an aromatic refinement that is reminiscent of a fine Puligny-Montrachet, with none of the cloying sugariness that Europeans so often associate with Australian Chardonnays. The same methods are followed in the production of the company's Shiraz, a wine where the role of the more fruity grapes from the MacLaren Valley, with their well-balanced acidity, has become increasingly important. We are delighted to see that producers believe that lovers of good wine prefer refinement and balance to brute strength.

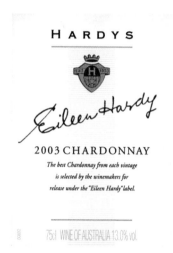

VINE VARIETY

6,178 acres (2,500 hectares) of vines distributed all over the wine-growing areas of Australia. All varieties and also large quantities of brought-in grapes.

OUR FAVORITE WINES

The company's fame owes much to the prestige Eileen Hardy cuvées, masterpieces of skilled, modern enological knowledge. We have recently been greatly impressed by the Chardonnay awarded a prize at the Adelaide Wine Show.

Henschke

The Henschke family is something of an institution, and one of the few to produce in every good year wines of an individuality and distinction of taste equaling that of the greatest crus of Europe. This success can be attributed partly to the terroir and a unique inheritance of old vines. Many of the vines planted on the Hill of Grace and Mount Edelstone sites have root stocks dating from the late 19th century. They have been lovingly preserved to serve as a basis for new planting. After an excellent training in Geisenheim (Germany) and at Adelaide University, Stephen and Prue Henschke have proved to be accomplished vine cultivators and winemakers, producing wines that express with naturalness and vigor all the tiniest nuances of the terroir. Their Lenswood Sauvignon Coralinga, for example, has discreet mineral notes and a smokiness only found elsewhere in the finest Pouilly Fumés, while the violet aromas of the Hill of Grace will only find an equal in a La Mouline. Another classic from this house, the Julius Riesling, recalls the family's German origins with its elegance of aromas, naturalness of balanced alcohol, acidity, and (slight) residual sugar – unique qualities linked to the genetic strengths of the old clones of this grape variety. French vine growers should be encouraged to come here to obtain rootstocks for planting to produce quality grapes with a direct link with previous centuries.

VINE VARIETY

Vineyards in Eden Valley.
Mount Edelstone, 40 acres (16 hectares). Hill of Grace,
20 acres (8 hectares). Eden Valley, 79 acres (32 hectares).
Also, in the Adelaide Hills at Lenswood, 32 acres (13 hectares).
All on Cambrian schist or iron-bearing granite.
Red: mainly Syrah.
White: Sauvignon, Semillon, Riesling.

OUR FAVORITE WINES

The two Syrahs – Hill of Grace and Mount Edelstone – are
arguably the most refined wines in Australia, with an elegance
of tannins that is reminiscent of the finest Côte Rôties, and
which sets them apart from other Barossa Valley and Great
Western wines.

Jasper Hill

The soil at Heathcote is heavy, volcanic, and rich in iron oxide. Wherever it occurs in the world, this combination of qualities will give red wines that have plenty of body, tannin, and color. On the other hand, it will also interfere with the aromatic refinement of white wines. Unlike most Australian producers who seek to create wines modeled on a vision of the expression of the grape variety and microclimate, the Laughton family decided, when they set up at Jasper Hill, to emphasize a European-style terroir approach. Selecting several acres of land made up of volcanic soil and lava flows from nearby Mount Ida, they planted ungrafted vines, cultivating them according to biodynamic methods, without irrigation. These conditions were perfect for a Syrah with an immediate and spectacular expression. That said, to refine the tannins, a small proportion of Cabernet Franc is sometimes added on the Emily Paddock vineyard, which produces the most complete wine. In recent years, the worldwide phenomenon of global warming has led to a worrying increase in the levels of alcohol, overwhelming the liveliness of the wine, which has not been counterbalanced by a compensatory strengthening of the tannic support, as has been achieved in the case of Penfolds Grange. Those who enjoy powerful, warm, and extrovert wines will certainly enjoy these.

VINE VARIETY

Two vines, as below.
Emily Paddock, 7 acres (3 hectares) red: Syrah.
Georgia Paddock, 42 acres (17 hectares):
Syrah (30 acres/12 hectares), Nebbiolo (2.5 acres/1 hectare),
Riesling (7 acres/3 hectares), Semillon (2.5 acres/1 hectare).

OUR FAVORITE WINES

The winery produces exclusively wines with a marked character
and alcoholic strength, uncompromising expressions of a
southern-Mediterranean type of terroir, and grapes that verge
on the overripe.

Leo Buring

Bringing together a vast beer business and the 20 wine marques formerly owned by Southcorp (Penfolds, Wolf Blass, Rosemount, Lindemans, and so on), the Foster's Group is a colossus on the international scene. The wines are produced from grapes from over 37,066 acres (15,000 hectares) of vines in all parts of the world. One of the mysterious and impressive things about the Australian system is that, despite its size, this enterprise is also capable of nurturing gems such as a wine like Grange, and of producing winemakers of the stature of a Leo Buring. Appropriately, given his German origins, this pioneer produces wine from Riesling grapes that have successfully adapted to the terroir and climate of the Clare and Eden Valleys in southern Australia. The existence here of very old, ungrafted vines, planted in the 19th century, has contributed enormously to the quality of his wines. His winery in Tanuda, Château Leonay, is still in use today, the Lindemans technical teams continuing its tradition of excellence. With a climate that is on the hot side for this grape variety, the wines have a high level of alcohol (12–13%). They are dry in character with pronounced mineral and kerosene aromas, related to the heavy pressing of the grapes. After ten years, the best cuvée, Leonay, develops a very rich, almost smoky bouquet, making this characterful wine with its perfect acidity the ideal companion to seafood and lobster from the colder waters of the Pacific.

VINE VARIETY
Vines under contract in the Eden Valley and Clare Valley and bought-in grapes.
White: Riesling.

OUR FAVORITE WINES
This small business, part of the enormous Foster's Group (formerly Southcorp), has always concentrated on producing just one type of wine: a Riesling. Dry and full-bodied, it has an astonishing personality that has managed to remain constant despite many recent changes. The Riesling Leonay 2005 is particularly fine.

Penfolds, a truly Australian enterprise, produces well over ten million bottles, including highly sought-after prestige crus as well as the cuvee Grange Hermitage, now known simply as Grange.

Moss Wood

Bill Pannell was the first wine producer in Margaret River to plant (in 1969) Cabernet Sauvignon vines. He was followed by the Cullen family. Since the estate was taken over by Keith and Clare Mugford, the reliable character of its wines has attracted the attention of many connoisseurs. Even in years when the alcohol levels are very high, the wine preserves its elegance and subtle aromas of cedar and red berries, but without any greenness. It is drier than many similar Australian wines, and has tannins of the Bordeaux type. Since 1989, the use of other grape varieties including Merlot and, very recently, Petit Verdot, has helped to diversify the taste, giving a better balance to each vintage. Another wine produced by this well-respected house is the generally successful white Semillon, very different in character from that of the Hunter Valley. Whereas in the Hunter Valley notes of honey and lanolin are dominant (even with a low amount of transformed alcohol), in the Moss Wood we find hints of white berries and acacia honey such as in a good Bordeaux. These are often found together with broom, box, and mint – possibly the result of the addition of a small amount of Sauvignon. This highly original style of wine – to our mind much more distinguished than that of Chardonnay – ages remarkably well. We will not forget the delicious 1986 drunk in 1996 and still in perfect condition.

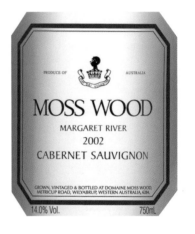

VINE VARIETY

Three vineyards, as below.
Mosswood, 29 acres (11.80 hectares): Cabernet Sauvignon, Merlot, Petit Verdot, Pinot Noir, Semillon, Chardonnay.
Ribbon Vale, 16 acres (6.60 hectares): Cabernet Sauvignon, Cabernet Franc, Merlot, Semillon, Sauvignon.
Amy's Vineyard, 6 acres (2.5 hectares).
Grapes bought in from Yallingup, Cowaramup, and Pemberton.

OUR FAVORITE WINES

The Cabernet Sauvignon was the first – pioneering – wine to be produced in Margaret River. These days, its consistency of style means it can be regarded as a classic. It has rather more delicacy and natural sweetness than some of its neighbors.

Mount Mary

Established and run by the forceful Dr. John Middleton, the cult estate of Mount Mary produces wine on a small, non-industrial scale. The vines are not irrigated and are cultivated according to organic principles. Winemaking methods keep intervention to a minimum and make very little use of new oak, making it hard to identify the place of origin of this wine in a blind tasting. Produced from vines grown on the gray soil over clay of a small hillside, cooler than average for the valley, and known since the 19th century for its suitability for producing good grapes, the wine has a personality closely resembling that of wines from the classic regions of Europe. It expresses the natural character of the grape varieties with great transparency and honesty. The Pinot Noir has not always been produced by the best of methods, but the astonishing quality of the 1989, for example, with its magnificent bouquet of morello cherries, must surely have persuaded more than one young wine producer in the Yarra Valley to adopt this variety of grape. Wine experts from Australia and New Zealand have confirmed that the more recent vintages are in the same style, as we discovered with the 2002. Availability of these wines is problematic; paradoxically, they can be more easily found in a London wine merchant's than in Australia.

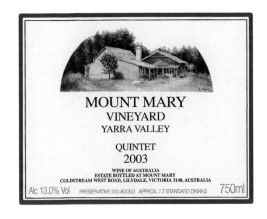

VINE VARIETY

33 acres (13.5 hectares) in a single estate: Pinot Noir; plus Cabernet Sauvignon, Cabernet Franc, Merlot, Malbec, Petit Verdot (the five varieties reflected in the name Quintet, given to the estate's blend of these Bordeaux varieties).

OUR FAVORITE WINES

Typically for a cult wine, it is produced in very small quantities, all sold in advance. It has a highly individual character, sometimes even slightly rough. The two main cuvées are a Pinot Noir that, in a good year, is deep and harmonious (for example, 1989) and Quintet, a blend of five Bordeaux varieties. In an outstanding year, this can be even more complex than the Pinot Noir (for example, 1988) but its quality can be irregular, since the Cabernet Sauvignon matures less successfully.

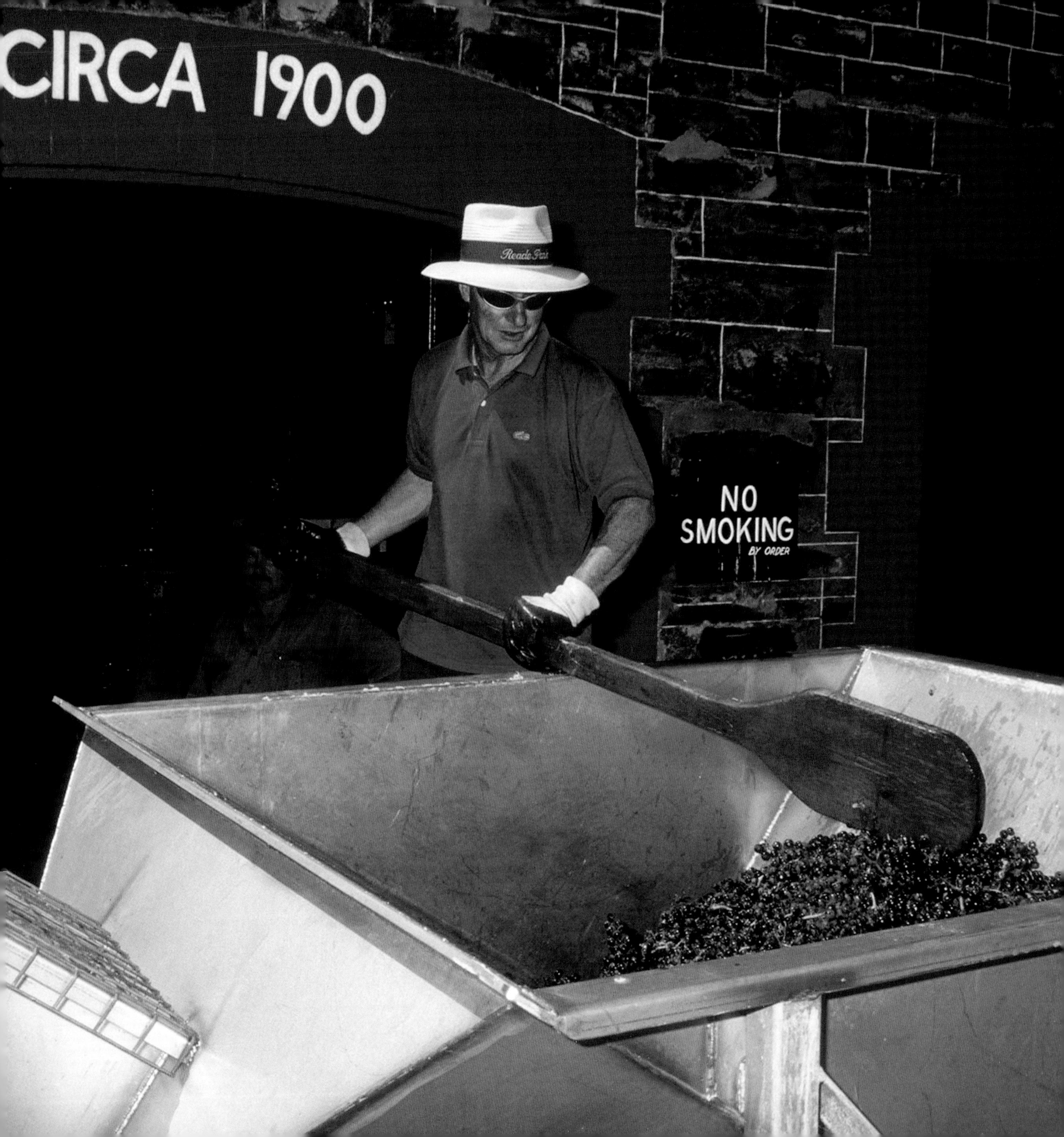
CIRCA 1900
NO
SMOKING
BY ORDER

Penfolds

Formerly the prestige marque of the Southcorp company, Penfolds now belongs to the Foster's Group. Penfolds itself is an enormous enterprise, producing well over ten million bottles. As in the case of Moët with Dom Pérignon (although with a lower volume of production), it owes its fame to Grange Hermitage, now known simply as Grange after European objections to the use of the French place name. This cuvée, created in 1951 by the great winemaker Max Schubert, is now justly famous as the best of all Australian wines. A skillful blend of the finest-flavored Syrah grapes from all the company's estates, with the addition of a significant amount of supplementary tannins and tartaric acid, fermentation is completed in casks of American oak. While it is probably the most powerful red wine in the world, it still retains an indisputable aromatic nobility that develops slowly in the bottle to give astonishing results some 20 or 30 years later (for example, the sublime 1962, and 1972). The bouquet of a fine Grange recalls simultaneously the greatest of the Hermitage la Chapelles (1961 or 1990, for example), and a vintage wine such as the Taylor. Recent vintages look to be equally promising. Another original and attractive combination from this company is the Koonunga Hill Shiraz Cabernet, a powerfully expressive wine, although nothing like the "claret" mentioned on the label.

It is strictly no smoking over the égrappoir (stemmer). The sunglasses are just for effect! Clare Valley is one of Penfold's main domaines.

VINE VARIETY

Total area not known. Many vineyards under ownership, plus bought-in grapes. Main estates as follows.
Magill, 12 acres (5 hectares): the oldest, created in 1844 by Dr. Penfold.
Kalimna, in the Barossa wine zone, 378 acres (153 hectares): basis of the prestige wines, including Grange.
Koonunga Hill, 74 acres (30 hectares).
Clare Valley, 539 acres (218 hectares): all varieties.
Eden and MacLaren Valley.
Coonawarra.

OUR FAVORITE WINES

The prestige crus Grange and Bin 707 deserve their international fame. A few individual batches can be even better than Bin 707, but limited production means that only the most attentive collector is likely to obtain a bottle (in 1962, for example, Bin 60A was the most sought-after wine in Australia).

Petaluma

Brian Croser, probably the best informed and most cultivated of Australian enologists, still acts in an advisory capacity at the winery he created and made famous worldwide. It is now the jewel in the crown of the Lion Nathan brewing company. He has successfully produced every type of wine, seeking inspiration from the best of the European traditions to raise them to an unusual degree of formal perfection. The microclimate and soil-type of the Piccadilly zone of Adelaide Hills give rise to grapes that are better balanced and less likely to suffer from the summer droughts than those in the neighboring Barossa zone. The character of the terroir is less marked, but the natural fruitiness of the grapes is able to emerge fully. While nothing can equal the red earth of Coonawarra for Cabernet Sauvignon, the Petaluma soil is perfect for Syrah and, since 1982, for Merlot grapes. The result is a supple but firm wine with noble aromas of cedar, spices, and dark chocolate. The rather too light Shirazes from Adelaide do not have the quality of those from Clare Valley despite its proximity. Fortunately, the Chardonnays have nothing to be ashamed of, offering a purity and mineral transparency very different from the excessive and vulgar lactic style often encountered in southern Australia. Worth keeping an eye on is a new Croser venture, this time associated with the Cazes family, from Pauillac in France, at their new winery on the borders of the Coonawarra zone with the lovely name of Tapanappa.

PETALUMA

2002 COONAWARRA

UNFILTERED

750ml

VINE VARIETY
309 acres (125 hectares) of vines in Coonawarra, Piccadilly, and Clare Valley.
Red: Cabernet Sauvignon, Merlot.
White: Chardonnay and Riesling.

OUR FAVORITE WINES
Three cuvées stand out for their reliability and character, which is very refined for Australian wines: the sparkling wine Croser, very pure and energetic with little dosage and much better than other more famous Australian sparkling wines; the Riesling, astonishingly complex and slow to age; and the red Coonawarra, a very well-balanced wine with a fine bouquet and long finish, the best years being 2002 and 2003.

Phillip Bass Wines

Phillip Jones, the founder, owner and winemaker of this very small winery on the southernmost coast of Victoria, is one of those enthusiasts prepared to take any risk to reach their goal, even if it involves occasionally making mistakes. He chose the situation – on the edge of the ocean – for its ideal microclimate. The great mass of water regulates the temperatures and humidity, making it possible to grow his favorite grape variety, Pinot Noir, without the need for irrigation. The grapes are grown and made into wine along organic principles; sulfur dioxide is not used. The first vintages, tasted in the mid-1990s, were a revelation: never before had Australian Pinot Noirs achieved such a level of refinement and aromatic subtlety. More recent vintages have been less reliable, the wine sometimes being oxidized and microbiologically unstable, or "live" as this type of wine is sometimes described. The South Gippland terroirs from where Jones gets his grapes are unlikely to reveal all the originality of their character without a more reliable aging method. He has a useful way of indicating to the customer those of his wines that he believes to be particularly successful: the smaller the label, the better it is. Those with a label the size of a postage stamp should therefore be worth a try!

VINE VARIETY

11 acres (4.5 hectares) red: Pinot Noir.

OUR FAVORITE WINES

This very small cult winery produces almost exclusively Pinot Noir wine. At its best, it has few rivals in the southern hemisphere, with a naturalness, refinement of aromas, and silky texture worthy of the greatest Burgundies. Unfortunately, as is sometimes the case with wines made without sulfur dioxide, a number of bottles are unstable and cloudy with an unpleasant smell.

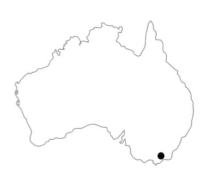

Shaw and Smith

One of the most recently established but influential wineries in Australia, Shaw and Smith set up in the Adelaide district. A wise choice, since this important city, with its mild climate and friendly people, plus its proximity to Melbourne, is rapidly becoming known as the wine capital of Australia. This is partly due to the presence of Adelaide University with its important, state-of-the-art Department of Horticulture, Viticulture, and Enology, and of the students trained here. But it is explained also by the potential of the vines grown on the hillsides around the city. The grapes grown around Adelaide are well sheltered from the wind and benefit from the cooler temperatures coming off the vast surrounding ocean. As a result they ripen better and have more flavor. Michael Hills Smith, not only Australia's first Master of Wine but also a much better taster than most of his colleagues, decided to plant Sauvignon vines and use them to make wines that would be as faithful to the fruit as possible. He is interested in wines that can combine well with good food – another of his passions. His knowledge and love of fine European wines have led him to develop a very pure, classic style, based on support from natural acids, that is a perfect advertisement for the pleasures of wine drinking. It is encouraging to see the extent to which he has influenced the new generation of enologists.

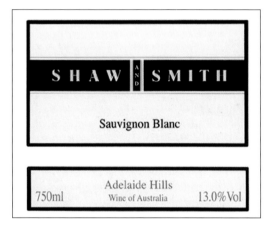

VINE VARIETY
*A single block of 69 acres (28 hectares),
mainly of white: Sauvignon, Chardonnay, Riesling.*

OUR FAVORITE WINES
*The white wines produced here suit the terroir well.
The Sauvignon, in particular, is fresh and pure, while the
unoaked Chardonnay has subtle mineral hints. The Riesling
lacks character at the moment, but is expected to improve.*

Rockford

Everything about this small-scale property in Barossa is suggestive of high-quality traditional methods and careful work. The buildings themselves are constructed in stone as in former centuries, while an old wine press is still in use. The robustly healthy and plain-talking owner, Robert O'Calaghan, worthy successor to his forebears, is the very picture of what the early pioneers of wine producing must have been: modest, hard-working, and stubborn, insisting on the essential principles of viticulture and winemaking. Wine lovers like this close relationship between grape and wine, and have enthusiastically adopted these honest, healthy, and original wines. Their muscularity and almost violent aromas can sometimes be somewhat disconcerting to a French palate. The white wines have less style, but we tasted some Rieslings from very old vines that were astonishingly muscular, with lemony aromas rarely encountered in Europe.

VINE VARIETY
No vineyards under ownership apart from 5 acres (2 hectares) around the winery, grapes being bought in from many small producers in the Barossa zone. Quantities unknown.

OUR FAVORITE WINES
The famous Basket Syrah concentrates all the spicy and balsamic taste for which the Barossa area is famous, resulting in a Syrah so different from that characteristic of the Rhône Valley that the change of name and spelling to Shiraz seems entirely justified. An excellent and daring Grenache, Rockford Dry Country, is similarly good, this time in a style resembling some Châteauneuf-du-Papes.

Barossa Valley. These robust, irrigated vines in the heart of Australia yield spicy and aromatic wine.

Rosemount

Rosemount is a huge enterprise that belongs in turn to the even bigger Foster's conglomerate. A number of its model wineries have become essential stops on the tour for any Australian or foreign tourist. The reliable, accessible, fruity wines produced in these wineries, with their clear and legible labels and large-scale production, are justly popular with the public. On the other hand, those seeking finer wines, or simply wines with more character, will be disappointed by the reds and most of the whites. The only real exceptions are the Chardonnays, which have the slight sweetness and smoothness characteristic of Hunter Valley, at least when the fall is not too wet. Two cuvées stand out. The first is Roxburgh, made from grapes from what is probably the most famous vineyard in Australia for this grape variety. An opulent wine with a rich bouquet, its notes of honey, almonds, and cream sometimes bring to mind a fine Bâtard-Montrachet. The other is the less well-known Giants Creek. Although not heavily promoted by the Rosemount company, it is perhaps even more original, with a powerful, mineral structure not dissimilar in style to a Corton-Charlemagne. The blended wines produced in Orange County have a better natural balance than the Hunter Valley wines. The very famous and carefully made red Shiraz Balmoral is nothing like as good as the best of the Henschke and Clarendon Hills cuvées and comes nowhere near Grange for quality.

VINE VARIETY

Numerous vineyards in all the zones, including 988 acres (400 hectares) in Hunter Valley, plus bought-in grapes. Two terroirs are particularly remarkable for Chardonnay: Roxburgh, 20 acres (8 hectares) on red marl; and Giants Creek on pebbly, sandy soil.

OUR FAVORITE WINES

Although more predictable today than in the days of the remarkable enologist Philip Shaw, the extraordinary personalities of two terroir Chardonnays stand out, Roxburgh and Giants Creek. The newly planted Chardonnay vines in the cooler part of Orange County have proved very successful.

These stainless steel vats are open to the elements, but the weather is fine during the winemaking period.

Seppelt

The Shiraz wines from Great Western are characterized by their tannins and their intensely peppery and spicy aromas suggestive of wild mint and other bush plants. After a short period when this type of wine fell out of favor (the public instead preferring the new wines produced in cooler regions of the country), these days it is once again justly famous worldwide. One wine that particularly stands out is Seppelt, a intensely colored cuvée that is a match for the very best of Barossa wines. Another equally good cuvée, of possibly even greater refinement but made in smaller quantities, comes from the St Peters vineyard. We should be grateful that the firm has continued to produce wine in the style created by two great pioneers: Colin Preece, and especially Maurice O'Shea. But the firm has other things to offer, including some highly unusual creations. It has become famous for a curious red sparkling wine, sold for a long time under the name of Burgundy. It is in fact made from Shiraz grapes from Great Western and Barossa, and has a delightful richness of bouquet and notable finish. This type of wine benefits from a long maturation in the cellar, losing some of its fizziness in the process and coming to resemble something like a classic Shiraz. Finally, there are the fortified wines made a century ago and still available today. The fame of the house's legendary centenary liqueur port, with its long finish rivaling the best Portuguese colheita ports, lives on.

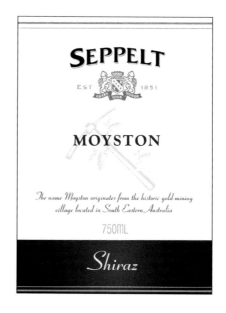

VINE VARIETY
Many vineyards under ownership in Great Western (including the famous pre-phylloxera vines of St Peters), Rutherglen, and Barossa.

OUR FAVORITE WINES
This historic company has the enormous advantage of owning the old Shiraz wines at Great Western, one of the birthplaces of Australian wine.

Virgin Hills Vineyards

It is little wonder that this wine has become something of a cult among local wine lovers. The vineyard was the result of the vision of Tom Lazar, a Melbourne restaurateur and expert on fine French wines who dreamed of producing a high-quality Bordeaux-style wine. He chose a spot some 1,969 feet (600 meters) above sea level in the Macedon Ranges near Lauriston, a cool hillside with a remarkably favorable climate. Here, he grows vines using strictly organic methods and without the use of irrigation. Protected from the untimely interventions so often practiced by Australian winemakers, the wines immediately develop a marked personality. The new owner, Michael Hope, continues to run the business along the same lines, remaining faithful to Tom Lazar's organic methods and refusal to add sulfur dioxide. His expert knowledge of fine European wines makes him a good judge of grape quality, allowing him to make wise and appropriate decisions during the winemaking process. During our visit, we were struck by the quality of the unusually elegant tannins in the most recent vintages, and also by the aromatic naturalness of the fruit tastes of a blend that often includes just the right amount of Shiraz and even a small quantity of Pinot Noir. It's a shame that this bottle is not known in Europe and America. Even a few bottles would reveal a very different aspect of Australian wine, one much closer to our tastes.

VINE VARIETY

30 acres (12.5 hectares) on a single holding.
Red: 60% Cabernet Sauvignon; 40% mixed Shiraz, Merlot, and Malbec.

OUR FAVORITE WINES

One of the most successful and original Australian reds, this wine has the elegance of bouquet characteristic of a very cold terroir, and a naturalness owing much to the instinctive but expert skills of the producer. The 1999 is very fine.

St Hallett

St Hallett can claim with some justification that it produces wines that are the quintessential expression of the Barossa Valley. A long and successful partnership with the many fiercely independent local grape-growers has made it possible to select the best terroirs and the varieties with the most individuality. Stuart Blackwell, St Hallet's enologist, knows the area like the back of his hand and his approach to winemaking – differing from general local practice because it involves very little intervention – results in wines with a strongly marked character made from the grapes of old, unirrigated vines. He uses French oak for the barrels in which the wine is carefully matured, giving toast and vanilla aromas that are less strident than those characteristic of wines matured in American oak. The best Shiraz wines produced here are a skillful blend of grapes from the Kalimna area lying to the north of the Barossa Valley (associated with wines with strong aromas of blackberry and blackcurrant) and Seppeltfield to the west (where the wines have a spicier bouquet and more aggressive tannins). Added to this is the freshness and elegance of wine from the Eden Valley with its cooler nights. Another admirable wine made here is the energetic but controlled GST, the name an indication of its unusual blend of Grenache, Shiraz, and Touriga grapes.

The scent of eucalyptus and pine that fills the surrounding air will reemerge in the wine.

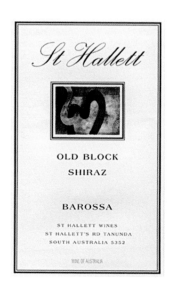

VINE VARIETY

Does not have its own vineyard but buys in grapes from local producers.
Red: Shiraz, Grenache, Touriga Nacional.
White: Semillon, Sauvignon, Riesling.

OUR FAVORITE WINES

Of the typically robust wines from the Barossa Valley, Old Block is arguably one of the finest wines in all Australia. This full-bodied and energetic Shiraz is refined by the addition of a small quantity of grapes from the cooler microclimate of Eden Valley.

New Zealand

At the beginning of the 1990s, New Zealand astonished the world of wine – the English-speaking portion of it at least – with Sauvignon Blancs bursting with fruit and Pinot Noirs displaying more Burgundian finesse than Californian opulence. It had taken the country barely ten years to develop a style of wine of such precision and seductiveness and another five for it to become really well known – a record that will no doubt prove difficult to beat! Despite the area's relatively high rainfall, vines were initially planted on the North Island close to Auckland, where Chardonnay now triumphs, then a little further south at Gisborne and Hawke's Bay, which is better suited to the red Bordeaux varieties. Contrary to all expectations, New Zealand's best Pinot-Noir-producing area (pending confirmation of the quality of the newly planted Central Otago vineyards) is the small Martinborough region at the southern tip of the North Island. Sauvignon Blanc reigns supreme in the vast Marlborough region in the north of the South Island with intense varietal aromas and vinification techniques imported from Australia. Throughout the whole country, in fact, the European varieties, often made heavier in this hemisphere by an abundance of sunshine, are rediscovering their original aromatic range with a distinctive finesse that explains their universal success.

List of domaines

Ata Rangi

Clive Patton, the founder of Ata Rangi, started out in the dairy business. In the late 1960s, he planted a small vineyard of Gewürztraminer grapes for his sister, but it was not long before his friend Neil McCallum of Dry River persuaded him that the terroir and climate would be suitable for ripening Pinot Noir. A passionate enthusiast of fine Burgundy wines, he took his chance, succeeding in a miraculously short time in producing an internationally medal-winning wine. Since 1993, Oliver Masters, who is now in charge of production, has not put a foot wrong. The cool nights at Martinborough, like those of the Marlborough region, bring out the natural fruitiness of the grapes, but a chronic shortage of water means that precise amounts of irrigation must be used as soon as it becomes necessary. However, these dry conditions have the one big advantage of preventing the grapes from rotting, as they tend to do in more humid conditions. They can be allowed to ripen as long as desired before harvesting. The richness of body characteristic of the Pinot Noir is less well suited to the Chardonnay, which can sometimes be a little too heavy. Its 2003 vintage, "Célèbre," a prestige blend of Syrah, Merlot, and Cabernet, looks set to become as famous as the Pinot Noir. One of the most fascinating mysteries of this "new vineyard" is its ability to ripen different grape varieties equally successfully.

ATA RANGI
·MARTINBOROUGH·
Pinot Noir
2003
WINE OF NEW ZEALAND

VINE VARIETY
Estate (comprising Ata Rangi, Craighall, Walnut Ridge, and Kahu, situated among the Martinborough terraced vineyards, and Petrie, near Masterton) of 86 acres (35 hectares), red: Pinot Noir, Merlot, Syrah, Cabernet Sauvignon; white: Chardonnay, Sauvignon, Pinot Gris.

OUR FAVORITE WINES
All Clive Patton and his associates' love and care has been lavished on the Pinot Noir. It remains unequaled in New Zealand for completeness, having a remarkable structure without heaviness, noble red berry aromas, and perfectly balanced tannins – a quality that is rare in the southern hemisphere.

Cloudy Bay

2002

World market forces have made Cloudy Bay not only the first New Zealand wine marque to be so widely exported, but also the representative of all New Zealand wines. While there is no doubting the commercial expertise of the owners, Veuve Clicquot, the wine needed to convince the public that it could surprise and delight. The first vintage Sauvignons created by the founder of Cloudy Bay, David Hohnen from Cape Mentelle in Australia, immediately conquered the British market with their precision and aromatic energy expressive of the grape variety. From Britain, the wine became known worldwide. With this wine, we find ourselves at the heart of the mystery of New Zealand wines. Instead of strongly individual wines that vary from one terroir and one winemaker to another, we find, particularly in the case of white wines, perfect types – or even stereotypes. Here, nature has created soils and microclimates that bring out the aromas of the grapes to an extent almost unmatched elsewhere in the southern hemisphere. The best winemakers wisely attempt to translate the flavor of these grapes as faithfully as possible in their wines. Kevin Judd, the house's brilliant but modest winemaker, has succeeded better than any. The high level of production requires absolute technical control, something that tends to make one vintage very similar to the next. However, since Tony Jordan took over as head of the winery, there has been a move towards a rather more transparent expression of the terroir.

VINE VARIETY

358 acres (145 hectares) over three vineyards (Matthews Lane, Wairau Valley; Mustang, Fair Hall; and Widow's, Renswick) red: Pinot Noir; but mainly white: Sauvignon, Chardonnay, Pinot Blanc, Semillon, Gewürztraminer. Grapes also bought in from the same areas and from Brancott Valley.

OUR FAVORITE WINES

The winery's signature wine is the Sauvignon. A frisky, highly scented wine, the normal cuvée tends to verge on the green. The Te Koko, given an exotic touch by being aged in oak casks, is much more vinous, requiring three or four years in the bottle before it settles down.

Bottles and barrels beautifully arranged.

Dry River

Although Dry Creek is now part of the small wine empire created by the Californian Julia Robertson (as is Te Awa in Hawkes Bay), the wine is still made by the founder of this small, traditional winery, Neil McCallum. With his friend Clive Paton at Ata Rangi, he was able to see the potential of the flat, gravelly terroirs of this area, despite their being so very different from the European limestone hillsides specializing in the Burgundian grape varieties. He also improved vine growing and grape treatment methods so as to bring out their best qualities. Good luck and, above all, skill led him to combine an innate love of the land and its products with rigorous enological science. Not interested in producing the intensely aromatic wines for which New Zealand has become famous, he is more concerned with creating wines that develop slowly and surely in the bottle as a result of traditional, non-interventionist production methods combined with strictly observed hygiene of fermentation and protection at all stages against any tendency to oxidation. Neil McCallum has paved the way for a new generation of wine producers who are becoming increasingly interested in expressing the character of the terroir and not just that of the grape variety.

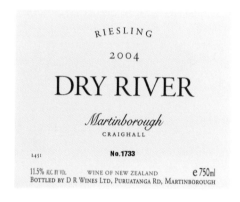

VINE VARIETY

22 acres (9 hectares) over three estates:
Puruatanga, white: Sauvignon, Vignier, Gewŭrztraminer,
Pinot Gris, Chardonnay; red: Pinot Noir.
Craighall, white: Chardonnay, Riesling; red: Pinot Noir.
Arapoff

OUR FAVORITE WINES

All Neil McCallum's wines impress with their excellent aromatic precision, clean, tight body, and beautifully honest finish. These qualities are particularly apparent in both the sweet and the dry Craighall Rieslings. The newly fashionable wines of the Central Otago region are as yet no match for his Pinot Noir; it is one of the best in the country, with a remarkable vinosity and vigor.

Herzog

Thérèse and Hans Herzog came to New Zealand from Switzerland. They did not, however, abandon the family vineyard there, returning to make wine in Switzerland during the New Zealand winter. While maintaining all the traditions of precision, rigor, and high qualities of cleanliness characteristic of winemaking in their birthplace, they quickly adopted the open, generous pioneering spirit of their country of adoption. Well aware of the quality of their wine, they immediately opened a restaurant where it could be tasted and appreciated. An excellent method of making their wine known nationally and internationally, it offers by far the best cuisine in Marlborough and has been awarded a Michelin star. Hans Herzog is a most conscientious winemaker, and his vines, looked after like precious exotic plants, are an example to his neighbors. Wishing to experiment with different grapes to see which would best suit his terroir, he planted a large number of different varieties (including, unusually, the Italian Montepulciano variety). To his surprise, each of the wines produced from the different grapes was better than he could have dreamed. This would appear to confirm that, while the land and climate of the Marlborough region do not have a strong personality of their own, they are able to develop the aromatic qualities of all grape varieties to an astonishing degree.

VINE VARIETY

*Own vineyard (size unknown) and bought-in grapes,
red: Pinot Noir, Syrah, Montepulciano; white: Chardonnay,
Pinot Gris, Viognier.*

OUR FAVORITE WINES

*All the wines from this winery are very attractive with a full
body, clean aromas, and a general elegance of style. Perhaps the
most original is the Viognier, which has such a pure and natural
perfume of apricot that it could easily be taken for a fine Condrieu
– unusual for the normally extrovert New World Viogniers.
The Pinot Noir from young vines looks to be very promising.*

The secret of the "cloudy bay": morning mists occur here all year round.

Kumeu River

Winemaking began in New Zealand in the area around Auckland. Although the climatic conditions were not, perhaps, ideal – grapes do not generally thrive in very hot and humid summers – the city-dwellers were ready to buy and drink wine. The exhausting work of planting vines was carried out a century ago by Croatian immigrants who were able to establish healthy grapes that ripened well. It soon became apparent that some areas had the potential to become great terroirs. Thus it was that the Brajkovitch family struck lucky with their vines in the Kumeu River area. By good fortune, Michael Brajkovitch had begun his studies of agriculture and enology in Australia, perfecting and extending his knowledge with an extended period in Bordeaux in 1983 with Jean-Claude Berrouet. He has planted his vines on the slope of the hill, and practices a system of crop rotation to reduce production. An important innovation is the use of the lyre vine-training system, which allows the sun to penetrate better into the fruit and discourages the growth of mold when it rains. Above all, he has respected the natural equilibrium of the grapes themselves, making no adjustment to the alcohol, acidity, or aromas of the fruit. Fine wines, with a just measure of well-integrated oakiness, they are very different from typical Australian wines. The whites deserve to be known throughout the world, where they will show up the unsophisticated character of many currently fashionable wines.

VINE VARIETY

74 acres (30 hectares) red: Merlot, Pinot Noir, Malbec; white: Chardonnay, Pinot Gris.

OUR FAVORITE WINES

This estate is famous for its Chardonnays, which have continued to get better and better. The aromatic purity, elegance, and graceful finish of the 2003 vintage was particularly admirable, losing nothing in comparison with the Californian wines tasted at the same time and that only a winemaker who is a true artist could create.

Palliser Estate

Palliser has worked hard to get New Zealand wines properly established in Europe, taking advantage of the market for New World Sauvignons, and producing an aromatic and surprisingly fresh-tasting wine. Richard Riddiford, who runs the company with great skill, has turned all the prizes won by his wine in international competitions to good account and is now developing a middle-price range – including, particularly, red wines from Pinot Noir grapes. These are beginning to take on the full-bodied Martinborough character. Here, too, the idea of marque and the confidence a marque inspires appear to be more important than any indication of origin. The microclimate of this area favors grapes that produce an immediate aromatic expression. The Chardonnay is highly fragrant with notes of lemon and fresh butter; the medium dry Riesling lacks the noble austerity of Dry River, but its lively acidity make it a delicious aperitif wine; the Pinot Gris, also medium dry, has a delightful spiciness. All these wines are notable for a certain vibrancy of texture and body, assisted no doubt by the significant amounts of carbon dioxide present and the use of screw caps in bottling to prevent any early oxidation.

VINE VARIETY
210 acres (85 hectares) over five vineyards (Palliser, Pencarron, Om Santi, Pinnacles, and Clouston) red: Pinot Noir; white: Sauvignon, Chardonnay, Riesling, Pinot Gris.

OUR FAVORITE WINES
The most striking wine produced by this estate is the Sauvignon, a very aromatic but pure wine that is, in some ways, more refined than those from the Marlborough terroirs.

Te Awa Farm

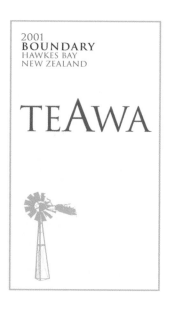

Gimblett Gravels is the first appellation of origin delimited and recognized by New Zealand viticulture. It has the great advantage over France of being open to a large number of different wines. The soil here, as its name suggests, is gravelly and so has the best natural drainage of the Hawkes Bay region. The microclimate allows the red Bordeaux grapes for which the area is known (particularly Merlot) to reach a state of perfect ripeness. The probity of the local producers is a pleasure to observe: no one would dream of making a false declaration regarding the harvest or origin of the grapes. Here the name attached to the wine is a matter of pride, and, unusually, indications of the type of grape seem to be of lesser importance. Te Awa farm is owned by Julian Robertson. It is run by a remarkable woman, Jenny Dobson, who learned how to make wine in Burgundy with Jacques Seysse, subsequently producing many vintages of Château Sénéjac in Médoc. She admires the balance of the great European wines and has succeeded in recreating it in Hastings. The wines go well with the excellent cuisine of the winery's restaurant, a popular local institution. Jenny is expecting great things from the recently planted Syrah vines, and plans to model these new wines on the French or Swiss style, rather than that of Australia.

Jenny Dobson at work in the winery: energetic and practical ever since her early days in the Haut Médoc, she is always seeking to perfect her art.

VINE VARIETY
124 acres (50 hectares) red: Merlot, Cabernet Sauvignon, Syrah, Gamay, Malbec, Pinotage; white: Chardonnay.

OUR FAVORITE WINES
All the wines produced here have a style and balance particularly suited to the European or American palate. The most ambitious and accomplished of these is the "Boundary," a red wine of blended Bordeaux varieties; the 2002 and, especially, the 2001 are outstanding.

Te Mata

No other wine-producing estate is as famous in New Zealand as Te Mata. Two of its cuvées – Coleraine (red), and Elston (white) – command the highest prices on the market and have done much for the global prestige of Hawkes Bay. Local wine connoisseurs are divided into Pinot Noir fans, who swear by the new vineyards planted in Central Otago, and supporters of a Bordeaux style of wine, who have no interest in developments in New Zealand's South Island. John Buck, one of the pioneers of the wine renaissance in his country, belongs to this second group, and he has made it his life's work to create, then constantly improve, production of a superior Bordeaux-style red wine. Success came swiftly with a wine produced from the two hectares of vines that he christened Coleraine. He was then able to increase production at Te Mata, while also further improving the quality. As in Bordeaux, his success can be explained by his skill in creating a final blend of grapes where the whole is infinitely greater than the sum of its parts. An excellent communicator, he was soon able to persuade people of the importance of soils and the value of exhibitions of Hawkes Bay wines. Their growing awareness of the existence of a significant cultural patrimony was due in great part to his efforts. Today, Te Mata has diversified its production, recent experiments with Syrah and Viognier appearing to hold promise for the future.

VINE VARIETY

Estate (comprising Havelock Hills, Woodthorpe Terraces, Ngatarawa District) of approximately 272 acres (110 hectares), red: Cabernet Sauvignon, Merlot, Cabernet Franc, Syrah, Gamay, Petit Verdot; white: Sauvignon, Pinot Gris, Semillon.

OUR FAVORITE WINES

Something of a cult wine, the estate's Coleraine is also the most remarkable and one of the two or three best wines in New Zealand. A blend of equal parts of Merlot and Cabernet Sauvignon (as opposed to the Elk Cove), it combines, to a remarkable degree, power, complexity, and refinement. The most recent vintages have been produced from even riper grapes than previously. Another prestige wine produced here, the Elston Chardonnay, seems slightly disappointing.

Villa Maria

Croatian in origin (like many of his fellow wine producers in Auckland), Georges Fistonich has, over a period of 35 years, created a credible marque capable of marketing with the same success several thousands of bottles of an esoteric wine at the same time as millions of bottles of table wine. With consummate skill, he manages an enormous enterprise – hundreds of hectares of vines and two immense, ultra-modern and highly competitive wineries. Having consolidated the business at its present size, the capital has been shared out between himself and his family. As well as having remarkable business acumen, his secret is nothing more than that of respect for the consumer. By regularly producing wines at the right price, the customer can be led gradually from a simple, fruity, and accessible type of wine to a wine that can fully express its vintage or its origin. He has got where he is today by placing his trust in others: first, in his technical teams, which are fully instructed in his vision of what wine should be; second, in the producers with whom he works closely, drawing up strict instructions, including, first and foremost, rigorous standards of viticulture. Now that he has brought his marque to the attention of the world, he has moved on to the next stage, which is to bring out all the originality of character of each region. He is currently offering wines from specific terroirs, the grapes being processed at the superb new wineries near Auckland.

VINE VARIETY

A large number of properties are under contract in Hawke's Bay (including the famous but tiny terraced vineyard in the Esk Valley) and Marlborough, planted with all varieties of white and red. The total figure is not known.

OUR FAVORITE WINES

The company is first and foremost a marque, producing blends designed according to price. That said, these blends are all technically irreproachable, a triumph only possible through enormous investment. The most expressive wines are the Marlborough Reserve Sauvignons, particularly good in 2003, and the incomparable Esk Valley "Terrace," a full, sensual Merlot reminiscent of a great Pomerol, and surely the best New Zealand red wine of any grape variety.

Japan

Although establishing itself as one of the most important markets for the consumption of fine wine, until recently Asia occupied no more than a back seat in terms of wine production. While the viticultural industry is now developing with a certain dynamism in India and China, it is in Japan that the most ambitious and well-made wines are to be found. Only reemerging in the 19th century (having been prohibited when the country's borders were closed two centuries before), Japanese viticulture relied initially on hybrid vines imported from America. Under the influence of both small winegrowers and large distillers and brewing groups, it has now turned toward higher quality varieties such as Cabernet Sauvignon, Merlot, and Chardonnay. Vines are generally trained onto overhead trellises in order to minimize the risk of rot due to the humid climate. The care devoted to winemaking in Japan, albeit in small quantities, testifies to the country's very real affection for wine culture.

Château
Mercian

Japan came to wine late in the day but has subsequently begun to pay much attention to this field. While the appreciation of fine wine is now a widespread phenomenon, a number of people have taken this enthusiasm further, even to the extent of creating and producing a great Japanese wine. In 1970, Mercian, an important company producing sake and also dealing in spirits, decided to create a vineyard in the Kikyogahara region in central Japan. Initially, Merlot vines were planted. Almost ten years later, Cabernet Sauvignon grapes were planted nearby, grown, rather unusually, on trellises. This classic combination of grape varieties led to the creation of Château Mercian's red wine. This was complemented, quite logically, by an equally classic white wine from Chardonnay grapes, also grown on trellises. Both the red and white Château Mercian wines go by the name of Signature. The perfect maturity of the grapes when harvested and the care involved in the winemaking are evident in the full, harmonious and well-balanced character of both. Unsurprisingly, they do not yet have a strongly individual personality; on the other hand, they have a refinement and balance that has all the elegance of Zen.

VINE VARIETY
Chardonnay, Merlot, Cabernet Sauvignon.

OUR FAVORITE WINES
The 2002 Merlot from the Kikyogahara vineyard has chocolatey aromas without heaviness. It has a fleshy mouthfeel that is not without a certain elegance. Its smooth and restrained character reveals a perfect technical mastery.

Index of châteaux and estates

Index of names

A

Abreu, David, 451
Adelsheim, David, 482
Albada, Eric, 50
Alban, John, 434
Allegrini, family, 243
Allied Lyons, 298
Alliet, Philippe, 162
Altare, Elio, 226
Alvarez, family, 313, 420
Ambrogini, Angelo, 268
Angerville, Jacques and
Guillaume d', 123
Antinori, family, 248
Antinori, Ludovico, 264
Araujo, Bart, 435
Arcaute, Jean-Michel, 520
Arena, Antoine, 179
Argiolas, Francesco
and Giuseppe, 282
Arnault, Bernard, 517
Arzuaga, Florentino, 310
Ausas, Xavier, 313, 323
Avril, Paul and Vincent, 195
AXA (company), 89, 345,
416, 417

B

Bacso, Andréas, 420
Badenhorst, Adi, 539
Barbadillo, family, 296
Barbier, René, 305
Barett, Bo, 441
Barlow, Peter, 539
Barton, family, 54, 428
Bassermann-Jordan, family, 374
Beau de la Morinière,
Jean-Charles, 112
Becker, Friedrich, 377
Benanti, family, 283
Bento dos Santos, José, 344
Ben Zaken, Eli, 429
Bergquist, family, 342
Berrouet, Jean-Claude, 588
Bertheau, Bob, 488
Bertrand, Giulio, 536
Beydon-Schlumberger,
Séverine, 14
Bilancini, Claudie and Bruno, 209
Billecart-Salmon, family, 129
Biondi Santi, family, 253
Bize-Leroy, Lalou, 98, 109,
461, 479
Bizeul, Hervé, 158

Blackwell, Stuart, 576
Bodenstein, Ilse and Toni, 393
Boisset, family, 108
Bonetti, Bill, 460
Bonnie, family, 78, 520
Borie, family, 46
Boscaini, family, 244
Boüard, Hubert de, 22
Bournet, Cyril de, 203
Bovard, Louis, 404
Brajkovitch, family, 588
Bratasiuk, Roman, 548
Bredell, family, 529
Breuer, family, 370
Brounstein, Al, 441, 449
Brumont, Alain, 209
Brun, Jean-Paul, 343
Bründlmayer, Willi, 386
Brunier, family, 204, 439
Buck, John, 592
Buring, Leo, 557
Bürklin, Dr. 373

C

Caloz, Charles, 411
Canet, André and Isabelle, 189
Carletti, family, 268
Catena, family, 514
Cathiard, Daniel and Florence, 80
Catoir, family, 376
Cazes, Jean-Michel, 57, 64,
417, 566
Ceretto, family, 221
Chadwick, Eduardo, 504, 506
Chapoutier, Michel, 180, 452
Chappaz, Marie-Thérèse, 406
Charlopin, Philippe, 95
Charmolüe, family, 60
Chave, Gérard and Jean-Louis,
182
Chevallier, Charles, 84
Chiquet, family, 136
Chivite, family, 315
Clape, Auguste and Pierre, 183
Clendenen, Jim, 438
Clerico, Domenico, 222
Clicquot, Nicole-Barbe, 149
Clubb, Megan and Martin, 492
Coche-Dury (Jean-François), 113
Cohn, family, 473
Cointreau, Anne, 534
Colombo, Jean-Luc
and Anne, 184, 404
Concha y Toro, 509

Confuron, Jean-Pierre, 425
Conterno, family, 227
Coppola, Francis Ford and
Eleanor, 473
Cordier, family, 47
Corino, Carlo, 284
Cottarella, Ricardo, 277, 281
Croser, Brian, 566
Cruse, family, 50, 69
Cullen, Diana and Kevin, 550, 560
Currado, Luca, 235
Cuvelier, Didier, 56, 520
Cvetic, Marina, 275

D

Dagueneau, Didier, 166, 541
Dal Forno, Romano, 245
Dalla Valle, Naoko and Gustav, 448
Dalmau Cebrian, Vincente, 322
Daniel, John, 454, 473
Dassault, Laurent, 502, 520
Davies, Jack and Jamie, 459
De Almeida, Joao Nicolau, 326
De Bortoli, family, 551
Debreczeni, Leanne and Pál, 425
Decelle, Olivier, 160
Deiss, Jean-Michel, 12
Delmas, Jean and Jean-Philippe,
76
Delon, Michel and son, 55
De Marchi, Paolo, 260
Devillard, Bertrand, 126
Diel, Armin, 366
Dobson, Jenny, 590
Doerner, Steve, 478
Domecq, 298
Dönnhoff, Helmut, 364
Draper, Paul, 469
Drouhin, family, 118, 483
Ducos, Commandant, 199
Dugas, Alain, 199
Dugat, Bernard, 94
Duhr, family, 397
Dunn, Randy, 442
Dupuy, Charles, 160
Dürrbach, Eloi, 177

E

Egly, Francis, 135
Eguzniza, Pablo, 315
Enjalbert, professor, 154
Errazuriz, Maximiano, 504
Estournel, Louis-Gaspard d', 44
Etchart, family, 525
Etzel, Michael, 479, 480

F

Falco, Carlos, 316
Faller, Colette and daughters, 19
Fay, Nathan, 476
Ferguson, Jean, 492
Fernandez, Alejandro, 311
Ferrari, Giulio, 238
Fèvre, William, 91
Figgins, Gary, 490, 495
Finlayson, Peter, 528
Fistonich, George, 593
Flatgate, family, 330
Foradori, Elisabetta, 240
Forrester, Ken, 533
Foster's, 557, 563, 572
Foti, Salvo, 283
Foucault, Charly and Nady, 173
Franzen, Martin, 376
Frère, Albert, 517
Frescobaldi, family, 262, 264
Frey, Jean-Jacques, 192
Fürst, Rudolf, 383

G

Gagey, Pierre-André, 119
Gaja, Angelo, 215
García, Mariano, 309
Garcin, family, 521
Gasqueton, Madame, 43
Gauby, Gérard, 159
Gautreau, Jean, 70
Gehry, Frank, 319
Gere, Attila and Monica, 414
Germain, Bernard, 167
Gerovassiliou, Evangelis, 430
Gerrie, Paul, 478
Giacosa, Bruno, 219
Ginestet, Bernard, 58
Girardet, Freddy, 402
GMF, 416
Goelet, John, 445
Golitzine, family, 493
Got, Bertrand de, 77
Grahm, Randall, 439
Gramona Marti, Jaume, 295
Gresy, Alberto di, 230
Grgich, Mike, 441
Gruaud, frères, 47
Gublin, Nadine, 126
Guffens, Jean-Marie, 127
Guibert, Aimé, 154
Guigal, Marcel and
Philippe, 188, 541
Guimaraens, family, 330, 333, 339

Guinaudeau, Jacques, 37
Guradze, Christian von, 373

H

Haag, Wilhelm and Oliver, 350
Hamilton-Russel, Anthony, 528
Hardy, Eileen, 554
Harlan, Bob, 451
Hasselbach, Fritz and Agnes, 379
Heitz, family, 442, 452
Henriot, Joseph, 91
Henschke, Stephen and Prue, 555
Herzog, Thérèse and Hans, 585
Hill Smith, Michael, 568
Hirtzberger, Franz, 387
Hochar, family, 428
Hohnen, David, 581
Hope, Michael, 575
Hua, Su, 464
Huet, Gaston, 168
Hugel, family, 15
Humbrecht, Léonard
and Olivier, 20
Hwang, Anthony, 419

I

Imparato, Sylvia, 277
Incisa della Rochetta, family, 248,
269

J

Jaboulet, family, 192
Jacquesson, Adolphe, 136
Jadot, Louis, 119
Janssens, Geneviève, 470
Jensen, Josh, 440
Johnston, Nathaniel, 46
Joly, Nicolas, 163
Jones, Phillip, 567
Jooste, Duggie and Lowell, 532
Jordan, Tony, 546
Judd, Kevin, 581

K

Karatsolas, Leon, 431
Keller, Klaus-Peter, 381
Kesseler, August
Kinigopoulos, Kyriakos, 485
Kistler, Steve, 460
Kongsgaard, John, 464
Kovács, Tibor, 416, 425
Kracher, Aloïs, 390
Krug, family, 137

The authors would like to thank Béatrice Boullier and Lacen Baata for their invaluable help, as well as Ernesto Gentile and Fabio Rizzari for their apposite and expert opinions on the subject of Italian wines.

And a thousand thanks to our editor, Nathalie Démoulin!

PHOTO CREDITS

Cover image: Isabelle Rozenbaum (Verre Riedel)

Page 1, 2: Cephas/Clay Mc Lachlan;
Page 6: Klein-Constancia;
Page 13: Christophe Meyer;
Page 16-17: Domaine Hugel, www.hugel.com;
Page 21: Scope/Jacques Guillard;
Page 24-25: Château Ausone;
Page 30-31: Scope/Michel Guillard;
Page 39: GHFP/Hoa Qui/Philippe Roy;
Page 45: Scope/Michel Guillard;
Page 48: Scope/Michel Guillard;
Page 53: Château Lafite-Rothschild architect Ricardo Boffill;
Page 59: Gamma/Eric Travers;
Page 63: Cephas/Mick Rock;
Page 67: Château Pontet Canet;
Page 68: Château Rauzan-Ségla © Burdin L'Image ;
Page 73: Domaine de Chevalier © Positif Bordeaux ;
Page 74: Scope/Jean-Luc Barde;
Page 79: Château Malartic-Lagravière;
Page 83: GHFP/Hoa Qui/Philippe Roy;
Page 86: Gamma/Eric Brissaud;
Page 88: Château Suduiraut, photo Alain Gariteai;
Page 92-93: Cephos/Mick Rock;
Page 101: Scope/Jean-Luc Barde;
Page 104-105: Scope/Michel Plassart;
Page 110-111: Le Figaro Magazine/Eric Martin;
Page 115: Scope/Jacques Guillard;
Page 116-120-125: Louis Jadot;
Page 121: Cephas/Ilan Shaw;
Page 128: Champagne Billecart-Salmon, photo S. Régnier/BS;
Page 131: Scope/Jacques Guillard;
Page 132: Anthony Blake/John Carey
Page 138-139: Champagne Krug;
Page 143: Cephas/Mick Rock;

Page 146-147: Atelier Michel Jolyot;
Page 151: Thierry Petit;
Page 152: Francedias.com/Serge Coupe;
Page 156-157: Paul Palau;
Page 161: GHFP/Explorer/Francis Jalain;
Page 164-165: Montevideo/Christophe Petiteau;
Page 170-171: Domaine Alphonse Mellot;
Page 175: José Nicolas;
Page 178: Cyril Le Tourneur d'Ison;
Page 181: Scope/Jacques Guillard;
Page 186-187: Cyril Le Tourneur d'Ison;
Page 190-191: Scope/Jean-Luc Barde;
Page 196-197: Scope/Jacques Guillard;
Page 202-203: Domaine du Vieux Télégraphe, photo Jean-François Cholley;
Page 206-207: Etienne-Follet.com;
Page 216: Gaja;
Page 223: Cephas/Clay Mc Lachlan;
Page 224: Cephas/Mick Rock;
Page 228: Luciano Sandrone;
Page 234 , 239: Cephas/Clay Mc Lachlan;
Page 243: Allegrini;
Page 247: Cephas/Herbert Lehmann;
Page 250-251: Castello di Brolio, photo Francesco Ricasoli;
Page 256-257: Castello di Ama Architecte Daniel Buren © Adagp, Paris 2006;
Page 260 , 265 , 266: Cephas/Mick Rock;
Page 272, 273: Sassicaia/Etienne Hunyady, www.etiennehunyady.com;
Page 278-279: Feudi di San Gregorio;
Page 284-285: Planeta;
Page 293: GHFP/Age/Roine Magnusson;
Page 297, 300-301: Cephas/Mick Rock;
Page 302: GHFP/Age/Javier Larrea;

Page 306-307: Cephas/Diana Mewes;
Page 312: Scope/Jacques Guillard;
Page 317: GHFP/Age/Daniel.P.Acevedo;
Page 320-321: Cephas/Mick Rock;
Page 328-329: Porto Taylor;
Page 335: Porto W.&J.Graham, photo Irmacos Braga;
Page 336: Scope/J.Guillard;
Page 340-341: Le Figaro Magazine/Jacques Torregano;
Page 346-347: Scope/J.Guillard;
Page 352-353: Scope/J.Guillard;
Page 358-359: Weingut Sankt Urbans-Hof;
Page 362: Cephas/Nigel Blythe;
Page 365: DWI/Martin Kämper;
Page 368-369: Scope/J.Guillard;
Page 375: Weingut Geheimer Rat Dr. von Bassermann-Jordan;
Page 378: Scope/J.Guillard;
Page 388-389: Cosmos/Toni Anzenberger;
Page 392: Cephas/Mick Rock;
Page 395: GHFP/Imagestate/Ethel Davies;
Page 400-405-408-410: Diapo.ch/Régis Colombo ;
Page 415: Attila Gere, www.gere.hu;
Page 418: GHFP/Top/Joël de Cange;
Page 421: Oremus, photo J. Mészaros;
Page 422-423: Réa/Benoit Decout;
Page 436-437: Cephas/R.& K.Muschenetz;
Page 443: Camus Vineyard;
Page 444 , 446-447: Corbis/Charles O'Rear;
Page 450: Cephas/C.MacLachlan;
Page 453: Cephas/R.& K.Muschenetz ;
Page 456-457: Kendall Jackson;
Page 462-463: Newton Winery;

Page 466-467: Cephas/Clay McLachlan Architect Scott Johnson;
Page 471: Cephas/Clay Mc Lachlan;
Page 474-475: Cephas/R.& K.Muschenetz ;
Page 475: Guillaume de Laubier;
Page 481: Ponzi Vineyards © Polara Studios;
Page 486-487: Scope/Sarah Matthews;
Page 491: Anthony Blake/Steven Morris;
Page 494: Leonetti Cellars;
Page 497: Inniskillin Wines;
Page 500-501: Cephas/Andy Christodolo;
Page 505: Cephas/Clay Mc Lachlan;
Page 510-511: Almaviva Architecte Martin Hurtado;
Page 515: Catena Zapata © Carlos Calise;
Page 516: Cephas/Kevin Judd;
Page 519: Norton © Augusto Foix;
Page 522-523: Cephas/Andy Christodolo;
Page 530-531: Klein Constancia Estate Vineyards ;
Page 535: Morgenhof;
Page 538: Cephas/Alain Proust;
Page 542: Guillaume de Laubier, architect Jean de Gastines;
Page 549: Clarendon Hills, photo Roman Bratasiuk;
Page 552-553: De Bortoli;
Page 558: Scope/Jean-Luc Barde;
Page 559: Fréderic Maury;
Page 562: Penfolds;
Page 564-565: Cephas/Andy Christodolo;
Page 570-571: Corbis/David Lawrence;
Page 573: Cephas/Clay Mc Lachlan;
Page 577: Fréderic Maury;
Page 582-583, 586-591: Cephas/Kevin Judd.

Published in 2006 by Stewart, Tabori & Chang
An imprint of Harry N. Abrams, Inc.

Copyright © 2006 by Editions Minerva, Geneva, Switzerland

Library of Congress Cataloging-in-Publication Data is on file with the Library of Congress.

ISBN-13: 978-1-58479-557-5
ISBN-10: 1-58479-557-3

Editor: Jennifer Eiss
Graphic design: www.francism.com
Photo research: Marie-Christine Petit

English-language edition produced by Cambridge Publishing Management Ltd
Translators: Richard Elliott and Caroline Higgitt
Copy-editor: Sandra Stafford
Proofreader: Deborah Murrell

The text of this book was composed in Helvetica Neue and Rotis Semi Sans

Printed and bound in France
10 9 8 7 6 5 4 3 2 1

HNA
harry n. abrams, inc.
a subsidiary of La Martinière Groupe

115 West 18th Street
New York, NY 10011
www.hnabooks.com